ANCIENT ISRAEL

ANCIENT ISRAEL

What Do We Know and How Do We Know It?

Revised Edition

Lester L. Grabbe

Bloomsbury T&T Clark
An imprint of Bloomsbury Publishing Plc

B L O O M S B U R Y
LONDON • OXFORD • NEW YORK • NEW DELHI • SYDNEY

Bloomsbury T&T Clark
An imprint of Bloomsbury Publishing Plc

Imprint previously known as T&T Clark

50 Bedford Square
London
WC1B 3DP
UK

1385 Broadway
New York
NY 10018
USA

www.bloomsbury.com

BLOOMSBURY, T&T CLARK and the Diana logo are trademarks of Bloomsbury Publishing Plc

First published 2007.

This revised edition first published 2017.

British Library Cataloguing-in-Publication Data
A catalogue record for this book is available from the British Library.

ISBN: PB: 978-0-5676-7043-4
ePDF: 978-0-5676-7044-1
ePUB: 978-0-5676-7045-8

Library of Congress Cataloging-in-Publication Data
A catalog record for this book is available from the Library of Congress

Cover image: Panel from the black obelisk of King Shalmaneser III.
www.BibleLandPictures.com/ Alamy Stock Photo

Typeset by Forthcoming Publications (www.forthpub.com)
Printed and bound in Great Britain

Dedicated to

Professor Loren R. Fisher
The European Seminar in Historical Methodology
My History of Israel students over a quarter of a century

CONTENTS

Part II
Historical Investigations

Abbreviations

AASOR	Annual of the American Schools of Oriental Research
AB	Anchor Bible
ABD	*Anchor Bible Dictionary*. Edited by David Noel Freedman. 6 vols. Garden City, NY, 1992
ACEBT	*Amsterdamse Cahiers voor Exegese en bijbelse Theologie*
ADPV	Abhandlungen des Deutschen Palästina-Vereins
AEL	*Ancient Egyptian Literature*. Edited by M. Lichtheim. 3 vols; Berkeley, 1971–80
AfO	*Archiv für Orientforschung*
AGAJU	Arbeiten zur Geschichte des antiken Judentums und des Urchristentums
AHI	*Ancient Hebrew Inscriptions: Corpus and Concordance*. Graham I. Davies. Cambridge, 1991
AJA	*American Journal of Archaeology*
ALASPM	Abhandlungen zur Literature Alt-Syren-Palästinas und Mesopotamiens
ALGHJ	Arbeiten zur Literatur und Geschichte des hellenistischen Judentums
AnBib	Analecta biblica
ANET	*Ancient Near Eastern Texts Relating to the Old Testament*. Edited by James B. Pritchard. 3rd ed. with Supplement. Princeton, 1969
AOAT	Alter Orient und Altes Testament
AP	Cowley, A. *Aramaic Papyri of the Fifth Century B.C.* 1923. Repr. Osnabruck, 1967
ARAB	*Ancient Records of Assyria and Babylonia*. Daniel David Luckenbill. 4 vols. 1926–27. Repr. London, 1989
ASOR	American Schools of Oriental Research
ATD	Das Alte Testament Deutsch
AUSS	*Andrews University Seminary Studies*
BA	*Biblical Archeologist*
BAR	*Biblical Archaeology Review*
BASOR	*Bulletin of the American Schools of Oriental Research*
BBB	Bonner biblische Beiträge
BCE	Before the Common Era (= BC)

BETL	Bibliotheca Ephemeridum Theologicarum Lovaniensium
BHS	*Biblia Hebraica Stuttgartensia*. Edited by K. Elliger and W. Rudolph. Stuttgart, 1983
Bib	*Biblica*
BibOr	Biblica et orientalia
BIS	Biblical Interpretation Series
BJRL	*Bulletin of the John Rylands Library*
BN	*Biblische Notizen*
BO	*Bibliotheca Orientalis*
BWANT	Beiträge zur Wissenschaft vom Alten und Neuen Testament
BZ	*Biblische Zeitschrift*
BZAW	Beihefte zur Zeitschrift für die alttestamentliche Wissenschaft
CAH	*Cambridge Ancient History*
CBC	Century Bible Commentary
CBET	Contributions to Biblical Exegesis and Theology
CBQ	*Catholic Biblical Quarterly*
CBQMS	*Catholic Biblical Quarterly* Monograph Series
CBR	*Currents in Biblical Research*
CHANE	Culture and History of the Ancient Near East
CIS	*Corpus Inscriptionum semiticarum*
CML	*Canaanite Myths and Legends*. Edited by J. C. L. Gibson, 2nd ed. Edinburgh, 1978
ConBOT	Conjectanea biblica, Old Testament
CoS	*The Context of Scripture*. Edited by W. W. Hallo. 3 vols. Leiden, 1997–2003
CRAIBL	Comptes rendus de l'Académie des inscriptions et belles-lettres
CRBS	*Currents in Research: Biblical Studies*
DDD	*Dictionary of Deities and Demons in the Bible*. Edited by K. van der Toorn, B. Becking, and P. W. van der Horst. 2nd ed. Leiden, 1999
DSD	*Dead Sea Discoveries*
DtrH	Deuteronomistic History
EA	el-Amarna letters
EB	Early Bronze Age
EI	*Eretz-Israel*
ESHM	European Seminar in Historical Methodology
ET	English translation
EvT	*Evangelische Theologie*
FAT	Forschungen zum Alten Testament
FOTL	Forms of the Old Testament Literature
FRLANT	Forschungen zur Religion und Literatur des Alten und Neuen Testaments

FS	Festschrift
HAT	Handbuch zum Alten Testament
HdA	Handbuch der Archäologie
HSM	Harvard Semitic Monographs
HSS	Harvard Semitic Studies
HTR	*Harvard Theological Review*
HUCA	*Hebrew Union College Annual*
ICC	International Critical Commentary
IDB	*Interpreter's Dictionary of the Bible*. Edited by G. A. Buttrick. 4 vols. Nashville, 1962
IDBSup	*Interpreter's Dictionary of the Bible: Supplementary Volume*. Edited by K. Crim. Nashville, 1976
IEJ	*Israel Exploration Journal*
IOS	Israel Oriental Society
JANES	*Journal of the Ancient Near Eastern Society of Columbia University*
JAOS	*Journal of the American Oriental Society*
JARCE	*Journal of the American Research Center in Egypt*
JBL	*Journal of Biblical Literature*
JCS	*Journal of Cuneiform Studies*
JEA	*Journal of Egyptian Archaeology*
JESHO	*Journal of the Economic and Social History of the Orient*
JNES	*Journal of Near Eastern Studies*
JNSL	*Journal of Northwest Semitic Languages*
JQR	*Jewish Quarterly Review*
JSOT	*Journal for the Study of the Old Testament*
JSOTSup	Journal for the Study of the Old Testament: Supplements Series
JSPSup	Journal for the Study of the Pseudepigrapha: Supplement Series
JSS	*Journal of Semitic Studies*
JTS	*Journal of Theological Studies*
KAI	*Kanaanäische und aramäische Inschriften*. H. Donner and W. Röllig, mit einem Beitrag von O. Rössler. Vols 1–3. Wiesbaden, 1962–64
KAT	Kommentar zum Alten Testament
KTU	*Die keilalphabetischen Texte aus Ugarit*. Edited by Manfried Dietrich, Oswald Loretz, and Joaquín Sanmartín. Münster, 2013. 3rd enl. ed. of *KTU: The Cuneiform Alphabetic Texts from Ugarit, Ras Ibn Hani, and Other Places*. Edited by Manfried Dietrich, Oswald Loretz, and Joaquín Sanmartín. Münster, 1995 (= *CTU*)
LB	Late Bronze Age
LC	Low Chronology (see §1.2.4.4)
LCL	Loeb Classical Library

LdÄ	*Lexikon der Ägyptologie*. Edited by Wolfgang Helck, Eberhard Otto and Wolfhart Westendorf. 5 vols. Wiesbaden, 1975–92
LHBOTS	Library of Hebrew Bible/Old Testament Studies
LXX	Septuagint version of the Old Testament
MB	Middle Bronze Age
MCC	Modified Conventional Chronology (see §1.2.4.4)
MT	Masoretic text
NEA	*Near Eastern Archaeology*
NEAEHL	*New Encyclopedia of Archaeological Excavations in the Holy Land*. Edited by Ephraim Stern. 4 vols. New York and Jerusalem, 1992. *5 Supplementary Volume* (2008)
NEB	Neue Echter Bibel
OBO	Orbis Biblicus et Orientalis
OEANE	*The Oxford Encyclopedia of Archaeology in the Near East*. Edited by Eric M. Meyers. 5 vols. New York, 1997
OLA	Orientalia lovaniensia analecta
Or	*Orientalia*
OT	Old Testament/Hebrew Bible
OTL	Old Testament Library
OTS	*Oudtestamentische Studiën*
PAPS	*Proceedings of the American Philosophical Society*
PdÄ	Probleme der Ägyptologie
PEQ	*Palestine Exploration Quarterly*
PJb	*Palästina-Jahrbuch*
RB	*Revue Biblique*
RBL	*Review of Biblical Literature*
RIMA	The Royal Inscriptions of Mesopotamia, Assyrian Periods
SAAS	State Archives of Assyria Studies
SAHL	Studies in the Archaeology and History of the Levant
SANE	Studies on the Ancient Near East
SBL	Society of Biblical Literature
SBLABS	Society of Biblical Literature Archaeology and Biblical Studies
SBLASP	SBL Abstracts and Seminar Papers
SBLBMI	SBL Bible and its Modern Interpreters
SBLDS	SBL Dissertation Series
SBLMS	SBL Monograph Series
SBLSBL	SBL Studies in Biblical Literature
SBLSBS	SBL Sources for Biblical Study
SBLSCS	SBL Septuagint and Cognate Studies
SBLSymS	Society of Biblical Literature Symposium Series
SBLTT	SBL Texts and Translations
SBT	Studies in Biblical Theology

SEL	*Studi epigrafici e linguistici*
SemeiaSt	Semeia Studies
SHANE	Studies in the History of the Ancient Near East
SHCANE	Studies in the History and Culture of the Ancient Near East
SJOT	*Scandinavian Journal of the Old Testament*
SNTSMS	Society for New Testament Studies Monograph Series
SWBA	Social World of Biblical Antiquity
TA	*Tel Aviv*
TAD	*Textbook of Aramaic Documents from Ancient Egypt: 1–4*. Bezalel Porten and Ada Yardeni. Hebrew University, Department of the History of the Jewish People, Texts and Studies for Students. Jerusalem, 1986–99
TDOT	*Theological Dictionary of the Old Testament*. Edited by G. Johannes Botterweck and Helmer Ringgren. Translated by John T. Willis et al. 15 vols. Grand Rapids, 1974–
TRu	*Theologische Rundshau*
TSAJ	Texte und Studien zum Antiken Judentum
TSSI	*Textbook of Syrian Semitic Inscriptions*. J. C. L. Gibson. Oxford, 1973–81
ThWAT	*Theologisches Wörterbuch zum Alten Testament*. Edited by G. Johannes Botterweck and Helmer Ringgren. Stuttgart, 1970–2000
TZ	*Theologische Zeitschrift*
UF	*Ugarit-Forschung*
VT	*Vetus Testamentum*
VTSup	Supplements to Vetus Testamentum
WBC	Word Bible Commentary
WMANT	Wissenschaftliche Monographien zum Alten und Neuen Testament
ZA	*Zeitschrift für Assyrologie*
ZAH	*Zeitschrift für Althebräistik*
ZAR	*Zeitschrift für altorientalische und biblische Rechtsgeschichte*
ZAW	*Zeitschrift für die alttestamentliche Wissenschaft*
ZDPV	*Zeitschrift des Deutschen Palästina-Vereins*
ZTK	*Zeitschrift für Theologie und Kirche*
§	Marks the sections of the text for cross-referencing

Preface to the Second Edition

The field of the history of ancient Israel is changing so rapidly that after only a decade it is time to come out with a new edition. A number of changes have been made, including both updating and new material. In many ways the volume remains 'prolegomena' as originally conceived, but the additions to the text put it on the road to a comprehensive history (albeit a short one). The following are some of the changes made:

- Chapter 1 has been slightly updated.
- Chapter 2 has been updated and expanded, especially in the sections relating to Egypt, including §§2.1.2, 2.2.1, 2.3.2.
- Chapter 3 on the beginnings of Israel has had the text considerably revised and also updated, including §§3.1 and 3.2.
- Chapters 4 and 5 have had a number of expansions, especially in §4.2 and §5.2, to give a more comprehensive survey of the Israelite and Judahite kings.
- For Egyptian dates, the system worked out by Hornung et al. 2006 is used.

I regret that it was not possible to take account of two recent histories that have just appeared: Frevel 2016; Knauf and Guillaume 2016. On a personal note, I would like to thank Professor William G. Dever for his helpful review of the first edition of this book in *BASOR* (357 [2010]: 79–83), and also for his kind and generous references to it in other publications. After an initial (somewhat hostile!) encounter, we came to better understand each other and, more important, for each to respect the work that the other does. Although we are far from being in complete agreement – and our individual rhetoric is quite different – I believe we share a similar view on many issues (not least, postmodernism!).

Kingston-upon-Hull, UK
4 July 2016

Preface to the First Edition

Throughout the writing of this book, its working title was, *Prolegomena to a History of Israel: What Do We Know and How Do We Know it?* In the back of my mind, though, I think I realized it would not be the final title. It was the publisher who objected on the grounds that it would not be readily understood by some of its intended readership. The subtitle expresses what I have been trying to do, and the 'Aims' (§1.1) explain in detail. It is with some regret that it has not been possible to use my original title, but perhaps to have done so would have been an act of hubris – at least, some of my colleagues might have thought so.

This book is, however, not a history of Israel but the preparation – the *prolegomena* – for such a history. It is aimed initially at scholars, with the intent of contributing to the current debate. By laying out as clearly as possible the main primary sources and drawing attention to the areas of debate and the arguments being advanced, I hope to give a snapshot of the field at the present time. Yet as always, I want to reach other audiences as well and have attempted to make some concessions for them, such as giving both the Hebrew script and transliteration. These secondary audiences include scholars who do not work primarily in history but who would like a useful overview and reference; scholars who may be historians but not specialists in Hebrew Bible or ancient Israel; students who might find that the book would serve as a useful text. In that vein, I have tried to make the data accessible and provide sufficient information even to non-specialists, even if this is sometimes by way of referring the reader to some relevant bibliography. Such a small book can cover only so much, but within the confines of the space allotted I hope to have given a helpful – and thoughtful – account about the problems and methods for writing a history.

There are many people whom I could thank for discussion, inspiration and other help provided, but this could be a very long list. In addition to those to whom the book is dedicated, I shall limit my thanks to the following: Jim Eisenbraun, for making available a copy of the Amihai Mazar Festschrift before formal publication; Benyamin Sass, for a copy of his book on the alphabet; my student Kwanghyun Ryu for bringing some bibliographical items to my attention.

My first class in the history of Israel was in 1970 with Professor Loren R. Fisher. Although my perspective at the time was not in line with his, I still managed to learn a great deal and to begin a journey on the road to learning a critical approach to the Bible.

In the decade since the European Seminar on Methodology in Israel's History (now shortened to European Seminar in Historical Methodology) had its first meeting, I have learned an enormous amount from my peers in the UK, on the Continent, from Israel and elsewhere. My main reason for founding the Seminar was to get scholars of different views and approaches to talk to each other. I was also hoping for a gradual narrowing of the range of opinions, which does not seem to have happened, but I think we have all become clearer about our own opinions and also those of others in the Seminar. In the process, I think some useful volumes have been produced for the wider scholarly world.

British universities have traditionally focused on undergraduates. For almost 25 years I have offered an optional module in the History of Israel on a regular basis. Because students in the class are new to the subject, most of my learning has come from repeatedly having to go over the material in preparation for the class rather than directly from students. But during that time I have had some interesting essays and found teaching the class very rewarding.

Kingston-upon-Hull, UK
13 October 2006

Part I

INTRODUCTION

Chapter 1

The Principles and Methods of Investigating the History of Ancient Israel

1.1 Aims

This book is not a history of ancient Israel as such (though this second edition takes it further down that path), but it is primarily the preparation for such a history. Its purpose is to survey the sources and summarize the data available for writing such a history, and then evaluate the various interpretations of these data for reconstructing a history of Israel. It is, in fact, 'prolegomena to a history of Israel'. It asks: What do we actually know? On what basis can we claim to have knowledge of ancient Israel? Simple questions, but the answers are far from simple. In order to address them, each chapter has three main parts:

1. Original sources. In this section the pertinent sources for a history of Palestine are surveyed and discussed, with relevant publications, translations and secondary studies.
2. Analysis. In this section specific topics will be examined, the data from the sources critically discussed and the various theories that have been advanced will be considered and evaluated.
3. Synthesis. Here the main issues will be summarized and an attempt made to outline how I would put all the data together and would understand the history of Israel for the period covered by the chapter.

The principles along which I shall work are summarized in §1.3.3 below, but first I want to survey some of the main questions that inform these principles and the main areas relevant for writing a history of ancient Israel today.

1.2 Concepts and Complications: The Question of Sources and Methods

This section will take up several different issues that are relevant for writing a history. These might seem somewhat miscellaneous, but each (potentially) affects the reconstruction of ancient history and requires some knowledge or background on the part of the reader.

1.2.1 The Place of the Social Sciences

Although many biblical scholars make use of the social sciences, it is probably fair to say that Hebrew Bible/OT studies have still not fully incorporated the social sciences into their frame of reference. Not all studies relating to the Bible require use of the social sciences, but many studies that one sees do not go behind the biblical text, even though making use of insights from anthropology or sociology would give a better and more complete perspective. There is no question that anyone working on the history of ancient Israel needs to make full use of the contributions that can be brought in from the many social scientific studies.

The world of the social sciences is too large for a proper survey here, but for many points within the present study social scientific literature will be cited. I shall not normally make a hard and fast distinction between the terms 'social anthropology' (normal British usage) and 'cultural anthropology' (normal American usage), and professionals themselves do not always find it easy to distinguish anthropology from sociology. Archaeology has benefitted from the social sciences in recent years, and archaeology of all periods now routinely incorporates a great deal from anthropology. Some examples of areas where social theory and anthropology are invoked in this study are the settlement (§3.2.4.2), nomads and tribes (§3.2.4.3) and state formation (§3.2.4.4), but the social sciences leaven the work at many points and are essential for proper historical work in antiquity.

Unfortunately, biblical scholars have tended to be quite naive in their use of social anthropology, seeming to follow a stereotyped formula as follows: fish out a theory found in an elementary textbook or – preferably – one that is starting to make ground as a respectable topic. Take this theory, pick a set of unsuspecting biblical data, read the theory into the data, throw in some half-understood sociological vocabulary and – presto! – another sociological study. Therefore, some points to be kept in mind include the following (cf. Grabbe 2001c: 121):

1. Theories derived from the social sciences are simply models to be tested against the biblical and other data, not conclusions to be imposed on the sources. They are simply analogies based on one or more cultures. They are not 'facts' that can then be taken as givens by biblical scholars but are interpretations, to be critically examined against the data and then modified or discarded where necessary.
2. The function of sociological theories is to interrogate the textual or other data. The texts themselves may be read uncritically, as if they provided immediate access to the ancient society. It is easy to forget that the biblical texts cannot be treated like anthropological reports.
3. A related danger is to overinterpret – to find a lot more data in a passage than is warranted because of applying the sociological theory. Cross-cultural comparisons allow us to ask questions, to look at familiar data in a new light, to think in new directions. However, we cannot go beyond the data there, and hair-splitting interpretations – sometimes based on dubious linguistic analysis (cf. Barr 1961) – should be treated as the speculation they usually represent.
4. One of the most problematic tendencies in scholarship is that of reading modern ethical and theological concerns into the data. Biblical scholars are in the habit of making statements about the text based on theological bias and calling it sociological analysis. What should be sociological description becomes in fact an ideological value judgment. Too often sociological theory is simply a vehicle to import preconceived views about the biblical text. The city/urban is bad; the country/rural is good. The rich/ruling class is bad; the poor are good. The Canaanite city-states are bad; the refugee slave/peasant/proto-Israelite highland settler is good. The monarchy, social status, the economic situation, class divisions, urbanism and the like are all presented from the point of view of what a modern liberal, middle-class biblical scholar with a social conscience would consider acceptable.

1.2.2 The *Longue Durée*

One of the insights often forgotten in historical discussion is the extent to which any history is shaped by long-term factors that are usually outside the actors' control: physical geography (the geology, climate, vegetation, types of agricultural land, routes of communication and other physical surroundings), the availability of natural resources and the necessities of life (traditional lifestyles and modes of making a living) and long-term historical events (population movements, rise and fall of empires and nations, traditional alliances, old feuds and rivalries). It was the insight of the *Annales* school of historiography that different aspects of history have their own rhythm and temporal progress (for example, I. Finkelstein has drawn attention to the long-term cycling between settlement and pastoralism [§3.2.4.2]). Some historical constituents tend to change very slowly; others change much more quickly. This led F. Braudel (1980: 25–54) to divide history into three levels: (a) the level of events (*histoire événementielle*), the individual happenings on a short-term basis (though these do not necessarily escape the influence or sometimes even the determination of geography and environment); (b) the medium-term processes (*histoire conjonctures*); (c) the changes over long periods of time, affected by such issues as landscape, geology and climate (*longue durée*).

1.2.3 The Model and Method of Classical Studies

What is sometimes forgotten by historians of ancient Israel is that historians of ancient Greece and Rome have had to work with sources often very similar to those relied on by 'biblical' historians. For centuries classical historians had to rely primarily on the ancient written accounts. Some of these, such as Thucydides, were high quality, but for vast stretches of ancient history the surviving accounts were of poor or uncertain quality. Classical historians had to try to extract historical data from dodgy sources, writings lost in antiquity but used by surviving accounts, histories of various qualities, accounts written long after the original events, and writings that were not intended to be histories as such. There were also some inscriptions, and more recently archaeology has begun to take on a more important place in historical reconstruction. As will be clear, many of the classical sources provide much the same sorts of literature, information, and methodological problems as the Bible does to historians of Israel. Those of us writing on ancient Israel have much to learn from the Greek and Latin historians who have been doing their work for far longer than we.

1.2.4 Using Archaeology as a Source

All historical work requires sources, by which is meant the source of data or information. Thus, 'source' includes not just literature or inscriptions but archaeology, surveys, demographic studies and so on. Any ancient history should depend as far as possible on 'primary sources', the principle already laid down by von Ranke (§1.3.1). This means that artifactual evidence – archaeology and material culture – is extremely important. In contrast to the old way of beginning with the text, historical reconstruction should start with the *longue durée* (geology, climate, environment), and then move on to inscriptions and archaeology. These furnish information not found in texts and also provide an objectivity not possessed by texts because they provide actual realia from the past. The importance of archaeology cannot, therefore, be overestimated.

1.2.4.1 General Comments

The use of archaeology for historical reconstruction is as complicated as the use of texts. The material data have to be interpreted just as much as textual data. Artifacts by themselves are mute. They speak only when interrogated and given a context by the archaeologist and the historian. Much depends on the skill and technical understanding of the excavators and the careful recording of the archaeological data. As David Ussishkin (2007b: 132) has put it:

> The need for objectivity in archaeological research must be emphasized: Firstly, most data can usually be interpreted in more than one way: this or that wall can be assigned to the upper level but it may also be assigned to the lower. Or this and that storage jar can be assigned to a floor, but also to a pit dug from above. Or the uncovered fragment could be part of a bowl but it also resembles a jug. And so forth. Secondly, the archaeologist bears a great responsibility as in most cases he cannot repeat the discovery: uncovering the data is also the destruction of the data. For example, the archaeologist uncovers a jar lying in the debris – once he has extracted the jar we cannot repeat the discovery and study afresh the context of the same jar. Taking into account all the above I feel that the work of the archaeologist resembles that of a police detective, whose primary task when dealing with a case is to sort out the facts, and to interpret them in the most objective manner possible. Indeed, as I often state in lectures and in writing, I feel that my mentors are Sherlock Holmes and Hercule Poirot and their colleagues.

The past four decades have seen some significant changes in archaeological theory and method, some of which has had its impact on the archaeology of Palestine. This can only briefly be surveyed here. It is probably fair to say that the 'Biblical Archaeology' mode of operation had dominated the archaeology of Palestine up to the death of Albright who was its foremost practitioner (Dever 2001: 57–9). Perhaps it might be characterized in the phrase often quoted from Yigael Yadin, working with a spade in one hand and the Bible in the other. In other words, the Bible constituted the guide for interpreting the archaeology. 'Biblical Archaeology' was very much in the traditional cultural-historical archaeology mode, in which an emphasis was placed on describing, reconstructing history, explaining developments by cultural contact and diffusion and migration, and the identification of ethnicity with material culture – 'pots equal people' (cf. Renfrew and Bahn 2004: 40–2). It was partly the changes more broadly in archaeology that caused a serious questioning of both the historicity of the Bible (§1.3.2) and the assumptions of 'Biblical Archaeology' in the 1970s. W. G. Dever (1981, 1985) was one of the main scholars who drew attention to how the changes happening in the broader field of archaeology were eroding the old 'Biblical Archaeology'.

What is usually termed 'processual archaeology' – though often called the 'New Archaeology' – arose in the 1960s (Redman 1999: 60–5; Renfrew and Bahn 2004: 41–2, 473–84). It was an attempt to put archaeology on a more scientific basis, looking to anthropology and statistical and systems analysis. The general view was that society was a system, made up of a set of subsystems (subsistence, trade, technologies, etc.), and cultural change was to be explained by the processes and interactions of systems, especially as these adapted to their environment(s). Archaeology was an objective discipline, with the aim of explaining (not just describing) by logical argument and by the use of hypotheses and models that were, however, to be rigorously tested.

In the late 1980s and early 1990s a reaction developed to what was seen as the excessively mechanistic approach of the New Archaeology: it was too determinative, ignored the place of the individual and did not recognize the subjective element in all archaeological interpretation. This was 'post-processual archaeology', or 'interpretive archaeology' as some preferred to call it (Redman 1999: 65–9; Shanks and Hodder 1995; Renfrew and Bahn 2004: 494–6). It had many parallels with the postmodernist movement in literature and other cultural fields taking place at the same time. Some of its main features are the following (Shanks and Hodder 1995: 5):

- It focuses on contextual concerns, including the natural environment but also the socio-cultural environment.
- All social activity (including doing archaeology) has to do with meaning and interpretation – making sense of things. Hence, the designation 'interpretative archaeology'.
- The person and work of the interpreter is explicitly recognized.
- Archaeology works in the present, constructing knowledge, narratives and the like from the remains of the past. It 'reads' material culture like a 'text'.
- There is no final or definitive account of the past; archaeology is a continuing process.

- Interpretations of society are less concerned with causes than making sense of things.
- Possible interpretations are multiple: different interpretations for the same set of data are possible.

This does not mean that the New Archaeology disappeared; on the contrary, its procedures still dominate the work of most archaeologists. But the insights of post-processual archaeology have also been recognized. It is probably the case that the dominant approach now is what has been called 'cognitive-processual archaeology', which seems to be the basic core of processual archaeology but well leavened by the interpretive approach (Renfrew and Bahn 2004: 496–501; cf. Redman 1999: 69–72). The main ways in which it differs from processual archaeology are given as the following (Renfrew and Bahn 2004: 496–7):

- It seeks to incorporate information about cognitive and symbolic aspects of society.
- It recognizes that ideology is an active force within society and on individuals.
- Material culture is an active factor in the process by which individuals and society construct their world.
- Internal conflict within societies has to be taken into account.
- The creative role of the individual has to be recognized.
- Facts can no longer be considered independent of theory, nor are there universal 'laws of culture process' on the analogy of physical laws.

Most Palestinian archaeologists would probably pay strong lip-service to the 'cognitive-processual' approach, though it appears that most do not agonize a lot over theoretical method: they excavate as they have been taught and as their experience has informed their work over the years. But it is also the same with historians of my acquaintance – they just get on with it without long debates over the historical method. As Dever noted, however:

> The result is that Syro-Palestinian archaeologists, despite some *rapprochement* with the field of anthropology in recent years, are still dismissed by our colleagues as parochial, naïve, and incapable of contributing anything to the advance of archaeology as a discipline. Again, some of our more Neanderthal colleagues ridicule any desire to be in the mainstream, but they are terribly wrong. (Dever 2003b: 515)

As is clearly evident, the debate still continues about the place of the Bible in archaeological interpretation. One can say that the 'biblical archaeology' of Albright and Yadin still has considerable influence on Palestinian archaeology. For some, at least, the Bible still seems to play a central role in the intepretation of Palestinian archaeology. Apart from that we need to consider two cautions relating to the use of archaeology in biblical interpretation.

First is the one that was being discussed above: failure to recognize that the use of archaeological data is just as subjective and interpretative as data from texts. Some archaeologists (and others) give the impression that it is objective, that archaeology somehow speaks by itself. Many times in the past we were assured that archaeology 'proved' this or that scenario. Some of that is still around, but most recognize the need for an interpretative context and the limitations of the science.

The second danger is the exact opposite: to assume that archaeological data is no more objective than textual data. Such an approach has mistakenly led some to discount its value:

> …in the modern period of historiography it has sometimes been assumed that archaeological remains offer us the prospect of grounding historical statements in something more solid than testimony… This kind of view of the nature of archaeological evidence has been common among historians of Israel, even where they have somtimes recognized that it cannot be entirely correct and have found space in one part of their minds for the contrary idea…that archaeological data are no more 'objective' or 'neutral' than other sorts… In fact, *all* archaeologists tell us stories about the past that are just as ideologically loaded as any other historical narrative and are certainly not simply a neutral recounting of the facts. (Provan, Long and Longman 2003: 63)

While this quote recognizes that artifacts indeed have to be interpreted, just as do texts, it ignores the major difference between the two sets of data: the archaeological data actually existed in real life – the artifacts are realia (apart from some faked artifacts – see below). Texts, on the other hand, are products of the imagination. The content of a text always contains human invention, and it is always possible that a text is entirely fantasy.

Archaeology is especially important because it has the potential of providing a separate witness to history and a source of distinct and independent data. Archaeology can help to confirm or disconfirm the reliability of texts. The proper attention to archaeology is vital for any history of ancient Israel, and it is my intention to try to give it the prominence it deserves. But a number of studies in recent years have pointed out some long-term problems of interpretation in Palestinian archaeology. Not everyone will agree with some of the interpretations proposed, but the reader should be aware that some major reorientations are being called for by some archaeologists. Notice some of these:

1.2.4.2 Terminology of Archaeological Periods

A number of slightly different archaeological schemes, divisions and datings are used. One scheme of EB and MB (Albright 1932: 8–18; *NEAEHL* IV, 1529) divides EB I (ca. 3300–3000), EB II (ca. 3000–2700 BCE), EB III (2700–2200 BCE), MB I (2200–2000 BCE), MB IIA (2000–1750 BCE), MB IIB (1750–1550 BCE), or possibly three MB divisions: MB IIA–C. However, MB I is often labelled EB IV or Intermediate Bronze (Dever 1977: 82–9; Finkelstein 1995a: 87–8), in which case the MB (Dever 1987: 149–50; Ilan 1998: 297) is divided into MB I (ca. 2000–1800 BCE), MB II (ca. 1800–1650 BCE), and MB III (ca. 1650–1500 BCE), though some want to divide MB only into MB I and MB II. In spite of these differences, this concerns only the background history of the second millennium BCE.

For the history of ancient Israel, a major issue arises over the end of LB, beginning of Iron I and end of Iron I (also, some divide Iron I into IA and IB). This, though, is not the main difficulty. The real problem is that at the moment there is no agreed terminology among archaeologists for the period from about 1000 BCE to the fall of Jerusalem in 587/586 BCE. Some schemes are based on supposed 'historical' periods, which can be question-begging since most schemes tend to associate certain artifacts with particular historical periods. After the Hazor excavations of the 1950s (so Barkay 1992: 305), Aharoni and Amiran proposed Iron II (1000–840 BCE) and Iron III (840–586 BCE), but the *Encyclopedia of Archaeological Excavations in the Holy Land* (when first published in Hebrew in 1970 but also maintained in the English translation [Avi-Yonah and Stern (eds) 1975–78: IV, 1226]), had the following scheme: Iron IIA (1000–900), IIB (900–800), IIC (800–586). W. G. Dever notes that American archaeologists tend to begin Iron II about 920 BCE, whereas Israeli archaeologists usually begin it about 1000 BCE (Dever 1998b: 416). His own treatment ends Iron IIA at 722 and Iron IIB at 586 BCE. However, the editor of the volume to which Dever contributes (Levy 1998: x–xvi, esp. xvi) divides as follows: IIA (1000–900); IIB (900–700); IIC (700–586). But even among Israeli writers Iron II is differently divided. Barkay proposed Iron

IIA (10th–9th centuries BCE), Iron IIb (8th), IIIa (7th and early 6th), IIIb (586 to the late 6th BCE). The *NEAEHL* used the terminology Iron IIA (1000–900 BCE), IIB (900–700), IIC (700–586), Babylonian and Persian periods (586–332). However, A. Mazar (1993) divided slightly differently, with Iron IIA (1000–925 BCE), IIB (925–720), IIC (720–586). H. Weippert (1988) differed from them all, with Iron IIA (1000–900 BCE), IIB (925/900–850), IIC (850–587).

This only-partially controlled chaos means that readers must always pay attention to the scheme used by the individual author, and the individual author ought (though does not necessarily do so) to indicate to the reader the particular scheme being used. The present book is divided into chapters that cover particular periods of time, without being water-tight compartments. But because it draws on a great variety of archaeological writings, it will quote the data according to the scheme used by the particular writer. I have tried to give preference to the archaeological period (LB, Iron I, Iron IIA, etc.) rather than a date; however, if a specific date or even century is given, an indication of who is doing the dating is normally provided. This has been complicated by the LC, since material culture conventionally dated to the tenth century BCE would usually be dated to the ninth according to the LC. However, as noted at §1.2.4.4, I do not normally use the LC because it is still so controversial (except where I note specifically that an author follows it).

1.2.4.3 Use of Survey Data

The archaeology of Palestine was transformed in the 1980s by the execution of large-scale surveys and the use of their results. The importance and value of these surveys will become clear in the archaeological survey of each chapter. Yet the proper use of survey data also requires that one be aware of the weaknesses of surveys, in comparison with actual excavation results. Two examples of those drawing attention to problems are G. Lehmann (2003: 123–5) and O. Lipschits (2004: 101–3; 2005: 259–60 n. 249). Some surveys have been conducted much more rigorously than others. A lot depends on the thoroughness of the collection of surface pottery, but surface pottery is not always a good indicator of the actual periods of habitation. Similarly, the estimation of site size – which is very important for demographical calculations – can be quite difficult. Yet Lehmann, Lipschits and others go on to point out the value and importance of surveys, in spite of potential problems. The same applies to salvage excavations (Lipschits 2004: 101–3).

1.2.4.4 The Debate Over the 'Low Chronology'

One of the most controversial but also potentially important developments is Israel Finkelstein's 'Low Chronology' (LC). This thesis, advanced in its first full form in the mid-1990s, dated most of the events and finds of the Iron I and Iron IIA about a century later than had been common among archaeologists. Finkelstein's original study (Finkelstein 1996a) argued that conventional chronology is based on the twin pillars of the stratigraphy of Megiddo and the Philistine Bichrome ware. Since then the debate has widened considerably to take in radiocarbon dating, correlation with the Aegean, the context of the Assyrian expansion in the ninth century and other factors. A major opponent of the LC has been Amihai Mazar (2005) who has developed what he calls the 'Modified Conventional Chronology' (MCC). This is similar to the traditional chronology but extends the Iron IIA from 980 to 830, that is, covering most of both the tenth and the ninth centuries. This allows three major pottery periods (Iron IB, Iron IIA, Iron IIB), each lasting about 150 years, in the 450 years between approximately 1150 and 700 BCE.

The following are some of the main issues around which the arguments – pro and con – have revolved:

1. The biblical data. Finkelstein points out that conventional dating is strongly – if not always explicitly – influenced by the biblical text (e.g., 2005a: 34). This sometimes leads to circular arguments in which the argument depends on the biblical text and moves around to arguing that the data support the biblical text. A good example is Shoshenq's invasion (see next point). Yet all parties have appealed to the biblical text in the discussion of the two key sites of Samaria and Jezreel (Ussishkin 2007a; Finkelstein 2005a: 36–8).
2. The invasion of Shoshenq. This event has been a central benchmark for dating historical and archaeological data, yet the dating of when it happened has depended on the biblical text, since 1 Kgs 14.25-28 puts it in the fifth year of Rehoboam (Finkelstein 1996a: 180). A recent Egyptological evaluation has dated the event to 917 BCE (Shortland 2005), but P. S. Ash has shown that it could be anytime in the period 970 to 915 BCE (1999: 30–1). Yet this is not the end of the matter, because it is not clear exactly what sort of measures were taken by Shoshenq. It had been assumed that his invasion resulted in widespread destruction of sites, but it has been argued that if Shoshenq planned to use Megiddo as the place to plant his royal stela, he would hardly have destroyed the site (Ussishkin 2007a). In

fact, it 'has not been proven that any sites were destroyed by Shishak in 925 B.C.E., and the attribution of destruction layers to the end of the tenth century at many sites is mere conjecture' (Barkay 1992: 306–7).

3. Implications for the Aegean and other Mediterranean areas. N. Coldstream (2003: 256) argues that the LC best fits the situation in the Aegean, but A. Mazar (2004) stands against this. Yet Killebrew (2008) also relates the situation in Philistia to the broader Mediterranean pottery context and agrees that the LC 'with some minor revisions' would best fit the situation elsewhere in the Mediterranean: see next point.
4. The development and dating of Philistine Monochrome and Bichrome pottery. It seems to be generally agreed that Philistine Monochrome (or Mycenaean IIIC:1b or Mycenaean IIIC Early to Middle) appears in the late twelfth century, developing from imported Mycenaean IIIC:la (Mycenaean IIIC Early or Late Helladic IIIC Early). The Egyptian Twentieth Dynasty and the Egyptian presence in Palestine came to an end about 1140/1130 (Mazar 2007). Yet no Philistine Monochrome ware appears together with Egyptian pottery of the Twentieth Dynasty, not even in nearby sites such as Tel Batash and Tel Mor, which suggests that Philistine Monochrome is post-1135 BCE, while Philistine Bichrome is even later – the eleventh and perhaps much of the tenth century but not before 1100 BCE (Finkelstein 1995b: 218–20, 224; 2005a: 33). A. Mazar (2008) responds: (1) Canaanite pottery assembly in Ashdod XIII and Tel Miqne is typical of the thirteenth and beginning of the twelfth centuries BCE, and Lachish VI must have been contemporary; (2) local Mycenaean IIIC is inspired by the Mycenaean IIIC pottery in Cyprus but this disappears after the mid-twelfth century; (3) although D. Ussishkin and Finkelstein claim it is inconceivable that locally made Mycenaean IIIC did not reach contemporary sites in Philistia and the Shephelah, this ignores cultural factors that could limit it to a few urban centres; the early stage of Philistine settlement lasted perhaps only a generation, and Lachish is at least 25 km from the major Philistine cities which is sufficient to create a cultural border; (4) the Philistine settlement was possible perhaps because of the state of the Egyptian domination of Canaan at this time, and Philistine Bichrome pottery slowly emerged as a hybrid style later, probably during the last quarter of the twelfth century.

Yet in a thorough study of the Aegean-style pottery A. E. Killebrew (2008) argues that the high chronology (two-wave theory) would date the Philistine Monochrome (Mycenaean IIIC:1b) to about 1200 BCE as the result of an early proto-Philistine wave of Sea Peoples, while the middle chronology would date this pottery to about 1175 BCE, with the Bichrome developing from it in the mid-twelfth century. Such datings are becoming more problematic in light of the increasing consensus that Mycenaean IIIC:1b should be equated to Mycenaean IIIC Early (into Middle) which is dated to the mid-twelfth. With some revisions (such as dating the initial appearance of Mycenaean IIIC Early phase 2 to about 1160 BCE), the low chronology would best fit the dating of Mycenaean IIIC Early to Middle at other sites in the eastern Mediterranean and would also provide a more reasonable dating of Bichrome to the eleventh continuing into the tenth, based on LB II–Iron I stratigraphic sequences at both Tel Miqne and Ashdod.

5. Pottery assemblages and the dating of various strata. Here there is a surprising difference of interpretation between professional archaeologists whom one would expect to agree about the facts in the ground: the relationship between the strata in the sites of Hazor, Samaria, Jezreel and Megiddo; the interpretation of Jerusalem; the dating of Lachish; the dating of the Negev destruction.
6. The gap in the ninth century. Current dating leaves a strange gap in the ninth century in the dating of archaeological remains (Finkelstein 1996a). We have much in the tenth and the eighth centuries but not the ninth, leaving a very thin stratigraphy over 350 years. For example, Tel Miqne and Tel Batash have thick accummulations related to Philistine Bichrome ware, a ninth-century gap, then limited Iron II remains. Other sites show a similar gap: Tell Halif, Tel Mor, Tell Beit Mirsim, Ashdod, Tel Haror, Gezer, Jerusalem. The LC closes the unexplained gap between monumental architectures of the tenth century and evidence of public administration for the late ninth to the eighth centuries BCE.
7. Downgrading or elimination of the united monarchy. The monuments previously associated with the united monarchy are redated from the second half of the tenth century to the early ninth. It strips the united monarchy of its monumental buildings, including ashlar masonry and proto-Ionic columns. We have evidence of fortifications in the tenth century, but the main mounds in the north (Megiddo and Gezer) and the south (Beersheba and Lachish) only date to the ninth century or later. This means that the strong and historically attested Omri

kingdom is the first state in Palestine and preceded the geographically weaker Judah. Taking a global perspective, this is what one would expect rather than the anomalous Jerusalem-centred and Judah-dominated kingdom of David and Solomon.

8. Radiocarbon dates. This is the most recent attempt to find a way to pin down the matter of dating and has great potential. Yet a database of radiometric dates from a wide variety of sites is needed; such is now being developed and may resolve the issue (Sharon et al. 2005; Sharon et al. 2008). In the meantime, there are significant differences in interpretation. The reasons for this have been well laid out by A. Mazar:

> The many stages of selecting the samples, the pre-treatment, the method and process of dating, and the wide standard deviation of Accelerator Mass Spectrometry dates may create a consistent bias, outliers or an incoherent series of dates. The calibration process adds further problems, related to the nature of the calibration curve in each period. In our case, there are two difficulties: one is the many wiggles and the shape of the curve for the 12th–11th centuries BCE. This leads to a wide variety of possible calibrated dates within the 12–11th centuries BCE. The other problem is the plateau between 880 and 830 BCE, and the curve relating to the last third of the 10th century BCE, which in certain parts is at the same height as the 9th century BCE plateau. In many cases the calibrated dates of a single radiocarbon date is [*sic*] in both the 10th and the 9th centuries BCE, and in the 9th century BCE more precise dates between 880 and 830 BCE are impossible. These limitations are frustrating, and make close dating during this time frame a difficult task. It seems that in a debate like ours, over a time-span of about 80 years, we push the radiometric method to the edges of its capability, and perhaps even beyond that limit. (Mazar 2005: 22)

The result is that a variety of radiocarbon dates have been made at key sites, with some arguing that they support the MCC (Mazar 2005: 22–3; Mazar et al. 2005); and others, that they support the LC (Finkelstein and Piasetzky 2003; Piasetzky and Finkelstein 2005; Finkelstein 2005b; Sharon et al. 2005; Sharon et al. 2008).

1.2.4.5 Estimating Population

One area where much has been learned in recent years is that of estimating the population of an area (town, village, region) in ancient times. The result is that current estimates are often greatly different from those found in older literature, which were often based on textual sources. In most cases the population estimate by scholars today is much lower than that in literature even a few decades old. See especially the articles of Zorn 1994; Geva 2014; cf. also Shiloh 1980; Van Beek 1982.

1.2.4.6 The Stratigraphy of Samaria

For many years Samaria was used as a model for interpreting other sites. The ancient site was excavated by the Harvard University expedition in 1908–10 and then under a combined expedition under J. W. Crowfoot in 1931–35; a few isolated digs have taken place since then. As part of the Crowfoot expedition, Kathleen Kenyon presented the stratigraphy of the site (1942). R. Tappy has compared the published interpretation from that in Kenyon's notes and found many discrepancies (1992, 2001; §4.1.1).

1.2.4.7 Reinterpretation of the Jochan Seal

The following bulla, once dated to the time of Jeremiah, should now be placed in the late eighth century: 'Belonging to Eliaqim servant of Yochan' (לאליקם נער יוכן: Gogel 1998: 467 [Beth Shemesh seal 2], 492 [Ramat Rahel seal 8], 494 [Tell Beit Mirsim seal 1]; *AHI*: 100.108; 100.277; 100.486; Garfinkel 1990). Impressions of this seal on jar handles were found at Tell Beit Mirsim and Beth Shemesh, and eventually at Ramat Rahel. When impressions of this seal were first found, the name Yochan or Yochin was thought to be a version of King Jehoiachin's name. Based on the interpretation of W. F. Albright scholars long took this as the seal of Jehoiachin's steward, which resulted in the misdating of the strata where they were originally found and those strata elsewhere thought to be parallel. In Garfinkel's words this caused 'sixty years of confusion' in Palestinian archaeology. Although this interpretation is still widespread, especially in more general works, it has now been completely reassessed by specialists (Ussishkin 1976, 1977; Garfinkel 1990). Even if some aspects of the seals and their owners have still not been clarified, they have now been dated to the period before 701 BCE.

1.2.4.8 Problems with Forgeries

Becoming much more prominent in recent years is another danger: the faking of antiquities being traded on the market (Rollston 2003). This has been especially a problem with seal impressions, but recently inscribed objects have appeared. A number of these have been exposed with more or less a scholarly consensus (e.g., the Jehoash inscription [see at §4.1.2]), but there are others still in dispute. The good side of this is that objects found in properly controlled excavations are accepted as authentic. A genuine archaeological context is usually sufficient guarantee that the finds are genuine. Very seldom has the authenticity of such objects been questioned (though some have queried the Tel Dan inscription [§4.1.3.1]).

As more and more items are obtained through the antiquities market, the bigger the potential problem becomes. We now find that a number of discoveries hailed as evidence of the biblical account are questionable or even out-and-out fakes. To take one cherished example, even the famous Berekyahu ben Neriyahu seal impressions, alleged to belong to the scribe of Jeremiah, now seem to be forgeries. The first one found was published by Avigad (1978). More recently another has allegedly been discovered and was published by Deutsch and Heltzer (1994: 37–8) and Shanks (1996). This latter seal impression was part of the indictment against Robert Deutsch and Raphael Brown (Rollston and Vaughn 2005: 4). It is hardly unusual that Avigad (1978; 1986) put particular emphasis on the Baruch seal impression when he set about publishing the lot of seals of which they were a part, the so-called 'Burnt Archive'. Avigad also asserted that there 'was no reason to suspect their authenticity, and I seriously doubt whether it would be possible to forge such burnt and damaged bullae' (1986: 13). The recent investigation by Goren and Arie seems to have settled the question: they are not authentic (2014).

We may be rapidly coming to the point of having to take a 'Popperian' view of the situation. By this, I mean that antiquities not obtained within a proper archaeological context can never be authenticated; they can only be falsified. That is, just as a scientific theory – according to Karl Popper (1959) – can never be proved but only falsified, so antiquities-market artifacts that have not been falsified will still retain a certain aura of uncertainty. There is an unfortunate air of naive arrogance on the part of some technical scholars. C. Rollston (2003: 183–6) tells of a laboratory which managed to create a fake patina that would pass most tests for authenticity, yet the very people able to do this took the stance that forgers would not be able to do the same. Many intelligent people through the ages have underestimated the ability of frauds and cheats to fool them, to their cost. When potentially large sums of money are at stake, it is worth the while of a good forger to invest the necessary time, money and equipment to produce a plausible counterfeit. And those who think that antiquities cannot be so cleverly forged that they cannot fool modern laboratory tests or the judgment of expert epigraphers ought to read some of the recent discussions of the subject (for a sample, see Cook 2005; Goren 2005; Goren et al. 2004; Lemaire 2005; Rollston 2003, 2004, 2005; Rollston and Vaughn 2005; Vaughn and Dobler 2005; Vaughn and Rollston 2005).

It is not surprising that some epigraphers do not accept the judgment of the Israel Antiquity Authority's committees on various objects, and it is quite fair for them to present their arguments (e.g., Lemaire 2005). But headlines such as 'Forgery Hysteria Grips Israel: Is Everything a Fake?' can leave non-specialists with a rather distorted picture of what is consensus and what is genuine controversy. Museums around the world are filled with artifacts relating to ancient Israel and Judah that no one questions. It is the unprovenanced objects sold on the antiquities market that cause the problems.

1.2.5 Ethnicity

The question of ethnicity has been much discussed in recent decades, not only in biblical studies but also in social anthropology. Particular problems are those of group identity and identifying ethnic groups from material culture (i.e., can this be done from archaeology alone?). There is a problem already at the beginning of the discussion: What does one mean by 'ethnic' or 'ethnicity'? At the most basic level, it has to do with the Greek word *ethnos* which is variously translated as 'people, nation, race'. But this only partially answers our question. The basic issue is that throughout the historical sources are the names of groups and peoples, from the frequent naming of 'Israel' and 'Judah' and continuing down to obscure groups mentioned only once or twice in extant sources. How do we characterize these groups, who are often little more than names? Do we think of them in social terms, kinship terms (lineal? segmental? tribal?), ethnic terms or what? Was the name in the source their name for themselves or something alien that they never used? How we treat these groups in a historical discussion needs to take into account recent discussions of 'ethnicity' and '(ethnic) identity'. In most cases, we have no information beyond the textual data, though sometimes there is also material culture – or at least some scholars have brought material culture into the discussion of ethnicity/identity.

There have been different approaches to ethnicity not only in biblical scholarship (Brett 1996; Sparks 1998; Killebrew 2005: 8–16) but extensively in anthropological study (Shennan [ed.] 1989; Hutchinson and Smith [eds] 1996; Sokolovskii and Tishkov 1996; Keyes 1997). A view that ethnicity should be seen mainly in biological terms (ethnic groups have a common ancestry or kinship or genetic pool) is widely rejected but has contributed the important insight that ethnic groups generally define themselves in kinship or quasi-kinship terms. Others saw the question in terms of distinct cultures, but this was problematic in that cultural groups do not always develop an ethnic identity or group consciousness. There is also the fact that there is a 'primordial' quality to ethnic identity in which the group's distinctiveness – 'we/they' – is essential (Geertz 1973: 255–310; Keyes 1997). The classic study is that of F. Barth (1969) who pointed to the importance of inter-group boundary mechanisms: ethnic groups define themselves in contrast with other groups ('self-ascription'), often by a minimum of explicit (even trivial) differences. He explicitly rejected the use of an inventory of cultural traits (as Kletter [2006: 579] points out, W. Dever [1993: 22*–24*; 1995b: 201; 2003a: 192–3] seems to have misunderstood Barth in this regard and adopted the very definition that Barth criticizes). But there has been a good deal of discussion since Barth (Kamp and Yoffee 1980; Shennan [ed.] 1989; Hutchinson and Smith [eds] 1996; Finkelstein 1997; Jones 1997; Bloch-Smith 2003; Kletter 2006).

Because our knowledge of groups in the ancient Near East is based on texts rather than a direct study of living peoples, we are limited by what the texts tell us. This means that the task of penetrating to identity and ethnicity is often very complicated. For example, the biblical text tells us what was distinctive about Israelites and Judahites that made them different from the surrounding peoples, but what we have are the views of the biblical writers, not necessarily of the average Israelite or Judahite who might have seen his or her identity in quite different terms. For many groups (e.g., the Canaanites) we have only the views of their opponents and do not know how they regarded themselves. An interesting example is the situation in the Persian period, with the text of Ezra making a sharp distinction between 'Israel' and the 'peoples of the land(s)', but there is reason to think that both groups were Judahites and did not necessarily regard themselves as separate in the way that the textual writer portrays it (Grabbe 2004a: 285–8).

Trying to find a definition of an ethnic group is still not easy. Recent treatments tend to recognize the fluidity of ethnic identity (an insight from Barth), and any definition must recognize that. Kamp and Yoffee stated that most sociologists and anthropologists saw an ethnic group as 'a number of individuals who see themselves as being alike by virtue of a common ancestry, real or fictitious, and who are so regarded by others' (1980: 88). Kletter follows A. D. Smith in seeing an ethnic group as:

> ...a group of people who share most – but not necessarily all – of the following: (1) a collective proper name; (2) a myth of common ancestry; (3) historical memories; (4) one or more differentiating elements of common culture; (5) an association with a specific homeland (which may be symbolic, without physical control of the homeland); and (6) a sense of solidarity among at least parts of the group. (Kletter 2006: 574)

Sokolovskii and Tishkov give a similar definition and suggest that it 'opens further avenues for integration of anthropological, political and psychological knowledge in understanding of ethnic phenomena' (1996: 192). Of particular interest is that self-identity may be strongly based on religion, myth and law, areas which have traditionally been studied with regard to ancient Israel.

Yet even such carefully thought out definitions can be in danger of restricting the recognition of how complex the matter is in the real world. Politicians may mount a self-serving campaign to encourage their constituents to think of themselves as of a particular ethnic group. Individuals might adopt a particular ethnic identity for the sake of social or economic advantage or even as a strategy for survival. An ethnic group can grow out of what were once different ethnic groups (as will be argued below in reference to Israel [§§3.2.4; 3.3]). The fact that a name occurs in a text does not necessarily tell us whether it represents an ethnic group. As will be discussed below (§2.2.1.5), the term 'Canaanite' probably applies to territory rather than ethnicity; that is, a 'Canaanite' seems to be the inhabitant of a region or land rather than the member of an ethnic group.

Finally, we come to an issue being very much debated at the present: the question of whether ethnic identity can be determined from material culture – also known as the 'pots equal people' debate. Relating material culture to ethnicity is fraught with problems (Edelman 1996b; Skjeggestad 1992). It is interesting that most of Kletter's six elements relating to ethnic identity leave no trace in the archaeology record. Also, differences or similarity in material culture do not necessarily show differences or identity in ethnicity: they may be the result of similar or diverse environments (Finkelstein 1998b: 359, 365) or similar or diverse lifestyles. Nevertheless, attempts continue to be made to find ways through the obstacles and develop approaches that can successfully relate ethnicity and archaeology (cf. Redmount 1995; Killebrew 2005; R. D. Miller 2004; Kamp and Yoffee 1980; Jones 1997; Finkelstein 1997; Dever 1993; 1995b; 2003a: 191–200). Yet any list of particular traits in the material culture is likely to be problematic, whether we think of pottery, architecture, diet or even language. The traditional list of 'Israelite ethnic markers' have evaporated as exclusive indicators: four-room pillared house, collar-rim jar, abstinence from pork (Bloch-Smith 2003: 406–11; Kamp and Yoffee 1980; Kletter 2006: 579; Hesse and Wapnish 1997). What is clear is that there 'is no list of material traits that can cause "ancient Israel to stand up" independently, without the help of written sources' (Kletter 2006: 579).

It is interesting that neither Dever nor Killebrew identify Israel and her neighbours from material culture alone. On the other hand, we do have some written sources for ancient Israel, and why should we not use them? Particular traits might not prove an ethnic identity, but the clustering of certain traits might be diagnostic if combined with particular types of textual data. From Killebrew's data it strikes me that the archaeology most clearly shows the presence of Egyptians (administrators, soldiers, etc.) and the Philistine settlement. Yet Bunimovitz (1990) argues that the actual material culture at the Philistine sites is a mixed one, and some 'Philistine' pottery is found in what are usually regarded as non-Philistine areas. Most importantly, for disputed sites the material culture has not been able to decide the question of who lived there (Finkelstein 1997: 220–1). We can end this preliminary discussion by asking three questions:

- Was 'Israel' an ethnic group? The answer is that both the people themselves and outsiders saw a group identity that we would call ethnic. The fact that a diversity of groups may have contributed to their makeup (cf. §3.2.4.4) – indeed, most probably did – does not negate ethnic identity (*pace* Lemche 1998b: 20–1).
- Were 'Judah/Judahites' to be identified as 'Israel/Israelites'? Within the biblical text they seem to be seen as one ethnic group, yet they are never identified as such by outsiders. Judah/Judahites are never called Israel/Israelites in any non-Jewish literature or documents until the beginning of the Common Era.
- How do 'tribes' relate to the question? This issue is discussed below (§3.2.4.3).

1.2.6 Ideology and Neo-Fundamentalism

A fact all historians and scholars live with is the subjective nature of much argument (Grabbe 2002). It has been explicitly recognized in postmodernism (§1.3.1), but it was known long before that. Complete objectivity is an unobtainable ideal (many reject it even as an ideal), but most historians think that an effort should be made to be dispassionate in evaluating and arguing a case (§1.3.1). Yet S. Sandmel (1979) drew attention to a tendency we all live with: to rely on the 'comfortable theory'. What he pointed out was the extent to which we as scholars – and despite our implied adherence to critical thought – tend to gravitate toward those theories or views that we find most congenial: 'A comfortable theory is one which satisfies the needs of the interpreter, whether theological or only personal, when the evidence can seem to point in one of two opposite directions' (Sandmel 1979: 139). To give my own interpretation of Sandmel's thesis, the comfortable theory is not a disinterested search for the 'facts', the 'truth' or whatever term one wishes to use, but a means of maintaining our position with the least amount of effort. When Sandmel exposed the 'comfortable theory', he did not exempt himself from his own strictures, nor can I. Sandmel admitted that he was as susceptible to the seductive comfortable theory as the next man, and I have to own up to the same temptations. We all have our own comfortable theories. Perhaps we would like to think that we have thought them through carefully and are willing to change our minds if the facts show otherwise, but whether in practice that is true is not something we individually can judge alone – our peers might have definite views on the matter! (For further thoughts along this line, see Grabbe 2011a.)

We also all have ideologies that make us gravitate toward certain 'comfortable theories'. Some use this, however, to argue that one theory is as good as another (some postmodernists) or that a fundamentalist interpretation of the Bible is as valid as a critical one. The postmodernist question is dealt with elsewhere (§1.3.1), but here we need to confront directly and explicitly the neo-fundamentalist approach to scholarship that is very much in evidence in some areas (Grabbe 1987; 2002). The term 'maximal conservatism' was coined by J. Barr (1977: 85–9). He notes that instead of advancing a dogmatic approach, conservative evangelicals will often adopt a position that can be defended from a critical point of view but is the one that is closest to the biblical picture. A 'maximal conservative' interpretation may be adopted by someone who is not a true fundamentalist. The old fundamentalism was generally easy to identify because it was blatantly and unequivocably apologetic about the Bible. Indeed, it was not unusual for the tone to be anti-intellectual. Neo-fundamentalism is just as fundamentalist, but it tends to cloak its defence of the Bible in the rhetoric of scholarship.

A truly fundamentalist approach will usually show itself by the assumption that the Bible is inerrant in the autographs, whereas a 'maximal conservative' approach will usually have moved away from such a stance. (Barr does not seem to make a distinction between 'conservative evangelical' and 'fundamentalist', but in my own experience there is a distance between those conservatively inclined and the true fundamentalist who believes in 'the inerrancy of the Scriptures'.) However, in practice it is not always easy to tell the difference between the two. The neo-fundamentalist will often adopt a maximal conservative approach without admitting the true guiding principle of his or her work in biblical studies. On the other hand, a fundamentalist approach does not have to be confined to the Bible-believers. A dogmatic scepticism that continually looks for a way to reject or denigrate the biblical text can be as 'fundamentalist' in its own way as a refusal to allow the Bible to be wrong. This attitude was well addressed by Hans Barstad in his essay on 'bibliophobia' (Barstad 1998).

There is no permanent state of purity nor any established chair of righteousness in scholarship. Even if one suspects that a scholarly position or theory is ideologically motivated – whether from biblical fundamentalism or some other ideology – one should evaluate the position on the basis of stated arguments. Trying to second guess motives has become too much of a pastime in the academy. This brings us to a related issue: the *ad hominem* argument.

1.2.7 'Maximalists', 'Minimalists' and the *ad hominem* Argument

As noted below (§1.3.2), the history debate took on an unwelcome shrillness in the 1990s. The tendency for *ad hominem* argument and personal attacks was especially evident in the debate over 'minimalism' and 'maximalism'. These terms have come into common usage in recent years to characterize the approach of scholars to reconstructing the history of Israel. These have been defined as follows: 'minimalist': one who accepts the biblical text only when it can be confirmed from other sources; 'maximalist': one who accepts the biblical text unless it can be proved wrong (Knauf 1991c: 171, though W. Hallo claims to have coined the terms [2005: 50; 1980: 3–5, nn. 4, 11, 12, 23, 55]). This designation has a certain usefulness in that it captures the dichotomy in how different scholars approach history and thus helps to explain and characterize some radical differences of interpretation of the same data. Yet in the end it is mainly a hindrance to discussion, for several reasons:

- Almost all scholars are minimalists in certain parts of history. That is, most scholars have now abandoned the picture of the biblical text for the 'patriarchal period' and the settlement in the land. Even though many still accept the concept of a united monarchy, few would follow the picture of David and Solomon's kingdom as found in Samuel–Kings or Chronicles.
- There are very few true maximalists, that is, those who accept the testimony of the Bible unless it be falsified. Indeed, the only history known to me so far written that one could call 'maximalist' is that of Provan, Long and Longman (2003; reviewed in Grabbe 2004c, 2011b).

- Some of those pursuing a minimalist interpretation sometimes give the impression that they alone are exercising methodological rigour and that they are eschewing the subjective interpretations of others. This can be misleading, since all historical work is done within a theoretical framework. Apart from total scepticism, all attempts to understand the past make certain assumptions and depend on certain data. Thus, reconstructing the history of Palestine based purely on archaeology might seem more methodologically 'pure' than using texts, but this fails to realize that the context for the archaeological interpretation has been created by considerable use of texts (J. M. Miller 1991; Ahlström 1991; Na'aman 2013; Dever [2001: 88; 2005: 77] seems to have misunderstood this point). Some who adopt the label 'minimalist' have drawn enthusiastically on reconstructions based on texts when it suits their purpose (for an example, see Grabbe 2000d).

It has become common in recent years to introduce personal motives into arguments: 'so-and-so takes this position because he/she is/thinks/believes this or that'. Unfortunately, we can always find reasons to say that someone takes a scholarly position because of personal or ideological motives (see the well-founded plea of Lemche 2000). Such statements have no place in scholarly argument. In fact, there is probably not a one of us who has not taken a position on some issue for personal reasons, even if totally unconscious of this motive. As suggested above (§1.2.6) I am very sensitive to arguments or positions that seem to arise from a fundamentalist stance with regard to the Bible. Yet, as John Emerton once remarked from the floor in a conference, we should reply to the specific arguments rather than what we think might lie behind them (cf. Grabbe 1987).

To take just one example, two British scholars published an article putting the case for dating the Siloam inscription to the Maccabaean period (§5.1.1). This was attacked in an article by a number of scholars which had the heading of 'pseudo-scholarship'. Some of those who published in the article made some relevant and serious points, but the main abuse of editorial privilege was the header of 'pseudo-scholarship'. No doubt it was supplied by the editorial staff, not the contributors, but it served to prejudice the readership from the start. The redating of the Siloam inscription may be wrong – and most so far think it is – but it is not 'pseudo-scholarship', and such *ad hominem* comments do not belong in scholarly writing or debate.

1.3 The Contemporary Practice of Writing Israel's History

It would probably not be an exaggeration to say that there is something of a 'crisis' – or at least a major impasse between two basic positions – with regard to the history of Israel. It is unfortunate but true that many of those taking a position are not really historians and do not seem to understand the issues well enough to qualify for entrance into the debate (not every biblical scholar is a historian!). But the existing fact – which underpins my reasons for writing this book – is that at present there is a major debate about writing the history of 'ancient Israel' (this term is used for convenience; some would prefer terms such as 'ancient Palestine' or 'southern Syria' or 'the Levant'). This has been widely – but inaccurately – characterized as a debate between 'minimalists' and 'maximalists'. Such a characterization is a caricature since it fails to note the wide variety of positions or principles of working among different scholars (on 'minimalists' and 'maximalists' see the discussion at §1.2.7).

In order to understand this debate – taken up in detail in the subsequent chapters of this book – it is useful to indicate how things have developed and where we stand generally in relation to historical study. I shall, first, give a survey of the debate about writing history in general, and then indicate how the writing, specifically of Israelite history, has developed in the past 40 years or so.

1.3.1 Developments in General Historiography

In order to discuss the history of ancient Israel, it is useful to survey how the science of historiography has evolved in recent times (for a more detailed survey and bibliography, see Grabbe 2004a: 2–10). It is fair to say that the principles developed by Thucydides almost 1500 years ago in many ways still guide the historian (cf. Grabbe 2001b), yet much has also been learned in the past couple of centuries.

In the nineteenth century, important developments toward the modern study of history were made by Leopold von Ranke, but he is often misunderstood: he belonged to the Romantic tradition and believed in the importance of intuition in historical reconstruction, as well as careful research based on documentation. Ranke's contributions can be summarized under three headings (Evans 1997: 16–18): (a) establishing history as a discipline separate from both philosophy and literature, (b) seeing the past in its own terms rather than judging by the standards of the present and (c) a critical method of source criticism based on philological principles. He made the important distinction between primary and secondary sources (Iggers 1997: 24). In his view the goal was to write history 'as it really [or "essentially"] happened' ('wie es eigentlich gewesen ist'). This famous quote, important as it is as a symbol, is often misapprehended. The context for Ranke's statement was that, contrary to previous historians who saw it as their right to pronounce judgment on history, he felt the responsibility of the historian was only to write what had happened, not moralize about it. Perhaps the most far-reaching impact came from the new discipline of the social sciences, toward the end of the nineteenth century. There was a shift in emphasis to social and economic trends rather than the actions of individuals in the political sphere. This application of the social sciences to historical study had its major impact after World War II. Especially important was the *'Annales* School', of whom one of its leading proponents was F. Braudel; they emphasized the significance of the *longue durée* perspective (§1.2.2).

A watershed was marked in the 1960s with what is often called the 'linguistic turn' in historical study. There were several trends. Some of these were important developments but did not cause a major break with the past, such as the desire to write history 'from below' – to focus on the effect events had on individuals, the common people; to write the story of the ordinary soldier or the ordinary citizen; to recognize the common omission of women and other minorities from conventional histories. The 'grand narrative' so characteristic of some world histories of the nineteenth century and earlier had by and large already been rejected, but the tendency for many historians was now to work on what some called 'micro-histories'. The optimistic view of continual progress gave way to a more sceptical view of such a perspective. Finally, there was the debate on epistemology that had been underway for a long time in philosophy and elsewhere, owing much to Friedrich Nietzsche and Jacob Burckhardt.

At this time a radical questioning undermined the two major assumptions that had undergirded historical work from Thucydides to Braudel: the correspondence theory of history and the view that human intentions were the basis of human actions. This fundamental questioning came from what has broadly been called 'postmodernism', though in fact a great many different considerations – philosophical, literary, linguistic, anthropological, feminist – fed into the debate on historical methodology. The view now championed by some was that objective historical inquiry was not possible. How to define or characterize 'postmodernism' as it applies to history is not an easy task since postmodernists themselves often seem to avoid a positive statement of their historical method. One useful way of summarizing the movement, however, may be the following (Appleby, Hunt and Jacob 1994: 198–237; Iggers 1997: 6–16, 118–33; Zagorin 1999):

- There is no essential difference between history and literature, between a historical narrative and a narrative of fiction. In the words of Hayden White, 'historical narratives are verbal fictions, the contents of which are as much *invented* as *found* and the forms of which have more in common with their counterparts in literature than they have with those in the sciences' (1978: 82, italics in the original).
- The world of the text is self-contained; nothing exists outside the text, because no reality can transcend the discourse that expresses it.
- There is no possibility of certain knowledge; there is no truth, only ideology. 'The basic idea of postmodern theory of historiography is the denial that historical writing refers to an actual historical past' (Iggers 1997: 118), that there is an objective truth separate from the subjective thought of the historian. Or one could point to the statement of Foucault that 'reality does not exist, that only language exists' (Iggers 1997: 133).
- The text can be interpreted in multiple ways. Authorial intent is an illusion. Texts conceal as much as they reveal, which means they need to be deconstructed to bring out the hidden assumptions, contradictions and gaps; furthermore, meaning is always deferred.
- The 'grand narrative' is at an end, to be replaced by fragmentation, with many different even competing histories and the inclusion of groups formerly omitted or marginalized. The key phrase is 'history from below' but also a shift to a focus on culture.

The radical antihistoristic elements of postmodernism are not in fact completely unexpected, as a close scrutiny of the developments in historical theory in the past two centuries shows (cf. Grabbe 2004a: 2–6). Nevertheless, the debate about postmodernism continues in a vigorous fashion among professional historians, at least in some parts of the Academy in English-speaking scholarship. One of the main advocates for a postmodern perspective in history, Keith Jenkins, has recently produced a 'postmodernist reader' (1997) that tries to bring together some of the most influential articles in the debate. In a long introduction he lays out the main issues, with a defence of his own approach. One can find a similar advocacy of postmodernism, though perhaps less flamboyantly presented, by Alun Munslow (1997), but the past few years have been especially characterized by a strong resistance movement. Joyce Appleby, Lynn Hunt and Margaret Jacob (1994) produced a book which might appear at first to have a postmodern agenda in its assault on the way 'outsiders' (women and other minorities) have been excluded or neglected. Yet a good part of their text is a strong attack on such postmodern gurus as Foucault and Derrida.

A book achieving widespread circulation in the UK is Evans's *In Defence of History* (1997), which is written for a non-technical readership. It actually tries to explain clearly the different approaches of recent writers on historiography and is not just an assault on the postmodern, but it ultimately rejects postmodernism from being the way forward even if the relevance of some aspects of it is accepted. A wide-ranging attack on a number of recent trends in history-writing, as the title *The Killing of History* already makes quite plain, has been carried out by Keith Windschuttle (1996). He covers more than postmodernism, and such figures as Derrida are mentioned mainly in passing; however, he has a long chapter attacking Foucault whom he sees as the main culprit in undermining the traditional study of history. Although the title and style might suggest an irresponsible blunderbuss attack on ill-defined targets, the book makes a number of effective points despite some shortcomings (D. Gordon 1999). C. B. McCullagh (1998) has tried to steer a middle way by recognizing that the critics have not always presented the arguments of the postmodernists fairly and by himself giving due weight to the postmodernist positions; nevertheless, taking into consideration the valid points about subjectiveness and the place of language in reality, he still concludes that historical knowledge is possible (cf. also McCullagh 1991).

In the end, however, one can only agree with the observation that 'the majority of professional historians…as usual, appear to ignore theoretical issues and would prefer to be left undisturbed to get on with their work while no doubt hoping the postmodernist challenge will eventually go away' (Zagorin 1999: 2). This certainly fits the attitudes of most historians I know in my own university who seem to have little interest in the debates on theory. Perez Zagorin has recently divided the reactions to the 'linguistic turn' into three sorts (1999: 3). Whether another division might be truer to the real situation is for others to say, but Zagorin's three-fold categorization is certainly clearer and more understandable than the rather confusing attempt to find five different positions by Jenkins (1997: 21–4):

- 'Some who evince great alarm at the incursions of postmodernism, considering the latter as a new kind of nihilism threatening the very existence of history as an intellectual discipline, and who tend to regard themselves as a beleaguered minority defending the citadel of reason against its hordes of enemies' (e.g., K. Windschuttle).

- A small number of those who have embraced postmodernism (e.g., K. Jenkins).
- Those who feel that historians still have something to learn from the challenges and questions raised by postmodernism but have rejected it as a framework or at least its more extreme conclusions (e.g., R. J. Evans).

Among historians there is at present no uniform answer to the question of the value – or not – of postmodernism in historical study. What we see is a reluctance among practising historians to give up the idea that there is some connection between what they write and past reality, though the cogency of some of the main features of recent theoretical movements is recognized (covertly if not overtly). Iggers summarizes it this way:

> There is therefore a difference between a theory that denies any claim to reality in historical accounts and a historiography that is fully conscious of the complexity of historical knowledge but still assumes that real people had real thoughts and feelings that led to real actions that, within limits, can be known and reconstructed. (Iggers 1997: 119)

So what might we conclude from this very brief survey of historical theory and methodology in the past few centuries? No doubt a number of points could be made, but I draw primarily four conclusions:

1. Although put in a particularly stringent manner by the postmodernists and their predecessors such as Nietzsche, the question of epistemology has been discussed at length by historians through the centuries.
2. The idea that past historians worked in a positivistic mechanical fashion, to produce what they saw as objective descriptions of 'what actually happened', is a caricature. The history of historical writing is one of self-critique (or at least criticism of the past generation), questioning of rules and attempts to come to grips with an often-difficult profession.
3. The place of the imagination and the subjective insight of the practising historian has been widely recognized through the past two centuries and more. Despite the occasional temporary reign of positivism, the subjective nature of the task and the important contribution made by the individual interpreter have usually been taken for granted.

4. Perhaps one of the most far-reaching developments has been the embracing of the social sciences and the recognition that history should include all facets of life – economics, the structure and complexity of society, the lives of ordinary people, the material culture, both high and low literature, ideology and beliefs.

1.3.2 Forty Years of Debate Among Biblical Scholars

The survey in the previous section was given as background to the present debate on the history of ancient Israel (for a more detailed discussion of the debate in this section, see Grabbe 2000b). If we go back to the 1960s we find a remarkable consensus on many issues, the differences often largely limited to those between the two schools of Albright and Alt–Noth. Their views on history were available in convenient summary in the histories of Israel by J. Bright (1959 [1st edn]; 1980 [3rd edn]) and M. Noth (1956/1960). At that time there were two views of the Israelite occupation of the land, the Albright interpretation and the Alt–Noth interpretation of a peaceful infiltration. The Albright interpretation was widely accepted in North America and strongly defended on archaeological grounds by Albright, G. Ernest Wright, Yigael Yadin and others. As far as the 'patriarchal age' was concerned, the Albright school accepted that the Genesis account was made up of a variety of sources and could not be taken at face value. Nevertheless, it argued for 'essential historicity', again claiming the support of ancient Near Eastern texts. The Alt–Noth school accepted the Wellhausen dictum that the narratives reflected the time when they were written, though Alt still wished to extract data about pre-settlement religion from the narratives.

Already, however, there were signs of changes to come. A little article by George Mendenhall (1962), only sparsely documented and really only a programmatic outline, presented a rather radical reinterpretation of the settlement as a peasant revolt. Then, not long after Albright's death, a study challenging some of his basic conclusions on the patriarchs was published by T. L. Thompson (1974). Some months later another work on the same subject with similar conclusions, despite a quite different approach, was published by John Van Seters (1975). The death knell to an American consensus was sounded; it was the beginning of a rapid end for the historical patriarchs. The year 1975 also provided what proved to be a diversion in the debate – perhaps more accurately described as a sideshow – with the discovery of the Ebla tablets. Exaggerated claims were made that soon had to be retracted, with much embarrassment (Freedman 1978). This should serve as a cautionary tale to those who leap in to 'defend' the Bible by new discoveries that have been studied only incompletely.

Following the rapid fall of support for the patriarchal narratives, the various models of the conquest came under scrutiny. The volume edited by Hayes and Miller (1977) represented the best of conventional scholarship but was already starting to move in new directions. On the patriarchal period, the knife continued to be driven in (e.g., William Dever's survey of the archaeology in the second millennium illustrated the difficulties for the patriarchal narratives). On the Israelite settlement, Miller's contribution gave a thorough critique of the Albright position and ultimately rejected it (Hayes and Miller 1977: 270–4; cf. Miller 1979). His conclusions present a picture emphasizing the development of Israel from internal populations and also from the Sea Peoples or tribes forced to migrate in their wake, and expresses some scepticism toward the significance of nomadic incursions. Then in 1979 appeared Norman Gottwald's long-awaited study that provided the academic underpinning for Mendenhall's programmatic article almost two decades earlier, and it caused immediate stir and debate. The conquest model was defended by Yigael Yadin in an article published only a couple of years before his death, but this was its swan song (Yadin 1982; cf. Yadin 1979); for practical purposes, it was already dead. A collection edited by Freedman and Graf and strongly espousing the Mendenhall–Gottwald thesis was published in 1983, though it was notable especially for the trenchant essay by Mendenhall attacking and disowning Gottwald's approach (Mendenhall 1983).

In the 1980s new developments and discussion shifted to a much more international arena (much of the debate through the 1970s had been carried on in North America). N. P. Lemche (1985) published a sociological study of Israelite origins that included a major critique of Gottwald, but while differing from Gottwald on many points, including the concept of an internal revolt, Lemche's final picture was of an internal development of the indigenous population. Several new histories of Israel appeared in the mid-1980s. Writing in Italian, A. Soggin (1984) began with David and waited until after dealing with the 'empire under Solomon' to discuss the pre-monarchic period (see the survey of Soggin's developing thought in Grabbe 2011c). H. Donner (1984, 1986) completed his history which was firmly in the Alt–Noth tradition. Miller and Hayes (1986) drew on the insights of both North American and Continental scholars. Sheffield Academic Press launched a new series, The Social World of Biblical Antiquity, with a number of monographs applying sociology and archaeology to late-second and early-first-millennium BCE Palestine (e.g., Frick 1985).

On the archaeological side, M. Weippert (1979) defended the classic Alt–Noth hypothesis of the settlement, but in an article appearing the next year V. Fritz (1980; cf. Fritz 1981) was already developing a model which looked remarkably like a synthesis of the Alt–Noth and the Mendenhall–Gottwald models, which he referred to as the 'symbiosis hypothesis'. The large-scale archaeological surveys undertaken in Israel brought to bear a whole new range of data, and a new generation of Israeli archaeologists began to break through the archaeological tradition strongly influenced by Albright. Israel Finkelstein (1988) appeared in English with a full-blown exposition of his model of the Israelite settlement which delineated a revised version of the original Alt model (but with the full archaeological backing which Alt had never had available) and also drawing on the Mendenhall–Gottwald model. Finally, Helga Weippert (1988) published an archaeological handbook which summarized the results of Palestinian archaeology to the Persian period. The impact of the new archaeological assessment cannot be overestimated, and the discussion gained a whole new basis which outdated all that had gone before.

Through the 1980s the areas of interest began to shift. The settlement and what preceded it remained of intense concern, but now the first part of the Israelite monarchy came firmly into focus. Up until this time, the debate about Israel's origins had concerned the patriarchs and the settlement, with history securely beginning at the reign of Saul. Yet already in 1986 Miller was asking questions about the reliability of the Saul, David and Solomon traditions:

> When it first appeared a decade ago, my treatment of Solomon generally seems to have been regarded as overly skeptical, especially in view of what was believed to be strong archaeological evidence in Solomon's behalf. Alan Millard and William Dever were particularly outspoken on this matter. Nowadays, my treatment seems to be viewed as rather traditional and conservative. (J. M. Miller 1997a: 12–13)

However, the real shaker was the collection of essays by G. Garbini (1986) whose rapid translation into English facilitated its impact. Garbini was known primarily for his work in Northwest Semitic philology, rather than biblical scholarship, and a number of his comments arise out of the particular tradition of biblical scholarship in Italy, which look somewhat odd to those in the Germanic/Anglo-Saxon tradition. Yet despite its weaknesses, Garbini's collection of essays attacked some fundamental consensuses in OT scholarship, not least that of the Solomonic kingdom.

Sometimes influenced by Garbini's radical book, but sometimes independently of it, a number of scholars were critiquing the consensus about the Israelite monarchy. R. Coote and K. Whitelam (1987) had done a sociological study which encompassed not only the settlement as such but took in the development of the Israelite monarchy. E. A. Knauf produced two books (1985, 1988) which ignored the emphasis on Israel and instead concentrated on other Palestinian peoples (anticipating the 'Palestinian' arguments of the 1990s – see below), but his critical treatment of all sources and his scepticism toward the biblical text, until verified, was very much in line with the work of others in this decade. H. M. Niemann (1993) argued that Israel did not become a state until the time of Omri; and Judah, until the time of Uzziah. Diana Edelman (1991, 1996a) did a search for the 'historical Saul'. Perhaps the most influential book, though, was ostensibly an investigation of another subject. D. W. Jamieson-Drake (1991) was asking about the existence of scribal schools, but to answer the question he addressed the issue of when Jerusalem might have become the capital of a major political entity, concluding this was not until the late eighth century.

It would be wrong to assume, however, that the sceptical trend was the only one. Although the abandonment of the patriarchal period and the conquest model was almost universal, the majority of scholars remained within the consensus that we knew a lot about Israelite and Judaean history at least from the time of David. Among the archaeologists a rigorous debate has been going on for some time between members of the 'Tel Aviv school' (e.g., Finkelstein 1981; Ussishkin 1980b; Finkelstein and Na'aman [eds] 1994) and several American archaeologists such as William Dever and Lawrence Stager over the attribution of certain finds to the Solomonic age. However, Dever in particular fronted opposition to those casting doubts on our knowledge of the David and Solomonic age (Dever 1982, 1996; cf. Dever 1998a).

With the coming of the 1990s there was a decade which saw a real explosion of new ideas and challenges to consensuses. Particularly eventful was the year 1992. The *Anchor Bible Dictionary* appeared (though many of its articles were actually completed in the late 1980s). The multiple-author entry on 'Israel, History of' (*ABD* III, 526–76) will probably become recognized as a classic, with Lemche on the Pre-Monarchic Period, Dever on Archaeology and the 'Conquest', and R. P. Carroll on the Post-Monarchic Period. Also published in 1992 was Thompson's book on the early history of the Israelite people, but the book which in many ways made the greatest impact in that year came from a surprising quarter: this was P. R. Davies' *In Search of 'Ancient Israel'*.

I say ‘surprising’ because Davies made no claim to originality; his aim was to translate and expound some of the recent trends and their basis for students (1992: 7). Yet his book caused a storm: eliciting reviews, such as that by Iain Provan published in the *Journal of Biblical Literature* (1995), along with responses from Davies and Thompson. The publication of the Tel Dan ‘Ben-David’ inscription brought a great flurry of claims and counterclaims (§4.1.3.1). G. Ahlström’s opus magnum was published posthumously in 1993. The title of Keith Whitelam’s 1996 book, *The Invention of Ancient Israel*, with the provocative subtitle of *The Silencing of Palestinian History*, was a harbinger of what has been probably the greatest stimulus to controversy. In the same year, Lemche brought out a full-scale treatment of the pre-monarchic period (1996a), and the next year a collection of essays on archaeology and history had papers from a number of the protagonists in the debate (Silberman and Small [eds] 1997). The most recent contribution on the issue of the early monarchy is the volume, *The Age of Solomon* (Handy [ed.] 1997), which lays out the main issues and positions for the early monarchy.

Unfortunately, the next few years saw the debate take on a shrillness and *ad hominem* character that it had not seemed to possess before. The long debate between the Tel Aviv and American archaeologists was made by those who differed in a good-natured way but had no personal animosity. The sharp exchanges which have come to the surface since the early 1990s are of a different and more ominous quality (e.g., Dever et al. 1997). The terms ‘maximalist’ and ‘minimalist’ began to be pejorative labels, and the term ‘nihilist’ came to be used of certain positions (Dever 1995a; cf. 1996: 45, where he clarifies and defends his use of the term, though with evident unease). Some said the ‘minimalists’ were dangerous; others, that they could be safely ignored. The curious anomaly of dangerous people who can be safely ignored serves as a symbol of the unhelpful way in which the debate has moved. One has the sense that it has ceased to be a matter of academic disagreement and has become an emotive and personal issue.

This was hardly a one-sided fight, however; there has been intimation that those who defended the status quo were nothing but biblical fundamentalists, which was not usually the case. This led to a hardening of stances and a tendency to defend established positions rather than debating the issues in a genuine desire to understand the other side. But when things become so ugly that some begin to use the term ‘anti-Semitic’ of particular academic positions, one begins to despair of any chance of a proper scholarly exchange. It was my frustration over this lack of genuine debate that led to the founding of the European Seminar on

Methodology in Israel's History in 1995, with the aim of moving past the 'minimalist'/'maximalist' dichotomy by assembling a group of mature scholars working in the field of history who were willing and able to talk to each other, whatever their positions or disagreements (see Grabbe [ed.] 1997; [ed.] 1998; [ed.] 2001; [ed.] 2003; [ed.] 2005; [ed.] 2007; [ed.] 2008; [ed.] 2010; [ed.] 2011; [ed.] 2017; [ed.] forthcoming).

The impression that one has now is that the debate has settled down. Although they do not seem to admit it, the minimalists have triumphed in many ways. That is, most scholars reject the historicity of the 'patriarchal period', see the settlement as mostly made up of indigenous inhabitants of Canaan and are cautious about the early monarchy. The exodus is rejected or assumed to be based on an event much different from the biblical account. On the other hand, there is not the widespread rejection of the biblical text as a historical source that one finds among the main minimalists. There are few, if any, maximalists (defined as those accepting the biblical text unless it can be absolutely disproved) in mainstream scholarship, only on the more fundamentalist fringes. Most who write on the history of ancient Israel now take a position that accepts some minimalist positions (as just noted) but is also willing to make use of the biblical text as one of the sources in reconstructing the history of Israel and Judah. (This, incidently, was the position of most of those participating in the European Seminar in Historical Methodology.) The European Seminar had its final meeting in 2012, since it was felt by most of us that this particular group had gone as far as it could (see Grabbe [ed.] forthcoming). However, some younger scholars in Europe and in North America seem to be carrying on the debate in some fashion, which is welcome.

Religion is properly a part of any discussion of the history of Israel. Alt, Mendenhall and Gottwald all seem to have been concerned to hold onto the religion in the early traditions while dismissing the history (Lemche 1985: 413–15). Yet the debate in this area has to some extent been carried on in its own way. For over two decades after Georg Fohrer's classic history (1968/1972) little of major significance appeared (Schmidt [1983] understood his work, strangely, as 'standing midway between a "history of Israelite religion" and a "theology of the Old Testament"', while Cross's [1973] sections on religion had mostly been published sometime before), though a number of relevant individual studies were published (e.g., Albertz 1978). Nevertheless, a great deal of work was being done in individual areas under the stimulus of new discoveries and new questions. Perhaps the most significant new finds were the Kuntillet 'Ajrud and Khirbet el-Qôm inscriptions which implied that Yhwh had a consort. A perennial question is when monotheism developed in Israel, and also whether aniconism was always a feature of Yhwh worship. Mark Smith's monograph came out in 1990, written primarily from a Northwest Semitic perspective (2nd edn 2002). This was followed in 1992 by the most thorough synthesis to date, by Rainer Albertz (ET 1994), which made use of all sources, textual, archaeological and ancient Near Eastern. Following Albertz's work, a plethora of monographs and collections have appeared, and the debate on Israel's religion is as energetic as that on the history in general (see further at §4.2.8).

1.3.3 Principles of Historical Method Used in this Book

As noted above (§1.1), the present book is not a full history as such but an attempt to discuss the issues relating to writing a history (cf. Grabbe 2004a: 13–16), though most of the areas that would be controversial are dealt with in one way or another. Therefore, the principles that follow do not form a full list of principles for writing a full history; rather they indicate why certain decisions are taken and paths followed in the discussion that follows in subsequent chapters of this book.

1. All potential sources should be considered. Nothing should be ruled out a priori. After a full critical evaluation has been undertaken, some sources might be excluded, but this is only a posteriori.
2. Preference should be given to primary sources, that is, those contemporary or nearly contemporary with the events being described (a concept expounded by L. von Ranke [Iggers 1997: 24; Knauf 1991a: 46]). This means archaeology and inscriptions. The biblical text is almost always a secondary source, written and edited long after the events ostensibly described. In some cases, the text may depend on earlier sources, but these sources were edited and adapted; in any case the source has to be dug out from the present context.
3. The context of the *longue durée* must always be recognized and given an essential part in the interpretation (§1.2.2). One of the factors often forgotten is the difference between Israel in the north and Judah in the south. There was a considerable disparity of natural resources and economy between the two, with Judah continually the poorer. There are reasons for this (Lehmann 2003: 149–62; Ofer 1994: 93–5). In Judah the agriculture was largely subsistence and disadvantaged by lack of good soil for grain-growing and rainfall of 300–500 mm per annum. The better soils around Hebron had their value reduced by low rainfall. This meant that pastoralism was an important pursuit. In competition with Israel, Judah definitely came

off second best. When Palestine enters the inscriptions of other nations, such as the Assyrians, in the first millennium BCE, there is already a division between Israel and Judah. This long-term division is also hinted at in a number of biblical passages (2 Sam. 2.4; 5.4; Judg. 5), in spite of a supposed twelve-tribe nation.

4. Each episode or event has to be judged on its own merits. Even secondary sources have their uses, while primary sources may well contradict one another. Historical reconstruction requires all data to be used, critically scrutinized, evaluated and a judgment made as to the most likely scenario in the light of all that is known.
5. All reconstructions are provisional. New data, new perspectives, new theories may suggest other – better–ways to interpret the data. This openness to new ways of thinking and new configurations of events always needs to be there.
6. All reconstructions have to be argued for. There can be no default position. You cannot just follow the text unless it can be disproved (sometimes expressed in the nonsensical phrase, 'innocent until proved guilty' – as if the text was a defendant in court; if there is a forensic analogy, the text is a witness whose veracity must be probed and tested). The only valid arguments are historical ones. Ideology, utility, theology, morality, politics, authority – none of these has a place in judging how to reconstruct an event. The only argumentation allowed is that based on historical principles. Naturally, subjectivity is inevitable in the process, and all historians are human and have their weaknesses and blindspots. This is why each must argue for their viewpoint and then subject the result to the judgment of peers, who are also human and subjective.

Part II

HISTORICAL INVESTIGATIONS

Chapter 2

SECOND MILLENNIUM: MIDDLE AND LATE BRONZE AGES (2000–1300 BCE)

The Bible begins the story of Israel with creation, or at least with the survivors from the Noachian flood. In many ways Abraham is presented as the first Israelite – even if Israel is made out to be his grandson. This is why most histories of Israel have begun their story sometime in the second millennium BCE, some earlier and some later. The second millennium is a lot of space to cover, but this chapter gives a brief survey, though focusing on those issues that have been associated with writing a history of Israel.

2.1 Sources

2.1.1 Archaeology

The Middle and Late Bronze Ages cover much of the second millennium BCE, MB extending over approximately 2000–1500 BCE, and LB about 1500 to 1200 BCE. These divisions are not exact and are to some extent artificial, but they broadly represent significant differences in culture and society, as well as historical background. As noted earlier, terminology for archaeological periods is not consistent (§1.2.4.2). The scheme used here (cf. Dever 1987: 149–50; Ilan 1998: 297) is:

MB I (ca. 2000–1800 BCE)
MB II (ca. 1800–1650 BCE)
MB III (ca. 1650–1500 BCE)
LB I (ca. 1500–1400 BCE)
LB IIA (ca. 1400–1300 BCE)
LB IIB (ca. 1300–1200 BCE)

These dates are in part based on historical events, whereas the cultures recorded by archaeology do not always follow the historical periods marked off by events. Needless to say, there is much disagreement, with many beginning the LB in 1550 or even 1600 BCE.

Middle Bronze Age I–III has become better known in recent years (Dever 1977, 1987; Finkelstein 1993; LaBianca 1997; Ilan 1998; Steiner and Killebrew [eds] 2014: 401–94). It seems to have been an era of considerable urbanism: one estimate puts the urban population at half as great again as the rural population (Ilan 1998: 305). Many sites were fortified (Finkelstein 1993), and 'a proliferation of massive fortifications is the single most characteristic feature of the fully developed phases of the period' (Dever 1987: 153): an estimated 65 per cent of the population lived in a few fortified sites of 20 hectares or more. In MB I an unprecedented surge in settlement swept the hill country, large sites including Shechem, Dothan, Shiloh, Tell el-Far'ah North, Hebron, Beth-zur and Jerusalem (Finkelstein 1993: 117–18). About 75 per cent of the population seems to have lived between Shechem and the Jezreel Valley. In the areas of Ephraim and Manasseh there was a definite extension into the western part of the regions. But this settlement in the central hill country began only later, in MB II. In MB II–III almost every site seems to have been fortified, down to as small as 8–16 dunums.

Dever (1987: 153) suggests that the larger sites were in fact city-states. How one is to relate this conclusion with S. Bunimovitz's argument that, following the Rank Size Index, the southern coastal plain and the Jezreel Valley were more integrated in MB than LB (1998: 323) is not clear. D. Ilan (1998: 300–301) suggests that the cultural changes coming about in MB were in part caused by immigration of a new population into Canaan (possibly the Amorites and perhaps others such as the Hurrians), even though the 'diffusionist' explanation has ceased to be very popular (on the Amorites, see §2.2.1.2). There is evidence of trade with Syria and Mesopotamia, with Hazor as the main 'gateway' for Canaan (Ilan 1998: 306–8). There was also extensive trade with Egypt, the main trading centre being Tell el-Dab'a. At first most commerce was with the northern Syrian coast (especially Byblos), but it gradually shifted south. The Middle Bronze Age ended with widespread collapse, often ascribed to the conquest of Avaris and the expulsion of the Hyksos from Egypt (ca. 1550 BCE), and/or subsequent campaigns by Thutmose III and other Eighteenth Dynasty rulers (Ilan 1998: 314–15). There is now a tendency to see other causes (or additional causes) and also to recognize that the collapse was complex and spread over a considerable period of time. Also, there was considerable cultural continuity with the following LB.

The socio-cultural changes at the end of MB 'reshaped the social landscape of Palestine and had a profound, long-term impact on Canaanite society' (Bunimovitz 1998: 320). Although some have seen a major shift away from urbanism in LB, Bunimovitz (1998: 324) argues against this: urbanism was different in scale but the balance between urban and rural remained much the same. The urban centres were considerably smaller but so was the rural sector. A region of major interest, because of its implications for the Israelite settlement, is the highlands: they contained hardly any settlement throughout much of LB (Finkelstein 1988: 339–45). The argument is that pastoralists were the main inhabitants of the hill country on both sides of the Jordan (Finkelstein 1988: 339–45; 1993: 119; 1998c; Ilan 1998: 324). In general the Canaanite city-states were underpopulated and short of manpower (Bunimovitz 1998: 326–7). This is no doubt to be related to the frequent mention in the Amarna letters of the ʻApiru and other groups on the margins of society (§2.2.1.3). The Late Bronze Age ended with a major collapse that seems to have affected the whole of the eastern Mediterranean (§3.1.1).

One issue concerns the cities or sites mentioned in Genesis in connection with the patriarchs (Dever 1977). Albright (1961) had argued that the patriarchal narratives fitted what is commonly called the EB IV period (2200–2000 BCE, though he attempted to date it as late as 1900 or even 1800 BCE). Unfortunately, neither his placement of the patriarchs nor that of others who have tried to put them in the early second millennnium BCE can be supported:

> A date in MB I [= EB IV or Intermediate Bronze] is ruled out for the patriarchs simply because the latest evidence shows that the main centres traditionally associated with their movements, *pace* Albright, are conspicuously lacking in MB I remains… To date, not a single MB IIA [= MB I] site has been found in all of southern Transjordan or the Negeb – one of the principal arenas of patriarchal activities in Genesis. (Dever 1977: 99, 102)

At Beersheba (Gen. 21–22) there was a settlement gap between the Chalcolithic and Iron I – no MB remains at all (Herzog 1997; Rainey 1984: 94). Attempts to find the ‘cities of the plain’ (Gen. 19.24-29) have failed (Dever 1977: 101). It is difficult to find a period in the early or middle second millennium BCE when all sites in the patriarchal narratives were settled; on the contrary, it appears to be not until Iron I that this was so (Clark 1977: 147). On the other hand, many of the main cities known to have existed in MB are completely absent from the patriarchal narratives (Finkelstein and Silberman 2001: 321–3). For further information on the patriarchs, see §2.2.2.

2.1.2 Egyptian Texts

The situation in Palestine is known mainly through Egyptian texts. Although the main source is the Amarna tablets, there are various royal and other inscriptions (see the basic collection in *AEL* I–III; also Redford 1992a). Some of these are cited in the discussions below. From a historical point of view, the Merenptah Stela is very important (§3.1.2).

2.1.2.1 Execration Texts

The Egyptian Execration Texts (Helck 1971: 44–67; Seidlmayer 2001; Redford 1992b; *ANET* 328–9; *CoS* I, 50–2) were ceramic objects on which the names of enemies or potential enemies to be cursed were written. The object was then broken to effect the curses. Two sets of broken pieces, dated to the Twelfth or Thirteenth Dynasty (nineteenth or eighteenth centuries BCE) have been found which included names in the Palestinian area. The main value of these is topographical, to show which cities existed in Palestine in particular periods, since only names and no other information is given. Included are apparently sites in Phoenicia (Byblos, Tyre), Syria (Damascus), some sites in Transjordan (such as Pella), but also Aphek, Ashtaroth, Akko, Laish, Hazor, Rehov, Megiddo, Beth-shean, Ekron, Beth-shemesh, Lod and Ashkelon; Shechem and Jerusalem are the only two highland sites in the extant texts (though the reading 'Jerusalem' has been questioned [Na'aman 1992a: 278–79]). Some personal names also occur, 'Amorite' in form, with apparently no Hurrian or Indo-Iranian ones. An argument has been made that the two sets of texts attest to a gradual sedentarizing and urbanizing of the countryside, but this view has been challenged (Redford 1992b). We do know that the Ephraimite hill country, as well as extensive sections of Syria, are absent from the texts.

2.1.2.2 Amarna Letters

Our most extensive information on Canaan comes from the fourteenth century BCE, in the Amarna letters (Moran 1992; *ANET* 483–90; *CoS* III, 237–42). At this time, Palestine was a part of the Egyptian New Kingdom. The letters belonged to the archive of Amenhotep IV, better known as Akhenaten (1353–1336 BCE), in the capital of Amarna that he built on a new site. After his death, the capital was abandoned, which is probably why the archive was not eventually discarded. The letters are written in Akkadian which seems to have been the language of international communication at the time. When the city was excavated in the nineteenth century, among the recovered archives were copies of correspondence between the Egyptian administration and their vassals in other regions, as well as with other major powers. Many of the letters are from local chieftains or city-states in Palestine (including Jerusalem) and tell of the situation there. These so-called 'Amarna letters' give us a unique insight into events in Palestine during this period.

The city of Ugarit is mentioned in the Amarna letters (e.g., EA 1, 45, 89, 98, 126, 151), though it was not a vassal of Egypt. But we know of a number of the northern polities in Syria that were south of Ugarit and under Egyptian control, including Amurru (EA 60–62, 73–76, etc.), Byblos (Gubla: EA 67–140, etc.), Sidon (Ṣiduna: EA 83, 85, 92, 101, 103, 114, 144–49, etc.), and Tyre (Ṣurru: EA 77, 89, 92, 101, etc.). Our information for the area of Phoenicia and Syria is more extensive than that for Canaan, because of the voluminous correspondence of Rib-Hadda of Byblos (most of the letters in EA 67–140). These letters tell us especially about the activities of 'Abdi-Aširta and Aziru of Amurru. Unfortunately, they tell us little about what was going on further south, except to affirm Egyptian control of the whole area. However, our concern is not primarily with the area of Lebanon and Syria but the area of Palestine or Canaan. Fortunately, we have quite a few letters from the area of Canaan itself. We know of the main city-states of Hazor, Megiddo, Shechem, Jerusalem, Gezer, Gath, Ashkelon and Lachish. The Amarna letters describe a situation in which the various city-states are jockeying for position, whether to gain power and territory or to defend themselves against takeover by neighbouring city-states or perhaps even a combination of both. Among those who wrote letters to the Pharaoh was the king of Jerusalem (Urusalim). We have six letters from him (EA 285–90), plus a couple of other letters that refer to him (EA 284, 366). The king of Jerusalem is called 'Abdi-Ḫeba. Other kings include Suwardata of Gath and Lab'aya of Shechem. Other cities mentioned are Gaza (EA 129, 287, 296), Ashkelon (EA 187, 320–1, 322, 370), Gezer (EA 253, 254, 287, etc.) and Lachish (EA 287, 288, 328, 329, 335).

The name of the king of Jerusalem (Urusalim), 'Abdi-Ḫeba, means 'servant of the (Hurrian) goddess Ḫeba'; however, as far as we can tell he was a native Canaanite, one of the many kinglets of the Canaanite city-states. In the passages that follow, the term used for the head of the various city states is usually *ḫazannu* which normally means 'mayor' or chief administrator of a city; however, it is used here of the petty kings of the city-states. The Akkadian term for king, *šarru*, seldom occurs for the rulers of the city-states. We have six letters from 'Abdi-Ḫeba (EA 285-90), plus a couple of other letters that refer to him (EA 284, 366). Here is one (EA 287):

> May the [kin]g know (that) all the lands are [at] peace (with one another), but I am at war. May the king provide for his land. Consider the lands of Gazru, Ašqaluna, and L[akis]i. They have given them food, oil, and any other requirement. So may the king provide for archers and the mayors will belong to the king, my lord. But if there are no archers, then the ki[ng] will have neither lands nor mayors. Consider Jerusalem! This neither my father nor m[y] mother gave to me. The [str]ong hand: …(arm) [of the king] gave it to me. Consider the deed! This is the deed of Milkilu and the deed of the sons of Lab'ayu, who have given the land of the king <to> the 'Apiru. (Moran 1992: 328)

As will be clear, we need to keep in mind that only 'Abdi-Ḫeba's side of the story is given in his letters. His claims to loyalty and being a victim of treacherous neighbours need to be considered alongside other letters, letters from those very same neighbours who accuse him of treachery, aggression and disloyalty toward the Pharaoh! (e.g., EA 280).

As already noted, what we can find from the various letters is that there were a number of competing city-states. They squabble among themselves and complain to the Pharaoh, each manoeuvring for position and seeking advantage for itself in competition with its neighbours, constantly playing off one another in relation to the Egyptian king. A combination of the Amarna letters, archaeology and a recent petrographic examination of the clay composition of the letters allows us to reconstruct some of the interactions of the various city-states at this time (Goren, Finkelstein and Na'aman 2004). Two of those who have written on the city-states in Canaan are Nadav Na'aman (e.g., 1992a, 1997c) and Israel Finkelstein (e.g., 1996c; 2013: 13–22). Although Na'aman and Finkelstein have a number of differences in their reconstruction of the system of city-states, the general picture they paint is still remarkably similar (in addition to Goren, Finkelstein and Na'aman 2004, see Finkelstein and Na'aman 2005). They agree that there were about 20–25 city-states in Canaan (not to mention the other city-states in Lebanon and Syria). They also disagree about whether the city-state boundaries included all the land (so Finkelstein) or omitted a certain amount of 'no-man's-land' (Na'aman).

One of the main players was Lab'ayu of Shechem. He protests his loyalty to the Egyptian king, but 'Abdi-Ḫeba and others accuse him of aggressive tactics (EA 244):

> Thus says Biridiya, the loyal servant of the king… May the king, my lord, be apprised that since the regular army went back (to Egypt), Lab'ayu has made war against me so that we are unable to pluck the sheep (or) complete the harvest. We can't even go out the city gate because of Lab'ayu since

> he found out that regular troops are not c[oming fo]rth. And no[w] he is determin[ed] to take Megiddo. So may the king please rescue his city; let not Lab'ayu seize it! (Rainey 2015a: 1, #244)

After his death, his sons are alleged to have carried on the same way (EA246, 250, 287, 289). What we appear to have here is a coalition of city-states, led by Shechem, that was seeking to seize control of territory that would allow them to control the main trade routes through Palestine: the coastal route connecting Egypt to Lebanon, Syria and beyond and the King's Highway that extended from the Gulf of Aqaba through the Jordan Valley and on up to Damascus (Finkelstein and Na'aman 2005). With Lab'ayu were Gezer, Ginti-kirmil, Tel Yoqne'am, Anaharath, and eventually Pehel or Pella (Piḫilu), Ashtaroth and the city of the kinglet Yashdata (perhaps Taanach). Opposing them (perhaps simply for self-defence) was another coalition of Megiddo, Rehov, Achshaph, Acco, Gath, and perhaps Hazor. The thrust of the Lab'ayu axis threatened to divide the rest of Egyptian Canaan into two disconnected parts, a northern grouping (the anti-Shechem alliance listed above) and a southern one of Jerusalem, Gath, Ashkelon and Lachish. Lab'ayu apparently intended to take Shim'on or Shimron (Shamḫuna) in the Jezreel Valley, which would allow him to encircle those opposing him in the rest of the Jezreel Valley, including the Egyptian centre at Beth-shean. If he had been able to achieve his evident territorial ambitions, this would have given him a base from which he could manipulate trade and might even endanger Egyptian control of the region. Eventually, Egypt acted to sort out Lab'ayu's rebellion and apparently executed him (cf. EA 245, 250, 253, 254, 280).

One term that appears several times is *'Apiru* (§2.2.1.3).

2.1.2.3 The Story of Sinuhe

Although some have taken this as an actual account of personal experiences, it seems to be a piece of literature (*AEL* I, 222–35; Baines 1982). Its main theme seems to focus on the disadvantages of being removed from one's country of Egypt, but it makes reference to a number of data relating to Syria and Palestine that seem to represent a contemporary description (Simpson 1984; Rainey 1972).

2.1.3 Ugaritic Texts

The city-state of Ugarit on the Mediterranean coast opposite Cyprus has become quite important for OT study. The city was known about through the Amarna letters but was not discovered until about 1928 in the area of Ras Shamra in Syria. Tablets written in an unknown language and script were unearthed quite quickly. The script was written on clay tablets in wedge shapes but, unlike cuneiform, was clearly an alphabet of 29 letters. The script and language were deciphered within a couple of years, and some of the important tablets were already translated before World War II. Excavations still continue, and tablets have even been found in recent years. The language belongs to Northwest Semitic, the sub-family which also includes Hebrew, Aramaic and Phoenician.

Ugarit already existed as an independent entity in the eighteenth century, but it reached its height during the Amarna period (fourteenth century). We have correspondence between Egypt and Ugarit in the Amarna tablets and in texts from Ugarit. The city was apparently destroyed sometime before 1200 BCE, whether by the Sea Peoples (as often alleged) or others. When the Ugaritic texts were first deciphered about 1930, their importance for the mythology and literary world of the Israelites was quickly recognized. Many of the texts are in alphabetic cuneiform and the Ugaritic language (*KTU*; *CML*; Parker 1997). But other texts were in Akkadian and even Hurrian, and many of these have more direct relevance for the history of the eastern Mediterranean in the second millennium BCE. Although Ugarit and the Ugaritic texts have often been used to reconstruct Canaanite culture, mythology and religion, Ugarit seems to have been considered outside of Canaan (Grabbe 1994b). The Ugaritic texts provide some historical information for the Amarna age, though this is usually in the way of general background since they do not usually mention Palestine directly. (For general information on the Ugaritic texts and the history of Ugarit, see especially Watson and Wyatt [eds] 1999.)

2.1.4 Mesopotamian Texts

Most of the Mesopotamian texts do not mention Palestine, though there seems to have been trade between Hazor and Mari (§2.1.1). These texts are important for other sorts of information, and they have been invoked in the past for information relating to the patriarchs. The Mari texts, first discovered in the 1930s, are still being published; a collection of letters in translation is now available (Heimpel 2003). The Nuzi tablets, which brought in the discussion about the patriarchs, are also still in the process of publication (for example, Maidman 1994).

2.1.5 Biblical Text

The main biblical source that might fit the Late Bronze is the Heptateuch: Genesis to Judges. The question is how much the author(s) or compiler(s) knew about the events described. Not long ago, it was a strong consensus of scholarship that the Pentateuch and perhaps even some of the other books were compiled mainly from four sources: the Yahwist (J), the Elohist (E), the Deuteronomist (D), and the priestly writer (P). Many would still agree with that, up to a point, but opinion is much more diverse (Dubovský, Markl and Sonnet [eds] 2016). Basically, the old consensus that had developed around the Documentary Hypothesis has gone, though there is nothing to take its place (Rendtorff 1997; Whybray 1987). Some still accept the Documentary Hypothesis in much its original form, but many accept only aspects of it or at least put a question mark by it. There has also been much debate around the J source (Rendtorff 1997: 53–55) and the P source (Grabbe 1997b). It seems clear that the Pentateuch was put together in the Persian period (Grabbe 2004a: 331–43; 2006c, 2013, 2016). If so, it seems unlikely that a substantial memory of second-millennium events is to be found in it. True, many traditions in the Pentateuch are accepted to be pre-exilic (for example, Deuteronomy is still widely dated to the seventh century BCE), but that is still half a millennium from the end of the Late Bronze, and a thousand years later than a conventional dating for the patriarchs. An evaluation of the patriarchal tradition on its own terms confirms this a priori position (§2.2.2). For a discussion of Joshua and Judges, as well as the Deuteronomistic History in general, see §3.1.6.2.

2.2 Analysis

2.2.1 Peoples/Ethnic and Social Groups

A number of different groups are found in our sources, mainly Egyptian inscriptions and Amarna letters, which have at one time or another been connected with the origins of Israel but are also important for the history of ancient Palestine. Here are mentioned those that are important in the second millennium BCE (for the Sea Peoples and Philistines, see §3.2.2; for the Aramaeans, see §4.2.5). On the general question of labelling such peoples as ‘ethnic groups’, see the discussion at §1.2.5.

2.2.1.1 Hyksos

This was a group of people who became temporary rulers of Egypt but were said to be foreigners associated with Asia (Weinstein 1997a; Oren [ed.] 1997; Redford and Weinstein 1992; Redford 1970b; the monograph of Van Seters [1966] marked a milestone in study of the Hyksos but appeared before major archaeological data were available from Egypt). They ruled during the Second Intermediate Period, making up the Fifteenth Dynasty of the traditional kinglist. One of the main textual sources remains Manetho, as mediated by Josephus and Julius Africanus (Waddell [ed.] 1940), but some native Egyptian sources are also available

(Redford 1997a), as is archaeology (Bietak 1997; Redmount 1995). The Egyptian name *ḥq3w ḫ3swt* means 'rulers of foreign lands' and seems to have been their name for the actual Hyksos rulers, whereas the people are often referred to as *'3mw* 'Asiatics'. The names known from scarabs and other written sources appear to be Northwest Semitic.

It was once argued that there was a 'Hyksos invasion', part of a large Amorite (§2.2.1.2 below) population movement. It is more commonly argued now that 'Asiatics' gradually settled in the eastern part of the delta during the late Twelfth and Thirteenth Dynasties, possibly as slaves or mercenaries. They took over rule to found the Fifteenth Dynasty, with six kings over 108 years. The question of whether it was a gradual process or a sudden coup is still debated. During the time of their rule there was evidently extensive trade with the Levantine coast, Cyprus and possibly even the Aegean (Betancourt 1997). According to the Egyptian texts, they were expelled into Palestine by Kamose and by his brother Ahmose who founded the Eighteenth Dynasty. Ahmose went on to take the Hyksos centre of Sharuhen (perhaps Tell el-'Ajjul or Tel Harar). The question of where the Hyksos came from seems to have a firm answer (or partial answer): the archaeology indicates a population largely (at least in the core Hyksos area) made up of those heavily influenced by Canaanite culture (Bietak 1997; McGovern and Harbottle 1997; Redmount 1995). Neutron Activation Analysis indicates that many amphora with imported goods were manufactured in southern Palestine (McGovern and Harbottle 1997), though Bietak (1997: 98–9) continues to argue a connection with the northern Levant, specifically Byblos, because of the architecture.

2.2.1.2 Amorites (Amurru)

The Amorites are often thought to be important for the early history of Israel (Buccellati 1966, 1997; Gelb 1961). The Bible presents them as a pre-Israelite people in the Palestinian region (e.g., Gen. 15.21; Exod. 13.5), sometimes associated with the hill country (Num. 13.29; Deut. 1.7, 44) but also with the Transjordanian region (Num. 21.13, 26). For example, they are mentioned as being among Israel's ancestors in Ezek. 16.3, though interesingly they were also supposedly one of the peoples opposing Israel on its way to Canaan (Num. 21.21-32). They are known mainly from two sorts of information: (1) their names in cuneiform sources which are Northwest Semitic in structure and different from the Akkadian names (Huffmon 1965; Gelb 1980); (2) references to them in cuneiform sources, usually by the Sumerogram MAR.TU. As far as archaeology is concerned, nothing distinctive has been found to relate to them.

From the late third millennium (2500–2000) they are referred to in texts from Ebla and southern Mesopotamia (usually by the label MAR.TU). In the Old Babylonian period (1900–1600), many northwestern names are found and are identified as 'Amorite' by their structure, though the individual who bore them is seldom said to be Amorite. They are especially associated with the city-state of Mari on the Euphrates. Amorite tribes include the 'sons of the south' (or 'southerners') and 'sons of the north' (or 'northerners'). The name of the first attracted attention since it was equivalent to 'Benjaminites'; however, the reading has been disputed. The last part of the name, *Yamīna*, apparently referring to the right-hand (or southern) bank of the Euphrates, is clear, but the first part of the name is written in Sumerograms DUMU.MEŠ 'sons (of)'. The question is whether it should be read as Akkadian *mārū(-yamīna)* or as Northwest Semitic *bini(-yamīna)* (Tadmor 1958a; Anbar 1991: 83–4 n. 324). Gelb (1961: 37–8) suggests that 'sons' is only a semantic indicator of a tribal name and that it is appropriate to refer only to Yaminites. In any case, there is the parallel tribe of DUMU.MEŠ-*si-im-a-al* 'sons of the north' (or 'northerners'). The similarity to the biblical Benjaminites seems coincidental, even if the name is read *Bini-Yamīna* and not *Mārū-Yamīna* or just *Yamīna.*

Many of the descriptions make them nomadic pastoralists, and one text refers to the Amorite as a 'tent dweller [buffeted?] by wind and rain… the one who digs up mushrooms at the foot of the mountain, who does not know how to…bend his knee, who eats uncooked meat, who in his lifetime does not have a house, who on the day of his death will not be buried' (Buccellati 1966: 92–3, see also 324–30). Although many of the Amorites were tribal and engaged in pastoralism, this was not true of all of them (Kamp and Yoffee 1980: 89–94). There are texts which refer to Amorites in an urban setting. Also, rather than being seen always as unruly, wild and hostile, they seem to be well blended into Sumerian society. In the Ur III period they are 'fully integrated in every facet of the Mesopotamian social landscape. Amorites were pastoralists, agriculturalists, country dwellers and city dwellers' (Kamp and Yoffee 1980: 98). By the late Bronze Age, references to Amorites (*Amurru*) disappear from the Mesopotamian texts except as a general reference for the region to the west. However, a 'kingdom of Amurru' in Syria is known from references in the Amarna letters, Ugaritic texts and the texts from the Hittite capital at Boğazköy in Anatolia (Gelb 1961: 41–2); some Mari texts suggest that it already existed several centuries earlier than the Amarna period (Gelb 1961: 47). It was located west of the Euphrates, in Syria, between Lebanon and Damascus; apparently a section of the territory extended as far as the Mediterranean (Gelb 1961: 42).

There are disagreements over Amorite origins. In the past it has been common to label them nomads on the fringes of civilization in the Euphrates region, and some texts seem to give support to this picture. Others think they were originally farmers in a narrow region of the mid-Euphrates who expanded their territory by moving into the steppe and taking up sheepbreeding. Some cuneiform texts consider them as uncultured, semi-wild people of the wilderness, but this is mainly a biased view. Their names are important because Semitic names had meaning, being sometimes a complete sentence (e.g., 'God has blessed'), which allows the grammar of the language to be partially reconstructed by names alone. Their language was Northwest Semitic and in the same language family as Hebrew, Aramaic, Phoenician and Ugaritic. This suggests a closer affinity with these people, at least in their origins, than to the eastern Assyrians and Babylonians. As for their descendants, it may be significant that several Aramaean groups and even states arose in the early first millennium in the same areas that the Amorites had earlier inhabited, which might suggest that the Aramaeans – at least in part – descended from the earlier Amorites.

2.2.1.3 'Apiru/Ḫaberu

One term that appears several times in second millennium texts is "Apiru' or possibly 'Ḫapiru' or 'Ḫaberu' (Na'aman 1986c; Lemche 1992a; Gottwald 1979: 397–409; Loretz 1984, but see the review of Na'aman [1988b]), often written in cuneiform with the Sumerograms SA.GAZ; Ugaritic: *'pr*; Egyptian *'prw*. When these texts were first studied a century or so ago, it was assumed that it was an ethnic term related to 'Hebrew'. Many modern scholars agree that the term 'Apiru and Hebrew are cognate, but that neither was originally an ethnic term but a social designation: the word seems originally to mean someone outside the social system or an outlaw (Gottwald 1979: 401, 404) or a refugee or migrant (Na'aman 1986c; Lemche 1992a). In the early texts it appears to have a merely descriptive meaning of 'migrant'. People were always temporarily in this category because they would soon be integrated into the (new) society and location. Yet migrants often took on employment that might be considered marginal by the natives, such as becoming mercenaries. Or on occasion they might become brigands as the easiest or even the only way to survive. Šuwardata (apparently ruler of Gath, though there are several possibilities) and 'Abdi-Ḫeba, ruler of Jerusalem, were able to make common cause when they were both threatened by 'Apiru, as indicated in EA 366 (letter from Šuwardata):

> May the king, my lord, be informed that the 'Apiru that rose up...against the lands, the god of the king, my lord, gave to me, and I smote him. And may the king, my lord, be informed that all my brothers have abandoned me. Only 'Abdi-Ḫeba and I have been at war with (that) 'Apiru. Surata, the ruler of Akka, and Endaruta, the ruler of Akšapa, (these) two also have come to my aid...with 50 chariots, and now they are on my side in the war. (Moran 1992: 364)

In the Amarna letters many of those labelled 'Apiru seem to have sold themselves as mercenaries to the highest bidder, while others turned to raiding or stealing. Therefore, the term not infrequently has a pejorative connotation along the lines of 'outlaw' or 'bandit', and was used of one's enemies, regardless of whether they were truly 'Apiru (EA 68, 185, 186). In some cases, the writer accuses fellow kings of city-states of siding with the 'Apiru or employing them against the Pharaoh's interests (EA 286, 287, 288, 289) or asserts that the 'Apiru would take over (EA 366) or even that the rulers themselves are becoming 'Apiru (EA 67, 288). In the biblical text the word has become an ethnic term, used by Israelite and Judahite writers only for themselves, or by outsiders such as the Philistines, perhaps as a way of satirizing the outsiders (Na'aman 1986c). In some passages in the laws, however, it seems to have much of the original base meaning of one who was likely to be vulnerable and poor and in need of legal protection, perhaps even a slave (Exod. 21.2; Deut. 15.12; Jer. 34.9, 14). Idrimi, king of Alalakh, joins 'Apiru when he himself becomes a refugee:

> An evil deed happened in Halab, the seat of my family, and we fled to the people of Emar... (So) I took with me my horse, my chariot, and my groom, went away and crossed over the desert country and even entered into the region of the Sutian warriors...but the next day I moved on and went to the land of Canaan. I stayed in Ammia in the land of Caanan [*sic*]; in Ammia lived (also) natives of Halab, of the country Mukishkhi, of the country Ni' and also warriors from the country Ama'e... There I grew up and stayed for a long time. For seven years I lived among the Hapiru-people. (*ANET* 557; Greenberg 1955: 20)

2.2.1.4 Shasu (Shosu, Š3św, Sutu)

A group referred to in a number of Egyptian texts (Giveon 1971) are the *Š3św*, usually transcribed as Shasu or Shosu (Redford 1990: 68–75; 1992a: 269–80; M. Weippert 1974; Ward 1972, 1992); Akkadian texts, such as the Amarna tablets, seem to refer to the same group as *Sutu* (EA 16, 122, 123, 169, 195, 297, 318). They are often associated with the area of southern Transjordan in Egyptian texts (Redford 1992a: 272–3). Seti I conducted an Asian campaign in which he defeated the Shasu from the fortress of Sile to (the city of) Canaan (= Gaza?) (*ANET* 254; Giveon 1971: #11). In a frontier report from the Papyrus Anastasi VI (*ANET* 259; Giveon 1971: #37) the Shasu tribes are allowed to pass the fortress with their cattle. Several texts mention geographical areas associated with the Shasu (Giveon 1971: ## 6a; 16a): 'the land of the Shasu Samath' (*t3 š3św smt*; *šsw smt*), 'the land of the Shasu Yahu' (*t3 š3św Yh*[*w*]; *šsw yhw*), 'the land of the Shasu Trbr' (*t3 š3św trbr*); 'Seir (in the land of) the Shasu' (*šsw s'rr*); 'Laban (in the land of) the Shasu' (*šsw rbn*); *šsw psps* 'Pyspys (in the land of) the Shasu'; *šsw wrbwr* 'Arbel (?) (in the land of) the Shasu'. Ramesses II claimed to have destroyed the land of the Shasu and captured the mountain of Seir (Giveon 1971: #25). Reference is also made to the tribes of the Shasu of Edom (Giveon 1971: #37). This locates the Shasu in the area of Edom, Seir and Transjordan east of the Arabah.

But the question is complicated by the fact that Shasu are mentioned in lists that include toponyms from other areas, some as far away as Mesopotamia (Giveon 1971: ## 4, 5, 6, 7, 48). Also, Ramesses II's version of the battle of Qadesh refers to the capture of two Shasu who are spying for the Hittites (Giveon 1971: #14). None of these examples proves that Shasu came from other regions, since the topographical lists have diverse names, and the spies accompanying an army would not necessarily remain in their home territory. But another list seems to include mainly names from northern Palestine or northern Syria (Giveon 1971: #13; cf. #12); however, since not all sites can be identified, it is not decisive. The term 'Shasu' is variously taken as a socioethnic group, a sociocultural group, or a geographical location (Hasel 1998: 220). However, up to the time of Ramesses II, the hill-country determinative is consistently used of them in texts, and differences from that in some later texts is explicable, which means that the name refers to a geographical location (Hasel 1998: 220–5). From the data so far known, it seems most likely that where there are geographical indications, the Shasu are usually associated with a specific area around the southern and eastern part of the Dead Sea (Redford 1992a: 272–3), the old area of Edom, Seir and southern Transjordan. If this is correct, it undermines Ward's statement (1992) that the Shasu represent 'not an ethnic group but rather a social class'. His is a peculiar assertion since a social class is not usually said to be a people and to have their own country, while the text and the normal determinative used with the Shasu indicate both a people and a territory.

It also often seems to be assumed that the Shasu were all pastoral nomads (or just 'nomads' or 'semi-nomads'). We shall be discussing the question of nomads generally (§3.2.4.3), but as noted in the discussion, nomadic pastoralism covers a wide-ranging spectrum and can include those who raise crops, engage in trade, or even go raiding or robbing caravans, alongside their livestock husbandry. A nomadic lifestyle would have been best suited to the desert fringe around the southern end of the Dead Sea, but the Shasu may also have inhabited more fertile areas and engaged in farming, arboriculture, raiding, trade, and perhaps even copper smelting (Levy, Adams and Muniz 2004; Levy 2009b). One Egyptian inscription does say that Ramesses II destroyed the 'tents' of the Shasu, using the common Semitic term *'ōhel* (Hasel 1998: 224). But it is not at all established from the few texts that we have of the Shasu that their lifestyle is exclusively nomadic: we do not appear to have enough information from texts or archaeology to be definitive. The Shasu do not just wander around indiscriminately but make up a Shasu country or territory (though, as we shall see, nomadic pastoralists do not just 'wander' but migrate purposefully). Although we know that pastoralism was characteristic of some or possibly even most Shasu, we cannot say that this was the sole means of livelihood of all of them: pastoralism is part of the general way of living among settled peoples as well. But some inscriptions seem to suggest that Shasu also live in towns (Giveon 1971: 114–15, #32; 240–1). On the question of the Shasu and Israel, see §3.2.4.2.

2.2.1.5 Canaanites

In the biblical text the 'land of Canaan' is the common way of referring to the area on the western side of the Jordan; similarly, the 'Canaanites' are the inhabitants of this region. The Canaanites (sometimes listed as several different tribes [see below]) are the traditional enemies of the Israelites and also the bad example of the traits and practices that they are to avoid (Lev. 18.3; Deut. 12.29-31; 18.9). Lemche (1991) makes a good case for the biblical picture of the Canaanites being a literary construct, based on certain ideologies. If he is correct, one cannot rely on the Bible for information on the historical Canaanites. Lemche goes on to argue that in other sources as well the term 'Canaan/ites' had no precise geographical or ethnic content. Contrary to Lemche, however, original sources from the second millennium BCE and elsewhere indicate a geographical content to Canaan and Canaanite that is as specific and meaningful as many other such names in the texts (Na'aman 1994b; Hess 1998; Killebrew 2005: 93–148; Rainey 1996; cf. the response in Lemche 1996b, 1998c).

I see no difference in the many references in the Amarna letters to other geographical or ethnic entities. Many passages are not very specific, of course, but a 'passport' from the king of Mitanni to the 'kings of Canaan' to allow his messenger to pass (EA 30) must have had some practical purpose. Similarly, a number of the texts available are legal texts, such as a note of indebtedness in which the debtor is identified as a 'man of Canaan' (LÚ URU *Ki-in-a-ni*$_7^{KI}$: Rainey 1996: 3; Na'aman 1999: 32).

Lemche (1991: 152) makes the point that no one would have referred to himself as a Canaanite. Whether that is true is debatable (cf. Na'aman 1994b: 408), though it might be true if the term was primarily a geographical designation. But there are many examples in history of a group of people who are known mainly by a name – even a pejorative name – given to them by outsiders (for example, the names for the Sioux Indians and the Eskimos in North America meant 'enemy'). The present-day trend to call aboriginal groups by their own designation does not negate the fact that the group had an identity – even an ethnic idenity – in spite of the use of a name that they themselves might have rejected. Also, we do not have to know precise borders to a geographical area or territory before the name has meaning. How many of us could give a precise delineation of the Sahara, even though we all know basically what it refers to?

From the indication in the Egyptian, Ugaritic and Mesopotamian sources 'Canaan' referred to what we call Palestine and Phoenicia (Killebrew 2005: 94). Within that territory was a variety of ethnic groups. Perhaps all the inhabitants of this region had a tribal or ethnic name for themselves, in which case 'Canaanite' was an outsider's term for any inhabitant of the region. If so, our term 'Canaanite' as a contrast with 'Israelite' is nonsense: Israelites were as much Canaanite as anyone else (Grabbe 1994b). Most of the references to Canaanite/Canaanites seem to be geographical and support Killebrew's decision to use it as a purely geographical term. Yet the term seems to be ethnic in the biblical text (and this might also be the case in a few ancient Near Eastern passages). It is easy to explain this as a misunderstanding, especially in the light of other biblical distortions with regard to the historical Canaanites. But there is enough imprecision in our data to make us back away from dogmatic statements. 'Canaan/ite' had meaning in antiquity, but whether we yet have the precise usage pinned down might still be debated.

The biblical text's references to Canaanites sometimes appears to be generic, including all the inhabitants of the land of Canaan (Gen. 12.6; Deut. 11.30; 21.1; Josh. 3.10; 5.1; 17.16, 18; Judg. 1.9-17, 27-33). At other times, the Canaanites seem to be just one of a number of peoples living in the land: Kenites, Kenizzites, Kadmonites, Hittites, Perizzites,

Rephaim, Amorites, Canaanites, Girgashites, Jebusites (Gen. 15.19-21); Canaanites, Hittites, Amorites, Perizzites, Hivites, Jebusites (Exod. 3.8; 23.23; 34.11; Deut. 20.17; Josh. 9.1; Judg. 3.5); Hittites, Girgashites, Amorites, Canaanites, Perizzites, Hivites, Jebusites (Deut. 7.1; Josh. 24.11); Canaanites, Hittites, Perizzites, Jebusites, Ammonites, Moabites, Egyptians, Amorites (Ezra 9.1). Also of interest are the Horites, though these are associated with Seir/Edom and do not feature in the other lists (Gen. 14.6; 36.20-30; Deut. 2.12, 22). How are we to understand these lists? Na'aman (1994c: 239–43; 1994d) argues that a major displacement of peoples occurred at the end of LB, at which time a number of 'northerners' migrated into Palestine, including a number of peoples from Anatolia, such as the Hittites, Hivites, Girgashites and Jebusites (the Perizzites are so far unattested outside the Bible). If so, far from being enemies of Israel, they may have been one of the constituents of the developing ethnic group in the Palestinian highlands (§3.3).

To confuse matters, there is the archaeological usage of 'Canaanite' to refer to the material culture in Palestine that preceded Phoenician, etc. (Sharon and Gilboa 2013).

2.2.2 Question of the Patriarchs

The question of the narratives about the 'patriarchs' – those who are made the ancestors of Israel in Genesis – was strongly debated in the mid-twentieth century. A variety of views was advanced. Perhaps the most exotic was that of C. H. Gordon (1958, 1963) who argued that Abraham was a 'merchant prince' who lived in the Amarna period, for which he found parallels in the Ugaritic and other ancient Near Eastern texts. Alt and Noth had followed Wellhausen's dictum that the contents of the texts reflected the history of the age in which they were composed. Alt's interest in the patriarchal texts was mainly in the religion reflected there (cf. Alt 1966). But the Albright school was particularly effective in promoting the idea that the patriarchal traditions contained 'substantial historicity'; the following statement by J. Bright is exemplary:

> When the traditions are examined in the light of the evidence, the first assertion to be made is that already suggested, namely, that the stories of the patriarchs fit authentically in the milieu of the second millennium, specifically in that of the centuries sketched in the preceding chapter [twentieth to seventeenth centuries BCE], far better than in that of any later period. The evidence is so massive and many-sided that we cannot begin to review it all. (Bright 1980: 77)

The basic problem was that the only information preserved was what could be found in the text of Genesis – there was no direct external confirmation, either epigraphic or literary. A number of further problems presented themselves, such as the following:

1. Except for Jacob/Israel the references to the patriarchs are attested in Israelite tradition only late. Apart from the Genesis texts, Abraham (1 Kgs 13.36; 2 Kgs 13.23; Isa. 29.22; Micah 7.20) and Isaac (1 Kgs 18.36; 2 Kgs 13.23; Amos 7.9, 16; Jer. 33.26) are little mentioned. R. E. Clements expressed the view that 'in the preexilic prophets, there is no authentic reference to the Abraham traditions. Mic. 7:20 is a postexilic oracle, as is also probably Isa. 29:22' (*TDOT* I, 57).
2. The patriarchal narratives in Genesis in their present form reflect a later time, with many anachronistic details: the Philistines are in the land long before the migration of the Sea Peoples; Arameans (Gen. 22.21; 24.10) who are first attested about 1100 BCE in an inscription of Tiglath-Pileser I; Arabs who first occur about the ninth century (Gen. 26.12-18); the Chaldaeans (Gen. 11.28) are attested after 1000 BCE but are mainly important in the Neo-Babylonian period (Ramsey 1981: 40–2) – while the migration from Ur has an interesting parallel to the return from exile. There has been something of a debate over the presence of camels in Genesis: Albright had argued that this was anachronistic and made Abraham a donkey caravanner, but Gordon and also some conservatives had claimed evidence for the domestication of camels at an earlier time. The most recent evidence for the domesticated camel in Palestine, however, seems to be no earlier than the Iron Age, with the concentration of bones at Tell Jemmeh, apparently a caravan centre, focusing on the seventh century BCE (Wapnish 1997; Zarins 1978; Na'aman 1994c: 225–7; Finkelstein and Silberman 2001: 37).
3. Archaeology has sometimes been drawn on in support of 'substantial historicity', but the most recent study is mainly negative (see §2.1.1 above).
4. Chronology is a significant issue: if the patriarchs are historical, when did they live? If the narratives are reliable, reliable for when? Some writers act as if the chronology can be taken for granted, but it cannot be. Having asserted how well the narratives fit the early second millennium (as quoted above), Bright then went on to admit:

> Granting the above, does the evidence allow us to fix the date of the patriarchs with greater precision? Unfortunately, it does not. The most that can be said, disappointing though it is, is that the events reflected in Gen. chs. 12–50, for the most part, fit best in the period already described,

> i.e., between about the twentieth and seventeenth centuries (MB II). But we lack the evidence to fix the patriarchs in any particular century or centuries and we have, moreover, to face the possibility that the patriarchal stories combine the memory of events that took place over a yet wider span of time. (Bright 1980: 83)

In fact, a number of other scholars dated the patriarchs many centuries later than Albright and Bright: later in MB, in LB and even in Iron I (Dever 1977: 93–6; Clark 1977: 143–8).

5. Mode of life. It was once assumed that the patriarchs were nomadic and that this was uniquely in line with the early-second-millennium BCE context (Ramsey 1981: 34–6). Much discussion has taken place in the past few decades, undermining this argument (§3.2.4.3).
6. Names. Many parallels can be found to the names in the patriarchal narratives. Bright asserted that they fitted the early second millennium, but a number of his examples actually came from later than the first few centuries of the second millennium. Names cannot be proof, of course, because the patriarchal names can all be found in the telephone book of almost any large Western city today; however, it is interesting that a number of the names do not recur in the Israelite tradition until the Graeco-Roman period. But as Thompson (1974: 35) points out, most of the names are typical Northwest Semitic in structure. Some of the names for Abraham's ancestors in Gen. 11.20-32 are actually topographical names in the region of Haran, as known from Mesopotamian texts (N. Schneider 1952: Serug, Nahor, Terah, Haran). On the name Benjamin, supposedly known from the Mari texts, see §2.2.1.2.
7. Customs have been one of the main pieces of evidence. A good example of this is E. A. Speiser's commentary on Genesis (1964). Drawing extensively on the Nuzi texts, he used them to illustrate many passages in the patriarchal narratives. Yet at times his argument was not that the biblical custom could be found in the Nuzi text but that the custom from the Nuzi text was not understood by the biblical writer – a rather strange way of arguing for authenticity and reliability. In fact, many of the customs are not parallel to the biblical passage, or either the Nuzi text or the biblical text have been misunderstood or misrepresented: for example, the idea that Eliezer was an heir because he was an adopted son of Abraham but would not inherit once Isaac was born was actually contrary to the Nuzi custom (Thompson 1974: 203–30; Donner 1969). Abraham's and Isaac's passing of their wives off as sisters (Gen. 12.10-20; 20.1-2; 26.1-11) was said to reflect a Hurrian custom of adopting the wife as a sister.

The biblical text does not actually suggest such an adoption (Speiser argued that the Genesis writer no longer understood this custom), but the Nuzi practice was actually misapprehended by some modern scholars (Greengus 1975; Eichler 1977). The best parallel to Genesis 23 seems to come from the Neo-Babylonian period (Tucker 1966; Petschow 1965). In the end, none of the alleged customs demonstrating an early-second-millennium background for the patriarchal stories seems to have stood up.

2.3 Synthesis

The story of Israel and Judah began as such only at the end of the second millennium BCE. Yet a full understanding requires a knowledge of the history of Palestine throughout the second millennium and even more broadly the history of the ancient Near East. Only a brief outline can be given here, the main sources being the *Cambridge Ancient History* (*CAH*), Klengel (1992), Kuhrt (1995) and Van De Mieroop (2004). In the discussion that follows I shall divide treatment into early and later second millennium, but the line dividing the two is really a broad band stretching from about 1600 to about 1500 BCE.

The Middle and Late Bronze Ages cover much of the second millennium BCE. Approximately 2000 BCE marks the end of the Early Bronze IV (or Intermediate Bronze, in some terminology) and the beginning of the Middle Bronze but also the end of the Ur III Period and beginning of the Old Assyrian Period in Mesopotamia and the end of the First Intermediate Period and beginning of the Middle Kingdom in Egypt. Then the point of about 1600/1500 BCE marks the transition to the Late Bronze Age and also the end of the Second Intermediate Period and beginning of the New Kingdom in Egypt, and the beginning of the Hittite Old Kingdom. The late Bronze Age is usually seen as ending about 1200 BCE, though some have argued that it should be later, perhaps in the latter half of the twelfth century, while a recent article would put it much earlier (Meitlis 2008).

Chronology for the second millennium BCE is often not certain (Van De Mieroop 2004: 4). There are a few astronomical dates, which are very precious but not very frequent. Events can also be co-ordinated by linking them to the same event as recorded or mentioned in other regions. For the most part, there are only a few fixed dates, with everything else fitted around them. Basically, the earlier an episode the less certain its dating. Over the years, three basic chronological schemes have been proposed, a high, middle, and low chronology. In Mesopotamia, it all depends on the dating of Hammurabi. In the early second millennium, up to 50 or more years separate the higher from the lower chronology; in the late second millennium, the differences are more like a decade (see further Dever 1990; Weinstein 1991, 1992; Hoffmeier 1990, 1991).

About 3000 BCE writing seems to have originated in both Egypt and Mesopotamia, beginning the historic period for both regions. The Egyptian priest Manetho, writing in Greek under Ptolemaic rule about 300 BCE, divided Egyptian history into 30 dynasties (Waddell 1940). Although it is now recognized that Manetho's divisions were not always justified and some of these dynasties were contemporaneous rather than consecutive, the dynasties became the framework for writers on Egyptian history even to the present, despite better sources for certain periods. According to Manetho, the first real king of Egypt was Menes who united Upper and Lower Egypt about 3000 BCE and initiated the First Dynasty. The Early Dynastic Period consisted of Dynasties 1–2 (ca. 3000–2700 BCE). The Old Kingdom covered Dynasties 3–6 (ca. 2700–2150 BCE), during which time most of the pyramids were built. The Old Kingdom ended with what is called the First Intermediate Period (ca. 2150–2050 BCE), a time of turmoil which Egyptian writers, with their emphasis on order, found particularly abhorrent. This included the short-lived Dynasties 7 and 8, when order (in the sense of strong central government) began to break down, and then Dynasties 9–10, and finally Dynasty 11 during which central control was re-established.

The first civilization in Mesopotamia was in the southern region of Sumeria. The Sumerians spoke a language not related to any other known language, and it was for this language that the writing system on clay tablets was developed. This was originally pictograms, but it soon became clear that it was easier to outline the figures by jabbing the triangular point of the stylus into the clay than to try to draw with it. Thus, the pictograms soon evolved into characters made up of wedge-shaped marks; hence, the name *cuneiform.* Sumeria as a power came to its peak with the Ur III period (ca. 2100–2000 BCE), when the city of Ur dominated the region. After that the history of Mesopotamia belongs mainly to the Semitic peoples further north, known as Akkadians (from the city Agade or Akkad), a collective term for both the Assyrians in the north and on the Tigris and the Babylonians on the Euphrates. They adopted Sumerian culture (much as the Romans adopted Greek culture), including the writing system even though it was not well designed for writing a Semitic language such as Akkadian. Texts in the Sumerian language continued to be copied and even new ones written well into the first millennium BCE, but Sumerian was probably a dead language during most or all of this time and used only for literary purposes, much as Latin was in the Middle Ages.

2.3.1 First Part of Second Millennium (ca. 2000–1600/1500 BCE)

2.3.1.1 Egypt

The Middle Kingdom (ca. 2050–1700) was made up of Dynasties 11–12. The Twelfth Dynasty was one of the most famous, reaching a height of power and culture. However, it ended in the Second Intermediate Period (ca. 1700–1550). This encompassed Dynasties 13–17. The length of the individual dynasties is uncertain, but some of them were contemporaneous. In many cases we have nothing more than the names of the kings within the dynasties, though even here there are questions. The Second Intermediate Period was dominated by the Hyksos (§2.2.1.1).

2.3.1.2 Old Assyrian Period (ca. 2000–1750)

With the collapse of Sumerian power, the Assyrians and Babylonians tended to dominate Mesopotamian history for the next 1500 years until the Persian conquest. The Assyrians were known much of this time for their military prowess, but early in the second millennium they conquered through trade, by establishing a trading empire in Anatolia. This was done by merchants (rather than government) who set up trading colonies in different cities by agreement with the city rulers (Larson 1976). Charters were drawn up giving the merchants certain rights, some of which have been preserved. The trade was mainly in textiles and tin (needed to make bronze, the principal metal of this time). One of the figures who promoted this sort of trading empire was Shamshi-Adad I (ca. 1800 BCE) who was an older contemporary of Hammurabi and (like Hammurabi) of Amorite ancestry (see §2.2.1.2 on the Amorites). He also conquered Ashur and brought the variety of Assyrian city-states under his control, but the empire collapsed after his death. For the next two or three centuries, we know little about Assyria.

2.3.1.3 Old Babylonian Period (2000–1600)

The height of Babylonian greatness came in the early second millennium, not to be equalled until the brief Neo-Babylonian empire (605–539 BCE). There were several rival states (Isin, Larsa and Babylonia), but the area was united by Hammurabi of Babylon. The date of his reign is very important for the chronology of this period but varies widely between those advocating the high, middle, or low chronology: his dates vary from ca. 1850–1800 to 1800–1750 to 1730–1680 BCE. Hammurabi conquered many cities of the region, including the city-state of Mari on the Euphrates. After the death of Hammurabi, Babylonia declined over the next 150 years. It was finally devastated by a Hittite attack under Mursilis

I about 1600 BCE. This weakened the state considerably and allowed it to be taken over by the Kassites, usually thought to have come from the Zagros mountains. The Kassites are usually seen in much the same way as the barbarian tribes who destroyed Rome. Babylonia was controlled by the Kassites for the next three centuries until about 1150.

2.3.1.4 Hittites

The original inhabitants of Asia Minor were a group often referred to as the Hatti. During the early second millennium BCE an Indo-European people, the Hittites, infiltrated the country and became the ruling class. They developed their own writing system, Hittite hieroglyphic, but also used Akkadian cuneiform writing. It is uncertain how the empire developed (compare the situation in the Old Assyrian period). The Hittite Old Kingdom straddled the line between the Middle and Late Bronze Age (ca. 1650–1500). A number of historical texts have survived from this period. Mursilis I conquered Aleppo and Babylonia, opening the way for the Kassite invasion; however, palace revolutions and Hurrian pressure weakened the state.

2.3.1.5 Northern Syria

The sources for Syria are limited, but there are two main ones: the Mari texts and the Alalakh tablets. Mari was a city-state on the Euphrates in northern Syria. It has become quite famous because excavations beginning in the 1930s have turned up many texts of diverse sorts, including prophetic texts that predicted the defeat of Hammurabi. The kingdom was ruled by various Amorite dynasties. Alalaḫ was further west. About 500 texts were found in the excavations of the city, mainly from two periods: about 1700 BCE and the fifteenth century. They are mostly lists of various sorts: inventories, rations, landholdings, loans, etc. They thus tell us mainly about social, legal and economic aspects of the people, though there are some documents about historical events. We also know something about the city-state of Yamhad (modern Aleppo). There are only scattered references, but these indicate a substantial state during the Old Babylonian period, strong enough to resist the moves of Shamshi-Adad I to take control. The city of Yamhad was destroyed by the Hittite king Mursilis I about 1600 BCE.

A group of people known from Mari and northern Syria – but also in central Mesopotomia – were the Amorites; on them see §2.2.1.2.

2.3.2 Second Part of the Second Millennium (1600/1500–1200 BCE)

2.3.2.1 Egypt

For this period the most important background is Egyptian history, though this of necessity brings in the Hittites and Mitanni at various points. The end of the Second Intermediate Period (on this see especially Ryholt 1997) ushered in the Egyptian New Kingdom, consisting of Dynasties 18–20 (ca. 1550–1050 BCE), which was a high point in the history of Egypt. It was also the time in which we first find mention of Israel in an extra-biblical source and provides the possible background to the supposed events of the exodus and conquest of the land by Israel (but see below). Dynasty 18 was responsible for the 'expulsion' of the Hyksos (see §2.2.1.1 for the complications to what had happened). The New Kingdom rulers first secured their northern and southern borders and then began to expand into Nubia and Syro-Palestine. Ahmose (ca. 1539–1515 BCE) is conventionally the founder of the New Kingdom and first king of the 18th Dynasty. He conquered the city of Sharuhen, which seems to be the city mentioned in Josh. 19.6 and is often identified with Tell el-Far'ah South. This meant that Egypt had nothing immediately to fear across the Sinai, because with Sharuhen gone, there was no other metropolitan state in Canaan of significance south of Hazor (Redford 2003: 190 + n. 24).

Some reference books mention expeditions by other early New Kingdom rulers, such as Amenhotep I, Thutmose II, and Hatshepsut. These campaigns are deduced from small amounts of information. Redford (1992a: 149) is dubious of all but the excursion of Thutmose I in the period of 70 or 80 years between Ahmose's expulsion of the Hyksos and Thutmose III's taking of Megiddo. What we find is that for the next three-quarters of a century after the expulsion of the Hyksos, the Egyptian pharaohs concentrated on extending their borders south into Nubia. However, during this period the new state of Mitanni was developing its strength and extending its territory. Egypt ignored it for the time being, but Thutmoses I (ca. 1493–1483 BCE) may have begun to see a danger (so Redford 1992a: 146–9) and responded with an expedition to the Euphrates and the Mitanni territory. We know little about this, though he apparently set up a stela on the Euphrates. For the next 40 years, however, the Mitanni threat seems to have been neglected. A razzia against the Shasu is sometimes ascribed to Thutmose II (ca. 1482–1480). His wife, the famous queen Hatshepsut, ruled jointly as regent with their son Thutmose III, though she claimed sole rulership at times (ca. 1479–1458 BCE).

Because of his habit of having his various activities recorded in day-books (Redford 2003), we happen to know a lot about what Thutmose III did during his long reign which covered a good portion of the fifteenth century (ca. 1479–1425). He already began his campaigns into Palestine during his co-rulership with his mother and made many expeditions when he became sole ruler. A couple of his campaigns to the north can be mentioned in which he exhibited brilliance as a battlefield strategist. Perhaps the most famous exploit of Thutmose III was in his 22nd year (the 1st year of sole reign) when he took Megiddo by the bold move of leading his army directly through a narrow pass in the Carmel ridge. This was followed in year 33 by an exploit in which he defeated Mitanni. It was under Thutmose III that the Egyptian empire reached its farthest expansion to the north.

He was followed by Amenhotep (Amenophis) II (ca. 1425–1400 BCE) who continued to keep the pressure on the northern frontier. He made forays into Syria-Palestine during his 3rd, 7th, and 9th regnal years. In his 7th year, he came against Mitanni and its allies, including Ugarit. Following him, however, there seems to be a hiatus for several rulers, though this could be because the internal administrative system in Canaan and Syria was working reasonably well. For example, there were apparently no expeditions to the north under either Thutmose IV (1400–1390 BCE) or Amenhotep III (1390–1353 BCE). But this was supposedly because these territories had been brought thoroughly into line (Redford 1992a: 169).

It was mainly under Amenhotep IV, better known as Akhenaten (1353–1336) that the Amarna texts were written (Redford 1984). The priesthood and temples had been dominated by the cult of Amen Re, but Amenophis promoted the cult of Aten (the sun disc). This ‘religious reform’ is still debated by modern scholars, though the idea that it was the first example of monotheism is probably exaggerated. Amenophis changed his name to Akhenaten and built an entirely new city as his capital, what is now Tell el-Amarna, giving the name ‘Amarna period’ to the mid-fourteenth century BCE. After Akhenaten’s short reign of 16 years, his name was blackened and even erased from inscriptions and monuments. The powerful priesthood of Amen Re seems to have been partly behind this. In any case, his new capital was abandoned. During the ‘Amarna period’ most of the territory of Palestine and Syria seems to have been claimed by the Egyptians and by various vassal city-state rulers. Some of the Amarna tablets were written during the reigns of the last Amarna kings (including Smenkhkare‘ [1336–1334 BCE] and Nefernefruaten [1334–? BCE]), but apart from Horemheb, these Pharaohs seem to have accomplished little. Horemheb (1319–1292 BCE) was apparently the real leader of the country when Tutankhamun (?–1324 BCE) came to the throne as a boy. Reliefs in his tomb (found in 1975) indicate that he undertook campaigns into Syria and Nubia on Tutankamun’s behalf. He claims that ‘his name was famous in the land of the Hittites’ (H. D. Schneider 2001: II, 116). He was outmanoeuvred by others at the end of Tutankamun’s life, and Aya

(1323–1320 BCE) succeeded him. It was only when Aya's short reign ended that Horemheb took the throne, though we know of no campaigns to the north after this.

The founder of the new 19th Dynasty was Ramesses I (1292–1291 BCE), though Horemheb is credited with guiding the transition. Ramesses I was aged and reigned only a year or so before Seti I (1290–1279 BCE) took over to act like a new Thutmoses III. The thirteenth century is dominated by active pharaohs who exerted themselves in maintaining their northern possessions. Seti led an expedition against the Shasu in southern Palestine. This campaign took place as part of one directed at Tyre, which was also subdued, and brought the chiefs of Palestine in general into line. He later attacked Amurru and retook the town of Qadesh. In another campaign he marched against the Hittites in the Orontes Valley of northern Syria. His successor Ramesses II (1279–1213 BCE) had a long reign of 66 years and was a great military leader, at least in his younger years. He had a campaign up the Mediterranean coast to Phoenicia and perhaps to Amurru in his 4th year. The next year was the famous battle of Qadesh. Although Ramesses retrieved the battle from a Hittite ambush and it was more or less a standoff, on balance it was probably a defeat for the Egyptians. The result was that Palestine rebelled against Egyptian rule; however, after three years he retaliated and took many towns. He continued to pacify his northern territories in year 10 and also in some undated expeditions. In year 21 Hatti proposed a treaty, which Ramesses accepted, but Egypt never recovered Qadesh, Amurru, or Ugarit. Strangely, though, it is often proposed that the exodus and/or conquest of Canaan by the Israelites took place under his reign – apparently overlooking that he was one of the strongest of the pharaohs who had a firm hold of the whole region well into Syria and reigned for so much of the thirteenth century.

Ramesses II's long life meant that he outlived several of his sons who had been designated his successor. He was succeeded by his thirteenth son Merenptah (1213–1203 BCE) who was already middle aged. Merenptah had been a successful military leader, but this was behind him. However, Egypt suffered a Libyan invasion allied with a number of the Sea Peoples in the 5th year of his reign. They were met in the western Delta region and defeated. Merenptah's inscription is mainly devoted to the Libyan victory but also includes some Palestinian cities plus Israel at the end (§3.1.2). How they relate to the Libyan invasion – if at all – is unclear. Several short-reigning figures, some perhaps reigning simultaneously, followed Merenptah. Sethnakhte (1190–1188 BCE), who was probably a military leader, began the 20th Dynasty when Towsre (wife of Seti II) died without issue. His son became Ramesses III (1187–1157 BCE), the second king and one of the most successful rulers of the dynasty. His reign is best known for at least two alleged defeats of the Sea Peoples in his eighth year (ca. 1175 BCE). There are many questions about the Sea Peoples (see §3.2.2). Ramesses III was succeeded by his fifth son (the others all having died) who became Ramesses IV (1156–1150 BCE).

By this time Egyptian power over Canaan was weakening, but Ramesses IV might still have maintained an Egyptian toehold since scarabs of him have been found in Beth Shean and Lachish (Yasur-Landau 2010: 316). The problem is that scarabs of Ramesses III are not followed by Ramesses IV in Ashkelon XII (but instead by those of Ramesses VI). The Egyptians might even have clung on to some power until Ramesses VI (1145–1139 BCE), since a statue of him was found in Megiddo: it is hardly likely that a hostile population would have erected or maintained this statue. (Also, scarabs of him are found with those of Ramesses III in Ashkelon XII, but strangely not those of Ramesses IV, as we noted.) Toward the end of the 20th Dynasty, Egypt became divided into north and south, and control over Palestine was gradually lost (probably ca. 1130 BCE [§3.1.1]). It was succeeded by the Third Intermediate Period which lasted 400 years until the Saite period (beginning 664 BCE).

2.3.2.2 Mesopotamia

The period of Kassite rule in Babylon was a lengthy one (1600–1150 BCE). Not much is known, though the older view that the Kassites were seen as foreigners and illegitimate probably requires revision. Interestingly, the rulers were designated as 'kings of Babylonia', that is, the whole region, whereas previous kings had been kings of a particular city-state. The Amarna archives contain communications between Egypt and Babylonia, indicating that Kassite Babylon was an international power. Kassite rule was weakened by conflict with the Assyrians, and rule of Babylonia was replaced by rule from the city of Isin (Second Dynasty). The Aramaean incursions caused problems, as did Elam (a power in the area later to be settled by the Persians). Nebuchadnezzar I (ca. 1100 BCE) defeated Elam and brought a revival of Babylonia's fortunes for a time.

In Assyria there was a 400-year 'dark age' from about 1750 BCE to the beginning of the Middle Assyrian period (ca. 1350–1050 BCE) during which time we have little information on Assyria. The expansion of Mitanni had brought about the loss of Assyrian independence (ca. 1400 BCE), but the defeat of Mitanni by the Hittites gave Assyria its chance to regain independence and begin to exert itself again. The Assyrians took some territory from Mitanni, including the region of Nineveh, and eventually Mitanni itself (ca. 1300 BCE), now setting their borders directly on the Hittite Empire. Contacts were re-established with Egypt (known from the Amarna archives), and the Babylonians began to worry about the new Assyrian strength as the latter shifted the boundary between the two powers further south. It was not long before the Assyrians took control of Babylon for a time (ca. 1200 BCE). Toward the end of this period the Aramaeans became a threat by launching raids on Assyrian territory and even taking some of it temporarily (§4.2.5).

2.3.2.3 Hittite Empire (ca. 1400–1200 BCE)

The term 'Hittite Middle Kingdom' was once used but has now generally been rejected as a concept. The Hittite empire is also known as the 'Hittite New Kingdom'. As the Hittite strength grew, Egypt and Mitanni attempted to counter it. The powerful Šuppiluliumas I (ca. 1350 BCE) conquered northern Syria and made Mitannni into a protectorate. An attempt to establish good relations with Egypt was thwarted, however. The conflict with Egypt culminated in the battle of Qadesh (ca. 1300 BCE) between Ramesses II and Muwatallis II, leading to a treaty between Ramesses and Muwatallis's successor Hattusilis III (ca. 1275 BCE). The kingdom seems to have come to an end by internal decline rather than being destroyed by the Sea Peoples as was once thought. It was succeeded by a series of Neo-Hittite states that carried on for another 500 years.

2.3.2.4 Mitanni Kingdom (ca. 1600–1350 BCE)

The kingdom of Mitanni was once thought to be composed of two different populations. The main group were the Hurrians, a people who penetrated into northern Mesopotamia and Syria in the early second millennium BCE. We know that Hurrians were found among the populations of many cities across Asia Minor and northern Syria, though most of the penetration into Syria came after 1500. Their leaders were believed to be Indo-Aryan, some of the ancestors of the migration of people from southern Russia into Iran and northern India. Their names and some of the few words of their language were also thought to support this. One word borrowed by many languages across the region was *maryannu* 'charioteer', a word supposedly known from Sanskrit. However, although Indo-Iranian influence can be demonstrated, it is now thought to have been exaggerated, and claims are now made that the word *maryannu* is Hurrian in origin.

The kingdom of Mitanni was made up of a union of Hurrian and Amorite states. As it expanded it clashed with Egypt, but it concluded a treaty with Thutmose IV about 1400 BCE. The Hittite king Šuppiluliumas made Mitanni into a protectorate (ca. 1350 BCE), which allowed Assyria to gain independence and expand. Not long afterward (ca. 1300 BCE), Mitanni was destroyed by the Assyrians who took control of their territory, despite its being a supposed Hittite possession.

Table 2.1

CHRONOLOGY OF THE ANCIENT NEAR EAST (3RD/2ND MILLENNIA BCE)

3000		First writings in Egypt and Mesopotamia		
2500		City-state of Ebla		
2000	Middle Bronze I (2200–2000)	End of Ur III Period (ca. 2000)		
	Middle Bronze IIA (2000–1750)		Egyptian Middle Kingdom (2050–1700) 12th Dynasty	
1900		Old Assyrian Period (2000–1800) Shamshi-Adad I (ca. 1800) Old Babylonian Period (1900–1600)		
1800	Middle Bronze IIB (1800–1550)	'Mari Age' (19th/18th century)		
		Hammurabi (1825/1775/1700)		
1700			Second Intermediate Period (1750–1550) 15th Dynasty (Hyksos [1650–1550])	Hittite Old Kingdom (1650–1500)
1600				
	Late Bronze I (1550–1400)	Kassite Period (1600–1150)		Mursilis I (ca. 1600)
1500		Kingdom of Mitanni (1600–1350)	Egyptian New Kingdom (1550–1050) 18th Dynasty (1550–1300) Thutmose III (ca. 1450)	Hittite New Kingdom (1450–1200)
1400	Late Bronze II (1400–1200)	'Nuzi Period' (15th century)	Thutmose IV (ca. 1400) Amarna Age (14th century)	
		Middle Assyrian Period (1350–1050)	Akhenaten (ca. 1350) 19th Dynasty (1300–1200)	Šuppiluliumas I (ca. 1350–1325)
1300				
		End of Mitanni (ca. 1250)	Ramesses II (ca. 1280–1215)	Battle of Qadesh (ca. 1275)
1200	Iron IA (1200–1150)		Merenptah (ca. 1215–1200)	End of Hittite Empire (1200)
			Ramesses III (ca. 1190–1160)	
	Iron IB (1150–1000)		Defeat of Sea Peoples (Philistines) (ca. 1175)	
1100				
1000				

2.3.2.5 Ugarit

On this city-state, see §2.1.3.

2.3.3 Palestine

Once the biblical text is eliminated as having little to tell us about the second millennium BCE, we are mainly dependent on archaeology (summarized at §2.1.1), but we do have some inscriptions. It is important to bear in mind that throughout the second millennium BCE, Palestine was mostly under the thumb of Egypt. The history of the region is the history of an Egyptian appendage. The Execration Texts (§2.1.2.1) give the names of some cities. There are also a few texts describing individual episodes, such as the capture of Joppa by the commander Djehuty under Thutmose III (Goedicke 1968, though this seems to be legend with a historical core), as well as accounts of military forays into Palestine and Syria by various Egyptian kings (e.g., the taking of Megiddo by Thutmose III [*ANET* 234–8] or the campaigns of Seti I into Palestine and Syria [*ANET* 254–5]). The story of Sinuhe also offers insights (§2.1.2.3). It is the Amarna Letters, however, that give us a real look through the keyhole into the Palestine of the fourteenth century BCE (§2.1.2.2). The rulers of a number of cities are named and an account (often distorted, of course) of their activities is recorded for the Pharaoh by their neighbours (and rivals). Of particular interest are the kings of Shechem and Jerusalem who seem to dominate the highlands. The important period of transition between the LB and Iron I Ages is discussed in the next chapter (§§3.1.1; 3.2.4).

Chapter 3

Late Bronze to Iron IIA (ca. 1300–900 BCE): From Settlement to Statehood

This chapter covers a long period of about four centuries or more. No doubt many will feel that this is too long a period of time to be covered by one chapter, especially considering the importance of this period for the current debate. Yet this chapter encompasses such a long period of time precisely because interpretations vary so widely. If Iron I had been dealt with in a separate chapter from Iron IIA, it would give the impression of favouring one side of the debate over the other. For Finkelstein's Iron I extends through much of the tenth century, contrary to conventional chronology. Thus, it seemed best to treat this whole period together, even if it makes for a rather long chapter.

3.1 Sources

3.1.1 Archaeology

One of the most significant areas of discussion is that relating to chronology, specifically the debate about the 'low chronology'. This is summarized above (§1.2.4.4), with that section presupposed in the discussion here. Because of the debate over chronology, the following archaeological survey will attempt as far as possible to refer to archaeological periods (Iron I, Iron IIA, Iron IIB) rather than specific dates. Note that the LC and MCC coincide from the eighth and seventh centuries onward (Finkelstein 1999a: 39). It is generally agreed that Iron IIB ends, and Iron IIC (or, as some prefer, Iron III) begins, with the fall of Samaria and/or the invasion of Sennacherib (ca. 720/701 BCE; see the charts in Mazar 2005; cf. Ofer 2001: 30–1). The stratigraphic and chronological framework for the Iron Age in Palestine is based on several key sites: Megiddo, Lachish, Jerusalem and Samaria (Ussishkin 2007b). Jerusalem is probably the most contested site of all those in the whole of Palestine. It is vital for the period covering the so-called 'united monarchy'. Finally, as noted above, the invasion of Shoshenq has been used extensively to date specific sites with a destruction layer. Yet whether Shoshenq's topographical list relates an actual invasion of his or is only a traditional compilation is very much a debatable point. In any case, a widespread destruction by Shoshenq is by no means a certainty. Also, as Ussishkin points out, Shoshenq's treatment of various sites may have differed; for example, the stela erected in Megiddo suggests a site occupied rather than destroyed.

The LB ended with a major collapse that seems to have affected the whole of the eastern Mediterranean (Cline 2014; Drews 1993; Ward and Joukowsky [eds] 1992). This is no doubt to be related to the frequent mention in the Amarna letters of the 'Apiru and other groups on the margins of society: the rural decline left a vacuum that 'Apiru and Shasu moved into (Steen 2017). In any case, the general prosperity of the LB age in Palestine came to an abrupt end sometime about 1200 BCE with the destruction of the main centres: Akko, Hazor, Megiddo, Beth-Shean, Lachish, Ashdod. Yet the 'conventional wisdom' that the Palestinian city-state system came to an end at this time oversimplifies what happened (Finkelstein 2003a: 75–9). Some city-states probably did decline or disappear with the destruction of their urban centres, but the rural sector generally experienced continuity, both demographically and culturally, as is indicated by such sites as Tel Menorah, Tell el-Wawiyat and 'Ein Zippori. The peasants in the vicinity of the ruined LB cities lived as they already had, and the northern valleys remained densely settled. In Iron I (eleventh century, according to Finkelstein) the main centres began to recover, the main exceptions being Lachish and Hazor. This 'new Canaan' was prosperous because of stability in the rural sector and trade with Phoenicia, Cyprus and even further afield.

If we begin with the site farthest north, the current excavators of Hazor have retained Y. Yadin's assignment of stratum X to the tenth century and stratum VIII to the Omride dynasty (Ben-Tor 2000; Mazar 2008). Although some ^{14}C dates contradict this, Mazar notes that it seems difficult to compress strata XB to VIII into 70 years in the ninth century, as required by the LC (see Finkelstein's response in 2005a: 38). The conventional view equates Megiddo VA–IVB, Hazor X, Gezer VIII and Beersheba V – all seen as evidence for the united monarchy (Finkelstein 1996a: 177). Thus, according to Mazar (2008), Yadin's thesis of Solomonic architecture at the three sites (Megiddo, Hazor and Gezer) might still be correct. Finkelstein (1999b: 59) argues, however, that Yadin's equation of Hazor X with the time of Solomon creates chaos with strata IX, VIII and VII, leaving no place for the important activities of Hazael in northern Israel. A. Zarzeki-Peleg's study of the pottery assemblages connects Megiddo VIA with Jokneam XVII, while Hazor XB is later (1997: 284). Thus, Finkelstein (1999b: 60) argues, Hazor X was built by the Omrides.

If we move back to LB, A. Ben-Tor (1998) is apparently still of the opinion that the Israelites destroyed Hazor XIII and then settled it in stratum XII (thus continuing to agree – more or less – with Yadin's interpretation). D. Ben-Ami (2001) gives a somewhat different interpretation. He makes several corrections to previous interpretations (2001: 165–70, my formulation). First, the destroyers of LB Hazor (stratum XIII) left the site desolate and uninhabited. However, the 'impressive Late Bronze city of Hazor with its magnificence, monumentality, high status and influence...underwent a violent destruction that apparently cannot be related to the process of early Israelite settlement in Canaan' (Ben-Ami 2001: 168–9). Second, there was a gap in settlement for a period of time. Third, the settlement of Iron I was a temporary encampment whose presence was indicated by a large number of refuse pits. Fourth, although the identity of those in this encampment is unknown, the material culture is new, with substantial differences that suggest a different population. Fifth, Yadin's identification of two separate settlement strata (XII and XI) is unsupported and only one occupational phase is indicated by the remains.

In the upper Galilee the ceramic continuity from LB II to Iron I indicates that the population was indigenous rather than immigrants as pictured by the biblical text (Josh. 19.24-48; Bloch-Smith and Nakhai 1999: 81). Settlement of the Jezreel and Beth-Shean valleys flourished in LB, with a significant Egyptian presence at the administrative centres of Megiddo and Beth-Shean. The collapse of Egyptian dominance resulted in a general decline, with an impoverished culture (Bloch-Smith and Nakhai 1999: 81–8). A number of small settlements existed in this area, the majority established in the twelfth and eleventh centuries, with a material culture suggesting continuity with LB (Gal 1992: 84, 92). The suggestion that a new population took control (Bloch-Smith and Nakhai 1999: 83) appears to have little or no archaeological support.

Late Bronze II Megiddo (strata VIII/VIIB–VIIA), with an estimated area of 11 hectares, was one of the most prominent cities of Palestine (Finkelstein, Ussishkin and Halpern 2000: 593). With its monumental buildings it appears to have been the city-state centre for the king and his elite supporters. Megiddo thus seems to provide a good example of the nature of the major city-states in Canaan during the later part of LB (over 30 sites were apparently subordinate to Megiddo), though the LB city was apparently unfortified. The absolute dating of the LB II strata is not clear: according to Finkelstein, stratum VIII can hardly post-date the mid-fourteenth century; it is unlikely that there was no palace during the Amarna period. Stratum VIIB alone would represent the city of the thirteenth century. Stratum VIIA was then built in the late thirteenth century and destroyed in the second half of the twelfth. Strata VIII–VIIA therefore all represent one phase of urban continuity. Ussishkin agrees that Megiddo was continuously settled throughout LB, including the Amarna period, but the character of settlement was not uniform throughout the time. Significantly, most or all the monumental buildings were constructed after the Amarna period, while the Amarna settlement was relatively modest. The conclusion seems to be that the stratum VIII royal palace and gatehouse and some other public buildings were constructed in the thirteenth century.

Megiddo VIIA was destroyed in the second half of the twelfth century; rebuilt as VIB in Iron I it began to prosper again in VIA (Finkelstein, Ussishkin and Halpern 2000: 594–5). This city was destroyed in a major conflagration. Megiddo VB was very different in character, with Iron Age traits in its material culture and layout (Finkelstein, Ussishkin and Halpern 2000: 595–6). In the transition from VIA to VB there is a change both in the pottery tradition and the layout of the city; nevertheless, it remained an imposing administrative centre (Finkelstein, Ussishkin and Halpern 2000: 597). Ussishkin (2007a) argues that Megiddo stratum VA–IVB or parts of it preceded the Omri dynasty and that this stratum (or the preceding stratum VB) was probably the city captured by Shoshenq in the late tenth century; however, Shoshenq did not destroy the city but intended to make it his administrative centre. For a discussion of Megiddo in relation to Samaria and Jezreel, see §4.1.1.

Thus, it seems that at least in the northern part of the country, LB Canaan rose again in the late eleventh and early tenth centuries from the blow of the mid-twelfth century (Finkelstein 2003a: 77). Other city-states seem to have emerged at that time, at Tel Kinneret, Tel Rehov, Tel Dor and possibly Tel Keisan. Iron I Kinneret replaced LB Hazor as the centre of the upper Jordan Valley, while Iron I Tel Rehov was probably the focus of a territorial entity that covered the Beth-Shean and eastern Jezreel Valley. Late Bronze Tel Keisan continued to prosper and seems to have served as the central site of the northern coastal plain (including Akko, and Tell Abu Hawam IVA as its port). Iron I Dor dominated the coastal plain of the Carmel Ridge and possibly replaced LB Gath (Jatt) as the main centre of the region.

It has long been suggested that a number of innovations in technology took place in the central highlands: terracing, plastered cisterns, the 'Israelite house', collared-rim jars and iron (Dever 2003a: 113–25). Unfortunately, it seems there is no list of technologies that is exclusive to this region and time or that can serve as 'Israelite ethnic markers' (§1.2.5; Killebrew 2005: 171–81; Bloch-Smith 2003: 406–11; Kletter 2006: 579; Hesse and Wapnish 1997). Terracing was used as early as EB; the early Iron Age settlers in the highlands made use of an existing technology

(S. Gibson 2001). It is now argued that the collared-rim jar was already in use in the thirteenth century along the Levantine coast and is the product of a particular lifestyle or economy (such as the distribution of rations to employees) and is not exclusive to the Cisjordan highlands or Israel (Killebrew 2001; Raban 2001; Herr 2001). A. Faust and S. Bunimovitz (2003) recently argued that the four-room house was particularly Israelite, though they admit that a few such houses occur elsewhere, including in Transjordan. Iron seems to have been little used, despite the name 'Iron I': weapons and tools were mainly bronze (Bloch-Smith 2003: 417–20).

In this context of unique technologies, the question of pork consumption has also often been discussed, as an ethnic indicator. The subject is a complicated one, though there is a considerable drop in evidence for swine in the highlands during Iron I and Iron II, in contrast to LB and also the coastal plain where pigs remained a part of the diet. But Hesse and Wapnish conclude that 'no human behavioral evidence exists to indicate that pig avoidance was unique to any particular group in the ancient Near East… Lots of people, for lots of reasons, were not eating pork' (1997: 261). S. Bunimovitz and Z. Lederman (2008) found that the total absence of pig bones in Beth-Shemesh in Iron I was consistent with the minimal percentage of pig bones in the hill country, in contrast to sites identified as Philistine. Beth-Shemesh became a sensitive seismograph for social changes between the regions, one such conspicuous boundary being pork avoidance. This allows that the pig taboo as an ethnic marker might have begun in the Shephelah and extended into the highlands, rather than the other way round.

For the area of Ephraim we have the preliminary survey results (Finkelstein 1988–89: esp. 144–54; Finkelstein 1988: 121–204). The late Bronze Age had seen a demographic decline, but Iron I produced a 'settlement wave of unprecedented intensity', especially in the desert fringe and the northern central range (Finkelstein 1988–89: 146). This produced a pattern of major centres accompanied by a peripheral population. Finkelstein (1988–89: 148) argues that the population was densest in the east at the beginning of Iron I but then moved toward the west, with the cereal/animal husbandry economy also shifting toward a horticultural one; however, Bloch-Smith and Nakhai (1999: 71) assert that the archaeological data do not support either of these conclusions. Yet a comparison of Iron I and Iron II does indicate just such a population shift (Finkelstein 1998b: 357). Regardless, it does appear that the Ephraimite and Manassite regions had the densest population of any region west of the Jordan. Settlement of the less favourable slopes and foothills, with trees and brush to be cleared, came later in Iron I and continued into Iron II. In Iron II almost all the regions of Ephraim were intensively settled (Finkelstein

1988–89: 151–4). Compared with Iron I, the population had shifted west, with some of the large sites in the east abandoned: Shiloh, ʻAi and Khirbit Raddana. Sufficient grain was grown in some regions, apparently, to allow the western regions to concentrate on the important wine and oil production. In the southern central range of the Ephraimite hills some sites were abandoned and a fall in the population generally occurred in this region.

In LB and early Iron I, a clear difference separated the north and south in the central hill country between the Jezreel and Beersheba valleys (Finkelstein 1998b: 361; 1999a: 43–4). The north experienced significant continuity, with most of the main sites continuing from LB into Iron I. The Negev and Judaean hills had hardly any sedentary sites in LB; this long settlement gap came to an end in early Iron I. There was a large increase in small sites in early Iron I, especially in the central hill country (Stager 1998b: 134–7; Dever 2003a: 97–100). This increase was largely in the north, especially in the areas of Ephraim and Manasseh, and almost entirely north of Jerusalem. The Judaean hills had hardly any new sites in the early Iron I, and the region still remained highly pastoral (Finkelstein 1988: 52–3).

With regard to the Judaean hills, however, we find a significant difference of opinion. Most of the early Iron I sites were between Jerusalem and Hebron, with hardly any south of Hebron. According to A. Ofer the mid-eleventh to the tenth centuries saw a rapid growth in the Judaean hills, including the more peripheral areas (Ofer 1994: 102–4). Based on his survey results, Ofer (1994, 2001) argued that from the mid-eleventh to the eighth century the population nearly doubled in each century. To Iron IIA (a single identifiable ceramic stage) are to be assigned Tel Qasileh XI–IX, Izbet-ṣartah II–I, Beersheba VIII–VI, Tel Edar III–II and Arad XII–XI (Ofer 2001: 30–1). We see the beginning of settlement in the pasture areas, and the first inhabitants of the desert fringe sites (e.g., Tekoah, ha-Qain, Ma'on, Carmel). The Shephelah only began to be populated at this date.

Some of Ofer's interpretation has been challenged. G. Lehmann (2003) criticized Ofer's survey from a methodological point of view (citing a recent publication of A. Faust). He noted that deciding between the conclusions of Ofer and Faust was currently impossible because the political situation prevented the necessary testing. Nevertheless, Lehmann (2003: 133, 141, 157) went on to argue, in contrast to Ofer, for a much smaller settled area and a population more like 10,000 in Iron I and 16,000 in Iron IIA Judah (including Jerusalem), but these are maxima: he reckoned Iron IIA at 5000 to 10,000, with Iron I correspondingly less. The built-up area of the Shephelah was twice as large as Judah in Iron I and perhaps even three times as large in Iron IIA (2003: 134). Yet Z. Herzog and L. Singer-Avitz (2004: 220) critiqued Lehmann for nevertheless accepting too many of Ofer's data without question, though their study confirmed the view that the highlands of Judah (including Jerusalem – see below) were relatively sparsely settled, in contrast to the lowlands.

From a broader perspective the population density of the Judaean hills was significantly less than the areas to the north. Ofer (1994: 107) notes the difference between the results of the Judaean hills survey and those of the Manasseh hill country and the land of Ephraim surveys. In Iron I Ephraim and Manasseh were four times that of the Judaean hills, and twice that in Iron IIA. In the northern highlands most of the LB sites continued to be inhabited in Iron I, in contrast to the Judaean highlands which had almost no LB settlements (Finkelstein 1999a: 43–4). Many highland settlements disappeared in the later Iron I (Bloch-Smith and Nakhai 1999: 78). Growth in the Judaean hills was slow from Iron I to Iron IIA, in contrast, for example, with Benjamin where the growth was 243 per cent (Lehmann 2003: 134). Penetration into the desert fringe and an increase in the population of the southern regions of the Judaean hills in general characterized Iron IIA (Ofer 1994: 104). The continuity of settlement from Iron I to Iron II was over 70 per cent, but the villages increased in Iron II, with 60 per cent new (Lehmann 2003: 147–50). Unlike Iron I, the sites were not at the highest elevation but tended to be in the middle slopes, suggesting that the settlers were feeling more secure. The more important settlements lined up with the north–south watershed in both Iron I and IIA. The settlement peak came about in the eighth century (Ofer 1994: 105). This all suggests that developments in the central territory of Judah lagged significantly behind those of the north, which has implications for evaluating state development in general and the united monarchy in particular.

As noted above, Jerusalem is probably the most contested site in Palestine. The main question is what kind of a settlement Jerusalem was in Iron IIA: was it a minor settlement, perhaps a large village or possibly a citadel but not a city, or was it the capital of a flourishing – or at least an emerging – state? Assessments differ considerably, with Ussishkin, Finkelstein, Steiner, Herzog, Lehmann and Singer-Avitz supporting a minimal settlement; but many (including A. Mazar and, especially, Cahill) arguing for the latter. Using Rank Size Theory, Ofer had argued that the graph of settled sites required Jerusalem to be included as the capital for the Judaean hill country to follow the expected pattern (1994: 97–8, 102–4); however, Lehmann's Rank Size analysis shows just the opposite (2003: 149–51). D. W. Jamieson-Drake (1991) was one of the first who queried the status of Jerusalem, concluding that it did not have the characteristics of a capital city, including monumental architecture, until the eighth century BCE. Jamieson-Drake has been much criticized for gaps in his data, but it seems that he was right as far as he went, though he gave an incomplete description (Steiner 2001: 284).

J. M. Cahill (2003, 2004) has been one of the most vociferous voices arguing for a substantial city as early as the tenth century. She dates the 'stepped stone structure' to the Late Bronze/early Iron transition, arguing that both the stepped mantle and the terraces below it were built together as a single architectural unit (Cahill 2003: 42). The fortification wall built during the Middle Bronze Age remained standing and was repaired and used until Iron IIB (2003: 71). Cahill summarizes her conclusions for the tenth century:

> My own view is that the archaeological evidence demonstrates that during the time of Israel's United Monarchy, Jerusalem was fortified, was served by two complex water-supply systems and was populated by a socially stratified society that constructed at least two new residential quarters – one located inside and the other located outside the city's fortification wall. (Cahill 2004: 20)

Reinforcing Cahill's interpretation, it has recently been argued that a building at the top of the 'stepped stone structure' dates to David's time and could be his palace (E. Mazar 2006), though the proper archaeological details have not been published; however, acceptance of her interpretation is by no means universal, if conversations with other archaeologists are anything to go by. The 'stepped stone structure' is itself the subject of considerable dispute, with several positions being taken (Lehmann 2003: 134–6). In contrast to Cahill, Steiner (1994; 1998; 2003b: 351–61) argues from Kenyon's excavations that the stepped stone structure was quite different in extension and construction method from the terrace system. Where the terraces existed, only a mantle of stones was added, but where there were no terraces the structure was built up from bedrock. The dating and construction is confirmed by the pottery in the fill of the terraces which was Iron I, with no mix of later material. Steiner would date its construction to the tenth or early ninth century. In sum, the terrace and stepped structure systems do not have similar boundaries, identical pottery or the same construction techniques. From Kenyon's excavations she feels there is enough evidence to show that the structure went out of use in the late eighth or early seventh century BCE when a new city wall was built further down the slope.

As described by Steiner (2001, 2003a, 2003b), Jerusalem of the tenth and ninth centuries was a small town occupied mainly by public buildings, not exceeding 12 hectares and with approximately 2000 inhabitants (compare this with Lehmann's 2 hectares and 300–600 inhabitants in Iron I, and 4 hectares and 600–1200 inhabitants in Iron IIA [Lehmann 2003: 135–6]). It exhibits the characteristics of a regional administrative centre or the capital of a small, newly established state, the towns of Megiddo, Hazor, Gezer and Lachish showing similar characteristics at the same time. Excavations on the Ophel show the earliest buildings there date only from the ninth century. E. Mazar had argued that the fortified complex of this area south of the Temple Mount had been constructed as early as the ninth century, but the more likely date is between the eighth and the early sixth centuries BCE (Killebrew 2003: 336). E. A. Knauf (2000a) argues that the centre of the Davidic city has not been found because it would have been the area north of the Ophel, the area of the Temple Mount. Although it is not possible to test this hypothesis now, that section of the hill was a militarily strategic area and would have had to be incorporated into any settlement on the southeastern hill.

The argument that the MB wall was used as a city wall in LB, Iron I, and Iron IIA and IIB has no archaeological support: Jerusalem lacked a fortification wall until the mid-eighth century when the MB IIB wall was partially built over and partially reused for a new fortification wall (Killebrew 2003: 334; Ussishkin 2003b: 110–11). This is supported by recent excavations, such as the one at the Givati parking lot, which showed that there were no IA IIA fortifications on the southeast ridge ('City of David' settlement); rather, 'all Iron Age fortification components unearthed in Jerusalem are the outcome of one comprehensive building operation that took place at the close of the 8th century BCE' (Ben-Ami 2014). The lack of other finds relating to fortification suggests that Jerusalem was unwalled and unfortified between LB and Iron IIB (sixteenth to mid-eighth centuries), and thus Jerusalem was 'at best modest' (Killebrew 2003: 334). Also, the elaborate water system of MB IIB went out of use until the eighth/seventh centuries (Warren's shaft never served as a water system), as shown by the excavations of Reich and Shukron (Killebrew 2003: 334–5).

In the transition from LB to Iron I the Shephelah suffered a massive demographic decline, with 67 sites in LB but 25 in Iron I, and a reduction of settled area from 105 hectares to 60 hectares (Finkelstein 1999a: 44). The Shephelah sites seem to have prospered in the later Iron I (Bloch-Smith and Nakhai 1999: 102–3). A number of lowland features of Iron

I later became characteristic of highland Iron II, primarily the collared-rim storejars, the four-room house and the bench tombs. This indicates a movement of some lowland peoples to the east and north (Bloch-Smith and Nakhai 1999: 103). Y. Dagan (2004: 2680–1) concluded that in Iron IIA the sites developed slowly as the process of Judaean settlement began, with many 'dispersed' and 'isolated' structures, a situation unknown in earlier periods, indicating a period of stability. With regard to the central site of Lachish, it was rebuilt after a long habitation gap in Iron I (Ussishkin [ed.] 2004: I, 76–87). Although little remains of this city (level V), the inhabitants seem to be a new people with a new material culture. Some have wanted to date level V to the tenth century and connect it with the invasion of Shoshenq, but the latter's inscription does not mention Lachish (nor any place in Judah proper except Arad), nor has any destruction layer been uncovered. Based on O. Zimhoni's study of the pottery (2004: IV, 1707) Ussishkin dated level IV to the mid-ninth century BCE and level V to the first half of the ninth. (This incidentally supports the LC, but Ussishkin notes that the interpretation is not conclusive.) If Lachish V dates to the ninth, Rehoboam could not have fortified the site (2 Chron. 11.5-12, 23) nor would Shoshenq have destroyed it.

The recently excavated Khirbet Qeiyafa has been the occasion of much discussion, in large part because of the claims of the excavators that the site was Judahite and disproved those who doubted the biblical account of David (Garfinkel 2011; Garfinkel, Ganor and Hasel 2012a, 2012b; Garfinkel et al. 2012). Their conclusions about the archaeology of the site were criticized by Yehuda Dagan (2009) who had done a surface survey of the area. Although Dagan's objections are well-taken, there is the caveat that surface surveys have some problems of their own (§1.2.4.3). The excavators noted that Qeiyafa seemed to be a short-lived site that was in existence only for some decades before being destroyed or abandoned (until the Hellenistic period). Based on ^{14}C dating, they put it in the period of about 1025–975 BCE (Garfinkel and Kang 2011; Garfinkel et al. 2012; Garfinkel et al. 2015); however, this dating has been attacked on methodological grounds with the argument that raw ^{14}C dates need to be integrated with all the data, including pottery and other aspects of material culture. Based on this approach, Finkelstein and Fantalkin (2012) argue for a broader dating of about 1050–915 BCE; they even suggest that the site might have been brought to an end by Shoshenq I's invasion. There is also controversy over whether the site is Judahite, as the excavators claimed, or whether it might be Israelite (Finkelstein and Fantalkin 2012) or even Canaanite (Na'aman 2010). The argument that it is to be identified with biblical Shaaraim has also been opposed, with others identifying it as Gob (Na'aman 2008; Finkelstein and Fantalkin 2012: 46–8). In short, the implications of the site are still hotly disputed, and it is likely to take some time for any sort of consensus to develop. (On the Qeiyafa ostracon, see §3.2.5.)

It is often assumed that Judah controlled the Shephelah from an early time, but a number of scholars have recently argued that this important foothill region remained a source of contention until well into the ninth century BCE or even later. N. Na'aman (2013: 263–4) argued that Judah was already making inroads by perhaps the first half of the ninth century. However, a recent study by G. Lehmann and M. H. Niemann (2014) argued that the Shephelah settlements show a material culture independent of both Philistia and the highlands; however, as the largest city in the region (Maeir 2012b) Gath dominated the area, including the Shephelah. It was only after the destruction of Gath by Hazael about 835 BCE that Judah was able to expand into the Shephelah. Na'aman (2013) is quite correct that Judah probably had a non-aggression pact with Gath, but such an agreement is unlikely to have allowed Judah to expand at Philistine expense. On the other hand, Israel and Judah may well have been vassals – or at least junior partners – with Damascus, who allowed them to expand into new territory. Yet based on his excavations of eṣ-Ṣafi/Gath, Maeir (2012b: 247–50) argues that Gath was probably occupied by Judah in perhaps the mid-eighth century, which means that Judah occupied the whole of the Shephelah (as far as Philistia) only in the late eighth century, perhaps as late as the reign of Hezekiah.

In the Negev there was a settlement gap throughout LB but a renewal in population came in Iron I. The Beersheba valley is normally too arid for farming, but there have been a few periods of sufficient rainfall, including the period from the thirteenth to the tenth centuries (Herzog 1994: 125–6). This increased fertility and the peaceful conditions (apparently), and led to population growth (approx. 1000 in the eleventh century). New settlements included Tel Masos, Arad, Tel Haror, Tel Sera', Tel Esdar, Tel Beersheba, Nahal Yattir and other sites. Some sites (e.g., Tel Sera' and Tel Haror) were settled by Philistines, but the identity of those moving into other sites is controversial (see the survey in Herzog 1994: 146–8). The biblical text mentions a number of groups associated with this region: Judah and related groups, Simeon, Amalekites, Canaanites, Kenites, Calebites and so on.

A large number of sites were identified in the Negev Highlands around Qadesh-barnea in archaeological surveys, about 50 of which were identified as 'Israelite fortresses', perhaps built by Solomon (e.g., Aharoni 1967). However, a number of scholars have now questioned this interpretation, arguing that they were desert settlements of local people who were possibly changing from a nomadic to a more settled lifestyle (see the summary in Finkelstein 1995a: 103–14; also Na'aman 1992c). The main reason is that the location of the sites and their construction does not fit what would be expected of fortresses; furthermore, there was no renewal of them at a later time when Judah definitely controlled this area. Finkelstein went on to develop the thesis of a polity, perhaps a 'chiefdom', centred on Tel Masos that grew up when the population took control of trade in the region (Finkelstein 1995a: 114–26; 2013: 126–7; Fantalkin and Finkelstein 2006). Copper from the area (see below) probably formed an important part of this trade, and when the copper trade declined, the 'Tel Masos polity' also declined. The Tel Masos 'chiefdom' was not conquered by Shoshenq I; on the contrary, Egyptian interest in the copper trade led to its expansion at this time

The transition from Iron I to Iron IIA was marked by a significant abandonment of settlements. Tel Masos was destroyed or abandoned, but it was rebuilt as a small fortress, and a number of other fortresses were also established. It has been argued that these changes were the result of intervention by the Jerusalem monarchy, but 'the spatial distribution of the sites in the valley and the demographic estimates does not support this model'; rather, a good case can be made that the cause was environmental (Herzog 1994: 143–5). Other suggestions are expanding highland settlements or Shoshenq's invasion (Finkelstein 2003a: 78–9). Certainly, the sites most uncontroversially associated with the campaign of Shoshenq are found in the Negev. The 'Greater Arad' of Shoshenq is generally agreed to be Tel Arad (Finkelstein 1999a: 38–9). Arad has been much debated over the years, with later studies substantially disagreeing with the original excavator's. Stratum XI had been identified with Shoshenq's invasion, but Zimhoni (1985) and A. Mazar and E. Netzer (1986) concluded that XI must be later than the tenth century, which would make stratum XII the Shoshenq level. The latest excavator Z. Herzog (2001; 2002: 58–72) agrees with this. Thus Arad XI and Beersheba V (with the first Iron Age fortifications in Judah) must be in the ninth century.

An important aspect of the economy at this time (as already mentioned above) is copper production and trade. This centred primarily in the Arabah around the sites of Khirbat en-Nahas and Wadi Faynan (or Feinan). (On these sites, see §3.2.3.) Yet copper was also produced elsewhere, including Khirbet Mana'iyah in southern Transjordan and Timna in the southern Negev (Ben-Yosef 2012; Ben-Yosef et al. 2012). According to a number of hypotheses, control of the copper supply was the primary driver behind a number of events in the Late Bronze/Iron I (see further above and at §3.2.3)

3.1.1.1 Analysis

There is wide agreement that Arad XII and related Negev sites are to be related to Shoshenq's invasion (Mazar 2007, 2008). The use of Shoshenq's list of cities provided a chronological anchor of crucial importance (Ussishkin 2007b). Albright's assumption that Shoshenq destroyed the whole country has been widely accepted, but his actions might have been varied: the erection of a royal stela at Megiddo shows that Shoshenq aimed to hold the city, not destroy it. Thus, his list is useless as a secure archaeological and chronological anchor, the only possible exception being Arad XII. If Arad XII dates to the second half of the tenth century and not later, this affects the dating of Lachish V, Tel Beit Mirsim B and Tel Beersheba VII; however, Ussishkin (2007b) has some doubts about the reliability even of this synchronization.

The main advantage of the 'low chronology' is that it closes the 'dark age' of the ninth century (Finkelstein 1996a: 184–5). Its main disadvantage is that it changes the entire understanding of the emergence of the Israelite state. The monuments previously associated with the united monarchy are redated from the second half of the tenth century to the early ninth. The 'low chronology' forces reconsideration of several issues relating to the archaeology of proto-Israel. In the hill country, settlements of the tenth century are not much different from those of the eleventh; thus, the real transformation came about 900 BCE rather than about 1000 BCE, which has consequences for a united monarchy. In the northern highlands this transformation brought significant growth in the number and size of sites and expansion into new frontiers and niches, while the southern highlands were only sparsely settled in early Iron II.

'Accepting the Low Chronology means stripping the United Monarchy of monumental buildings' (Finkelstein 1996a: 185). According to Finkelstein (1999b: 39) many of the strata dated to the eleventh century should now be dated to the tenth (Megiddo VIA; Beth-Shean Upper VI, Tel Hadar IV, Jokneam XVII, Beersheba VII, Arad XII). Important for our purposes are those redated to the ninth century according to the LC: Megiddo VA–IVB, Beersheba V, Arad XI. Those strata dated to the eighth and seventh centuries are not affected. The main mounds in both the north and the south (Megiddo, Gezer, Beersheba, Lachish) would be dated to the ninth century BCE or even later. Although inscribed seals and impressions are known from the mid-ninth century, they are mainly found from the eighth century onwards. Finally, the LC closes the unexplained gap between the monumental architecture traditionally assigned to the tenth century and the evidence of public administration for which we have clues in the late ninth to the eighth. In sum, the tenth century is closer to the previous period than to Iron II; the real revolution came in the ninth century, more in the north than the south. The line between Iron I and Iron II came in the early ninth century rather than about 1000 BCE. The kingdom of David and Solomon would have been a chiefdom or early state but without monumental construction or advanced administration (cf. the early Ottoman Turks or Shechem in the Amarna age).

Mazar's MCC seems to have been fairly widely accepted (even by Finkelstein's colleague, Na'aman [2013: 262]), but its extended Iron IIA spanning both the tenth and ninth centuries means that 'it would make the position of those who wish to utilize archaeology for secure historical interpretation of the tenth–ninth centuries BCE harder to sustain' (Mazar 2007; cf. 2008). It also means that events that were dated to the tenth century in conventional chronology – and which the LC dates to the ninth century – are left unspecific in the MCC. Ussishkin has expressed his pessimism about resolving the issues about chronology by normal archaeological methods, referring to the:

> ambiguity of clear stratigraphic evidence in many sites, and the difficulty of comparing pottery from different regions of the country. Hence there are possibilities for different interpretations and different chronologies. In my view, as long as no new additional data are available, it would be impossible to solve the chronological differences being debated at present. (Ussishkin 2007b: 139)

He goes on to refer to radiocarbon dating, a 'method that has been enthusiastically adopted' by some scholars on both sides of the debate, but 'this method is far from providing conclusive and perfect results', for 'the interpretation of the same ^{14}C tests can be fitted to different ideologies' (Ussishkin 2007b: 139). As quoted above, Mazar has noted the problems with radiocarbon dating but, nevertheless, refers to the results that he feels support his case. It may be that radiocarbon data will lead to a resolution or partial resolution of the debate, but this is likely to be only after a substantial database has been established (Sharon et al. 2005).

Another conclusion (only partially divorced from the chronology debate) is the difference between the development in northern Palestine as contrasted with southern Palestine. This was largely due to geographical factors: topography, geology, soil, rainfall, climate in general. The northern region, both the hill country and the lowlands, was much more suited to settlement, farming and fertility in general. The region of Judah was less fertile, had a lower density of population, and developed economically more slowly than Samaria. When one considers the *longue durée*, it would have been extraordinary for the Judaean highlands to dominate the north in Iron I or IIA. A number of archaeologists argue that the archaeology does not support the text which depicts a Judaean-highland-centred united monarchy. Those who do argue for archaeological support for the united monarchy generally do so by explicit – or implicit – appeal to the biblical text as the guide for interpreting the archaeology.

Jerusalem remains an area of considerable controversy, but those who maintain that Jerusalem did not develop into a substantial city until Iron IIB have current archaeology on their side (though the building recently found by E. Mazar has intriguing possibilities). Those who maintain an earlier development must argue on the basis of what is presumed to have disappeared or what might be found in the future. This is why a substantial argument is now made that the Northern Kingdom (in the form of the Omride dynasty) was the prior development to a state in the ninth century, with Judah coming along more slowly, reaching its height only in the eighth century. But the debate continues.

3.1.2 Merenptah Stela

An inscription in the name of Merenptah, dating to his fifth year (conventionally dated to 1207 BCE, though Kitchen insists it is 1209/1208, while Hornung et al. 2006 also seem to put it the same as Kitchen), has the first known reference to Israel and the only reference until the ninth century. Accompanying it are reliefs from the Karnak temple that have been associated with some of the events described in the poem (on these, see below). Most of the inscription is about Merenptah's defeating the Libyans who attempted to conquer Egypt, along with help from a revolt in Nubia. It is only right at the end that statements are made about other peoples supposedly conquered by Merenptah, one of which seems to be Israel:

> Tjehenu is seized, Khatte is pacified,
> Pekana'an (Gaza) is plundered most grievously
> Ashkelon is brought in and Gezer captured,
> Yeno'am is turned into something annihilated,
> Israel is stripped bare, wholly lacking seed!
> [*Ysr3r fk(w) bn prt.f*]
> Kharu has become a widow for Egypt
> And all lands are together at peace.
>
> (translation of Redford [1986b: 197];
> textual quote from Niccacci 1997: 64)

Although the reading 'Israel' (for Egyptian *Ysr3r*) has been widely accepted, not everyone agrees. For example, the name *Ysr3r* has been read as 'Jezreel', as well as some less credible renderings (Eissfeldt 1965;

Margalith 1990: 228–30; Hasel 1998: 195–8; Hjelm and Thompson 2002: 13–16). From a philological point of view, this seems an unlikely reading, as do some of the other suggestions (Hasel 1998: 197–8; Kitchen 2004: 270–1; cf. Dever 2009). All in all, it seems that the reference to Israel is reasonably secure. Much debate has centred around the determinative (cf. Yurco 1986: 190 n. 3; Hasel 1998: 198–9). The other three names have the three-hills and throw-stick signs, which are normally used for a foreign territory, whereas Israel has a seated man and woman with the throw-stick, which suggests a people rather than a fixed geographical site. These data have been used in arguments about Israel's origins (§3.2.4.2). Another question concerns the phrase 'his seed is not' (*bn prt.f*). It has often been taken metaphorically to refer to 'descendants, offspring' (e.g., Niccacci 1997: 92–3), but recently it has been argued that this means 'grain', suggesting that Israel is a sedentary community of agriculturists at this time (Hasel 1998: 201–3; 2003: 20–6). Rainey (2001) argues strongly that it should be understood as 'descendants', though this translation is taken as evidence for his own interpretation of how Israel originated.

The question is, is this inscription only a piece of royal propaganda – a triumph-hymn – with little or no historical value (cf. Hjelm and Thompson 2002)? It is one of four sorts of royal inscription and includes extravagant praise of the king as a matter of course, but this by itself does not resolve the matter because factual material is also included at relevant points in such inscriptions (Kitchen 2004: 260–5). The argument – really, more of an assertion – that Israel is only an eponym ('analogous to Genesis' Israel: the patriarch of all Palestine's peoples') ignores the determinative, which is plural and which refers to a people. According to Kitchen (2004: 271) the oft-made statement that a number of errors in determinatives are found in the inscription is incorrect. As for Israel's being paired with Kharu, this is only one possible analysis. In fact, a number of different literary structures have been seen in the passage (summarized in Hasel 1998: 257–71). There is also the question of whether *Pekana'an* refers to 'Canaan' or 'Gaza' (Hasel 2003 argues it is the former). In spite of Hjelm and Thompson, the conclusion that this inscription 'has been considered correctly as concrete proof of an Israel in Palestine around 1200 BCE' (Lemche 1998a: 75) remains the most reasonable one.

More controversial are the reliefs (Redford 1986b; Yurco 1986; 1997: 28–42; Hasel 1998: 199–201; 2003; Dijkstra 2011, 2017). The reliefs in question depict ten different scenes: the first four are the main ones, which picture the Pharaoh triumphant in battle; the fifth pictures bound Shasu prisoners; and the sixth shows Canaanite captives being led to a chariot. Redford (1986b) has argued that the inscriptions originally related to

Rameses II and have been altered to fit later rulers, and there is no reason to associate all of them with Merenptah who was in poor health and decrepit when he came to the throne. There 'is absolutely no evidence that Merenptah attacked all these places during his short reign. To the best of our knowledge, during his rule there occurred no triumph over Khatte… nor any defeat of Gaza or Yeno'am' (Redford 1986b: 197).

F. Yurco has argued (against Redford) that the first four reliefs can be equated with the four names in the inscription (Yurco 1986; 1997: 28–42). In other words, scene 1 describes the conquest of Ashkelon; scene 2, of Gezer; scene 3, of Yano'am; and scene 4, of Israel. He concludes that the scenes pictured agree with the determinative that accompanies each name, with the first three shown as cities and the fourth (Israel) as a people but not a city. Yurco's argument that the reliefs are to be ascribed to Merenptah seems to have won over some (cf. Kitchen 2004: 268–70) – though Redford seems to maintain his position (1992a: 275 n. 85). But the equation of the reliefs with the four names in the inscription is rather less secure (Rainey 2001: 68–74). In only the first scene is the site named (Ashkelon), but no names are found in scenes 2–4. Also, it may be that there were once other scenes on the wall that are now missing because of deterioration of the structure. Thus, the relating of specific names to specific scenes is much more hypothetical than Yurco seems to allow.

The interpretation of the reliefs is important to the various antagonists primarily because of the identity of the peoples being defeated. Yurco's main concern seems to focus on the dress of those fighting the Egyptians. He argues that the defeated Israelites have the typical dress of the Canaanites, providing evidence that Israelites were like (and thus arose from) the Canaanites. Rainey (2001: 72–4) argues that, on the contrary, the Israelites are to be identified with another group who are pictured in scene 5: the Shasu (also Redford 1986b: 199–200). Although this seems to be a definite possibility, his arguments for a positive identification seem to be no stronger than those of Yurco for the Canaanites.

M. Dijkstra (2011, 2017) agrees with Redford that a succession of rulers copied or imitated reliefs of Ramesses II at Karnak, so that the reliefs are best seen as examples of long-term political claims about the Levant. The 'Victory' inscription is mainly about the Libyan war in which the Libyan leader used elements of the Sea Peoples as mercenaries. The Sea Peoples are not always easy to distinguish from the Shasu, and the lower register on the wall seems to picture a standard coalition of Asiatics, Shasu and representatives of the Sea Peoples. There is considerable doubt about a clear parallelism between the reliefs and the text, and we cannot be sure that an attempt is being made to represent 'Israel'. 'Israel' was on the margin of Egypt's interest until at least 1100 BCE.

Finally, there is the question of where Israel is supposed to reside. A number have asserted that it refers to the hill country (e.g., Dever 2001: 118–19). Kitchen (2004) argues that each name refers to a section of Palestine: Ashkelon to the coast, Gezer to the inland area, Yano'am to the Galilee; therefore, Israel would refer to the hill country. This is far from cogent. There is nothing in the inscription to suggest that the individual names were meant to refer to a specific part of the country – Merenptah may just be listing sites and peoples conquered. Also, the sections of Palestine listed for the first three names by Kitchen do not cover all the territory except the hill country: what of the valley of Jezreel, the Jordan Valley, the Negev, the Transjordanian region, the plain of Sharon and so on? N. Na'aman (1994c: 247–9) points out that it is possible that the author mentioned the cities first and then the people, so there was no sequential listing. The conjectured location is highly speculative: some put 'Israel' in the area of Shechem, but the Egyptians called it 'the land of Shechem' or 'the mountain of Shechem'; putting Israel in Manasseh is nothing more than guesswork. In conclusion, it is 'best to refrain from building on this isolated reference any hypothesis concerning the location and formulation of Israel at that time' (Na'aman 1994c: 249). Thus, no argument has so far been presented to pin down the exact location in the land of this entity Israel. Ultimately, the only thing we can say is that the inscription proves there was an entity called 'Israel' in Palestine about 1200 BCE. This is an important datum, but it does not allow us to be certain of where it was located (if indeed there was a single location) or the precise organization or status of this entity 'Israel'.

3.1.3 Medinet Habu and Related Inscriptions

Rameses III's temple at Medinet Habu is very important for reliefs and inscriptions that relate to the invasion and defeat of the Sea Peoples (*ANET* 262–6; *ARE* IV, §§59–82; O'Connor 2000; Wachsmann 2000), along with a few other sources of lesser importance (Redford 2000: 8). These are not straightforward historical accounts but require a fully critical approach; nevertheless, with a careful reading much can be learned (Redford 2000; see also §3.2.2 below). The following excerpt is taken from *ANET* (italics and square brackets in the original):

> (16) …The foreign countries made a *conspiracy* in their islands. All at once the lands were removed and scattered in the fray. No land could stand before their arms, from Hatti, Kode, Carchemish, Arzawa, and Alashiya on, being cut off *at* [*one time*]. A camp [was set up] in one place in Amor. They desolated its people, and its land was like that which has never come

> into being. They were coming forward toward Egypt, while the flame was prepared before them. Their confederation was the Philistines, Tjeker, Shekelesh, Denye(n), and Weshesh, lands united. They laid their hands upon the lands as far as the circuit of the earth… I organized my frontier in Djahi, prepared before them: – princes, commanders of garrisons, (20) and *maryanu*. I have the river-mouths prepared like a strong wall, with warships, galleys and coasters. (*ANET* 262)

For further on the interpretation of this text, see §3.2.2 below.

3.1.4 Report of Wenamun

One interesting text is the *Report of Wenamun*, about a journey to the Phoenician and Palestinian area (*AEL* II, 224–30; Helck 1986). The text is usually dated to the early eleventh century BCE, allegedly before Egypt lost its hold on the region. It is evidently a work of fiction but appears to give some useful insights into the relationship between Egypt and the Phoenician area and may contain some helpful incidental details.

3.1.5 Shoshenq I's Palestinian Inscription

According to 1 Kgs 14.25-28 a King Shishak of Egypt came up against Jerusalem in Rehoboam's fifth year and took all the treasures of the temple. When an inscription of Shoshenq I (ca. 943–923 BCE), founder of the 22nd Dynasty, was found at Karnak listing many topographical sites in Palestine, a connection was made with the passage in the Bible and has been the standard view ever since. All seem to agree that Shoshenq's expedition was a signal event in Israel's history, but precisely what happened on the ground and even when the invasion took place is considerably disputed. The conventional view is heavily informed by the Bible. According to it, Shoshenq's army made a number of destructive raids on various parts of Palestine, destroying many sites in the Negev and even as far north as Megiddo; however, Jerusalem did not fall because the Pharaoh was bought off by Rehoboam.

A number of studies have addressed the issue of Israel/Judah and Shoshenq's 'invasion' beginning with M. Noth's study in 1938 (for a survey of earlier studies, see K. A. Wilson 2005; also Helck 1971: 238–45; Schipper 1999: 119–32; Ash 1999: 50–6; Na'aman 1992c; Finkelstein 2002c). Most have assumed that Shoshenq conducted an invasion of Palestine, that the inscription gives some sort of invasion route, that the inscription can be reconciled with the biblical text and that the archaeology matches the inscription. There have, nevertheless, been some problems, especially the fact that Israel and Judah are not mentioned specifically, that no site in Judah occurs in the inscription, that the toponyms cannot be worked into any sort of itinerary sequence and that the biblical text says nothing about an invasion of the Northern Kingdom.

It might not be surprising that a Jerusalem scribe did not record the details of Shoshenq's raids on Israel, but why omit the destructive attacks on the Negev, which was a part of Judah – at least, in the eyes of the Bible? Leaving aside the Jerusalem question, there is still considerable disagreement about how to interpret Shoshenq's inscription. Was it a raid or primarily an occupation – albeit temporary – of the land? Various explanations have been given of the order of toponyms as they might relate to the progress of the invasion, but none has been completely convincing. Now, however, K. Wilson has investigated Shoshenq's inscription in the context of other Egyptian triumphal inscriptions. He concludes:

- Triumphal inscriptions were designed to extol the Pharaoh's exploits, not provide historical data.
- The reliefs glorify all the exploits of the king rather than a particular campaign.
- The topographical lists are not laid out according to any system that allows a reconstruction of the military route.
- The sites listed may in some cases be those attacked, but others not attacked – indeed, friendly towns and allies – might be listed as well.
- The lists were apparently drawn in part from military records and onomastical lists, which means that some data of value for certain purposes may be included.

The implications of these conclusions are considerable. Rather than recording a particular campaign into Palestine, Shoshenq's inscription may include more than one (as maintained by Knauf 2008a). This would help to explain the vague nature of the inscriptions that accompany the topographical lists, without clarifying the reasons for or objectives of the 'invasion'. In any case, the precise nature and progress of the campaign(s) cannot be worked out. More puzzling is the lack of any reference to Judah or Jerusalem as such. The argument is that this was in a section of the inscription that is no longer readable. This argument is still maintained by the latest study of the Shoshenq inscription by Kevin Wilson (2005). It must be said that this argument, while possible, is not compelling. Another obvious interpretation is that Shoshenq bypassed Judah – or at least, the Judaean highlands – because it did not suit his purpose, and the biblical writer got it wrong. Interestingly, the solution that seems to be agreed on by both A. Mazar (2008: 107–10) and Fantalkin and Finkelstein et al. (2008: 37–9) is that Shoshenq was indeed interested in Judah because of the copper trade. This could make Jerusalem not just a stage in the invasion but its main object (though not Finkelstein's view). This is an interesting interpretation, though one might ask why Shoshenq then pushed on north as far as the Jezreel Valley if he had already reached his objective.

Finkelstein, among others, argues that the main phase of prosperity was post-Shoshenq and that the sites in the south were primarily not destroyed but abandoned (Finkelstein et al. 2008). They point out that Shoshenq also does not mention the Philistine cities, which could be significant. Finkelstein interprets this as evidence for their control of the copper trade. But whether or not that is right, we have to ask why the Philistines were omitted. If the Egyptian expedition was a general attack on Palestinian cities in Israel and Judah, why should the Philistine plain be left out? Could these cities have a particular relationship with Egypt? Or was the Shoshenq operation a more complex one? David Ussishkin (2008: 205–6) makes the reasonable argument that Shoshenq would hardly set up his stela in a ruined city, but suggests that Megiddo was not just attacked but was occupied to become a regional headquarters. To me, this calls for a rethink of how destructive Shoshenq's raid was, as opposed to dominance and intimidation.

A final question is when this raid took place. The biblical text places it under Rehoboam, but some have wanted to put it earlier, under Solomon's time (see the discussion and references in Finkelstein 2002c: 110; see also Niemann 1997: 297–9). We do not know within Shoshenq's reign when the excursion took place: some want to place it early in his reign but others prefer later. Too many simply project into Egyptian history the date they have calculated for Rehoboam's reign. Thus, the lack of knowledge about the date of Shoshenq's campaign, its precise nature and the dating of Solomon's rule all contribute to a great deal of uncertainty

3.1.6 Biblical Text

Most of the texts of relevance to this time period are from the Pentateuch or the Deuteronomistic History (DtrH). Both of these are collections that scholarly consensus regards as late compilations but possibly having early material in certain sections. A detailed analysis is not possible here, but some of the main issues relating to historicity will be touched on.

3.1.6.1 Pentateuch

The Pentateuch has already been discussed (see §2.1.5). The main texts relevant for Israel's settlement in the land are the books of Exodus and Numbers. These revolve around the exodus and are discussed below specifically with regard to the exodus (§3.2.1). For texts relating to the settlement, see the next section and §3.2.4.1.

3.1.6.2 Deuteronomistic History (DtrH)

The composition of DtrH continues to be debated (Römer 2005; Lipschits 2005: 272–304; O'Brien 1989; Campbell and O'Brien 2000). Most specialists choose between an ascription to either a twofold composition, the first edition in the late seventh century and the second in the exilic period, or a single composition in the sixth century (though there are several variants of these, especially of the latter, since edits and additions are proposed for the single composition). In each case, the compiler(s) would have used a variety of traditions, as well as making their own edits and additions. On the question of Joshua and history, see N. Na'aman (1994c) and E. A. Knauf (2008b; 2010a). A survey of recent scholarship on Judges is given by K. M. Craig (2003): see also Knauf (2010b). The historicity of Kings has also been much discussed, recently summarized by Avioz (2005); also Grabbe 2016. I have argued that the DtrH used a Judahite chronicle for information on the Judahite and Israelite kings from the early ninth century (§4.1.7.2), but this generally does not help us in this chapter. For further information on Joshua and Judges as they relate to the Late Bronze Age, see §3.2.4.1.

3.2 Analysis

Several controversial issues need to be discussed at some length in this section, relating to the history of biblical scholarship (e.g., the exodus and conquest) as well as to current issues. Some of these may no longer be live issues in the minds of many but are still discussed and still accepted by some.

3.2.1 The Question of the Exodus

The idea that the ancestors of Israel were in Egypt for a period, that they were oppressed, that they came out of Egypt 'with a high hand' (Exod. 14.8) and that they entered the promised land after a period in the wilderness is a major concept in the biblical text. How historical is this? The last part of the picture – the conquest of the land of Canaan – will be discussed below, but here we focus on the general question of the exodus. Two recent works have a good deal of information on this question (Grabbe 2014; Levy, Schneider and Propp [eds] 2015). Several issues are involved:

1. The exodus tradition in the biblical text. The vast bulk of the Pentateuchal text describing the exodus and related events seems to be quite late (Albertz 1994: 23–4, 42–5: 'exilic or early post-exilic'). The question is whether the exodus is presupposed in early

texts. It was once widely argued that the exodus was embodied in certain passages quoting an early Israelite 'credo' (Rad 1965), but subsequent study suggested that some of these passages (e.g., Deut. 6.21-23; 26.5-9; Josh. 24.2-13) were actually late (Nicholson 1973: esp. 20–7). Some point out that Hosea (12.1; 13.4), for example, presupposes the exodus tradition. Not everyone is confident any longer in such literary analysis; in any case, this would take us back only to the eighth century, long after the alleged event. Whatever the reality, it is clothed in a thick layer of mythical interpretation (cf. Assmann 2015; Berner 2015; Finkelstein 2015; Hendel 2015; Maeir 2015; Propp 2015; Römer 2015; Russell 2015; Schmid 2015). The Pharaoh is a generic figure, without a name. A series of ten miracles is enacted – and attempts to find naturalistic explanations (e.g., Hort 1957) miss the point: the aim of the narrative is to magnify the power of Yhwh and his servant Moses. In looking at various naturalistic models, Mark Harris (2015) is quite right to 'question whether such a model provides a good reading of the text of Exodus 14–15' (italics in the original omitted). According to the plain statement of the text, 600,000 men of military age came out; with the elderly, women and children, the number would have been at least three or four million (Grabbe 2000c). The crossing of the Red Sea seems to mix a more naturalistic account, in which an east wind moves the waters (Exod. 14.21), with a more miraculous one in which the sea divides and the water stands on either side like walls (Exod. 14.22-29). F. M. Cross (1973: 121–44) attempted to argue that a naturalistic account, in which the Egyptians died in a storm as they pursued the Israelites across the sea in boats, is reflected in Exod. 15.7, but his philological analysis is flawed (Grabbe 1993b). Thus, even if Exodus 15 is an example of early poetry as some argue (e.g., Robertson 1972; Cross and Freedman 1955; Cross 1973: 121–44; Hendel 2015), it does not appear to give a picture different from the surrounding narrative (for the argument that Exodus 15 is not early, see Noth 1962). The biblical text does not provide any particular time for Israel's coming out of Egypt, and a number of the dates assigned to the event depend on data not really relating to the exodus itself (e.g., the settlement, the Merenptah Stela).

2. Semites in Egypt. A number of Egyptian texts from the second millennium BCE mention peoples who were non-Egyptian and probably Semitic (see the survey in Malamat 1997). The Egyptian texts refer to 'foreigners' under the categories of 'Asiatics' (*'3mw*), Nubians and Libyans (Leahy 2001: 548). None of the 'Asiatics' mentioned in Egyptian texts is referred to in such a way as to make

one identify them with Israelites (though see the discussion on the Shasu at §2.2.1.4). What it does indicate is that the idea of people from Syro-Palestine – including possibly some early Israelites – living for a time in Egypt is not in and of itself problematic. One text refers to Shasu bringing their livestock into Egypt (Giveon 1971: #37). Yet there were also Egyptian traditions of a Semitic (or Asiatic) people in Egypt who were driven out, probably based at least in part on a memory of Hyksos rule (Redford 2015). In that sense, the biblical story has an Egyptian precedent.

3. The Merenptah Stela (see §3.1.2 for a full discussion). Appeals to this text as evidence for the exodus are very problematic. The inscription provides no evidence for any sojourn in Egypt for those identified in the text as 'Israel'. The 'Israel' mentioned there seems to be a people not yet settled, while the country is firmly under Egyptian control. The inscription does not presuppose an Israel anything like that depicted in Joshua or Judges.
4. References in Egyptian texts (Frerichs and Lesko 1997; G. I. Davies 2004). There is nothing in Egyptian texts that could be related to the story in the book of Exodus. It is not just a question of the official ignoring of defeats of the Pharaoh and his army. There is no period in the second half of the second millennium BCE when Egypt was subject to a series of plagues, death of children, physical disruption of the country and the loss of huge numbers of its inhabitants (cf. §2.3.2.1). Occasionally, a scholar has seen a remarkable resemblance between Moses and an Egyptian official, but the arguments have not met widespread acceptance. At most, one could say that a memory of the Egyptian figure was used to create the figure of Moses in the biblical text. G. I. Davies (2004) surveys almost all the evidence available, but little of it is very compelling; indeed, he finds the attempts to equate the exodus tradition with certain figures known from Egyptian sources 'not very convincing'. (Thus, his conclusion that the exodus 'tradition is a priori unlikely to have been invented' appears tacked on rather than arising from his data.)
5. Egyptological elements in the exodus narrative. Some have argued that elements within the text fit the period of Rameses II (Hoffmeier 1997), but this is not sufficient; one must show that they do not fit any other period in history (see nos. 6–7 below). It has been widely accepted that there are names and other references that suggest some knowledge of Egypt in the exodus narrative, but how early are they? What is notable is that there are few incidental or accidental references to Egypt, such as one might expect, unlike some other

biblical passages such as found in Isaiah and Jeremiah; most of what is present is topographical (Redford 1987: 138). More important, a number of the Egyptian elements in the exodus story are anachronistic (see next points). There is no agreement among Egyptologists about elements that could only be dated to an early period.

6. Exodus 1–11: topographical names. A reference to the 'land of Goshen' does not occur in texts (Redford 1987: 138–49); most now agree that the name arose from the name of the Qedarite leader Geshem in the Persian period (Van Seters 2001: 267–9; cf. Grabbe 2014: 70–1). The cities Rameses (Pi-Ramesse) and Pithom (Exod. 1.11) are not clearly from the Ramesside period. The first problem is identification of the sites in question. Pi-Ramesse is widely identified with Qantir (Pusch 2001; Bietak 1987: 164; Hoffmeier 1997: 117), though Redford asked where the 'Pi' (Egyptian *pr* 'house') of Pi-Ramesse had gone (1963: 408–10; 1987: 138–9; but cf. Helck 1965). Also, the Hebrew spelling of the name is a late form of transliteration (Hoch 1994). No agreement about the identity of Pithom (Egyptian *pr-'Itm* 'the house of Atum') has been reached (Wei 1992). Many argue for Tell el-Maskhuta (Redford 1963: 403–8; Holladay 2001), but this site was not settled between the sixteenth and the seventh centuries. The nearby site of Tell el-Ratabah is another possibility, but it was reoccupied only about 1200 BCE (Wei 1992; Dever 1997a: 70–1). It is therefore difficult to understand Davies' statement that 'they are more likely as a pair to belong to a tradition that originated in the Ramesside period than to a later time' (2004: 30). If Tell el-Maskhuta was known as 'Pithom' from about 600 BCE (G. I. Davies 2004: 30) and topographical names with 'Rameses' were also widespread in the first millennium BCE (Redford 1987: 139), this argues that the tradition of Exod. 1.11 was likely to be late, rather than Ramesside. Sile (*Ṯrw*) was an important site in the New Kingdom, and the Israelites would have had to pass it, yet it is not mentioned in the text of Exodus. To sum up, a number of the toponyms cannot be Ramesside; on the other hand, all are known in the Saite or later periods (eighth–fifth centuries BCE: Grabbe 2014: 70–7).
7. The supposed route of the exodus from Egypt. Some have argued that the route of the Israelites' journeyings in the Bible matches the actual topography and Egyptian settlements on the ground (Hoffmeier 2005; Krahmalkov 1994). A more careful look shows, however, that the text does not reflect the fifteenth or thirteenth centuries BCE but the seventh or eighth (MacDonald 2000: 63–100; Dever 2003a: 18–20;

Finkelstein 2015). Some of the itineraries are rather vague, showing little actual knowledge of the topography supposedly being described (Deut. 2.1-25; Num. 21.10-20), with Num. 33.1-49 going the farthest in suggesting knowledge of a real travel route (MacDonald 2000: 98). Only at the end of Iron II (but not Iron I or early Iron II) were most of the sites that can be identified actually occupied. Most scholars argue that the itineraries in Exodus and in Numbers 33 are the result of late editing of several different traditions that do not presuppose the same route (Haran 1976; G. I. Davies 1990).

8. Conquest of the Transjordanian region. Trying to extract historical data from this tradition is difficult. There is some indication, for example, that at least some of the peoples listed in the tradition are simply creations from the names of mythical figures. Some of the most feared inhabitants of the land are the Anakim who are descended from the Rephaim (Num. 13.35; cf. Deut 1.28; 2.10, 11, 21; 9.2; Josh. 11.21-22; 14.12, 15; 15.14). One of the main figures is Og of Bashan. He is said to be from the remnant of the Rephaim and dwells in Ashtarot and Edrei (Num. 21.33-35; Deut. 1.4; 3.10-11; Josh. 9.10; 12.4; 13.12; cf. Num. 13.33). These names are significant. Other passages (such as Job 26.5; Ps. 88.11-13; Isa. 26.14, 19; Prov. 9.18), as well as the Ugaritic texts, associate the Rephaim with the dead. The god Rapha'u of an Ugaritic incantation seems to dwell in Ashtarot and Edrei (*KTU* 1.108). Thus, it appears that myth has been historicized, and the shades of the dead have been turned into ethnographical entities. The writer seems at times to have taken traditional or mythical names and used them to create a narrative about ethnic groups. There is also some evidence that the writer has drawn on topographical knowledge of the eighth or seventh centuries to draw up his list of journeys.
9. Archaeological evidence. No event of the size and extent of the exodus could have failed to leave significant archaeological remains. Israel's itinerary has already been discussed (point #7 above). According to the book of Numbers (10.11; 12.16; 13.26; 20.1, 22; 33.36) much of the 40 years of 'wandering' was spent near Qadesh-Barnea. This and related sites in Sinai and southern Palestine should yield ample evidence of a large population in this region. Yet we find nothing (Finkelstein and Silberman 2001: 62–4). Qadesh (Tell el-Qudeirat) itself has been extensively excavated but shows no habitation between the Middle Bronze Age and the tenth century BCE (Cohen 1981, 1997; Dever 2003a: 19–20) or even later (Ussishkin 1995a).

Opinions about the historicity of the exodus are divided. Despite the efforts of some fundamentalist arguments, there is no way to salvage the biblical text as a description of a historical event. A large population of Israelites, living in their own section of the country, did not march out of an Egypt devastated by various plagues and despoiled of its wealth and spend 40 years in the wilderness before conquering the Canaanites. The situation can be summarized as follows:

- Although there may well be early elements within the exodus narrative, some perhaps even going back to Ramesside times, the form of the story as we presently have it in Exodus and Numbers contains data that are most closely associated with the Saite and Persian periods, or about the seventh to fifth centuries BCE. Only some of the details could fit the Egyptian New Kingdom, but almost all could have a home in the Late Kingdom. It is not sufficient to point to early elements in a text to demonstrate an early date for it. Early elements can be found in late texts, but not vice versa. Ultimately, judging the date of a text depends on a variety of factors, but the final form of a text can be no earlier than the latest element in it. In some cases, it has been argued that an early text has 'only been updated'. But how is 'updating' different from editing or revising or rewriting that literary critics have traditionally appealed to? It means that the text has been interfered with and does not necessarily reflect the data or message of the original text.
- No Egyptian document, inscription, or piece of iconography depicts, describes, or refers to an exodus as described in the Bible. There are no Egyptian references of any kind that relate to Joseph, the descendants of Jacob, Moses, the ten plagues, or the exodus. It does seem strange that there is not even a hint in Egyptian literature, iconography, or legend that any of this happened. The Israelite narrator never puts a name to Pharaoh or any of the other Egyptians, a surprising omission if we were dealing with a contemporary historical document.
- It is even stranger that there is no early archaeology relating to the Israelites in the major areas of the exodus, especially around Qadesh-barnea or further north in the Transjordanian region.
- The Amarna texts do not describe a situation in Palestine anything like the narrative in Joshua or Judges. This rules out an exodus before the mid-fourteenth century BCE, contra some conservatives who still opt for a fifteenth-century date. Other Egyptian texts in fact rule out an exodus at all during the 18th and 19th Dynasties (see §2.3.2.1).

- The reference to Israel in the Merenptah stela does not presuppose an Israel anything like that of Joshua or the Judges. The 'Israel' mentioned there seems to be a people not yet settled, while the country is firmly under Egyptian control. Where this Israel is located is also unclear.
- The exodus story has a place in the Israel of the eighth century BCE or perhaps a bit earlier. Some argue that the earliest version of the story is found in Exodus 15, yet it probably does not take us much further back in time. In any case, the exodus narrative of the Pentateuch is not so early, with influences and details from a much later time. The story as we have it is not a monolith but is made up of elements from a variety of periods and milieus. On the other hand, various naturalistic explanations (whether of the plagues or a volcanic eruption or an earthquake/tsunami) do violence to the text and provide no support to the literalistic interpretation of some fundamentalists.

This does not rule out the possibility that the text contains a distant – and distorted – memory of an actual event. Some feel that the tradition is so strong in the Bible that some actual event must lie behind it, though it might be only a small group of (slave?) escapees fleeing Egypt (a view long and widely held). This is accepted even by some of those proposing theories about the indigenous origin of Israel in Canaan (see §3.2.4.2; Na'aman 2015 suggests the tradition originates from Egyptian oppression in Canaan itself). Some think it might even be a hazy remembrance of the Hyksos expulsion from Egypt in the sixteenth century BCE (e.g., the Egyptologist A. Gardiner [1933]). E. A. Knauf (2010c: 242–3) suggests it might originate from the return of Israelites initially taken captive by Merenptah.

Yet others point out that there is no necessity for assuming there was an exodus in the early history of Israel (Dever 2003a: 7–21). There is no external evidence for such an event, and any arguments must depend on the biblical tradition; however, since we know of many Egyptian connections with Israel and Judah at later times, from the time of the monarchy to the Persian and Hellenistic periods (cf. Isa. 19.19-25; Jer. 42–44), this could have been sufficient to give rise to the story in the biblical text. Many scholars now agree that there is little clear evidence that the biblical tradition is an early one.

3.2.2 The Sea Peoples and the Philistines

3.2.2.1 The Coming of the Sea Peoples

We know about the Sea Peoples from a number of sources (see the survey in Noort 1994; also Oren [ed.] 2000; Ehrlich 1996: 1–21). The main sources for the Philistines are the Egyptian texts, primarily the Medinet Habu reliefs and inscriptions (§3.1.3), and the material culture. About these, however, there is considerable debate.

The Philistines were one of the components of the Sea Peoples who migrated from the wider Aegean area in the late second millennium BCE. As C. Ehrlich (1996: 9–13; cf. also Morris 2005: 694–707) indicates, there are two main interpretations (depending heavily on the Medinet Habu inscriptions and other documents but also bringing archaeological data into the question). The 'maximalist' interpretation argues that Ramesses III fought a coalition of Sea Peoples (Peleset [Philistines], Sherden, Tjeker, Shekelesh, Denyen, Tresh and Weshesh) in both sea and land battles, defeated them and forced (or allowed) them to settle in fortresses and cities in the Palestinian (Philistine) coastal plain (Dothan and Ben-Shlomo 2013). This would have been in his eighth year (roughly 1175 BCE). This view is still found in much secondary literature.

This has since been partially contradicted by archaeology, which shows that Egyptianizing material culture preceded the coming of the Philistines in the area but disappeared with their settlement. The main indication of the Sea Peoples/Philistines in the coastal plain of Palestine is the material culture. Important in this discussion is locally produced Mycenaean IIIC:1 pottery (sometimes referred to as 'Philistine monochrome'). It was not itself imported but was influenced by the LH IIIC:1 pottery of the Aegean and/or Cyprus. These indicators of Philistine settlement are generally found unmixed with Egyptianizing material remains. This is important because it strongly suggests that the Philistine settlement and Egyptian rule were opposed to one another.

Recently, however, scholars have emphasized the need for a more nuanced reading of the sources which recognizes the diversity of possibilities of interpreting Philistine origins. A second or 'minimalist' interpretation argues that the nature of Pharaonic inscriptions needs to be taken into account. Ramesses III's claims are conventional propaganda, either created from a long literary tradition or a compilation building up a minor episode into an earth-shaking threat to Egypt from which the divine Pharaoh delivered her, as was his duty and function (cf. Morris 2005: 696–9). (It should be noted that at least two of Ramesses III's campaigns celebrated in Medinet Habu, his victories over the Nubians and Asiatics, are completely made up according to Noort [1994: 108], though

Morris [2005: 782–85] accepts there was minor military interaction with Nubia.) These leave the interpretation much more open, ultimately taking into account the material culture from the archaeology. The result for some was to argue that rather than being due to an invading force, the Aegeanizing material culture is the product of trade. Such a conclusion illustrates the need for reevaluating the evidence, considering new ideas and possibilities. Yet after a period of rethinking, most researchers at the present reject purely trade influence (however important it may have been in the process) but favour the idea of an outside population coming to settle in the area of Philistia, as the Egyptian inscriptions suggest, though the process was probably a more complex one than a simple reading of the Egyptian material indicates (as we shall discuss below). Although there are many problems of interpretation, several points about the Sea Peoples emerge with a reasonable probability from the reliefs and inscriptions (cf. Redford 2000: 12–13; Morris 2005: 691–715; Yasur-Landau 2010; Killebrew 2005: 197–245):

1. They come from 'islands in the midst of the sea', which meant Crete and the Aegean archipelago to the Egyptians (cf. the biblical 'Caphtor' [Amos 9.7; Jer. 47.4] which seems to mean the same thing [Drews 1998]).
2. They seem to have been well organized and well led (though this does not appear in the reliefs which, by their very nature, picture defeat and chaos); however, it was not necessarily a unified movement, but different groups at different times. Five (sometimes more) tribes are listed, of which the 'Philistines' (*prst*) are only one (see the list above).
3. The presence not just of warriors (the only ones pictured in the sea battle) but also of families and livestock, with household goods in ox carts, suggests the migration of peoples rather than just an army of conquest. These migrants (women, children and elders are depicted) evidently came overland from Anatolia. The Egyptian and other ancient Near Eastern texts have been interpreted to conclude that the Sea Peoples assisted in bringing an end to the Hittite empire, the kingdom of Ugarit and the city-state of Amurru. But more recent study has been more sceptical and noted that a good deal has been read into the texts; in any case, there were probably multiple causes for the downfall or destruction of these civilizations (Kuhrt 1995: 386–93). The archaeology shows no destruction for the Phoenician area, however, which leads to the proposal that at least the march south down the coast between Byblos and Dor was more or less peaceful (Yasur-Landau 2010: 168–71).

4. A sea battle seems to have taken place in the region of the Nile delta (as *r-ḥ3wt* 'river mouths' implies), but the land battle is more of a problem. Some (e.g., Redford 2000: 13) think the land battle was also in northern Egypt, but the inscription names 'Djahy' which can refer to the Phoenician coast. Three permutations concerning the relationship of the land and sea battles are possible (Ehrlich 1996: 9 n. 45), but the main question relates to the land battle. Ussishkin (2008) argues that since Egypt controlled Megiddo, the land part of the movement would have been stopped in northern Palestine. Ussishkin's view is supported in some ways by the recent book by E. Morris who comments in a footnote:

   > There is nothing in either the reliefs or the texts that supports the supposition…that the land battle had occurred near the mouth of the Pelusiac branch of the Nile. Indeed, Ramesses III's referral of the matter to vassals, garrison troops, and maryannu-warriors would argue strongly *against* an Egyptian locale. (Morris 2005: 697 n. 16)

   The strength of the Twentieth Egyptian Dynasty is attested by Morris (2005: 703–5) who notes the number of Egyptian fortresses and sites, yet Yasur-Landau still doubts that the Egyptian garrison severely hindered the movement of the migrating Sea Peoples (2010: 340). Ramesses III's 'victory' might have been an attack on a few contingents of migrating peoples but hardly the bulk of them.
5. There is a debate over whether the Philistines were forcibly settled in the coastal plain by the Egyptians or whether they took the area by force, in spite of what the Egyptians could do. Barako has recently argued, primarily from archaeology, that the 'Egyptians were not in Philistia during this period because the Philistines were there instead; and not as garrisoned prisoners-of-war but, rather, as an intrusive population hostile to Egypt' (2013: 51). While Morris presents both views, he also argues that Ramesses III may well have encouraged the Sea Peoples to settle the Philistine plain (2005: 698–709).
6. The immigration into the Philistine coastal plain may have been a prolonged one (Yasur-Landau suggests 'a time frame of fifty to seventy-five years' [2010: 320]; Killebrew [2005: 234] suggests a century or more). This is rather wide of the single invasion and battle in Ramesses III's eighth year that the textual data and some past interpretations have given us. In any case, by the later twelfth century BCE, Egypt no longer had the strength to prevent the Sea Peoples' migration.

We shall consider this picture in more detail after considering another pressing question: When did the Sea Peoples settle in Palestine? This question has been given three different answers (Yasur-Landau 2010: 315–20; Killebrew 2005: 232). One theory, the 'high chronology' (or two-wave theory), would date the Mycenaean IIIC Early (Mycenaean IIIC:1b) to about 1200 BCE, the result of an early proto-Philistine wave of Sea Peoples. However, with the finding of Myc IIIC:1 pottery, another view developed that a first wave of Philistine settlement appeared perhaps in the later thirteenth century BCE, but the main settlement (with Philistine Bichrome Ware) in the early twelfth century. This 'high chronology', which was favoured by Moshe and Trude Dothan, pioneers in excavating the Philistine area, has now been generally rejected (even by Trude Dothan [see Dothan and Zukerman 2004; Dothan and Ben-Shlomo 2013]).

The most widely followed theory, the 'middle chronology', depends on Ramesses III's inscription that he defeated the Sea Peoples in his eighth year or about 1175 BCE. This would date Mycenaean IIIC Early to about 1175 BCE and the Bichrome that developed from it to the mid-twelfth century BCE. This theory is becoming more problematic in light of the increasing consensus that Mycenaean IIIC:1b should be equated to Mycenaean IIIC Early to Middle, which should be dated to the mid-twelfth (Killebrew 2005: 232).

Israel Finkelstein (1995b) and David Ussishkin (2008), however, argued for a 'low chronology', which places the initial wave after about 1140 or 1130 BCE, after the Egyptian control of the area had effectively vanished. The low chronology theorizes that Mycenaean IIIC:1b appeared only after about 1140 BCE and the date of the Bichrome pottery even later into the eleventh century.

The choice at the moment seems to be between the 'middle' and the 'low' chronologies. A brief discussion of some of the arguments can be given here. Ussishkin (2008) has pointed out that, for all practical purposes, no Philistine pottery – Monochrome or Bichrome – was found at Lachish, even though such pottery was uncovered at the not-too-distant sites of Tel Zafit and Tel Miqne. This indicates that Philistine pottery postdates the Lachish settlement, viz., 1130 BCE. This argument (albeit, one from silence) goes against the 'Mazar-Singer-Stager hypothesis' that lack of 'Philistine' pottery is due to cultural factors. The inevitable conclusion (according to Ussishkin) is that the Philistine settlement of the coastal plain must postdate 1130 BCE.

Amihai Mazar (2008) responds that Ussishkin's and Finkelstein's arguments that contemporary sites should yield similar pottery assemblages in a geographical zone is correct in principle but should not be rigidly applied when dealing with specific cases such as this. They claim that it is inconceivable that local Mycenaean IIIC pottery did not reach contemporary sites in Philistia and the Shephelah but, according to Mazar, this ignores cultural factors that could limit particular pottery to a few urban centres. They think lack of such pottery means a settlement gap, but such a widespread occupational gap is unfeasible and also negated by finds at such sites as Gezer. The early stage of Philistine settlement lasted perhaps only a generation. Lachish is at least 25 km from the major Philistine cities, sufficient to create a cultural border.

These differences between archaeologists may seem confusing, but they are no more significant than those between interpretations of the inscriptional data. What we have to recognize are some major divergences between the various models for understanding the settlement of the Sea Peoples and the early history of the Philistines. The archaeology is vital, but it is also very interpretative at certain points. Yet the archaeology also provides data that seem to give a much clearer picture in certain areas. To take an example, Finkelstein (1996b) has compared the settlement patterns in the coastal plain between LB and Iron I, and this appears to lead to more definitive conclusions: in LB the area of the coastal plain that became Philistia seems to have been the most densely populated in Palestine, with many sites of a variety of sizes (about 100, covering about 175 hectares, though there were more sites in the Shephelah than in the coastal plain). About 80 per cent of the Iron I sites had been settled in LB, but there had been a drastic decline in numbers, down to about half the number in LB. On the other hand, the proportion of large sites is up (from about half to three-quarters), while medium-sized sites almost disappear. Even though the number of sites is considerably reduced, it is mainly the smaller sites that no longer exist. Because there are proportionally larger sites (even though fewer), the total built-up area remains much the same. The result is a major reduction in rural sites but a considerable expansion in urban settlement.

Finkelstein goes on to note that the major LB sites were Gezer, Gath, Lachish, Ashkelon, Gaza and Yurza. These continued into Iron I, with two exceptions: Lachish was abandoned (as was Tel Harasim), but Tel Miqne-Ekron had grown considerably. Ashdod and Ekron appear to be the strongest towns in the region, with Ashkelon and Gath the weakest (unless Ashkelon controlled Jaffa). The estimated population is 35,000 for LB and 30,000 for Iron I. This compares with 44,000 for the central hill country in Iron I (but only 2,200 of these were in the Judaean hills). Considering that few new sites were established in Iron I, and the total built-up area was also very similar, this suggests that the number of new settlers – the

Philistines – were few. This confirms what a number of scholars had been arguing: the Philistines settled among the indigenous Canaanite population, perhaps as an elite. One result of this is that the material culture in the region included both Philistine and Canaanite elements (Bunimovitz 1990). But if the Philistines were so few, this argues against a major invasion force that some postulate (25,000 or 30,000, for example).

The recent studies of the pottery by A. E. Killebrew (2005: 219–30; 2008; cf. 2000) are an important addition to our knowledge of the period. At Tell Miqne/Ekron stratum VII shows the sudden appearance of quantities of locally produced Aegean-inspired Mycenaean IIIC Early and associated assemblages. In stratum VI Mycenaean IIIC and Bichrome appear together throughout, showing the development from Mycenaean IIIC to Bichrome. Finally, in stratum V Mycenaean IIIC disappears and Bichrome becomes the predominant decorated ware. Killebrew concludes that, with 'some minor revisions', the low chronology would best fit the dating of Mycenaean IIIC Early–Middle at other sites in the eastern Mediterranean and would also provide a more reasonable dating of Bichrome to the eleventh century (continuing into the tenth [2008: 64–5; 2005: 232]). This conclusion is based on the LB II to IA I stratigraphic sequences at both Tel Miqne and Ashdod. This seems to provide some support for the interpretation of Finkelstein (1995b) and Ussishkin, that the Philistine settlement was later than Ramesses III's eighth year. Yet she emphasizes the complexity of the Philistine immigration process, which militates against a simple chronological reconstruction.

T. J. Barako (2013) has tackled the problem by comparing the contiguous cities of Ashdod and Tel Mor (and Killebrew and Lehmann [2013: 9] cite it with approval). Ashdod shows a destruction layer at the end of the LB. The LB stratum (VIII) shows Egyptianizing pottery and other finds that suggest that the Egyptians were controlling a Canaanite population. The early IA I stratum (VII), however, is completely dominated by Philistine material culture, and without an Egyptianizing admixture. On the other hand, Tel Mor's remains in both LB and early IA I show Egyptianizing without any break.

The solution may lie in the nature of the 'Philistine invasion' (as Killebrew already hinted at above). It appears that its violent character, at least in part, cannot be brushed aside, as Aren Maeir comments:

> the cause behind these destructions is very likely the Sea Peoples – even if this is not to be seen as a uniform conquest of Philistia. Thus, while I would hardly adhere to a 'D-Day like event'…, I believe that one cannot see the process of the arrival of the Philistines as a peaceful event in which foreign groups slowly arrived and were amicably accepted by the local Canaanites.

> Rather, this most probably was a complex process – including both violent interactions and peaceful integration. I would suspect that a likely scenario… would be that non-local leaders deposed the local Canaanite elites (and the destruction of the LB building in Area E which is most probably a public oriented building would fit in with this scenario) – while in most cases retaining connections and integrating with other elements of the original Canaanite population. This then would explain the evidence of partial destructions such as at Ekron and Ashdod, and the fact that the Philistine cities retained their original Canaanite names… (Maeir [ed.] 2012: 18)

Yet Maeir has been among those who have argued for looking at the Philistine settlement in all its complexity. He and several colleagues have recently tackled the question of the Philistine invasion/settlement from the point of view of 'acculturation', 'hybridization', or whatever term one wishes to use (Davis, Maeir and Hitchcock 2015; Hitchcock and Maeir 2013). This recognizes the complicated product that arose from the Philistine settlement in Canaan. Maeir and his colleagues have adopted the term 'entangled' to describe the way in which the culture of native Canaanites and the incoming Philistines affected one another to produce the culture that is sometimes called 'Philistine' but which also includes clear Canaanite aspects. It helps to explain the complex nature of the cultural processes reflected in the literary and archaeological records.

Thus, Maeir is not espousing a return to the old simplistic picture of a Philistine invasion. On the contrary, he cites with approval the scenario suggested by Assaf Yasur-Landau (2010: 315–34) which resolves the problem of chronology by proposing that the Philistine settlement took place over a lengthy period of time, with different phases, as is normal for migration and settlement processes that have been studied. According to Yasur-Landau (cf. also Killebrew 2005: 230–1), the immediate origin of the Sea Peoples may have been Cyprus and perhaps even Asia Minor (even if the ultimate origin was the eastern Aegean), and the settlements there may have been established not many years before those in Palestine. The number migrating was probably only a few thousand, far fewer than the 25 or 30 thousand often proposed. The first wave of a small number of scout or pioneering immigrants could have come shortly after 1200 BCE, to be followed by much larger waves. When Ramesses III realized what was happening, he attempted to stem the flow about 1175 BCE (though probably not a single event in that year but over a period of time) but is likely to have had only small success.

The incoming Philistines and the other tribes of the Sea Peoples settled to some extent independently along the coast and in the coastal plain. Trade links were no doubt a part of this process, but trade alone does not explain the southern settlement (the areas to the north may have a different history [see Sharon and Gilboa 2013; Gilboa 2005 on the situation in Dor]). There was some destruction of the earlier Canaanite settlement, but a massacre of the previous inhabitants and a wholesale destruction of their habitation was not to the Philistine advantage. In many cases, the new settlers took their places without major violence, though they seem to have dominated the original population. The material culture shows this creative synthesis made up of elements from the two sides, the Canaanite and the Sea People.

3.2.2.2 The Development of the Philistines

According to the biblical text the Philistines were the main enemy of Israel through much of its early history. This picture is manifestly wrong in certain parts; for example, the Philistines have been anachronistically projected back as settled in the land in the early second millennium BCE (Gen. 21.22-34; 26.1-18; Finkelstein [2002b: 152–4] suggests that this reflects an eighth- or seventh-century context). Yet other parts of the biblical picture may be correct; we can know only after looking at it carefully. They surface again in the book of Judges, especially in the story of Samson, but the main account is in the books of Samuel.

At this point, there is potential engagement between biblical text and archaeology. Israel Finkelstein, for example, has argued that the actual context for the main Philistine narrative in 1 Samuel is the seventh century BCE (2002b). Others see evidence of some earlier memory there (Na'aman 1996a, 2002b); for example, the Ark Narrative is not intrinsically unbelievable overall. Unfortunately, many of the welcome archaeological finds do not impinge directly on the Bible. For example, the pebbled hearth that Aren Maeir has noted as characteristic of the Philistine area for many centuries seems to have no reflex in the biblical text (2012a: 354–5). Here are some examples where text and archaeology interact:

Lists of Philistine Cities. Several lists of Philistine cities are found (Josh. 11.22; 19.43; Judg. 1.18; 1 Sam. 6.17; Jer. 25.20; 2 Chron. 26.6). 1 Samuel 6.17 lists five cities that have become known as the Philistine Pentapolis: Ashdod, Gaza, Ashkelon, Gath and Ekron. Gath was destroyed by the Aramaean king Hazael about 830 BCE and ceased to be a major Philistine site (2 Kgs 2.18; Maeir and Uziel 2007: 31–5). The biblical text seems to remember the original importance of Gath, which suggests an early memory (Na'aman 2002b: 210–12). Whether the cities were united into some sort of Pentapolis, with a council of *seranim* making decisions for it as pictured in the text (e.g., 1 Sam. 5.8, 11), is a separate question. With Gath and Ekron both roughly the same size but also much larger than the other three cities in the Iron I and early Iron IIA (Maeir and Uziel 2007), would they have been content to share power and authority equally with the smaller cities? Would they not have been rivals in at least certain ways? These data do not seem to be reflected in the text in any way. As Niemann notes, 'The treatment of the five Philistine main sites as a unified block was not historical: it was an element of "theological historical writing" projected back' (2003, my translation). We also have the statement in 1 Sam. 7.14 that the cities of Gath to Ekron were returned to Israel after the ark incident. This is clearly unhistorical in the light of archaeology: we have no evidence of Israelite/Judahite occupation in the material culture of this time. Indeed, 1 Sam. 17.52 evidently has Ekron in Philistine hands when David was young, not too many years afterward (Gath will be further discussed at §3.2.4.5).

Architecture of Philistine Temples. The placement of the pillars supporting the roof in the Philistine temple in Judg. 16.25-30 looks like a match to those found in archaeological excavations, where pillars placed closely side by side support the roof (Maeir [ed.] 2012: 29–30). Yet we must qualify this positive statement with two more negative ones. First, the statement that there were people on the roof who could observe events on the ground floor of the temple (as if overlooking an unroofed courtyard) is not confirmed by anything so far found. Secondly, this description of a Philistine temple could be quite late, since temples existed in Philistine towns until very late (note 1 Macc. 10.84; 11.4).

Achish, King of Gath. A number of biblical passages refer to Achish, king of Gath (מלך גת: 1 Sam. 21.11, 13; 27.2-4, 11; 1 Kgs 2.39). This is the only evidence for such a person; however, we have an inscription from the seventh century that reads partially as follows (in the translation of the publishers: Gitin, Dothan and Naveh 1997: 9):

1. The temple (which) he built, *'kyš* son of Padi, son of
2. *Ysd*, son of Ada, son of Ya'ir, ruler of Ekron,
3. for *Ptgyh* his lady….

Thus, in the seventh century there was an Achish (אכיש) who was ruler (שר) of Ekron. Finkelstein suggests that the author of the narrative (written in the seventh century) made use of the name of a contemporary ruler in the area of Philistia, but because Gath was already strongly in the David tradition, he made Achish a ruler of Gath (2002b: 133–6). This is a reasonable argument, but it seems to me that those who see Achish as a ruler of Gath in an early tradition about David also present a reasonable picture. W. Dietrich (2012: 94) argues against Finkelstein's interpretation, citing the label of Achish as *king* of Gath (1 Kgs 2.39). However, the reference to the figure of Achish in the Ekron inscription as שר, which seems to me likely to be equivalent to מלך, would actually bolster Finkelstein's argument. At the moment, I see no way of demonstrating for certain whether Achish is a late introduction into the narrative or an early element in the tradition.

Metallurgy. One passage that is often mentioned, though seldom discussed in proper depth, is 1 Sam. 13.19-21. The translation of the passage is quite different in modern translations from traditional ones, such as the Luther Bibel and the Authorized Version, partly because of archaeology (though the text is difficult and probably corrupt), primarily because of the finding of weights of two thirds of a shekel with the word *pym* on them, which seems to be the import of the word *pîm* in this passage. Basically, this passage says that the Philistines control the working of metal, and that for repair or sharpening of farming implements Israelites had to travel to the Philistines and pay them. The passage is somewhat difficult, partly because it may be corrupt and partly because the instruments listed are not all clearly identified, though their status as metal farm tools seems obvious from the context. What is done to them by the Philistine metal workers is also not certain. To renew a ploughshare that had been blunted or even damaged by stones would probably cost two-thirds of a sheqel (the value of a *pîm*), but this would seem extremely expensive simply to sharpen a sickle. Moreover, the Israelite farmer could easily have found appropriate whet stones in the environment to use to sharpen a sickle or mattock.

In the last few years several excavations have turned up data about metalworking in the Levant at the end of the Bronze and beginning of the Iron Age. The basic situation that emerges from what is presently known is that bronze dominated metal usage until about 1000 BCE, at which point the balance shifted heavily to iron. Yet in the Late Bronze Age and the early Iron Age, both copper-based and iron-based tools and weapons were in use. Carburized steel technology had developed by the twelfth century, so what had changed around 1000 BCE was one of proportions of use, not a change of technology (Gottlieb 2010: 89–90).

It was once claimed that the Hittites first monopolized iron production and that the Philistines then took that position in the Levant; however, it is now widely believed that that position has been disproved (Stech-Wheeler et al. 1981). Yet quite a few commentators have still accepted the view that 1 Sam. 13.19-21 was basically true and showed that the Philistines controlled or limited Israelite metallurgical skills (cf. Niemann 2013: 262–3; Dietrich 2007: 156, 213). It should be noted that 1 Sam. 13.19-22 does not specify iron; the tools and weapons in the passage could just as well have been bronze. A recent survey by Yulia Gottlieb (2010), which takes into account a variety of earlier studies, looks at the beginnings of the use of iron in Palestine in the early Iron Age. It is only in the Iron IIA (tenth century), that iron begins to displace bronze as the technology to make carburized steel develops. However, she notes that our data for the Shephelah and the highlands are sparse, and her statistics are primarily reliable for the North (especially Megiddo and Beth Shean) and the South (the Negev and the Beersheba Valley). In the central highlands the stratigraphy is problematic, but in Iron I and early Iron IIA bronze seems to have prevailed for agricultural implements in sites like Khirbet Raddana, though iron is predominant at Bethel and et-Tell. Interestingly, older settled areas seem to have been more conservative and continued to prefer bronze even while newer settlements (such as in the Negev) had focused on iron.

For the Shephelah, copper-based artefacts predominate until late Iron IIA, while for the area of Philistia, the first iron tools seem to be as late as Iron IIB. Gottlieb's article was written before the important metal-working facility was found at Gath/Tel eṣ-Ṣafi (Maeir 2012a: 367–8; Maeir [ed.] 2012: 27–8; Eliyahu-Behar 2012). Gath has provided the first physical evidence on the state of metallurgy technology in Philistia in the early Iron Age. Both bronze and iron working are attested for the early Iron IIA, once again indicating the importance of both metals at this time. But what we do not find is any indication that the Philistines controlled metal technology. As Aren Maeir notes, 'one cannot speak of a Philistine monopoly on metal production in the late Iron I and early Iron IIA (the available evidence from the ancient Levant does not support this supposition)' (2012a: 367). It seems to me an absurd notion that Israelites had to go to Philistia just to sharpen their farm implements, not only paying a very high price but also taking the time and trouble to travel there and back. What we find in 1 Sam. 13.19-22 is a statement of theology, not contemporary metal technology.

Military Data. We first have the question of Goliath's armour. Although there are a few who argue that it reflects Iron Age I (Singer 2013: 20, 25, 27), many have followed Kurt Galling in maintaining that 'the narrator… has put together the wholly singular weaponry of Goliath from diverse elements of military equipment known to him' at a rather later time (1966). Finkelstein has argued that Goliath's armoury represents a Greek hoplite soldier of the seventh century, though he also recognizes that some parts of the description fit Assyrian equipage (2002b: 145–6). This last point complicates matters: is an actual soldier with his weaponry being described, or is the image of Goliath simply made up eclectically (as Galling seems to be saying)? In either case, though, a later time than the Iron I or early Iron II is being represented.

As for the Cherethites and Pelethites, Finkelstein notes that Cherethites and Pelethites do not occur among the groups of Sea Peoples (2002b: 148–50). He follows Albright in interpreting Pelethites as a reference to Greek peltasts (*peltastai*) or light infantry (from their *pelte* or light shield). Again, he relates them to the Greek mercenary troops widely used in the seventh century. John Van Seters has similarly argued the question at some length (see at §3.2.4.5).

3.2.3 Transjordan

Until the coming of the Assyrians, most of our knowledge about the Transjordanian region derives from archaeology and the biblical text. A small amount of information occurs in Egyptian texts (Kitchen 1992; Worschech 1997; see also, with regard to the Shasu, §2.2.1.4), and beginning in the late ninth century or about 800 BCE we have some native inscriptions. The documentation is not great, but it is fortunate that several recent treatments of the archaeology are available (Routledge 2004, 2008; Steen 2004; MacDonald, Adams and Bienkowski [eds] 2001; Finkelstein 1995a; Bienkowski [ed.] 1992; Edelman [ed.] 1995a; J. M. Miller 1991; Sawyer and Clines [eds] 1983). This includes the important sites of Tall Hisbân (Geraty and LaBianca [eds] 1987–98) and Tall al-'Umayri (Herr et al. [eds] 1989–2002). Much of what we know about the archaeology depends on surface surveys since only relatively few sites in the areas of ancient Ammon, Moab and Edom have been excavated. As already noted (§1.2.4.3), surface surveys have certain limitations. This is evident in the Transjordan surveys since they have yielded surprisingly different results in some cases, especially disconcerting when this involves overlapping areas in the surveys. These can generally be explained (Miller 1992: 79–80), but it illustrates some of the problems.

In his well-known survey of the Transjordan, Nelson Glueck reached some conclusions that are still influential (see the references and discussion in Sauer 1986). His two main conclusions were (1) that the southern Transjordanian region showed a settlement gap between EB and the end of LB (also between late Iron II and the Persian period) and (2) that a chain of defensive forts marked the borders of the three kingdoms already in Iron I. Sauer questioned the first of these conclusions, arguing that more recent research showed major tell sites in the MB and LB in northern and central Transjordan, suggesting a system of city-states similar to those on the west side of the Jordan. The second of Glueck's conclusions has been widely criticized: the evidence for a chain of border fortresses is skimpy at best (J. M. Miller 1992: 79, 87–8; Steen 2004: 80–1).

In the twenty years since Sauer wrote, his conclusions have themselves been subjected to scrutiny, especially since, in the meantime, a number of surveys have reported. Many scholars now feel that Glueck had it largely correct: only a sparse sedentary population was present in MB and LB, but there was an explosion of settlement in the early Iron Age (Miller 1992: 80; Dearman 1992: 72–3; Steen 2004: 89–90). The problem seems to be the interpretation of the surface surveys, for the excavated sites have generally shown little in the way of LB settlement. The indications are that there was a greater sedentary population in the north: in general, the density of settlement decreases as one moves from north to south in Transjordan (LaBianca and Younker 1998: 406). Glueck's southern gap in LB (south of the Wadi Mujib) largely remains: not that there were no inhabitants but that the population in that region was almost entirely nomadic.

Borders are usually difficult to determine from archaeology, and the borders indicated in the biblical text cannot be considered as necessarily accurate (MacDonald 1999: 30–9; Bloch-Smith and Nakhai 1999: 106–7). Yet the textual indications for the locations of Ammon, Moab and Edom are reasonably consistent around a core region in each case. New Kingdom Egyptian texts already have references to Moab (Rameses II), Edom (Merenptah) and Seir (Rameses II) (Kitchen 1992; J. M. Miller 1992: 77–8; Ahituv 1984). Ammon seems to appear first by name in an eighth-century inscription of Tiglath-pileser III (Tadmor 1994: 170–1 [Summary Inscription 7:10]), though it is now argued that there may already be a reference in the Kurkh Monolith inscription of Shalmaneser III a century earlier (ca. 853 BCE; Tyson 2014: 72–5). Although it has been proposed that some Ammonite settlements are mentioned in Egyptian texts, this has also been doubted (Steen 2004: 11–12, 50); however, the archaeology suggests that the collapse of city-states toward the end of the LB II led to many rural villages with agricultural settlements (Fischer 2014: 573). Ammon is associated with the section of the Transjordanian plateau south of the Jabbok River (Wadi az-Zarqa) (Steen 2004: 50–1). At its largest extent it was perhaps the territory between the Jabbok and Arnon (Wadi al-Mujib) and between the Jordan and the desert to the east (MacDonald 1999: 38–9). The southern border probably fluctuated as the fortunes of Ammon and Moab waxed and waned. Although in Ammon the settlement gap inferred by Glueck has been shown not to exist, since several fortified sites have subsequently been excavated (Tall al-Umayri, Tall Sahab, Tall Safrut, Khirbat Umm ad-Dananir), the LB settlement was nevertheless sparse (Bienkowski 1992a: 5–6; Steen 2004: 51). The existing settlements centred on Amman and the Baq'ah Valley (Bloch-Smith and Nakhai 1999: 109–11); this area seems to have been the end of a trade route and served as a trade market (Steen 2004: 297–8). The end of LB saw an increase of settlements, but they tended to be small and fortified (Steen 2004: 304). At the transition into Iron I, however, some of the major sites were destroyed or suffered reduction, perhaps as a consequence of the collapse of the market system and trade with the Jordan Valley (Steen 2004: 305–6). Then, many sites were abandoned or even destroyed at the end of Iron I. For example, 'Umayri was apparently destroyed by hostile attack and extensively reoccupied only in the seventh century BCE. Two-thirds of excavated sites show a gap in late Iron I, though it has been suggested that this is a scholarly artifact resulting from poor pottery chronology or survey information (Bloch-Smith and Nakhai 1999: 111). Herr notes: 'The early centuries of Iron II are presently very difficult to document in all of Transjordan' (1997: 132). Little has been found that can be related to the tenth century, which has implications for the biblical passages relating David and Ammon.

Moab seemed to have been focused on Wadi al-Mujib (Bienkowski 1992a: 1). Its southern border is usually seen as Wadi al-Hasa, but most of the places associated with Moab are in fact north of the Mujib. Moab's northern border probably moved up and down, depending on the balance of power in Ammon and Moab's relationship. Although the settlement of LB is meagre overall, there may have been an increase in settlement in the area south of Wadi Mujib; in any case, there was a sudden growth in fortified settlements at the beginning of Iron I (Steen 2004: 305), with a steady increase of occupation through Iron I to a peak in Iron II (Bienkowski 1992a: 5–6; Miller 1992: 80; Bloch-Smith and Nakhai 1999: 114). Others assert that walled settlements were infrequent in LB and Iron I, but with fortified outposts and watchtowers reaching a high point in Iron II (Dearman 1992: 73; LaBianca and Younker 1998: 407). It has been argued that the archaeology of Iron IIB reflects the situation described in the Mesha Stela, though the incompleteness of the data at present is admitted (Harrison and Barlow 2005: 184–5, 188). The radiometric dates determined from Tall Madaba samples cluster either side of the date 850 BCE, which well fits the time of Mesha and his activities.

The area of Edom was originally south of Wadi al-Haba (perhaps down to Wadi Hisma) and east of the Wadi Arabah (Bienkowski 1992a: 1). Sauer (1986) attempted to show that Glueck was wrong about the sparseness of settlement in this region in the Late Bronze and early Iron Ages; his efforts have been both rejected (Hart 1992: 93) and accepted (Finkelstein 1995a: 135). MacDonald (1994: 242) noted that there was no LB evidence and also Iron I evidence only in the northern part of the traditional Edomite territory to the east of the Wadi Arabah. Since the occupation of the main sites of Busayrah, Tawilan and Umm al-Biyara showed no settlement before the seventh century BCE, it was possible that the 'Iron I' sherds were actually from Iron II (Bienkowski 1992b; Bloch-Smith and Nakhai 1999: 114). This has initiated an on-going debate between Bienkowski and Finkelstein; the latter has argued that Glueck was right and that there was continuous Iron Age settlement in southern Transjordan.

Bienkowski (1992b, 1992c) argues that Finkelstein has mistakenly dated sherds to Iron I by using parallels from Palestine and northern Transjordan, and that he has further ignored the fact that Iron II strata lie directly on the bedrock in many excavated sites (though Busayrah has not been sufficiently studied to say for certain). Finkelstein responds that the dating of Edomite sites has depended on C. M. Bennett's chronological sequence based on the find of a seal impression at Umm al-Biyara with the royal name 'Qos-Gabr', an Edomite ruler known from the inscriptions of Esarhaddon and Ashurbanipal (Finkelstein 1992a, 1992b; 1995a: 131–2; also Bienkowski 1992b: 99; Levy et al. 2005: 132). The stratigraphy of Edomite sites is far from clear, and it was the highland custom to remove earlier material in order to establish walls on bedrock. The differences between these two scholars hinges a good deal on pottery assemblages: a debate for archaeologists to carry on. For example, a recent study of the collared-rim pithoi (a pottery type appealed to specifically by Finkelstein) concludes that the pithoi are found in Iron II at al-'Umayri and are thus not diagnostic for Iron I (Herr 2001). In any case, the two different interpretations lead to different reconstructions of early Edomite history.

All seem to agree that in LB the inhabitants were nomadic groups whom the Egyptians referred to as *shasu.* According to Bienkowski (1992a: 8) and others, this would have continued through Iron I as well (except for some settlement in northern Edom) before a major process of sedentarization in the eighth or seventh centuries (though the extent of mountainous terrain meant that it did not become fully urban). The resumption of mining in Faynan may have helped with this (the mining activity, which began in the EB there, had been in abeyance for a millennium), as well as the Arabian trade and the general conditions of peace and stability under Assyrian domination. According to Finkelstein (1995a: 135–7) settlement in Edom was parallel to the settlement of the hill country in Palestine and northern Transjordan, though the southern Transjordan was more marginal and yielded small sites. The Edomite state of Iron II had its roots in the sedentary occupation of Iron I. The settlement history was thus not particularly different from that of Moab and the northern Transjordan. All seem to agree that the peak of settlement was in the eighth to seventh centuries and allowed Edomite influence to spread west of the Wadi Arabah.

Now a new perspective has been given by excavations at Khirbat en-Nahas and the application of ^{14}C analysis to samples taken from slag heaps (see especially Levy, Najjar and Ben-Yosef [eds] 2014; also Levy et al. 2004; Levy et al. 2005; Higham et al. 2005). They point to two crucial physiographic attributes: (1) an abundant ore deposit that allowed major copper mining and production and (2) a landscape divided between highlands, with some sections having sufficient rainfall to provide fertile agricultural land, and lowlands that could be farmed only with irrigation but also containing the copper deposits. The debate about early Edomite chronology seems to have been partially settled by radiocarbon dating (so Levy et al. [2004] argue) because their sampling shows that copper-working at Faynan (Feinan) took place at least as early as the tenth century BCE, with an expansion from about 950 BCE (Higham et al. 2005: 177). This metal production occurred over a century or a century and a half but ceased by the end of the ninth century. Levy et al. (2005: 160) argue against Finkelstein (2005c), making the point that the fortress at the site is associated with metal production dated to the mid-ninth century at the latest and thus pre-Assyrian (with contemporary radiocarbon dates found at satellite sites) and that the fortress at Khirbat en-Nahas did not exist in the eighth century when the Assyrian palace was extant at Busayra. But their argument relates primarily to Finkelstein's LC thesis in general (though they admit that the sample size is too small to resolve all of the issues of the LC [Levy et al. 2005: 158]). In fact, the early dating of metal-working at Faynan seems to provide some support for Finkelstein in his debate with Bienkowsky over the settlement of Edom in the early Iron period (Levy et al. 2005: 158).

However, some of the conclusions of Levy et al. have been strongly critiqued by E. van der Steen and P. Bienkowski (2005, 2005–2006, 2006). One area of particular focus is the technical side of ^{14}C dating and Bayesian analysis. They argue that the figures of Levy et al. look to be skewed to give a result about a century earlier than normal calibration would lead to. Attempts at clarification by Levy et al. have not laid these concerns to rest. A further question concerns the conclusion from the Khirbat en-Nahas excavations that 'perhaps the emergence of the kingdom of Edom...began some 200–300 years earlier than previously assumed'

(Levy et al. 2005: 157). This seems to ignore the level of settlement evidence known from actual excavations and surveys (Herr and Najjar 2001: 338; Bienkowski 1992a: 3). The existence of metal working does not contradict the other archaeological evidence nor necessarily imply a complex social organization in Edom at this time. E. A. Knauf – who had anticipated some of the Khirbat en-Nahas Project's findings – argued that the Faynan mining concern was controlled from west of the Wadi Arabah during Iron I (1992: 49), a point also made by van der Steen and Bienkowski (2005, 2005–2006). Neither do the new radiocarbon dates have to confirm the statement about Edomite chiefs in Gen. 36.31 (Levy et al. 2005: 158; similarly Finkelstein 1995a: 136). The argument that Genesis 36 is a description of the situation in the seventh or sixth century is still a strong one (e.g., Knauf 1992: 49). The new information from Khirbat en-Nahas is to be welcomed and will no doubt have implications for the history of Edom, but it has to be evaluated with other evidence. It is still too early in the debate to start drawing far-reaching conclusions.

The Transjordan in Iron IIB and beyond is discussed in subsequent chapters.

3.2.4 From Settlement to Statehood

The end of the LB was marked by decline and widespread destruction of cities (§2.1.1). However, this varied from region to region. In Palestine the decline or destruction of coastal cities was not always matched by inland sites. In the northern valleys (especially Jezreel and Beth-Shean) and the northern hill country in the regions of Ephraim and Manasseh, the small settlements show a large continuum in material culture, suggesting that it was the indigenous population that settled there.

The first certain mention of Israel is by Merenptah, in relation to a campaign about 1208 BCE. This shows that Israel was already in existence at the end of the LB, even though developments in the IA I have often been emphasized in publications on the subject. However, Manfred Görg has argued that the name occurs even earlier in another Egyptian inscription (Görg 2001; Veen, Theis and Görg 2010; Veen and Zwickel 2014). If he is correct, nothing is added to our knowledge except the occurrence of the name, yet it would show that such an entity – whatever it consisted of – existed at an earlier time than 1208. The inscription has been dated to the time of Ramesses II (early thirteenth century) or possibly even earlier in the fourteenth century BCE. However, some Egyptologists are not convinced, for philological reasons (e.g. Hoffmeier 2007). Thus, the approximate date of 1208 BCE remains the first clear reference to Israel.

A further consideration is the obvious one (as pointed out by Knauf 2017): Israel originated in the LBA. If an 'Israel' was already in existence about 1208 – or possibly even as early as the fourteenth century BCE – this raises the question of where it was located. Since the expansion in the central highlands was mainly a phenomenon of the IA I, could that region and/or the people in it be called 'Israel' already in the rather more sparsely populated end of the LBA? (This will be discussed below: §3.2.4.2.) The question is how to interpret this information from archaeology and inscriptions: How did Israel originate? How useful are the data in the biblical text, or did Israel and Judah come into existence in largely different ways?

3.2.4.1 Joshua and Judges

Joshua and Judges are also placed by many scholars in the Deuteronomistic History (DtrH; on the DtrH, see the discussion at §3.1.6.2). The book of Joshua describes how the Israelites crossed the Jordan (Josh. 1–5) and conquered the land in only five years, the major cities taken being Jericho, Ai, Makkedah, Libnah, Lachish, Hebron, Debir and Hazor (cf. also Josh. 12.9-24), while Gibeon and Kiriath-Jearim submitted without a fight (Josh. 9). Some decades ago the broad picture of the conquest of Canaan by the Israelites was widely accepted in parts of scholarship, especially in North America, where the 'Albright hypothesis' was very influential (see §3.2.4.2). The surprising thing is that when the reader moves from Joshua – where the land was conquered and divided up – to Judges, there is something of a shock, since the land seems far from under Israelite control. Granted, here and there are statements in Joshua that suggest that everything was not conquered all at once (e.g., Josh. 17.14-17), which means that something of a mixed message comes across. Nevertheless, the dominant impression is that it was all settled after five years. This is especially the impression left by Josh. 11.23; 14.15; 21.41-43 and Joshua 13–19 where the land is divided up among the various tribes. The 'Albright' or 'conquest' hypothesis is generally not accepted anymore, and the question to be asked is whether any of the book of Joshua can be taken as historical. Many would now answer this in the negative (e.g., Na'aman 1994c: 249–81; Van Seters 1990; J. M. Miller 1977). Some lists seem to relate to a much later time and situation (cf. Na'aman 2005 on Josh. 15.21-62; 18.21-28; 19.2-8, 40-46).

Judges comes across quite differently from Joshua: far from being conquered and under Israelite rule, the lowlands and many of the main cities are still controlled by the Canaanites who fight with chariots of iron (Judg. 1). As noted above, if one had read Joshua for the first time and then moved to Judges without knowing anything about its contents, it would produce considerable consternation, because a number of the things supposedly accomplished in Joshua have to be done again (e.g., Judg. 1.19-36 versus Josh. 16–19). The book of Judges is mainly made up of a series of episodes which follow a common pattern: Israel sins, is punished by being made subjects of a foreign people, cries to Yhwh and has a deliverer sent who leads them in throwing off the the foreign yoke – following a 40/80 year cycle. This structure is clear through much of the book. These stories, in addition to their entertainment value, had an important moral content, which is probably the main reason they were told. But our concern is with their historicity.

The general picture of Judges has often been one of an authentic representation of pre-state Israelite society, and this may indeed be the case. As has long been recognized, the narrative of Judges is divided between heroic deliverers ('major judges') and civic leaders ('minor judges'). The latter get little actual space but are presented in two brief lists (Judg. 10.1-5; 12.7-15). Shamgar ben Anath has a curious name, because it suggests a worshipper of the goddess Anat (Judg. 3.31; 5.6; cf §4.2.8). The judge named Jerubbaal is only later identified with Gideon (Judg. 6–8; 6.32 gives a nonsensical etymology of his name; it means something like 'Let Baal be great'). Abimelech (son of Gideon) looks like the king of a Canaanite city-state (Judg. 9). Jephthah occurs in the list of 'minor judges' but also appears as a heroic figure, whereas Samson seems independent of the other deliverer stories. One cannot rule out that some actual historical core can be found in the 'deliverer' stories, but when we turn the statement around, demonstrating such a core of history is very difficult. B. Halpern (1988) argued for such a core of historicity in the Ehud/Eglon story, but E. A. Knauf (1991b) has cast considerable doubt on his argument by showing that 'Ehud' was a Benjaminite clan, and Eglon a town in the Judaean foothills. Despite references to 'all Israel' only one or two tribes are normally involved in the action in an episode; the Song of Deborah (Judg. 5) is the only passage with more than two tribes. Thus, here and there may be reliable early traditions, but demonstrating them is difficult; the book is generally too problematic to use as a historical source. Two points relating to history, however, can be made about the book of Judges: first, the picture of a tribal society without a unified leadership engaging in uncoordinated local actions seems to fit the society of the hill country in IA I, as evidenced by the archaeology. To what extent the individual episodes and individuals laid out in the text relate to history is another question, very difficult to answer: the book is generally too problematic to use as a historical source. Knauf (2010b) has suggested some elements within the book that meet the criteria for historical data, but these are few. Secondly, perhaps the one exception to the historical ambiguity of the text is the Song of Deborah in Judges 5 (cf. Knauf 2005b). It has often been argued that the 'Song of Deborah' is an example of early poetry (Robertson 1972; Knauf 2005b), which would suggest that it was written close to the events described (Stager 1988a; see the summary of arguments in Lindars 1995: 212–17). The list of Israelite tribes differs in several ways from all other lists (see below), which might demonstrate an independent tradition and one possibly earlier than other traditions. Nevertheless, a number of scholars have argued that the Song of Deborah shows signs of lateness (e.g., Diebner 1995; Lindars 1995: 213–15), and assuming that it is more trustworthy as a historical source is misplaced confidence. As A. E. Knauf (2005b) argues, the original poem was perhaps tenth or ninth century BCE, but it was likely composed in an Israelite court and also underwent a later redaction. P. D. Guest has recently argued that far from being a compilation of different sources, the book of Judges shows the marks of unitary authorship that produced a 'crafted history' of the period: 'Although the text presents itself as history, it should not be mistaken for such' (1998: 61). In one area, however, Judges may reflect an older linguistic usage: the title 'judge' (Hebrew שופט *šôfēṭ*). Although the word means 'judge' in a judicial sense in most Hebrew usage, the reference to an individual in Judges means something like 'political/military leader' (Niehr 1994). All in all, here is an early text that may be the closest we have to a primary source in the Heptateuch.

Judges 5 ostensibly covers the same ground as the narrative in Judges 4 – the oppression of Sisera and his subsequent defeat and death. The archaic language of the poem has made it the earliest or one of the earliest passages in the Hebrew Bible. Estimates of the date vary, but the tenth century BCE may not be too far wrong (Knauf 2005b). One of the significant features of the poem is its listing of many of the tribes of Israel. Yet this list is remarkable for several reasons. First, two tribes which are otherwise unknown are named: Machir and Gilead (Judg. 5.14, 17). Machir seems to stand in place of Manasseh which is found in other lists (in some genealogies, Machir is said to be a son of Manasseh [Gen. 50.23; Num. 27.1]). Similarly, Gilead is found instead of Gad (Gilead is elsewhere said to be the son of Machir [1 Chron. 2.21; 7.14]). What this shows is that the list of 12 tribes (or 13, if Ephraim and Manasseh are listed separately instead of Joseph), known from a number of lists (e.g., Deut. 27.12-13; 1 Chron. 2.1-2), is not the original list but the final development.

The second feature of the poem is the absence of Judah, Simeon, and Levi. As the priestly tribe, the Levites' absence might be expected. Simeon sometimes had a close association with Levi (e.g., Gen. 34.25-31; 49.5); in any case, Simeon is strangely said to have its heritage inside Judahite territory (Josh. 19.1-9); finally, the tribe seems to disappear from the text after Judges 1. The absence of Judah is very notable, however, because it shows what can also be inferred from other passages: Judah was originally separate from Israel. This is important, because the relationship of Judah with Israel is one of the areas in which the data clash strongly with the surface narrative of the biblical text. According to Gen. 35.22-26 and many other passages, Judah was one of twelve brothers of a single father, Jacob/Israel, and Judah was thus just one of twelve tribes. There was nothing about his birth to single Judah out from his brothers or to single out the tribe of Judah from the other tribes. Yet it is obvious historically that Judah had its own national identity and was separate from and a rival of Israel from an early period. It is worth noticing some of these points, even though they are by no means new:

- Judges 5: Judah is not even mentioned in this early poem which names most of the tribes.
- Elsewhere in Judges Judah is seldom mentioned with other tribes. In ch. 1, they take Simeon with them in conquering their territory (1.3, 17), but as is well known Simeon then disappears from the text. In ch. 11, Judah is attacked by the Ammonites, but the resistance is "Israel" (the situation with "Ephraim" is a side issue [12.1]). Judah is supposed to go first in attacking Benjamin in 20.18.
- There is no evidence that Saul's territory included Judah.
- David ruled first over Judah alone for seven years (2 Sam. 2.11).
- After the reigns of David and Solomon, Israel and Judah split – or did they simply revert to their original situation?

Thus, the Song of Deborah gives us a peek through the keyhole, as it were, to see an earlier situation that the text has generally displaced with other traditions or interpretations.

A third point is that two of the tribes seem to be maritime figures: Dan and Asher (5.17). Since the tribes are not otherwise associated with the sea, this is sometimes explained away as a misunderstanding (e.g., Stager 1988). Although other explanations are possible, the association with the sea seems to be the most immediate interpretation. Again, this might show a different tradition about these two tribes than is found elsewhere in the Hebrew Bible.

Finally, there is the allegation that some of the tribes (e.g., Reuben) did not participate in the fight against Sisera because they were pastoralists (Stager 1988). This is possible, but it seems doubtful that the mode of livelihood was a primary factor in whether or not a tribe joined with others. Historically, pastoralists have often combined their livelihood with raiding and fighting. The inference seems to be based on insufficient data.

3.2.4.2 The Settlement

Over the past 40 to 50 years a great deal of debate has centred on the question of how Israel got into the land and eventually became a nation (see the survey in Ramsey 1981; McDermott 1998; Killebrew 2006). Until the 1960s most scholars favoured one of two models, the 'conquest model' of the Albright school and the 'peaceful infiltration model' of the Alt–Noth school. Then, in 1962, a programmatic article by G. E. Mendenhall in a semi-popular journal outlined a third theory, but its real development came in the late 1970s: the Mendenhall–Gottwald theory of an internal revolt. Much debate has centred on these, and understanding them is still important for getting at the historical situation

The Albright model of a unified conquest was heavily influenced by the biblical text, though it would be incorrect to conclude that it was only a paraphrase of Joshua. Albright initially dated the conquest to the fifteenth century BCE, but then N. Glueck conducted a survey of the Transjordanian region in the years 1932–47 (Glueck 1934–51; 1970: 152–4; §3.2.3). Since Glueck concluded that these regions were uninhabited until the thirteenth century, Albright redated the conquest to the thirteenth century, a position he continued to maintain until his death. Although ostensibly based on archaeology, it had an uncanny resemblance to the first half of Joshua. In some ways, this was more apparent than real, but it allowed the conservative tendency to maintain academic respectability while still really following the biblical text. In 1977 J. M. Miller gave a thorough critique of the Albright position and ultimately rejected it (Hayes and Miller 1977: 254–62, 270–7; also J. M. Miller 1979). His conclusions presented a picture emphasizing the development of Israel from internal populations and also from the Sea Peoples or tribes forced to migrate in their wake, and expressed some scepticism toward the significance of nomadic incursions. The position continued to be stoutly defended by Y. Yadin, even in one of the last of his articles to be published (Yadin 1979, 1982), but by then it was being widely abandoned by scholars. There have been a few die-hard defences by conservative evangelicals (e.g., Wood 1990; cf. Bimson 1981; discussed below). Thus, one is somewhat disconcerted to find a mainstream archaeologist trot out the thesis again, apparently without realizing that biblical scholarship has abandoned the position (Ben-Tor 1998, but cf. Ben-Ami 2001). The 'conquest' model is now only of historical interest, but it should alert scholars to the fact that vociferous adherence by large numbers of academics is no guarantee that a particular theory will stand the test of time.

As already noted in the discussion of the exodus, a couple of conservative evangelical scholars continue to argue for a fifteenth-century exodus and conquest much as the Pentateuch and Joshua describe them. These are John Bimson (1981) and Bryant Wood (1990, 2005, 2007). Whereas the views of Albright and others became dominant in their interpretation that Joshua came at the end of the Late Bronze, Bimson's main contribution to the debate was to show how fragile the archaeological support was for the Albright thesis, although his aim was to undermine Albright's dating rather than the conquest model as such. Similarly, Wood has argued from archaeology for a redating of the exodus and conquest, even though his arguments have not been published in a proper peer-reviewed context. The problem with their redating of the exodus was already discussed above. Their views on the 'conquest' also seem to have gained no followers (even the conservative James Hoffmeier [2007] has attacked Wood's arguments for the fifteenth century). Further evidence against their views are found in §2.3.2.1.

The 'peaceful infiltration' model of Alt and Noth has better stood the test of time in certain ways than Albright's. It continued to find adherents among archaeologists in the 1980s and even the 1990s (e.g., Zertal 1994). Yet a number of criticisms had been levelled at it that rendered the thesis in its original form untenable. One was that the desert could not produce sufficient nomads to populate the hill country in Iron I (see Chaney 1983; but this is disputed by Finkelstein 1988: 308; cf. Rainey 2001: 67–8). Another was that nomads adopt this lifestyle out of necessity and want nothing more than the chance to settle down: in fact, the 'nomadic' mode of life takes many forms, and those who engage in it are no more likely to change than those in other forms of subsistence agrarian activity (see the discussion in Lemche 1985: 136–47; Dever 2003a: 50–2). Yet recently Thomas Levy and Augustin Holl (2002) have pointed to the analogy of the Shuwa-Arabs of Chad and argued that the situation there is very similar to that postulated by the peaceful infiltration thesis (see below), showing that at least aspects of the theory are still viable.

The 'Mendenhall–Gottwald thesis' is widely used to designate the internal revolt model. Gottwald's 1979 study was the academic underpinning for Mendenhall's programmatic thesis almost two decades earlier. A collection strongly espousing the Mendenhall–Gottwald thesis was notable for the trenchant essay by Mendenhall attacking and disowning Gottwald's approach (Mendenhall 1983). Although noting some of the genuine differences between the two scholars, it has not stopped the hyphenated designation for this model. N. P. Lemche, while expressing his appreciation of Gottwald's use of sociology, presented a major critique of his work (1985; also Finkelstein 1988: 306–14). Although differing from Gottwald on many points, including the concept of an internal revolt, Lemche's final picture was of an internal development of the indigenous population. In his view, though, it was not urban residents who fled oppression of the city-states but members of the rural peasantry who went up into the hill country to escape taxes (Lemche 1985: 427–32).

The three models that dominated the twentieth century are no longer equal alternatives. An examination of their strengths and weaknesses has already suggested which way scholarship has moved. The Albright thesis of a unified conquest has all but been abandoned by mainstream critical scholarship and continues to be pressed only by a few conservative scholars. The reason is that much of the support has simply evaporated, in particular the evidence that was once seen as its main strength: the archaeology. In the past quarter of a century most of the discussion has revolved around the Alt–Noth and the Mendenhall–Gottwald theories and has focused on archaeology and on social-scientific models. Neither model is seen to be adequate in itself, and much of recent thinking has combined aspects of both.

A number of variants of these three have subsequently been developed. The 'symbiosis theory' of V. Fritz (1981, 1987) is really a variant of the Alt–Noth thesis, though it also incorporates insights from Mendenhall–Gottwald (yet, surprisingly, Levy and Holl [2002: 89] regard it as one of the least likely models). Fritz points to the similarity of the material culture of the highland settlers to that found in the territories of the Canaanite city-states, but also differences. This shows that the new population (assumed to be pastoralists) was not the same as the Canaanites but was in close contact with them over several generations. This population eventually settled down, their material culture showing a lot in common with Canaanite culture but also with enough differences to distinguish them. The problem with this theory is that all objections to the Peaceful Infiltration theory apply.

We can summarize by saying that the three main models that dominated the twentieth century have long since ceased to be equal alternatives in the twenty-first century; indeed, none of them seems to be accepted anymore in its original form.

However, a new consensus looks to be emerging. Although there are a number of variants of it, it seems to cluster around the view that Israel emerged in the highlands of Canaan largely from native inhabitants. A. E. Killebrew (2005: 149–96; 2006) has used the term 'mixed multitude' for this thesis, which serves as a good description for many of the views. Although Killebrew gives a succinct and persuasive argument for her case, she admits that the thesis did not originate with her. Indeed, it has been put forward in some form or other (though often briefly and without supporting argumentation) by a number of researchers going back at least to the mid-1980s (Ahlström 1986: 57–83; cf. Dever 1992a; Finkelstein and Na'aman [eds] 1994: 13–14). According to this theory, the population that became Israel was made up of a diverse group of people:

> ...demographic redistribution and an increase in the settled population, especially in the central hill country and Transjordanian highlands. These inhabitants most likely comprised different elements of Late Bronze Age society, namely, the rural Canaanite population, displaced peasants and pastoralists, and lawless *'apiru* and *shasu*. Outside elements probably included other marginal groups, such as fugitive or 'runaway' Semitic slaves from Twentieth-Dynasty New Kingdom Egypt... Other nonindigenous groups, such as Midianites, Kenites, and Amalekites, perhaps connected with the control of camel caravan trade routes between Arabia and Canaan, may have constituted an essential element of this 'mixed multitude'. (Killebrew 2006: 571)

Although most accept that early Israel was made up of a variety of groups, some tend to favour a single group as making up the bulk of the people. A survey of some of the more recent views will help to illustrate both the common core and the diversity of the specific theories.

I. Finkelstein produced what seems to be a true merging of Alt–Noth and Mendenhall–Gottwald, with a firm archaeological base (Finkelstein 1988). Much of his study is on the archaeology of developments during Iron I and documents the unprecedented growth of population in the hill country through this period. Although accepting that the new population included a number of elements, he especially argued that the spectacular growth came about because a large nomadic population settled down. The nomads did not come from the 'deep' desert region, however, but were the descendants of those who left settled life for a pastoral lifestyle in the Middle Bronze Age because of adverse conditions. He argues that the region went through a regular long-term cycle of people moving from settled life to nomadic life and back again, depending on climatic and economic cycles. Thus, the new population of the hill country was made up of nomadic pastoralists different from the Canaanites (as Alt–Noth proposed) but they were part of the indigenous population (as argued by Mendenhall–Gottwald). He notes that the earliest settlements in the areas of Ephraim, Manasseh and Benjamin were on the desert fringe; they also often settled near Canaanite cities (Finkelstein 1988: 310).

Finkelstein's thesis has been critiqued mainly on the basis that the archaeology of the Iron I hill-country settlements does not indicate nomadic influence on the material culture (Dever 1992a, 1998a). Also, the studies of pastoralists indicate that pastoralism is often not an exclusive lifestyle but one activity of people who also engage in agriculture (Lemche 1985: 136–47; Killebrew 2006: 565). This is true, but it does not strike at the heart of Finkelstein's proposal. More important are studies of Palestinian nomads in recent times who lived and moved freely among the settled areas and peasant farmers. Dever refers to these in his criticisms of Finkelstein (Dever 1998a: 222–9). As G. Lehmann (2003: 155) points out, however, 'it is impossible to estimate the number or the impact of nomadic pastoralists in Iron Age Judah'. More important is the context argued for by Finkelstein: the alternating cycles of sedentary agriculture and pastoralism that he sees as determining settlement and the lifestyle of the inhabitants in Palestine from at least the third millennium BCE.

N. Na'aman (1994c) associates the origins of Israel with the wider developments in the eastern Mediterranean. The thirteenth to eleventh centuries brought the settlement of peripheral areas contemporary with the collapse of urban culture in the entire Aegean–Anatolian–Syro-Palestinian region and the migration of large groups on the boundaries of Mesopotamia. At no other time was the disruption of urban culture in Anatolia and Syro-Palestine (reaching as far as the Aegean and the Balkans) so complete as in the twelfth century. The Arameans gradually took over large tracts in Mesopotamia and Syria. Large-scale migration in Iron I because of destruction in Asia Minor means that various groups reached Canaan and played an important part in settlement: Hittites in Hebron; Hivites in western Benjamin and perhaps around Shechem; Jebusites from the Hittite empire; Girgashites from Anatolia. Only two of the alleged seven pre-Israelite nations were autochthonous. These groups may have helped break Egyptian rule. Traditions about patriarchal migrations to Egypt are best understood against this background; similarly, stories of coming out of Egypt such as the exodus should be understood as vaguely remembered background rather than routine migration of pastoral groups. Thus, the overall picture does not support the assumption that the Iron I settlement was only an internal Palestinian one or settlers only from local Canaanite elements. The various groups entering Canaan joined the local uprooted and pastoral groups, which led to an increase in pastoral and bandit splinter groups that upset the urban–nomad balance and induced the nomads to settle down: 'The model that emerges from my analysis is of small and larger groups of variegated ethnic and cultural background who settled during a long period and slowly and gradually started cooperating in the new environment' (Na'aman 1994c: 246).

The recent study of E. van der Steen (2004: 306–10) lends support to this thesis. She argues that the trading collapse in Ammon caused inhabitants to migrate not only into Moab but also into the Jordan Valley. There the pressure of population caused further migration into the hill country west of the Jordan. It may be that there was a partial vacuum there at this time because Merenptah (or Rameses II) had 'laid waste Israel' (Merenptah Stela) who may have been living in the northern hill country, in her interpretation.

Z. Herzog (2002: 89–92) draws attention to the current 'fluid' concept of ethnicity that undermines attempts to identify ethnic borders. In the Beersheba valley in Iron I a variety of different groups seems to have lived (according to the bibical text), with a relatively uniform material culture. Here the groups mixed and combined in a complex social composition. Using the Beersheba valley as a model, Herzog argues that the larger settlement and the emergence of an Israelite identity should be understood from an 'interactive-combined model' in which 'a community identity is created from the development and combination of various social groups. Clearly, in different regions there were different combinations of communities, simultaneous with inter-regional mixing and blending' (2002: 92). Accepting the 'mixed multitude' thesis for the origin of Israel still leaves a number of questions unanswered. Some researchers have argued that the early Israelites were primarily from one particular group. At the moment, there is a considerable debate between those who say that the early Israelites were mainly 'Canaanite' and those who argue that they arose from the Shasu. For example, although differing from Gottwald on many points, including the concept of an internal revolt, Lemche's final picture was of an internal development of the indigenous population. In his view, though, it was not urban residents who fled oppression of the city-states but members of the Canaanite rural peasantry who went up into the hill country to escape taxes (1985: 427–32).

More recently, Dever has been a major voice in urging the case for postulating the Canaanite origin of the highland settlers who became Israel (his 'Proto-Israelites'). In his view, the basis of the highland settlements were farmers and others withdrawing from the systems collapse of the Canaanite lowlands (see especially Dever 2003a: 167–89). The idea that these new settlers were 'nomads' or 'semi-nomads' settling down is anathema to him. He argues that there is no evidence that nomadic types are generally willing to become agriculturalists; also, there would not have been sufficient nomadic pastoralists in the region to account for the population growth. This position is somewhat surprising in light of Dever's recent archaeological report on two Early Bronze IV sites (Dever 2014). Although the sites are some centuries before the IA I and Dever ascribes them to nomadic pastoralists, he notes that pastoral nomadism covers a broad spectrum of habitation styles, including those who planted crops in their summer pasture area and returned to harvest them, as well as engaging in trade and perhaps even metallurgy (Dever 2014: 231–5). He also suggests that the pastoral nomads who occupied these sites were Canaanites who left a sedentary lifestyle for particular reasons.

But if they could become pastoral nomads, could not they revert to a more settled lifestyle? Modern anthropological studies have shown that there are a variety of examples of a shift from a nomadic lifestyle to a sedentary one (see §3.2.4.3 on the whole question). This is not theoretical but comes from study of societies which have actually made the voluntary move from nomadism to sedentarianism. To give three examples of different forms of adaptation, the first example is of the Sebei of East Africa who made the shift from nomadic pastoralism to sedentary cultivation (Goldschmidt 1980). This was not from coercion but done voluntarily because it was seen as advantageous to themselves. For the second example, some of the Yoruk of southeast Turkey remained pastoralists but others chose to settle down and become village cultivators. This was because of economic circumstances which militated against the entire group's remaining pastoralists. Although the process was subject to adverse conditions, the shift in lifestyle was entered into voluntarily by those who left pastoralism for cultivation. A third example is nomadic groups who drastically reduced their adherence to the nomadic way of life while not giving it up entirely. This includes the Bedouin of the Beqaa Valley of Lebanon (Chatty 1980) and nomads of Baluchistan (Salzman 1980b). Thus, to argue that pastoralists do not settle down is to ignore many known examples where this has precisely taken place.

Others have argued that the Israelites arose from the Shasu. Such has been proposed by Rainey (2001) and Redford (1990: 73–5; 1992a: 267–80), plus a number of others. This is partly based on the reliefs associated with Merenptah's supposed conquests. Some argue that the 'Israel' of the inscription is to be identified with the Shasu of the reliefs. In my view, this goes far beyond the evidence. The equation of the reliefs with entities in the inscription is more ingenious than convincing. In any case, it seems that the texts distinguish the Israelites, Canaanites and Shasu. This does not mean that both Shasu and Canaanites could not have joined the settlers who became Israel, but once Israel had its own identity (as indicated by the Merenptah inscription) it was seen as separate from both the Canaanites and Shasu. (See further §3.1.2 in relation to the Merenptah inscriptions.)

Recently, Avraham Faust (e.g., 2006) has been an outspoken defender of the Shasu thesis. His position is that the highland culture shows mainly discontinuity, which militates against the settlers being Canaanites. Rather, they are mainly the Shasu who have changed their lifestyle because of various circumstances. Faust is quite right to argue that some of the settlers in the highlands could have been Shasu settling down (in opposition to Dever), as discussed at §3.2.4.3. Yet his rejection of the importance of Canaanites in the settlement process seems misplaced, based mainly on the argument of discontinuity between LB material culture and that of the IA I. The general view among other archaeologists seems to be that there is a great deal of continuity (see especially Killebrew 2005: 171–81). The most important of these continuities is in the pottery: 'Iron I highland pottery…is remarkable for its continuity with Late Bronze Age ceramic traditions', including the collared-rim jar which is a continuation of the Canaanite jar tradition (Killebrew 2005: 177–81). Also, contrary to Faust, many argue with regard to the three- or four-room house that 'its roots go back to Late Bronze Age Canaanite architecture' (Killebrew 2005: 174 plus n. 65). The main discontinuity Faust can point to is that of burials, but this is a disputed area (cf. Kletter 2002; the IA cemetery at Wadi Fidan 40 [Levy, Adams and Muniz 2004; Levy 2009a]); in any case, one expects a certain amount of discontinuity in light of the different environment and circumstances of the highland settlers.

Furthermore, Faust discounts or ignores some important continuities pointed out by Dever (2003a: 168). Two of these are language (the Israelites spoke a form of Canaanite) and religion (Israelite religion was essentially the Northwest Semitic religion shared by Canaanites and others in the region). Finally, we need to consider the arguments of Hasel about the Shasu. He draws up a comparison of Israel as described in the Merenptah inscription and the characteristics of the Shasu, and concludes that they differ from each other in three main points (Hasel 1998: 236–9). This would seem to support Israel's origins from Canaanites. Hasel's arguments are well taken and have weight; however, each characteristic is also based on slender evidence and can be debated. What his arguments do not seem to do is rule out that Israel could (whether in part or as a whole) have originated from a Shasu population settling down.

However, an important fact must be emphasized with regard to the two main authors being compared here: each author – Dever and Faust – undermines his own argument! This is because Dever accepts that some of the new settlers were likely to have been pastoral nomads, including Shasu (Dever 2003a: 181–2). Likewise, Faust allows that some of the settlers came from the Canaanite lowlands: 'it seems as if ancient Israel was composed of peoples who came from various backgrounds:...[including] settled Canaanites who for various reasons changed their identity... In the end it is likely that many, if not most, Israelites had Canaanite origins' (Faust 2006: 186). So, in making such a concession in the individual positions, each actually negates his main argument which focuses only on one group. From a broader perspective, though, these two positions reinforce the 'mixed multitude' thesis because each concedes that there is more than one component to the original highland settlements.

To conclude this discussion, I want to make several observations that are relèvant the highland settlements and the rise of Israel:

1. Many of the inhabitants of Canaanite cities were not 'urbanites' as we think of the term. That is, they were not scribes or administrators but simply agriculturalists who lived in the city. We have plenty of evidence of this even in modern times in quite large Third World cities where the majority of the inhabitants leave each day to tend their cultivated areas (Grabbe 2001c). Therefore, the idea that Canaanite city dwellers could not be among those in the IA I highland settlements is mistaken.
2. Some of those settling the highlands would logically have been Canaanite peasants and farmers from villages and farmsteads surrounding the Canaanite cities, but also those who had lived within the city walls.
3. As discussed above with regard to the Shasu, the assumption that they were all 'nomads' or 'semi-nomads' is not at all established from the few texts that we have of them (§2.2.1.4). They do not just wander around indiscriminately but make up a Shasu country or territory. Although we know that pastoralism was characteristic of some or possibly even most, we cannot say that this was the sole means of livelihood of all of them: pastoralism is part of the general way of living among settled peoples as well. Some inscriptions indicate that Shasu are also associated with certain cities.
4. Although the idea that nomads naturally settle down or even want to settle down has been shown to be an outdated concept, this does not mean that pastoralists do not sometimes move to cultivation and a

> settled lifestyle. It is true that among modern examples, we often find that pastoralists who give up their lifestyle do so because of governmental coercion. Yet it is also a fact that we have many examples in which pastoralists change – without government coercion – to a more settled way of living (§3.2.4.3).

It seems a reasonable conclusion that the highlands settlers included Shasu, either because the Shasu were less monocultural in their way of living than often assumed or because some of them moved from mobile pastoralism to a more settled way of living (or perhaps both). Yet it is also likely that the settlers included people of the Canaanite lowlands who left their villages and farms, and even the Canaanite cities, and made these remote regions their home. Those who fled to the highlands were often designated as *'apiru* in Egyptian sources, but that tells us little other than that they were seen as displaced persons and potential troublemakers. The term is not necessarily a designation of a particular lifestyle. It is true that the *'apiru* might well be raiders or mercenaries, and some of those living in the highlands might well have taken up both occupations. But just as the medieval Vikings were also farmers and settlers, as well as warriors and raiders, so those called *'apiru* pursued more than one way of making a living. Many or perhaps even most of them engaged in raising crops and livestock instead of or even in addition to those activities that the Egyptians objected to.

Yet we still face a further problem: the large expansion of settlement in the highlands took place in IA I, yet Israel seems to have originated *before* this, in the LBA. If an 'Israel' was already in existence by 1208 BCE or possibly even earlier, then where was it located? Could the highland population already be called 'Israel' even before this significant expansion? This seems unlikely. Thus, we have to assume either that a population associated with the highlands was already called Israel before the IA I settlement or that Israel actually originated elsewhere and only subsequently became associated with the population of the hill country. In the former case, it might be that some of the Shasu or related groups were called 'Israel'. So far, no such group is attested in our literary or archaeological sources, but we might need to look harder. With regard to the latter case, we are hard put to find a group, in the Egyptian realm but outside the Palestinian highlands, that could identified with Israel.

Faust has suggested that the settlement process already started in the thirteenth century (2006: 160). A recent study by Yitzhak Meitlis (2008) seems to go even further. Based on LB pottery found in IA I contexts, he argues that LB pottery was not easily distinguished from early IA I pottery. He concludes that IA I began much earlier than often dated. If he is right, it may be that the highland settlement was underway earlier than the time of Merenptah. This would also fit with those Egyptologists who think they have found references to Israel perhaps even as early as the fourteenth century BCE. Thus, either the highland settlements began much earlier than normally dated, or the Israel of the early Egyptian sources was located elsewhere. This is a case where new archaeological (or perhaps even textual) discoveries may help us to resolve what remains a difficulty in our historical reconstruction.

3.2.4.3 'Tribes' and 'Nomads'

Several issues debated among social anthropologists have been intertwined with the discussions on the origins of Israel, including 'tribes/tribalism' and 'nomads/nomadism'. First, 'tribes' and 'tribalism' are an aspect of the debate over ethnicity (Rogerson 1978: 86–101; Lemche 1985: 202–44; McNutt 1999: 75–94; Gottwald 1979: 293–341). 'Ethnic group' is now often used where 'tribe' would have been used in the past. 'Tribe' is of course the English word but is frequently the translation of Hebrew שבט (*šēveṭ*) and מטה (*maṭṭeh*). The term has been widely discussed in anthropology (Helm [ed.] 1968; M. H. Fried 1968, 1975; Kamp and Yoffee 1980: 88–9; Lemche 1985: 202–44; Khoury and Kostiner [eds] 1990) without any consensus, except that the term is problematic. M. H. Fried (1968: 4–5) stated that the 'single most egregious case of meaninglessness' was the word 'race', but 'tribe' was not far behind: thus, many anthropologists avoid using the term. Yet because of its frequent application in the context of Hebrew Bible study, the word 'tribe' cannot be avoided. Many seem to agree that ancient Israel was a segmentary society, that is, one organized according to (supposed) descent and kinship (but see Rogerson 1986, though he suggests that Israel might have been closer to a segmentary state). The relationship between various Israelites (and also other peoples) was expressed by the creation and use of genealogies (R. R. Wilson 1977; Johnson 1988; Levin 2001). In most societies, ancient and modern, genealogies do not necessarily show actual biological relationship or descent but social relationships between members and sections of society. Biblical genealogies also seem to have had this function.

A theory once popular among biblical scholars was that pre-monarchic Israel was organized as an 'amphictyony' (Noth 1930; 1960: 85–109; Gottwald 1979: 345–57), a tribal league organized around a central shrine. After considerable critique of the thesis in the 1960s and especially the 1970s (e.g., Geus 1976; Mayes 1974; Lemche 1977), this model was generally abandoned. Both it and Gottwald's alternative model placed a great deal of emphasis on tribes and a specific confederation of Israelite tribes (Gottwald 1979: 358–86; but see the more cautious view in Gottwald 1993: 177–82). One of the problems is making the tribe the key social unit. Apart from the book of Judges, the text gives little collective function to the tribes. Most collective activity is carried out by small groups, and the tribes appear to be mainly territorial units (H. Weippert 1973; Geus 1976: 211; Lemche 1985: 71). That is, references to tribes were usually a reference to geography; this clarifies most of the Bible references to Israelite tribes. The people within a specific territory were generally assumed to be of a common lineage, but since property was seen as belonging by right to a specific lineage (Lev. 25.13-16, 23-28), the two went together.

The essential problem is that 'tribe' has come to be used of social and/or political units of different sorts. The difficulty is not unique to English usage but extends to the biblical text itself. A variety of terms are used in Hebrew to designate divisions of the Israelites, and their significance is widely assumed to be the following (Rogerson 1978: 93–4): שבט (*šēveṭ*); מטה (*maṭṭeh*) 'tribe'; משפחה (*mišpāḥāh*) 'family, clan'; בית אב (*bêt-'āv*) 'extended family'. Yet the terms are often used interchangeably, as Rogerson points out (cf. Exod. 6.16-25; Judg. 17.7; Amos 3.1). Furthermore, an entity that would be called a tribe in the modern context of any east African ethnic group would correspond to the entirety of the Israelites, not the individual members of the 'twelve tribes' (Mojola 1998: 26). What this means is that we should be careful about making any social assumptions about the individual Israelite 'tribes'. It seems likely that the system of twelve tribes in the biblical tradition is a late development, perhaps as late as the sixth century (Macchi 1999: 272–80). M. Noth's (1930; 1960: 85–7) analysis of the various lists, showing two types of lists (one with Levi and Joseph, another without Levi but with Ephraim and Manasseh instead of Joseph), has been quite influential. More recent study confirms that there are two systems, but argues that they have been edited together into the scheme of twelve tribes; that is, the twelve-fold system is a late development (Macchi 1999; Kallai 1995, 1999).

Associated with the question of tribalism is that of nomads or pastoral nomads and the nomadic lifestyle. Through much of the twentieth century many biblical scholars saw the origin of Israel from a nomadic lifestyle (or 'semi-nomads'). The assumption of the Alt–Noth school (§3.2.4.2), but also others, was that a nomadic existence explained much about the early Israelite traditions (with special emphasis on their religion [§4.2.8]). One of the critiques coming from those who embraced the Mendenhall–Gottwald thesis was that nomadism was not the key to understanding early Israel (Chaney 1983), but the place of 'nomads' (or 'pastoralists') in the origins of Israel has not been given up (see the discussion of Finkelstein above [§3.2.4.2]). But now there is a much more sophisticated understanding of the question, though some of the anthropological studies one still sees cited have been superseded.

Earlier discussions especially focused on the work of J. R. Kupper, J. T. Luke and M. B. Rowton (see the summary in Kamp and Yoffee 1980: 90–2). Unfortunately, models were developed on these studies by biblical scholars who were apparently unaware of the wide range of nomadic/pastoralist modes of living (Irons and Dyson-Hudson [eds] 1972; Nelson [ed.] 1973; Kamp and Yoffee 1980: 92–4; Lemche 1985: 84–163; Khazanov 1994; Staubli 1991; Salzman 2004; Szuchman [ed.] 2009). The main problem was the assumption of bipolar opposites: sedentary/nomadic, agriculturalist/pastoralist, rural/urban, village/city (Mohammed 1973; Kamp and Yoffee 1980: 93; Lemche 1985: 198–201). This is despite the fact that a number of researchers recognized that pastoralists and farmers generally had a mutually beneficial relationship and usually lived together in harmony.

What was often forgotten was that 'pastoral nomad' covers a wide spectrum of living modes, from those who grow crops alongside their animal husbandry and have close contacts with the settled community to those who live away from the settled areas and have a very mobile way of life. Philip Salzman summarizes the situation, by saying that we must reject an evolutionary view that

> would not at all correspond to life in the Middle East and North Africa, where nomadization and sedentarization have been ongoing complementary processes for millennia... People settled when it seemed beneficial to do so and became nomadic for the same reason... We must also keep in mind that 'settled' and 'nomadic,' rather than being two types, are better thought of as opposite ends of a continuum with many gradations of stability and mobility. (Salzman 2004: 34)

He suggests a model of sedentarization that is much more nuanced to the realities of actual groups studied by modern anthropologists:

> ...it is necessary to propose a further model...in which sedentarization is seen not so much as a forced, coerced, unavoidable process, to which no conceivable alternative but annihilation could exist, but rather as (in very many cases) a voluntary, uncoerced shift from one available pattern to another in response to changing pressures, constraints, and opportunities both internal and external to the society.

Salzman (2004: 23–41) went on to make a number of proposals that give a perspective rather different from that found in many writings on the subject. I list some of the ones that seem most relevant here (my own formulation):

- Nomadism is a way of coping with a situation of scarce and unpredictable resources.
- Nomads do not usually concentrate on only one activity of production such as pastoralism but combine it with other activities such as grain cultivation, arboriculture, viticulture, fishing, or trading. There are nomadic agriculturalists as well as nomadic pastoralists.
- Nomadism is not necessarily connected to political structure or economic situation. The nomads' relationship to the political and economic situation varies greatly from community to community.
- Nomads vary greatly in structure, from egalitarian, acephalus, decentralized peoples to weak chiefdoms to very hierarchical and centralized entities. Nomadic pastoralists tend to be the former (decentralized) and in the more remote regions, while the more centralized and hierarchical tend to be sedentary or associated with agricultural settlements, cities, etc.
- Nomads are not a particular kind of people but a variety of peoples who use a particular strategy (household mobility) to carry out productive activities and to defend themselves. Nomadism is not their life goal or *raison d'être*: they migrate to live. Given other circumstances they might choose a non-nomadic way of life.
- Those that we call 'nomads' might in other contexts go by a variety of other names: peasants, warriors, tribal people, peaceful civilians. The label 'nomad' (or 'pastoralist') captures only a portion of their way of life, characteristics, and identity.

It is important to keep in mind that (a) a people might include both pastoralists and agriculturalists, or (b) even the same individuals might carry on both crop-growing and animal-herding, and (c) people could cycle lifestyles, being sometimes pastoralists and sometimes settled agriculturalists, not to mention the many stages in between.

Some general comments will summarize the discussion:

1. The ubiquitous reference to 'tribes' in the Bible, including in some possibly early passages, suggest that Israelite society was eventually 'tribalized'. Yet if Israel and Judah grew out of a coalescing of various elements (pastoralists, agriculturalists, Transjordanians, etc.), 'tribes' may have developed later rather than earlier.

2. In any case, tribalization seems to have had little practical effect, since we see little evidence that society was organized by tribes for administrative purposes or collective action. The twelve-tribe scheme, known from many biblical passages, is likely to be a late development, created for ideological purposes.
3. The once-common assumption that early Israel consisted of a tribal league (whether Noth's 'amphictyony' or something related) is still influential in some circles, even though generally thought to have been refuted.
4. If, as argued (§§3.2.4.2; 3.3), Israel and Judah developed from a variety of indigenous peoples who inhabited the highlands, it is likely that this mixture included pastoralists and transhumants. Thus, the study of 'nomads' in its broadest sense is still relevant to early Israel, but the great variety of types, lifestyles and combinations has to be recognized: 'categories and labels (such as "nomadic pastoralists") tend to over-simplify and distort the multiresource economies that most nomads have and the versatile, multipurpose nomadism that they use to the fullest' (Salzman 2004: 24).

3.2.4.4 Anthropological Models of Statehood

The question of statehood for Israel and Judah cannot easily be disassociated from that of the settlement: the settlement and the rise of the monarchy seem ultimately to be part of the same process. This does not suggest that, once those who became Israel settled down, a state was inevitable, but the settlement – its nature, its development, the resources available – are all determining factors in the progress toward statehood. One followed from and presupposed the other.

In recent years there has been much discussion among anthropologists and archaeologists about the nature of states, the types of states, how states develop and what precedes them. It is not unusual for discussions about the rise of Israel to make some reference to this discussion, but it must be said that most writings by biblical scholars do not give a thorough treatment of the subject. It is fair to say that when anthropological studies on state development are mentioned, it is not infrequently to expound one and follow it without serious discussion of other possibilities or critique of the one being followed. The literature on the subject is quite substantial, especially if one takes into account everything written since the seminal work by M. Fortes and E. Evans-Pritchard (1940). No attempt will be made here to trace the discussion over the decades, but several points can be made in order to summarize the most important considerations for discussion in the present:

1. Much of the discussion, at least until recently, has been based on evolutionary models (Redman 1999: 49–53; Gosden 1999: 476–82; Renfrew and Bahn 2004: 178–82; Yoffee 2005: 22–41). A popular one has been the model of E. R. Service (1962) in which civilization developed through the stages of bands, tribes, chiefdoms and finally states. Evolutionary models do not have to force everything into a rigid pattern nor suggest inevitability (Feinman and Marcus [eds] 1998: 5–6). N. Yoffee fully accepts the concept of social evolution, but his recent study is a sustained critique of the widely regarded 'neo-evolutionary model' (Yoffee 2005: 22–41).
2. The various models of statehood are ideal types, but there is a danger of elevating ideal types to reality. Reality is always much more complicated, while ideal types only serve as a means of investigation and comparison. Within the various types there is a great deal of variation. To pick one sociological model and argue from it without considering others or without critiquing the models themselves is to be naive and uncritical.
3. The concept of chiefdom – so beloved of studies on the development of statehood in Israel and Judah – has been much criticized (Yoffee 2005: 22–31). See further on this below.

The types of early states have been discussed in the anthropological literature, with a bewildering variety of models: city-states, territorial states, regional states, segmentary states, tribal states, ethnic states. The term 'city-state' frequently comes up in discussions relating to ancient Palestine, yet a recent collection found the term problematic (Feinman and Marcus [eds] 1998: 8–10). B. Trigger (2003: 92–113) divides early states into the 'city-state' and 'the territorial state'; yet, disconcertingly, toward the end of his discussion he suddenly introduces the 'regional state/kingdom' without discussing what it is or how it relates to the other two. 'Regional state' is also used by T. J. Barfield (1990), but he seems to be using the term in a different sense from Trigger.

A number of the recent theorists on the rise of the Israelite and Judahite states have worked with the model of the chiefdom. Of recent works R. D. Miller II argues that Israel began as a 'complex chiefdom' (2005: esp. 6–14):

> Those having an intermediate level or levels of 'subchiefs' between the paramount and the people… It is complex chiefdoms that develop into states and that one would expect to find in Israel on the threshold of Monarchy. (Miller 2005: 8)

Three main characteristics are said to be associated with complex chiefdoms: (1) tribute mobilization, (2) cycling (between two or three levels of control) and (3) sacralization. Unfortunately, Miller does not appear to take account of the debate. For example, he makes little reference to the critique of the chiefdom concept (e.g., Yoffee 2005: 22–31) and none to those who argue that the chiefdom is an alternative to the state, that is, that chiefdoms do not develop into states (cf. Yoffee 2005: 26–7). His statement that it is the complex chiefdom that develops into the state also does not seem to recognize that the complex chiefdom might well cycle into a 'simple chiefdom'.

N. Yoffee (2005) both critiques the 'neo-evolutionary' thesis and also makes his own proposals about the development of the state. His thesis seems to be expressed in the following statement:

> New social roles and new forms of social relations emerged alongside, and to an extent supplanted, exclusive kinship rules (of marriages and the status of children) that also functioned as the framework for relations of production. Leadership, exercised by shamans, expert hunters, and charismatic individuals, gave way to formalized ideologies in which the accumulation of wealth and high status were seen as rightfully belonging to leaders whose roles were, among other things, to 'make inequality enchant'. As social relations were transformed into relations of domination, new ideologies led to the acquiescence of subjects in their own domination and the production of their own subordination (Godelier 1986). The new ideologies of state, which were inextricable from the changing social relations that gave them birth, thus depicted how dominant leaders 'served' those who daily and perpetually served them... The earliest states, thus, consisted of a political center with its own leadership structure, specialized activities, and personnel, but also included numerous differentiated groups. These social groups continuously changed in their organization and membership in relation to the needs and goals, strengths and weaknesses of the political center. (2005: 32–4)

According to Yoffee (2005: 34–8) the critical processes of social and economic differentiation and political integration come about through the various forms of power that had to be in place before the earliest states could evolve: economic power (agricultural production, mercantile activity), social power (elites at both the state and local level, creation or adaptation of symbols of cultural commonality) and political power (bureaucratic administration, military organization, legal system, taxation structure). Although ancient states were unlikely to have passed through a chiefdom-like stage, he accepts and even presses the concept of city-state (2005: 42–62). He mentions in passing 'Yoffee's rule': 'If you can argue whether a society is a state or isn't, then it isn't' (2005: 41).

A. H. Joffe proposes the model of the 'ethnic state' for the rise of secondary states in the southern Levant, meaning Israel, Judah, Ammon, Moab and finally Edom. By 'ethnic state' he means:

> Polities integrated by means of identity, especially ethnicity, and which are territorially based…they are novel and historically contingent political systems which appear in the Levant during the first millennium BCE thanks to the confluence of several factors, not least of all the collapse of imperial domination and the longstanding city-state system. (2002: 426)

Joffe focuses on the archaeology and extra-biblical texts rather than the biblical accounts.

Based on fragmented evidence from the material culture (e.g., a series of palatial structures in *bit-ḫilani* style; proto-Aeolic capitals; red-burnished Phoenician-style tableware) Joffe identifies a state in the Cisjordan region already in the tenth century (2002: 440–6). The similarity of construction styles at Megiddo, Hazor and Gezer indicates they were part of a larger political unit, but all three seem to be in border areas. What the centre might be is not known. In spite of some marks of royal ideology, other significant ones are missing: representational art, monumental inscriptions, inscribed or decorated objects, inscribed or uninscribed seals or weights. Although Joffe insists on calling it a state, he admits it was fragile, hardly integrated and had little in the way of meaningful ethnic unity. In any case, much depends on following the conventional dating: if the LC turns out to be correct, the postulated development of the ethnic states will be somewhat different.

Other types of early state are sometimes postulated. The term 'segmentary state' seems to have been coined by A. W. Southall (1956). In a more recent article, J. W. Rogerson argued that ancient Israel was not a segmentary society but approached being a segmentary state (1986). The concept has come under considerable criticism, and Southall himself eventually gave it up (Marcus and Feinman 1998: 7–8). Another is 'tribal state', of which three sorts are proposed: (1) one tribal elite or dynasty conquers and rules over a heterogeneous population; (2) a non-tribal dynasty is brought to power by and depends on tribal support; (3) the rulers attempt to eliminate tribalism but promote a national ideology of integration that resembles tribal ideology (Tapper 1990: 69). Inspired by

M. Weber, L. E. Stager (1985a: 25–8), followed by D. Schloen (2001) and D. M. Master (2001), proposed the archetype of the patrimonial state. This is modelled on the household, in which leadership is vested by tradition in the patriarchal figure. In a recent book on the rise of Moab as a state, however, B. Routledge considered but rejected both these popular 'local models' of state formation, 'tribal states' and 'patrimonial states' (2004: 115–23).

One of the points made in a number of studies is the importance of ideology to the founding of states (Caton 1990; also to ethnic identity: §1.2.4). 'Ideology' can of course cover a number of different perspectives, including that of religion. For example, E. Gellner (1981) has demonstrated the significance of saints and religious leaders for the development or maintenance of chiefdoms in early Islamic history (also Tapper 1990: 65). In this light, the suggestion of Gottwald and others that Yahwism was important to the development of early Israel takes on a new significance. We also have to consider the place of law, which can play a similar role. In Israel law included not just civil law but moral and religious law. Unfortunately, it becomes a matter of speculation at this point because we have so little evidence, but see further at §3.3.

3.2.4.5 The Early Monarchy: Saul, Samuel, David, and Solomon Traditions

It has often been assumed in the past that with the reigns of Saul and David we begin to get into the historical period. In Noth's classic theory, 1 Samuel 13 to 2 Kings 2 was thought to have been made up of several blocks of tradition that were given only minor editing (including some formulaic introductions and transitional passages) before being incorporated into the DtrH (Noth 1981: 54–7). More recent analysis has not been as optimistic about finding early narratives, but the stories of Saul and David show evidence of a variety of traditions: there is a pro-Saul bias in the Saul traditions and anti-David perspectives in the Davidic material. There are also some essential differences between them and the Solomon narrative.

Saul. He was a problem for the narrator of 1–2 Samuel, which is an excellent reason for believing he was a historical personage. It seems clear that the narrator wanted to tell the story of David but had to deal with Saul as well, even though he would rather have ignored or forgotten about him. According to narrative logic, the rulership and dynasty should have begun with David. The whole story of the monarchy is of the legitimacy of the Davidic dynasty and the illegitimacy of the northern kingship.

The Northern Kingdom should not have existed, and the northern kings were presented as usurpers. But how is this to be explained, if David was also a usurper – not part of the dynasty originally chosen by God? The narrator of 1 Samuel has to present it that Saul's dynasty was not just wiped out, but that his descendants were null and void as far as kingship was concerned – a rather strange concept, if it was the king and dynasty originally chosen and anointed by Yhwh. If Saul's rulership and dynasty could be overturned, why not that of David? Yet the narrative insists on treating them quite differently.

Thus, it seems that the narrator was stuck with Saul and his family. The existence of Saul as the first king of Israel does not strike one as a likely fictional scenario, even if some aspects of the relationship and interaction between Saul and David could easily find their place in a work of fiction. The tradition was too firmly settled and known to the people to be given major changes, such as dropping Saul altogether. Even though there is absolutely no evidence for Saul apart from the biblical text, there is a good prima facie case for believing there was a historical Saul.

What else can we say with more or less confidence about this figure? As has long been observed, 2 Sam. 2.9 describes Ishbaal (or Ishbosheth) as ruling over 'Gilead, the Ashurites, Jezrel, Ephraim, and Benjamin'. This is reasonably the territory ascribed to Saul. It is especially important because it does not include Judah, for reasons which will be discussed below under David. Apart from some territory on the other side of the Jordan, the core of the fiefdom is the central hill country, which archaeology suggests is the centre of the Iron I settlement area. Many of Saul's activities could have been accomplished in two years (cf. 1 Sam. 13.1).

Much of the Saul tradition involves fighting against the Philistines. Yet he was supposed to have originally made his name by fighting the Amalekites (1 Sam. 15). On the surface, this appears unlikely, since the territory of the Amalekites was presumed to have been in the Negev (Num. 13.29). That is a valid objection, since Saul's territory does not appear to have included Judah, much less the areas to the south of it. Diana Edelman (1986) has argued, however, that Saul attacked Amalekites who were living in the region of Samaria. This is much more credible as a historical event.

It is plausible that Saul fought the Philistines, but it is more likely that Saul attacked them than the other way round. Philistines had lived happily in the coastal region for well over a century. The Shephelah acted as a transition zone, and there was opportunity for Philistines to expand if they had wanted to do so, without moving into the highlands. The ones aiming to expand their territory seem to have been the Israelites. Probably, the highlanders made periodic raids into the prosperous lowlands, though that may have forced the Philistines to send troops occasionally on retaliatory incursions into the highlands. But the idea that the Philistines were wanting to expand their territory into the highlands at this time looks unlikely. This interpretation seems to be supported by the archaeology. The Galilee region prospered during the Iron I for the most part, but some of the main sites were destroyed at the end of IA I (Finkelstein). Radiocarbon dating now suggests that these destructions were not a unitary event but happened over a period of some decades. The subsequent material culture suggests that invaders from the highlands were the cause of the destructions. This would seem to confirm the view that the highlanders – Israel – were expanding out of their core territory. If so, they would probably have also been expanding south, into Philistine territory. Rather than being the victims in the clash with the Philistines, Israel may have been the instigators.

Let us note some salient points about the Saul tradition. First of all, Saul looks like a chieftain, with a court that meets under a tree (1 Sam. 22.6). We have two versions of how he became king: one is that he was anointed by Samuel (1 Sam. 9.1–10.16 [10.23] + 13.2–14.52), which looks like a biased account from a prophetic source that wants to make Saul subordinate to Samuel; the other – more likely to be reliable – is that he arose as a deliverer (1 Sam. 11.1-15). A recent analysis of the Saul tradition finds a historical core, though this has been filtered through the distorting lenses of Davidic court circles, prophetic circles, Deuteronomistic perspectives and anti-monarchic views (Shalom Brooks 2005). The stories of killing the priests of Nob or the Gibeonites are probably later calumnies. According to Shalom Brooks the population in the central highlands was already moving toward a new socioeconomic situation characterized by a developing centralization. This was the background for the rise of the monarchy. Saul was a successful leader, the first to develop a standing army, who had the support of the people. Saul was not only able to unite the Israelite tribes (she includes Judah, though I think this unlikely, as explained in the section on David) but also to incorporate Canaanites and other minority groups into the emerging state. Loyalty to Saul continued after his death, creating rebellions and other problems for David; indeed, David almost wrecked the monarchy by his sabotage of Saul's rule in order to gain the throne for himself.

Similarly, D. Edelman (1991, 1996a) sees the historical Saul as the petty king of Gibeon with Benjaminite roots who expanded into surrounding territory to create a state called 'Israel'. Attempts to control local trade routes and find markets brought him into conflict with the Philistines and other independent states. He died trying to expand into the Jezreel–Beth She'an corridor.

Samuel. At this point we should consider the figure of Samuel who plays such an important part in the account of Saul but also at the beginning of the story of David. Samuel seems to fill the role in the narratives about Saul and David that Merlin does in the King Arthur story. Although his activities are sometimes centre stage, his purpose is to choose and anoint the person to be king. Merlin is a sort of shaman figure, which means that he functions in both prophetic and priestly activities. Certainly, Samuel is both priest and prophet, but he is also a political leader for part of his life. We do not normally expect either priest or prophet to be the king (or a similar figure), yet after the fall of the monarchy the high priest of Judah was also a political leader of the Jewish community and sometimes had prophetic functions (Grabbe 2004a: 230–4).

In the present text Samuel is in many ways the linchpin that connects the Saul and David traditions. He anointed the first king but, after Saul was rejected by Yhwh, he then anointed David. Yet many literary critics have argued that the prophetic figure who first anointed Saul (1 Sam. 10.1) was originally an anonymous figure. This might suggest that Samuel should be better associated with David, and that he has been brought into the Saul tradition secondarily. Yet Samuel's original circuit of cities where he carried out his priestly duties were Bethel, Gilgal, Mizpah and Ramah, all places in the North, and not everyone wants to replace the Samuel anointing Saul with an anonymous holy man. Whether Samuel should be inserted into 1 Samuel 9–10 (as he is now) or not, he could well have been an important shamanistic figure and king maker in the period at the beginnings of an Israelite state. He could then have been active in the rise of Saul but became disillusioned with him, at which point he would have looked around for a replacement.

One would have expected a religious figure – priest or prophet – to have been associated with the rise of the monarchy in Israel. One might think of the archbishop of Canterbury in English history. Although the archbishop was a religious figure, he had considerable power, including the power to crown the monarch. We also know that some archbishops were very political, even holding political office along with their ecclesiastical duties. The history of the English monarchy includes the activities of many of the Canterbury archbishops. From that perspective, Samuel who had both priestly and prophetic functions, as well as a community leadership role, would have been a necessary figure. In that sense, his general activities in both the Saul and David traditions are credible.

However, some of the activities ascribed to Samuel are unlikely to be historical. His function as a mouthpiece for anti-monarchic speeches is one of these. Many of the passages that express hostility toward kingship for Israel (e.g., 1 Sam. 8) are probably late (though as so often, the matter is complicated [cf. Dietrich 2011: 42*–3*]).

David. A number of recent studies attempt to analyse the David story (Brettler 1995: 91–111; McKenzie 2000; Halpern 2001; Finkelstein and Silberman 2006). One of the concerns in the early part of the story is to legitimate David – strongly suggesting that David was a usurper, as we shall see. Another concern is that he is inextricably associated with Judah. This is important, because the relationship of Judah with Israel is one of the areas in which the data clash strongly with the surface narrative of the biblical text. It has long been known and accepted that Judah had its own national identity and was separate from and a rival of Israel from an early period (discussed at §3.2.4.1).

What we find in 1–2 Samuel is the story of a young Judahite warrior made good. He seems to have grown up in a society that was not heavily stratified; nevertheless, there was no doubt tribal leadership, with Judahite elders and perhaps even a tribal chieftain or chieftains. Was David the heir of one of these tribal leaders? There are also some hints that his family was not so humble. After all, he was brought into Saul's court, unlikely to happen to a complete nobody. In any case, David became some sort of *'apiru* leader: surprisingly, this image appears to be agreed on by two archaeologists who otherwise take somewhat different views on the 'United Monarchy' (Mazar 2007: 164–5; Finkelstein 2001: 107–8).

According to the text of 2 Samuel, David continued Saul's fight with the Philistines, especially in 5.17-25 and 8.1. Yet several scholars have argued that the reality was different, and that David may not have fought with the Philistines but arranged a truce that allowed a peaceful co-existence throughout his reign (Niemann 2013: 259–60; Dietrich 2012: 95–8). There are a number of arguments in support of this. First, David's wars with the Philistines in 2 Sam. 5.17-25 seem only a passing episode, with little consequence; indeed, taking little space to describe. The motive for the Philistines to attack him also looks rather trumped up. Niemann notes that these campaigns (and the statement in 2 Sam. 5.25) fit Saul better and were probably borrowed from the Saulide tradition. Secondly, David does not defeat the Philistines (only the tacked on summary statement in 2 Sam. 5.25 claims this), yet the threat simply disappears from the text. Thirdly, we also have the reference to the 600 warriors from Gath, under the command of Itai, who assist David at the time of Abalom's rebellion

(2 Sam. 15.18-22). Fourthly, Achish king of Gath is clearly at peace with Solomon after the time of David (1 Kgs 2.39-40). Finally, some argue that Judah had expanded into the Shephelah in the first half of the ninth century (but see at §3.1.1); in any case, there is no evidence of conflict with Gath which would have dominated the area as a large city at this time (Na'aman 2010: 516–17; 2013: 264). This indicates that an earlier agreement (presumably the one made in the time of David) was still in effect.

Yet if David did not fight with the Philistines, was he seeking an essential expansion of his territory? According to 2 Samuel, David fought a variety of the surrounding peoples and expanded his territory to the north and east and south, into Moab, Ammon, Edom and the region of Aramaean rule (2 Sam. 8; 10.1–11.1; 12.26-31). The extension of control into Edom and Transjordan is credible, but defeat of the Aramaeans – even placing a garrison in Damascus (2 Sam. 8.6) – looks contrived. Now, Nadav Na'aman has presented a compelling case that this fight against and defeat of Hadadezer of Zobah is a literary creation, based on the Aramaean king Hazael in the ninth century (Na'aman 2002b: 207–10). However, he goes on to argue that David's conquest of Moab was also a literary creation, aiming to counter the defeat of Israel by Moab under Mesha; that the defeat of Ammon was devised to compensate for the cruelty inflicted by the Ammonites on Israel as outlined in Amos 1.13; and that David's defeat of Edom was borrowed from Amaziah's later victory over the Edomites (2 Kgs 14.7 [Na'aman 2002b: 212–14]). In the end, Na'aman sees in the story of David's conquests only a few historical elements, viz., the conquest of Jerusalem and the subjugation of the Philistines (Na'aman 2002b: 215). As we have seen above, however, it looks as if the driving of the Philistines from the central hill country is also a literary creation! This leaves us with the taking of Jerusalem, though I would argue that here we do have a genuine historical datum.

With regard to Jerusalem, the stories in Judges seem to remember a Jerusalem that came into Israelite hands only relatively late and continued to have the earlier people as a part of the population for some time afterward. What the various traditions suggest, therefore, is that there was a collective folk memory of a time when Jerusalem was not Israelite, and even that it came into Israelite hands much later than some of the surrounding territory. This is a remarkable memory, especially if we keep in mind that it would have been more convenient to believe that Jerusalem was conquered with the rest of the territory and divided up by the Israelites without any complications.

Yet the text acknowledges complications: Jerusalem is sometimes the property of Judah (Josh. 15.63; cf. Judg. 1.8) and sometimes within the territory of Benjamin (Josh. 18.28; Judg. 1.21). In both cases, it recognizes that some of the original inhabitants, the Jebusites, continued to live in the city, alongside the Judahites (Josh. 15.63; Judg. 1.21) or Benjaminites (Judg. 1.21). In spite of this tradition, 2 Sam. 5.6-6 requires David to conquer the city from the Jebusites again. What sort of entity Jerusalem was is not clear. The story suggests a type of fortress, though this does not mean a large or grand settlement, as is confirmed by the image of the Jebusite king of Jerusalem who does his own physical threshing of grain at his threshing floor which occupies a central point on the ridge (2 Sam. 24.20-23). David's sons acted as priests at this time, possibly even before he took Jerusalem (2 Sam. 8.17). In any case, David made the Jebusite priest Zadok one of his two chief priests, as has long been recognized (cf. Grabbe 2003).

Having argued that there is a historical core to both the Saulide and Davidide traditions, we must now ask whether there is any connection between them. The David traditions in the present narrative are in part bound up with the Saul traditions, and they need to be evaluated together. Granted, the present redacted text has the traditions heavily intertwined, but was that the case in the beginning? Can we simply see two sets of traditions, one of which described in some way the first northern king, while the other independently had the first southern king at its core? Such an interpretation is quite believable in itself and has the merit of being simple. Why must we complicate the story more than is necessary, even though the redactors certainly did? Yet a closer examination exposes greater complexity. Note the following: There is first of all the saying, `Saul has slain his thousands, but David his tens of thousands' (1 Sam. 18.7; 21.12; 29.5). Not a major datum but nevertheless one worth noting, and one likely to be early according to some commentators (e.g., Dietrich 2007: 204–5). If this is an early saying, where did it come from if the David and Saul traditions were originally separate?

Secondly, one of the major characteristics of the David tradition is the extent to which his reign is legitimated (strongly suggesting that David was a usurper [Shalom Brooks 2005: Chapter 4]):

- Comes as an apprentice to Saul's court (1 Sam. 16.14-23).
- Performs personal duties for Saul's health (1 Sam. 16.14-23).
- Fights as a champion against Israel's enemies (1 Sam. 17).
- Marries the king's daughter (1 Sam. 18.17-27).
- Wins her hand by warrior-worthy deeds (1 Sam. 18.25-27).

- Anointed by a prophet-priest (1 Sam. 16.1-13).
- Even the king's son and heir recognizes David's right to rule (1 Sam. 18.1; 20.12-17; 23.16-18).

Why go to all this trouble to make David's rule legitimate if he had been accepted as the first king of Judah by the tradition? This suggests that the present picture of the text (that he was not the first king but actually effected a change of dynasty) was not a secondary creation but one already there in the tradition when the text was redacted.

Thirdly, one could take the example of Michal. She could have been added to the tradition simply to give a further negative picture of Saul, since her story is ultimately a negative one in which she is rejected and childless, though remaining David's wife. But her story is more complicated and interesting than this. For example, she helps David escape from her father by a clever deception (1 Sam. 19.11-17). After she was married to another man, David expended some effort to get her back (2 Sam. 3.12-16).

Fourthly, there is also the story of Jonathan. Again, he could serve just as another reason to bolster David's legitimacy: even the heir to the throne supports David's right instead of his own. But why make him such an integral part of the story, if that were his only purpose? Not least is the question of why Jonathan did not succeed his father. The many hazards to an heir not only growing up but acquiring the necessary military prowess and confidence of the troops meant that prime heirs did not always gain the throne. But we might have expected a different sort of story, if it was simply a literary invention to enhance David's right to the throne.

Finally, we have to ask: If the Saul tradition was simply about the first king of Israel, separate from Judah, what happened to his dynasty? We know that at a later time, kings well attested in historical sources ruled over Israel. But if the Saul tradition was completely independent of the David one, what happened to the Israelite monarchy that had begun with Saul? Did it simply peter out? If so, what filled the vacuum, and how did it get started up again? It is such questions that make us turn to the David tradition and ask whether it is perhaps correct that David in some way was the successor to the throne of the inchoate state of Israel begun by Saul.

It is as if the Davidic and Solomonic traditions are *necessary* to fill the gap between Saul and the history of the two kingdoms or monarchies of Israel and Judah. If so, then the concept of the 'united monarchy' is perhaps correct, after all – but only in a particular sense. That is, the first king Saul ruled over a portion of the central highlands, though apparently not Judah. The Judahite David – possibly a tribal leader of Judah or perhaps even a sort of king of Judah – took over from Saul (or Saul's son), establishing some sort of rule over both the northern highlands and the Judaean highlands.

We can now draw some conclusions about the historicity of the David tradition. In the biblical story, David fits the image of the hero figure; there are many folkloristic elements and a variety of traditions; yet there are also traditions with some interesting twists, such as the willingness to acknowledge some of David's weaknesses, the need to legitimate David from a variety of angles – suggesting that he was not seen as legitimate by everyone – and the admission that David did not do certain things that we might have expected. To summarize, we can note some of the points that emerge from a look at the Saul and David traditions:

- The tradition recognizes that David was not the first king.
- Saul came to the throne probably as a military leader by popular acclaim (1 Sam. 11.1-15), whereas the prophetic tradition that the king was subject to Samuel's choice and censure (1 Sam. 9.1–10.16; 10.23; 13.2–14.52) is unrealistic.
- The apparent boundaries of Saul's kingdom (2 Sam. 2.9) are reasonably in line with the natural and demographic resources in Cisjordan.
- A strong link is made between David's rise and Saul's court, but much of this looks like a deliberate attempt to legitimate David as king from a variety of angles: anointing by Samuel (1 Sam. 16.1-13); armour-bearer in Saul's court, who plays the lyre for him personally (1 Sam. 16.14-23); slaying of Goliath (1 Sam. 17); marriage to Saul's daughter (1 Sam. 18.17-27).
- Contrary to expectations David does not build a temple (though a strenuous effort is made for him to do everything short of the actual building, especially in 1 Chron. 28–29).
- Both Saul and David were mainly military leaders.
- The text itself does not suggest an extensive administrative apparatus in the case of either Saul or David.

Solomon. The narrative about Solomon's reign (1 Kgs 2–11) seems to be rather different from those about Saul and David. One is immediately struck by how uniform it is. Although the text shows signs of editing (for there are some repetitions and signs of unevenness), it is essentially a folktale about an Oriental potentate – it is a royal legend or *Königsnovelle*. Almost from start to finish Solomon fits the image of the great 'oriental emperor'. He controls a vast territory and possesses great wealth, with absolute sovereignty over his subjects. Of course, he marries the daughter of a country of similar power – suggesting equality with Egypt in this case – and harnesses the best craftsmen and materials from legendary Tyre to build his city. His capital city consists of great palaces and a magnificent temple, with gold like dust and silver so abundant it is of little account. His household overflows with luxuries, his table groans under the weight of exotic fruits, meats from rare animals and every sort of desirable food for consumption. His wisdom is legendary, and he exceeds all others in intellectual skills. His reputation reaches far and wide, and rulers from distant lands travel to see such a supreme example of power, wealth and wisdom – only to find that the reports were understated. His ships travel to the ends of the earth for rare and astonishing goods.

I find it difficult to discover much in the Solomon story that strikes me as likely to be historical. Although the story of David has him expanding his territory via conquests, there is nothing to suggest that he rules all the land between Egypt and the Euphrates, yet this is the territory that Solomon controls, even though he fought no battles (1 Kgs 5.1, 4). There is not a hint that David could monopolize the trade in horses between Egypt and Mesopotamia (1 Kgs 10.28-29). As for the wealth invested in the House for Yhwh, this is commensurate with the quantity of gold that Solomon receives each year: 666 talents plus the revenue from trade, etc. (1 Kgs 10.14-15). Only a great empire, such as that of the later Persians, could collect so much wealth: according to Herodotus (3.91) the Persians collected 14,560 talents of silver in tribute annually – the equivalent of 1120 talents of gold. The idea that Solomon could raise 666 talents of gold plus much additional wealth each year is a gross flight of fancy on the part of the writer. In this story, though, the height of marvels is Solomon's great wisdom (1 Kgs 10.3, 68, 23-24), even if we are given little in the way of examples of how this is demonstrated.

I do not discount the existence of a King Solomon. His name echoing the old god of Jerusalem (Shalim/Shalem) is suggestive of reality rather than simply the piety of the David story. Also, he began his reign with the bloody elimination of rivals, though the idea that he took his throne in the midst of adversity which he overcame could be a part of the stereotype, and the writer probably saw nothing bad in this. But, overall, I can find little in the Solomon story that looks on the face of it to be historically reliable. Yet I am intrigued by the story that he built the Jerusalem temple. This sort of story is what we might expect, and the description of the wealth and rare construction of the temple fits well the legend. Yet David – the expected temple-builder – did not construct it, and we find nothing in the stories of the later kings that might hide such a building (with the possible exception of Jehoash who is said to collect money to repair the temple: 2 Kgs 12). This suggests that a temple was built in Jerusalem at a fairly early time. If David did not build it, then who? Possibly here we have a genuine remembrance that has been expanded into a great legend.

E. A. Knauf (1997) thinks that Solomon was historical but that he differed considerably from the biblical picture. The king's name shows that he was non-Judaean in origin. The Bathsheba story was not suppressed because there was a worse story: Solomon was not David's son. Knauf has tried to reconstruct some early sources. He sees 1 Kgs 8.12-13 as an early text quoting an incomplete royal building inscription which confirms Solomon's place in association with the temple (though perhaps only establishing a cult in a pre-existent temple rather than a temple builder as such). In 1 Kings 1–2 (a text probably from the seventh century) he sees glimpses of Solomon as the puppet of the Jerusalem elite on whom he turns and whom he eliminates. He concludes that Solomon was the son of a Jerusalem mother but not necessarily of a Judaean father. He became king through a *coup d'état* by getting rid of the Jerusalem elite. He was no monotheist, because the Judaean tribal deity Yhwh had only a subordinate position in the Jerusalem pantheon.

In a long survey of the Solomonic tradition M. H. Niemann (1997) argues that Solomon's alleged building programme of cities and monumental buildings cannot be confirmed archaeologically. Instead, we find evidence of a series of representatives (often relatives) who were sent to the northern areas as the first attempt to build a network of loyalty in an area that had not yet declared for Solomon's rule. Solomon might have indeed married the daughter of an Egyptian pharaoh, according to Niemann, but this would have been because he was a vassal of that pharaoh (Shoshenq?). This could be the reason that Jerusalem is not found on the Shoshenq inscription (but see below on Solomon's alleged marriage).

N. Na'aman (1997d) also analysed the account of Solomon for the existence of sources. He accepts that the early 'chronicle of Israelite kings' was created in the eighth century and thus rather later than Solomon; however, the Deuteronomist also had the 'Book of the Acts of Solomon' (1 Kgs 11.41), which Na'aman tries to reconstruct. Some episodes were invented by the post-Deuteronomic redactor, including the Queen of Sheba and the description of the temple (based on a description of the temple of his own times). Na'aman concludes that only in the late redaction do we have a picture of a ruler of an empire and a great sage. Although I agree that there was a 'Chonicle of the Kings of Judah' (Grabbe 2006b), I am more sceptical of a 'Book of the Acts of Solomon'. If such existed, it might have provided some historical facts, but we could not be sure without a careful analysis. But were such writings being produced this early? Administrative documents, yes, but not the sort of biographical writing envisaged here (§3.2.5). Thus, here and there might be a verse that reflects the historical Solomon, but to my mind the Solomon story is the most problematic, providing the thickest cloud of obscurity over the history that lies behind it.

The episode relating to the queen of Sheba illustrates the historical problem (1 Kgs 10.1-13). Although I have characterized the Solomon story on the whole as an 'Oriental tale', the Sheba story has all the marks of a folk tale (though it has been incorporated into the text by a literary writer). The main figure has no name: she is simply 'the queen of Sheba'. She herself is a representative of wealth, wisdom and power. Yet her function in the story is to marvel at all that Solomon and Jerusalem have to show her: in spite of all her own wealth and wisdom, Solomon's are much greater. He leaves her speechless. The story is often defended as historical by explaining it as a journey to establish trade relations between southern Arabia and Israel (e.g., Malamat 1982: 191, 204; Kitchen 1997), yet the biblical text says not a word about such a purpose. On the contrary, according to 1 Kgs 10.1, the queen of Sheba came to Solomon 'to test him with riddles'. Attempts have been made to authenticate the story by appealing to developments in southern Arabia by the tenth century. However, Mario Liverani encapsulates the problem in a nutshell:

> It was easy to decorate details that were otherwise authentic, but far more banal, with colourful fictional features. For examples, opening up trading links with the Yemen in the tenth century is not anachronistic; but the story of the Queen of Sheba's visit is too much like a fairy-tale in style and in use of narrative themes to be regarded as anything other than a romance from the Persian era. (Liverani 2005: 315).

A major question relating to Solomon are the Israelite relations with Egypt. Solomon is not only said to marry Pharaoh's daughter but to have received Gezer as a wedding gift from her father. Some have identified the king in question as Siamun (ca. 986–968), the next to last king of the 21st Dynasty. There are a number of arguments against this interpretation (Schipper 1999: 19–35; Ash 1999: 37–46). Briefly, a relief that some have interpreted as showing an incursion into Palestine by Siamun has probably been misinterpreted, and Siamun is not likely to have made any such expedition to the east. Although there are some destruction layers in Gezer and elsewhere in Philistia, the cause is not known, and no indications of Egyptian involvement is found in the material culture. It also seems rather unlikely that the Pharaoh would have given a *destroyed* city as a wedding gift to Solomon. Finally, the main destruction layer in Gezer is probably to be ascribed to Shoshenq I. Indeed, some argue that Shoshenq's invasion was actually during Solomon's reign rather than after his death (see the discussion at §3.1.5). As for Solomon's marriage to Pharaoh's daughter, many Egyptologists are of the opinion that it is very unlikely since it was clearly the custom for the reigning king to marry his daughters only to those within Egypt itself, not foreigners (Ash 1999: 112–19). Although some have claimed to find examples in which this was done during the Third Intermediate Period, no examples of a marriage of a reigning Egyptian king's daughter to a foreign ruler have in fact been found (Schipper 1999: 84–90). Schipper mentions two possibilities that might explain this biblical tradition (2000: that the reference was to a building, not a person, or that the person was someone from the court perhaps distantly related to the Pharaoh), but neither allows a literal reading of the biblical tradition or supports the view that Solomon was seen as an equal with the Egyptian king. As Ash concludes, 'it is best at this time to avoid placing any weight on the reports of Solomon's marriage to an Egyptian princess' (1999: 119).

3.2.5 Writing, Literacy and Bureaucracy

The Proto-Canaanite alphabet is attested as early as the fourteenth century BCE, but the standard view of its development into the Hebrew, Phoenician and Aramaic alphabets of Iron IIA is now contested. A concomitant debate concerns the development of official written texts: seals, inventories, documents, records, diaries and the like. Finally, there is the question of how early and how widespread knowledge of writing was within the wider population. (See in general Schmidt [ed.] 2015.)

B. Sass (2005) has recently re-evaluated the development of the Northwest Semitic alphabet. The conventional view had been that the latest Proto-Canaanite inscriptions were to be dated to the eleventh century, followed by the early monumental inscriptions from Byblos in the tenth century (the Ahiram sarcophagus being placed about 1000 BCE). The earliest examples of the Aramaic and Greek alphabets were also placed in the eleventh century, even though the actual evidence suggested this was two and a half centuries too early (Sass 2005: 14). Sass himself sees no problem with the relative chronology but argues that the absolute chronology should be lowered by about 250 years for many of the diagnostic inscriptions (see the chart in 2005: 73).

Currently, there is a dearth of monumental and other inscriptions that one associates with a functioning state until the ninth century. Sass (2005: 60) argues that the lack of monumental inscriptions is a reflection of the true state of affairs – there were few such inscriptions produced at that time (the lack of finds after so much archaeological work over many decades is definitive). On the other hand, administrative documents have not been found because they were probably written on perishable material. The finds of bullae that once sealed documents is one of the main indicators (Lemaire 1981; Sass 2005: 51; cf. Reich, Shukron and Lernau 2008).

The recent find of the Khirbet Qeiyafa ostracon adds to the small repertoire inscriptional material from this period but hardly changes the overall picture, contrary to some exaggerated claims made about it (for an overview, see Rollston 2011; also Galil 2009). Some argue that the site is Judahite and connected with David's kingdom (see at §3.1.1) and that the language of the inscription is Hebrew (albeit in Early Alphabetic script), connecting it with the Judahite administration. Others argue, however, that the language cannot presently be identified with Hebrew, and a number of other possibilities remain (Rollston 2011: 71–6; Na'aman 2010: 512–13). At present, the attempts at reading have not yielded much in the way of an intelligent message, with considerable differences between specialists. As Rollston notes,

> It must be stated candidly that there are no references to precise kings or particular kingdoms, nor are there precise data about specific conquests, hegemony, military officials, military movements, border disputes, national public works, building projects, monumental dedicatory acts, precise administrative activities or provisions for those in the employ of the state… Furthermore, this inscription cannot be used as the basis for claims about the levels of literacy, the spread of literacy or the literacy of non-elites… In sum, the field of scholarship must be very cautious about saddling this document with freight that it cannot readily carry. (Rollston 2011: 79)

What does all this say about the development of a bureaucracy, which in turn is usually taken as evidence of a fully fledged state? We should first be aware that a state can exist without the existence of writing (Trigger 2003: 595–8). Bureaucracy can exist without writing, and a state does not need an enormously complicated bureaucracy to be a state. Ancient Israel and Judah were not Mesopotamia or Egypt. The scribal structure needed to carry out the necessary administrative tasks might have been a fairly minimal one, with scribes trained by apprenticeship rather than in scribal schools, and the scribal office perhaps handed down from father to son (Grabbe 1995: 160–1, 173–4).

On the other hand, the kingdom of Solomon as described in the biblical text would have required an extensive bureaucracy to co-ordinate all the various governmental activities ascribed to his reign. Rather than a sophisticated administrative apparatus at the beginning of Israelite statehood (which is the picture given to us in the Bible), there are increasing signs of the spread of writing and literacy as time goes on, with the climax reached in seventh-century BCE Judah. This 'explosion of writing' has been explained as evidence of an increase in the bureaucracy (Finkelstein and Silberman 2001: 270; Stern 2001: 169). The finds indicate a greater quantity of written objects preserved from the seventh century – seals, seal impressions, ostraca and inscribed weights (Finkelstein and Silberman 2001: 270, 280–1; Stern 2001: 169–200) – seeming evidence that Judah had become a fully developed state by this time (Finkelstein and Silberman 2001: 281, 284). Thus, the sorts of written objects catalogued here do look like the type of written material that would be the product of the bureaucracy and state administration, but this was long after the tenth century.

The extent of literacy among the population has been much debated, but in order to understand ancient Judaism fully, we must keep in mind that it was mainly an oral society, like most other societies of the ancient Near East (W. V. Harris 1989; Niditch 1996; Young 1998). Although writing was known in both Egypt and Mesopotamia from about 3000 BCE, writing in many cases was quite complicated and primarily in the hands of professional scribes. Most people in the ancient world were not literate, even in cultures with an alphabetic script, and we have no indication that the Jews were any different from their Near Eastern neighbours. Ability to write one's name or decipher a seal inscription implies a different concept of literacy than the capacity to read, understand and write long documents (cf. Street 1984; Niditch 1996: 39–45). A society can know writing and still be an oral society (M. C. A. Macdonald 2005). If Jewish literacy at the turn of the era was no more than about 3–5 per cent (Hezser 2001: 496), it would have been correspondingly less in a largely peasant population in the early centuries of Northwest Semitic writing. If there had been lengthy written material, who would have read it?

All examples of writing we have from Palestine in this era are short and functional. Estimates of how early we have inscriptions in Palestine vary. N. Na'aman (1994c: 219–22) pointed out that there were no pre-eighth-century alphabetic writings in the area of Israel and Judah (except for the Gezer calendar which he suggested was probably Canaanite). The spread of alphabetic writing did not antedate the mid-eighth century, and not a single inscription has been found in Jerusalem before the late eighth century. This was more than a decade ago; things have changed but not by much. To the tenth century Renz (1995) attributes the Gezer calendar and three short inscriptions from Tel Batash, Tel 'Amal and Rosh Zayit – to which he adds two brief inscriptions from Beth-Shemesh and Tel Rehov VI. In addition to the four Arad ostraca that Renz attributes to the ninth century, along with the short inscription from Tell el-Hammah and the

Kuntillet 'Ajrud inscription, he would include two from Tel Rehov IV (see also Mazar 2007: 164). Even if there had been widespread functional literacy, there was very little written material available.

As already noted above, by the seventh century there was a significant increase in written artifacts, which has been interpreted as demonstrating a greater degree of literacy in Judah at this time. Indeed, it has been associated with the rise of the Deuteronomic movement and the promulgation of Deuteronomy under Josiah:

> The very fact that a written law code suddenly appeared at this time meshes well with the archaeological record of the spread of literacy in Judah… The report of the appearance of a definitive written text and its public reading by the king accords with the evidence for the sudden, dramatic spread of literacy in seventh-century Judah… Writing joined preaching as a medium for advancing a set of quite revolutionary political, religious, and social ideas. (Finkelstein and Silberman 2001: 280–1, 284)

I am not so sure that the inferences drawn here are justified: the increases are generally those associated with the bureaucracy and scribal bureaucrats. The increase in written material of this sort would not necessarily indicate an increase of general literacy in the population. There are also levels of literacy: the ability to read the short inscription on a seal impression or even an administrative document does not demonstrate the reading of long religious documents. If Deuteronomy was really produced at this time – a view widely held but also disputed (§3.1.6.2) – the writers were naturally literate. But it does not follow that there was greater literacy in the general population. There is no evidence of multiple copies of the document or that people were reading it for themselves; on the contrary, it was by public teaching – perhaps including public reading – that it would have been promulgated (cf. Deut. 31.10-13).

The archaeological finds of seals, seal impressions and ostraca give no support to the view that 'writing joined preaching for advancing a set of quite revolutionary political, religious, and social ideas'. Where are such ideas promulgated in the seal impressions and ostraca? Granted, the apparent move to aniconic inscriptions on seals may be a datum giving evidence of the spread of Josiah's reform. But the mere presence of aniconic seals is not an overt means of propagating the revolutionary ideals that accompanied such a reform. The move away from iconography would be a consequence of such a reform, not the vehicle for advancing it. The changes in seal impressions would probably have been noted consciously only by a very few.

The much-debated issue of schools in ancient Israel (Lemaire 1981; Millard 1985; Crenshaw 1985; 1998: 85–113; Haran 1988; Grabbe 1995: 171–4) includes two separate questions. Did schools exist to teach scribes? The answer is, possibly, but the case is not proved. Although scribes were trained in schools in ancient Egypt and Mesopotamia, the scribal needs for a small entity such as Judah could probably be met by a form of apprenticeship. The second issue is, did schools exist for general public education? The answer is definitely negative. If there were schools for others than scribes, they would have been for the wealthy and aristocratic, though these could probably afford to hire tutors. Apart from scribal schools, schools are first attested in the Greek period.

3.3 Synthesis

The context for this chapter has been the eastern Mediterranean and ancient Near East during the latter part of LB and the beginning of the Iron Age. The end of LB saw a general collapse of trade and communication, with many cities destroyed along the Mediterranean coast and sometimes further inland. The late Bronze Age had been what S. Sherratt unapologetically refers to as a period of 'globalization' (Sherratt 2003), which means that the collapse had a far-reaching effect on the various cultures in the region from about 1200 BCE. It was about this time that Egypt withdrew from Palestine, now thought by many to be about 1130 BCE. Concomitant with this was a remarkable increase in settlement in the highlands, mainly small sites. Yet the city-state system of Palestine and Syria did not come to an end as such. The rural sector certainly experienced continuity, with the peasants in the vicinity of the ruined LB cities living as they always had. Especially in the northern valleys the population remained dense. Then, in Iron I the main urban centres began to recover, including the development of trade with Phoenicia, Cyprus and beyond. In a few cases, even new city-states emerged, especially to replace those that had declined or disappeared.

It was in the time frame of this chapter that we began the history of Israel proper, for in many ways, we can say that 'Israel' begins with Merenptah. Something called Israel existed in the Palestinian region about 1200 BCE, and it appears to have been a people. Exactly where this people lived, what/who constituted it, where it got its name and its relationship to the Israel of the Bible are all questions. Some will say that the answer is obvious, but others will point out that this is not the same as proof. It has long been suggested that a number of innovations in technology took place in the central highlands: terracing, plastered cisterns, the 'Israelite house', collared-rim jars and the use of iron; also the absence of pig husbandry has been seen as significant (§§1.2.5; 3.1.1). Unfortunately, it seems there is no list of technologies or practices that is exclusive to this region and time or that can serve as 'Israelite ethnic markers'. On the contrary, it seems that a variety of ethnic groups (Hittites, Hurrians, Jebusites, Girgashites, Amorites, Shasu [?], etc.), as well as social elements (*'apiru*, Shasu [?], pastoralists settling down, peasants fleeing the lowlands, etc.), settled the hill country on both sides of the Jordan in Iron I, if our written sources are anything to go by. Some of the tribal and other groups known to us from biblical genealogies might have originated in this period, though we know that others are probably much later creations. Local leaders might have given rise to some of the stories in the book of Judges, but it is doubtful if much historical memory remains here, even if the general picture of a disunited series of autonomous (or partially autonomous) peoples is quite believable. Some still invoke the exodus tradition: although mainstream scholarship has long rejected the origin of Israel in this way, there is still a widespread view that some of the Israelites may have come from a temporary sojourn in Egypt. It can be neither proved nor disproved.

Eventually the kingdoms of Israel and Judah developed in this region. What was the process? Perhaps one important factor was a growth in population: a critical mass of settlers was reached without which certain things could not happen, but this was more significant in the north and decreased as one went south, with the area south of Jerusalem still being mainly pastoral. It seems that at some point a dominant ethnic consciousness came about in this region. Part of the reason might be by force: an 'Israelite' group might have conquered or otherwise taken over some other smaller groups and assimilated them (as suggested in Joshua and Judges). But it is doubtful if that was sufficient. Here the suggestion of Mendenhall, Gottwald and others might have some theoretical validity, even if they provided no concrete evidence: Yahwism. One of the characteristics – and constituents – of an ethnic group is a set of common myths and ideologies, which can include religion (§1.2.5; §3.2.4.4). Israelite society was long polytheistic, but Yhwh did function in some way as a national god and seems to have been the most widely honoured deity (§4.2.8). Thus, it is possible that Israel partly coalesced around Yhwh but, even if true, this would have been only one factor; it would be simplistic to suggest that this was the only factor. Indeed, we do not know for certain to what extent the hill peoples saw themselves as a single ethnic group, but the question becomes relevant if we start discussing Israel as an 'ethnic state'.

We can now ask how and why Israel and Judah developed into states, for we almost all agree that they eventually became states. The problem is that the current debate makes it difficult to come to firm conclusions about the archaeology (§3.1.1), especially with the debate over the LC (§1.2.4.4), but the archaeology does put limits on what can and cannot have happened. For many anthropologists, the formation of the Israelite and Judahite states would probably be explained from impersonal social and political forces, but others would allow a personal element into the mix, such as the presence of a dynamic charismatic leader. For example, Coote and Whitelam (1987) explain the rise of Israel as a state as due to the combination of pressure on highland resources as the population expanded and pressure from the Philistines in the lowlands. This follows a long line of scholars seeing the 'Philistine threat' as in some way pressing the Israelites into initiating a monarchy.

Yet there are some objections to these proposals. First, there is no evidence that the 'bearing capacity' of the highlands had been reached; in other words, archaeological surveys suggest that the highland population could still have been sustained by local resources without having to expand: the same population or greater could be found there in other periods (cf. Finkelstein 1999a; Broshi and Finkelstein 1992). Second, was there any impetus for the lowlanders to expand into the highlands since they also still had room to grow (Finkelstein 1998c: 24)? Thus, if there was friction between the Israelites and Philistines, it is likely to have been the Israelites who initiated it – perhaps making raids on the Philistines. But considering this explanation inadequate does not answer the question of why the highland settlements coalesced into a state.

By rights we would expect the first secondary state in Palestine to arise in the coastal plain, but here the Philistine city-states were successful, and there seems to have been no impetus to form a larger unit. The next area would be the northern region, perhaps the northern valleys or hill country. It is precisely in this area that the Omride kingdom emerged, which is one of the reasons that some scholars think this was the first Israelite state. The problem is what to do with the biblical traditions about the rise of the Israelite kingship. The idea that Israel was under divine rule but had Samuel anoint a king chosen by Yhwh is of course pure theology, not history. Should we simply dismiss the whole of the biblical account as too difficult to deal with? This is perhaps tempting, and some have certainly followed this approach. Yet more considered analyses suggest that there is history behind the stories of the 'united monarchy', even if precisely what sort of history is a matter of debate.

I believe there is sufficient evidence to assert that Saul, David and Solomon existed. Saul was evidently the first king, was primarily a military leader and was overthrown by David who subsequently met a lot of opposition, including from Judah. If anything resembling a united Israel – a territorial state – came about under David, it would have been an unusual development. One can hardly claim that it would be impossible, but it seems reasonable to conclude that in the light of all circumstances it would not be very likely. On the other hand, perhaps a city-state, much like the city-states of Shechem under Lab'aya or of Jerusalem under 'Abdi-Ḫeba, would be feasible. Much in the David tradition would be compatible with that. The archaeology does not yet support this, but most do not see the existence of a citadel of the ruler in an otherwise small settlement at Jerusalem as being contradicted by the archaeology currently available. But a Jerusalem city-state is not the same as the 'united monarchy' of the Bible. It seems unlikely that David controlled anything beyond a limited territory centred on the southern hill country and Jerusalem. This might have overlapped with territory earlier controlled by Saul, which would lead to some of the biblical traditions that made David the usurper and successor of Saul.

When all is said and done, I fail to find a major distinction between the views of I. Finkelstein and A. Mazar. Mazar states:

> It is certain that much of the biblical narrative concerning David and Solomon is mere fiction and embellishment written by later authors... I would compare the potential achievements of David to those of an earlier hill country leader, namely Labayu, the *habiru* leader from Shechem... David can be envisioned as a ruler similar to Labayu, except that he operated in a time free of intervention by the Egyptians or any other foreign power, and when the Canaanite cities were in decline. In such an environment, a talented and charismatic leader, politically astute, and in control of a small yet effective military power, may have taken hold of a large part of a small country like the Land of Israel and controlled diverse population groups under his regime from his stronghold in Jerusalem, which can be identified archaeologically. Such a regime does not necessitate a particularly large and populated capital city. David's Jerusalem can be compared to a medieval Burg, surrounded by a medium-sized town, and yet it could well be the centre of a meaningful polity. The only power that stood in David's way consisted of the Philistine cities, which, as archaeology tells us, were large and fortified urban centres during this time. Indeed the biblical historiographer excludes them from David's conquered territories. (Mazar 2007: 164–5)

Finkelstein states:

> We may still be able to identify in them [the stories of David] the action of a local chieftain who moves with his gang to the south of Hebron, in the Judean Desert and in the Shephelah, far from the control of the central government in the highlands further to the north. David takes over Hebron, the second most important Iron Age town in the highlands of Judah and the centre of his theatre of operations, and then expands to the north and conquers Jerusalem, the traditional centre of government in the southern hill country. David, according to these stories, is a typical Apiru leader, who manages to establish a new dynasty in Jerusalem. (Finkelstein 2001: 107–8)

We now come to what many consider the central question: Was there a 'united monarchy'? The question cannot be given a proper answer at this time, certainly not until the question of the LC is settled. But a partial answer can be given with some emphasis: *not as the Bible pictures it.*

Chapter 4

IRON IIB (900–720): RISE AND FALL OF THE NORTHERN KINGDOM

For the first time since the Merenptah inscription, it is in the reign of Omri that we finally begin to find extra-biblical data (apart from archaeology) with which to compare the picture given by the biblical text. Some are arguing that this is where the story of Israel begins – that Omri founded the first state in Palestine. In any case, the ninth and eighth centuries are dominated by the kingdom of Israel or Northern Kingdom.

4.1 Sources

4.1.1 Archaeology

One of the most significant areas of debate for this period is that of chronology. Because of the arguments of the LC hypothesis, some events conventionally dated to the tenth century would be in the ninth instead, if this scenario should turn out to be correct (see §1.2.4.4 for a discussion). For example, as noted earlier (§3.1.1), Finkelstein dates Hazor X to the time of Omri, or the ninth century.

The lower Galilee and the Jezreel Valley contained sites that were key to Israel in this period. Jezreel was the second main urban site in the region of Samaria, alongside the city of Samaria. There is evidence that, like Samaria, Jezreel was already settled in the tenth century BCE, before Omride rule (Zimhoni 1997; Ussishkin and Woodhead 1997: 68). The excavations there have suggested a new correlation with other contemporary sites at Megiddo and Taanach. Although it is not certain, the city gate seems to be of a six-chambered variety (Ussishkin and Woodhead 1997: 69; Ussishkin 2000: 248–50). This phase of Jezreel seems to be contemporary with Megiddo VA–IVB, with both destroyed at the same time; however, Ussishkin (2007a) argues that Megiddo VA–IVB was constructed earlier, though not long before, and was taken by Shoshenq I (though only occupied by him, not destroyed). Based on the biblical narrative the main settlement Jezreel is usually ascribed to the Omrides (1 Kgs 18.45; 21.1), but it did not last long, perhaps being destroyed in Jehu's revolt (ca. 842 BCE), but more likely by Hazael in the late ninth century (Ussishkin 2007a; Na'aman 1997b: 125–7). (For N. Franklin's views on Megiddo, Jezreel and Samaria, see below.)

Samaria is a critical site because its founding is directly associated with a historical event known from the Bible (1 Kgs 16.23-28). R. Tappy (1992, 2001) found, however, that the interpretation and dating methods used by K. Kenyon were flawed (§1.2.4.6). D. Ussishkin (2007b) points out that Omri's Palace and Inner Wall (Wall 161) belong to Kenyon's Pottery Period I, and Casemate Wall, Ostraca Building and the building in the centre to Pottery Period II (though Franklin dates the Inner Wall to Period II). Structures in Pottery Period I continued in use in Pottery Period II. Since Ussishkin thinks the 'floors' are layers of natural soil, not laid floors, he argues that the structures of Periods I and II are all contemporary and built according to a single scheme and orientation. The dating of the acropolis is based primarily on the biblical evidence, with its construction assumed to be during the reigns of Omri and Ahab. That it was a sort of capital of the Omride kings is shown by the monumental architecture, as well as numerous Hebrew ostraca of an administrative nature and also Phoenician ivory carvings.

Building on Tappy's insights, N. Franklin (2004, 2005, 2006, 2008) has come up with a radically new interpretation of the remains from Samaria. The use of Samaria as a chronological anchor is based on the biblical narrative. Building Period 0 is the earliest, including primarily rock-cut cisterns and associated wine and oil preparation areas. Two rock-cut tombs have been identified as tombs of Omride kings below the Building Period I palace. In Franklin's view Building Period I covered all of the Omride dynasty and part of Jehu's. Building Period II consisted of a new regime during which time the summit of Samaria became a strictly administrative centre. A correlation between Megiddo VA–IVB and Samaria Building Period I is indicated by mason marks in situ at Megiddo and Samaria. Megiddo Palace 1723 and Samaria I Palace use a 0.45m Egyptian cubit. Both Megiddo VA–IVB and Samaria I, on the one hand, and Megiddo IVA and Samaria Building Period II, on the other, have architectural similarities. The ground plans of Megiddo IVA and Samaria II are laid out using the Assyrian cubit of 0.495 m. These considerations all show that Megiddo IVA and Samaria II building methods were very different from the previous strata. Thus Samaria Building Period II is not a sequential addition to Building Period I. Only Samaria I is dated to the ninth century.

Finally, we come to the end of the Northern Kingdom. According to 2 Kgs 17.5-6, 23-24, the Assyrians besieged Samaria for three years before taking it and deporting all the inhabitants of the kingdom to Mesopotamia, replacing them with peoples from Mesopotamia. From an archaeological point of view there are some problems with this scenario. There is no burn layer or other evidence of destruction for Samaria, raising questions about the 2 Kgs 17.5-6 statement that Samaria was besieged for three years. As for the displacement of peoples, A. Zertal (1989; 1990: 12–14) has analysed the finds of a wedge-shaped decorated bowl from a confined area in the old territory of Manasseh. He argues that this pottery feature shows the settlement area of those Mesopotamians brought into Samaria in the late eighth century. This region, with Tell el-Far'ah (north) at its centre but with Samaria on its edge, is only a small part of the province of Samaria. If Zertal's analysis is accepted, the entire former kingdom of Samaria was not involved nor was the entire population deported. Zertal (1989: 82–3) estimates that the imported population was no more than a few thousand, and deportation affected not more than 10 per cent of the Israelite population, the vast majority of which continued to live in Samaria. How all this might relate to the text is discussed below (§4.2.7).

Almost all the regions of Ephraim were intensively settled (Finkelstein 1988–89: 151–4). Compared with Iron I, the population had shifted west, with some of the large sites in the east abandoned: Shiloh, 'Ai and Khirbit Raddana. Part of the reason seems to be the economic importance of horticulture, for which the slopes and foothills were better suited. Sufficient grain was grown in some regions, apparently, to allow the western regions to concentrate on the important wine and oil production. In the southern central range of the Ephraimite hills some sites were abandoned and a fall in the population generally in this region is probably to be explained by border conflicts and tensions between the kingdom of Israel and the kingdom of Judah. The population seems to have reached its peak in the mid-eighth century.

The Shephelah only began to be populated in Iron IIA. In Iron IIB we witness an impressive growth of settlement numbers in the whole area of Judah. This included strata IV–III of Lachish and the parallel strata in other sites. Y. Dagan (2004: 2680–1) concluded that in the Shephelah in Iron IIA and IIB the sites developed slowly as the process of Judaean settlement began, with 731 sites in Iron IIB. The prosperity of the period reached its zenith in the eighth century. The Shephelah (with about 2500 settled dunams) and Benjamin overshadowed the Judaean highlands. This ends, of course, with the massive destruction by Sennacherib in all areas south and west of Jerusalem. Lachish III is an important chronological indicator since it seems to have been destroyed by Sennacherib in 701 BCE.

As for the Judaean hills, some of the differences in interpretation were discussed above (§3.1.1). A. Ofer (1994, 2001) had argued that from the mid-eleventh to the eighth century the population nearly doubled in each century. In the ninth century this included 66 settlements covering 50 hectares; in the eighth, 88 settlements covering 90 hectares, which would mean a population of about 22,000–23,000. Any discussion of Jerusalem has to take account of the debate over the state of the city in the tenth and ninth centuries and the question of the united monarchy, which is discussed in the previous chapter (§3.1.1). Regardless of the answers, all agree that the archaeology of Jerusalem in the eighth century shows a significant city and the capital of a fully fledged state. Excavations on the Ophel show the earliest buildings there date only from the ninth century. E. Mazar had argued that the fortified complex of this area south of the Temple Mount had been constructed as early as the ninth century, but they more likely date between the eighth and the early sixth centuries BCE (Killebrew 2003: 336). E. A. Knauf (2000a) argues that the centre of the Davidic city has not been found because it would have been the area north of the Ophel, the area of the Temple Mount. Although it is not possible to test this hypothesis now, that section of the hill was a militarily strategic area and would have had to have been incorporated into any settlement on the southeastern hill. The argument that the MB wall was used as a city wall in LB, Iron I, and Iron IIA and IIB has no support; Jerusalem lacked a fortification wall until the mid-eighth century (Killebrew 2003: 334). From the late eighth century there is plenty of evidence for Jerusalem as a major urban centre.

One of the main controversies over a number of decades has to do with the size of Jerusalem in the last part of the Judahite monarchy (Geva 2003). Researchers have been divided with regard to when the fortified area expanded out of the southeastern ridge to include the southwestern hill. The 'minimalist' view was prevalent in the mid-twentieth century, while the 'maximalists' disagreed among themselves as to when expansion took place. Minimalists pointed to lack of archaeological finds on the southwestern hill, because the excavations of Kenyon and Tushingham on the eastern slope of the southwestern hill found nothing from the end of the monarchy. However, N. Avigad conducted excavations in the Jewish Quarter in 1969–82 (Avigad and Geva 2000). A significant find was a massive wall that Avigad identified with the 'Broad Wall' of Neh. 3.8. This settlement on the southwestern hill began in the mid-eighth century BCE. It was natural to associate the Broad Wall and other building activity with the reign of Hezekiah. This wall went out of use not long after it was built, and a new wall was constructed north of it in the seventh century (§5.1.1). New suburbs seem to have been established: *mišneh* (2 Kgs 22.14; Zeph. 1.10: a new residential quarter on the southwestern hill) and the *maktēš* (Zeph. 1.11: apparently the name of the central valley). Jerusalem experienced unprecedented growth, reaching 60 hectares (the southwestern hill 45). Geva gives a conservative estimate of the population in the eighth century as 6,000–7,000 (in contrast to Broshi's 20,000 [2001]). The indications are that the southwestern hill was sparsely settled, but there was also an expansion to the north. The earliest tombs to the west of the city in Ketef Hinnom and Mamilla are also dated to the eighth century (Reich and Shukron 2003: 211).

Recent excavations near the Gihon Spring have yielded some results that have been dated to the eighth century BCE (Reich, Shukron and Lernau 2008). A house was built in an abandoned pool, with the floor level created by fill presumably taken from the immediately surrounding area. The pottery from this fill was different from other late Iron pottery found in the area in a decade of digging: this pottery was more like Lachish IV or at least the early eighth century BCE and possibly the late ninth (a final verdict awaits completion of the sifting process). Four scaraboid seals, four scarabs and fragments of approximately 150 clay bullae bearing impressions were found (probably the remains from documents that had been unsealed). All are anepigraphic, but motifs include pseudo-hieroglyphs, proto-Ionic capitals, winged suns, winged griffins and an almost complete Phoenician ship. Overall, the collection points to the Phoenician realm. The large number of bullae and the seals, plus a 15-holed plaque (apparently a scribal device with a time-keeping function), point to a nearby administrative centre in the late ninth century. It might be that this shows the introduction of record-keeping and bureaucracy into Judah directly or indirectly through the services of the Omride kingdom (with its Phoenician connections).

In the Beersheba valley, it is now accepted that Arad XI and Beersheba V (with the first Iron Age fortifications in Judah) must be in the ninth century (Herzog 2001; 2002: 58–72). Herzog associates strata XI–VI with the Iron II period. Much controversy has centred around the temple on the site. The building of the temple's intial stage was associated with stratum X, which now needs to be dated to the eighth century; the second phase, with stratum IX (the stela and incense altars were used with this phase); the temple no longer existed in stratum VIII. Thus, the temple was built in the eighth century and dismantled about 715 BCE, having lasted no more than about 40 years (see further at §5.1.1). Much of strata VII and VI were removed by Hellenistic and Roman builders.

Considerable changes took place in the Beersheba valley and region during the ninth and eighth centuries (Herzog 2002: 94–9). The climate worsened at the beginning of the ninth century, which made cultivation much more difficult in this marginal region. This seems to have coincided with the establishment of a regional administrative–military centre in place of the agricultural settlements, taking in Arad XI, Beersheba V, Tel Masos I and Tel Malḥata. The population of the area nevertheless appears to have remained much the same, no more than about 1,000. A major cultural shift took place between the ninth and eighth centuries, with a completely different pottery assemblage for Arad X–XIII and Beersheba III–II. The massive fortifications of Beersheba IV and Arad XI were razed to the ground, followed by a much weaker replacement build (Herzog and Singer-Avitz 2004: 230). If the initial destruction was caused by enemy action, the replacement defences would have attempted to be at least as strong as those that had stood there before. Hence, a natural disaster such as an earthquake seems to be the cause. In the eighth century Tel 'Ira VII was resettled, and fortresses were built at Kadesh Barnea and Tell el-Kheleifeh. The settled area was twice that of the ninth century. There is also evidence for Beersheba as a 'gateway community' (supply station) for the trade route(s) from Arabia at this time (Singer-Avitz 1999).

The archaeology does confirm some textual hints at outside influences (Phoenicia, Syria, Neo-Hittite) on the Northern Kingdom (Barkay 1992: 306, 335–8). Most basic was Cypro-Phoenician pottery (Barkay 1992: 338). The ivories found in Samaria and elsewhere tend to be seen as showing Phoenician influence (Barkay 1992: 320–3). Many of the monumental and administrative buildings in the north appeared to be influenced by *bit-ḫilani* architecture known earlier from Syria (Reich 1992: 202–6; Barkay 1992: 310). Ashlar masonry (including the paving of square areas) and proto-Aeolic capitals are also often thought to be Phoenician imports (Stern 1992: 302–5).

4.1.2 Hebrew Inscriptions

The number of Hebrew inscriptions for this period is surprisingly small. This fact is one of the supports used by those who argue that writing only began to be used extensively in the latter part of the monarchy (§3.2.5). What we have are mostly ostraca (Renz 1995: I, 40–144). The main texts – those with legible text of any length – are the Kuntillet 'Ajrud inscriptions (Gogel 1998: #6.1.14) and the Samarian ostraca (Gogel 1998: #6.1.21; *TSSI* #1; Lemaire 1977). The former are mainly of religious interest and are discussed below in that context (§4.2.8). The Samarian ostraca are usually dated to the early eighth century and explained as administrative documents relating to wine and oil brought into the city from outside

(Kaufman 1992). H. M. Niemann (2007) has recently explained them differently: they document attempts by Jehoash and Jeroboam II to integrate the traditional tribal links into their personal power network. It was the practice to have elite members of the clans reside as 'honoured guests' in Samaria for shorter or longer periods of time, stabilizing political links between the Samarian king (warlord) and the surrounding clans. Wine and oil were sent from their local constituents to the clan members residing in Samaria, and the ostraca are to be explained as receipts for these goods. The ostraca are an important source of data on names of people in ancient Israel.

A recent object of controversy is the so-called Jehoash inscription. This was not found in a proper archaeological context but appeared on the antiquities market, the provenance and acquisition history unknown. The owner of the object was taken to court by the Israel Antiquities Authority, but the judge eventually ruled that forgery by the owner was unproved, though he admitted that the court could not pronounce it authentic, according to news reports. One professional geological analysis found signs of a modern forgery (Goren et al. 2004), but another professional group (Rosenfeld et al. 2009) found no such indications but concluded that the inscription had an apparent age of about the third century BCE (long after the time of Jehoash but still ancient); yet they attempted to explain how a tablet originally from the eighth century BCE might acquire the characteristics dating it 500 years later. However, analysis by philologists has created a scholarly consensus that the inscription is a modern forgery whose language shows signs of a speaker of modern Hebrew (Greenstein 2012), a conclusion accepted here. Hence, this will not be used as a source. For a general discussion on forgeries, see §1.2.4.8.

4.1.3 Aramaic Inscriptions

4.1.3.1 Tel Dan

Perhaps one of the most interesting texts is the one recently found at Tel Dan, which already has a considerable bibliography (Athas 2003; Kottsieper 2007). The following is my reading of the first fragment found in 1993 (Biran and Naveh 1993) with a minimum of reconstruction:

] my father went up [
my father lay down (died?). He went to [Is-]
rael earlier in the land. My father [(or 'in the land of my father')
I – Hadad went before me [
x my king. And I killed of [them chari-]
ot and thousands (or 2000) of riders [
king of Israel. And I kill[ed

xx 'house of David' (*bytdwd*). And I set [
xx the land. They x[
another, and xxxx [ki-
ng over Is[rael
siege over [

The second fragment (actually two fragments that fit together) does not clearly join onto the first, and the reconstruction based on putting the two together strikes me as purely speculative (cf. Athas 2003: 175–91). I read the second fragment as follows, with little hypothetical reconstruction:

] and cut [
] battle/fought against xx [
]x and went up the king x [
] and Hadad made king [
] I went up from Sheva'/seven [
seven]ty tied/harnessed x[
]rm son [
]yahu son [

This inscription has been subject to a number of interpretations, some of which are quite compelling, but they rely generally on the reconstruction of the original editors. However, it does seem to me that in the last two lines above, the restoration of 'J(eh)oram' is virtually certain, and of 'Ahaziah' quite reasonable. If so, this favours assigning the inscription to Hazael and the interpetations that follow from it. Finally, there have been some isolated doubts about the authenticity of one or more of the fragments, but these have not been convincing (Athas 2003: 22–35, 70–2).

4.1.3.2 Melqart Inscription

This is dated to the ninth or early eighth century BCE. A number of the older readings must now be discarded in the light of recent study. It mentions 'Bir-Ha[dad], son of 'Attar-hamek, king of Aram' (Pitard 1988: 272; cf. Puech 1992).

4.1.3.3 Zakkur Inscription

The Zakkur Inscription is dated to about 800 BCE.

> The monument which Zakkur, king of Hamath and Lu'ash, set up for El-wer [in Apish]… Bar-Hadad, son of Hazael, king of Aram, united against me s[even]teen kings: Bar-Hadad and his army, Bar-Gush and his army, the king of Que and his army, the king of 'Amuq and his army, the king of Gurgum and his army, the king of Sam'al and his army, the king of Meliz and his army [ ] seven[teen], they and their armies. (*CoS* II,155 [text 2.35])

4.1.4 Mesha Stela

The importance of the Mesha Stela or the Moabite stone has long been recognized. The exact date of the inscription is difficult because it depends largely on assumptions about the historical context (Lemaire 1994a, 1994b; Na'aman 2007a). For the purposes of this exercise, we cannot take that context for granted; however, the text is likely to date from the ninth or eighth century BCE. Only lines 1–9 are given here:

> I am Mesha, the son of Kemosh[-yatti], the king of Moab, the Dibonite. My father was king over Moab for thirty years, and I was king after my father. And I made this high-place for Kemosh in Karchoh, [...] because he has delivered me from all kings(?), and because he has made me look down on all my enemies. Omri was the king of Israel, and he oppressed Moab for many days, for Kemosh was angry with his land. And his son succeeded him, and he said – he too – 'I will oppress Moab!' In my days did he say [so], but I looked down on him and on his house, and Israel has gone to ruin, yes, it has gone to ruin for ever! And Omri had taken possession of the whole la[n]d of Medeba, and he lived there (in) his days and half the days of his son, forty years, but Kemosh [resto]red it in my days. And I built Baal Meon, and I made in it a water reservoir, and I built Kiriathaim. (*CoS* II, 137 [text 2.23])

The historical implications are discussed in some detail below (§4.2.4).

4.1.5 Assyrian Sources

In the Kurkh Monolith which details Shalmaneser III's campaign in his sixth year (853 BCE), he describes the force that met him after he had worked his way as far as Qarqar on the Orontes in northern Syria:

> 1,200 chariots, 1,200 cavalry, 20,000 footsoldiers of Adad-idri 'of Aram-Damascus ([*šá* KUR]-ANŠE-*šú*)'; 700 chariots, 700 cavalry, 10,000 footsoldiers of Irhuleni, 'the Hamathite (KUR *A-mat-a-a*)'; 2,000 chariots [2 LIM GIŠ.GIGIR.MEŠ], 10,000 footsoldiers of Ahab ([m]*A-ha-ab-bu*) 'the Israelite (KUR *Sir-'-la-a-a*)'...these 12 kings, he brought as his allies. They came against me to [wage] war and fight. In the exalted might which Ashur my lord gave me (and) with the strong weapons which Nergal, who goes before me, presented to me, I fought with them. I defeated them from Qarqar to Gilzau. I slew 14,000 of their soldiers with the weapons (and) rained, like the god Adad, the destructive flood upon them. (Yamada 2000: 156–7, 162)

The Baghdad Text (Grayson 1996: 32–41 [A.0.102.6]) and the Calah Annals (Grayson 1996: 42–8 [A.0.102.8]) indicate that the coalition continued to oppose the Assyrians successfully for many years – Shalmaneser's 10th year: opposed by Hadadezer of Damascus, Irḫulēnu of Hamath, together with a coalition of twelve kings; 11th year: opposed by Hadadezer, Irḫulēnu, together with a coalition of twelve kings; 14th year: Shalmaneser has an army of 120,000; opposed by Hadadezer, Irḫulēnu, together with a coalition of twelve kings. However, in his 18th year, the situation is different (Aššur Basalt Statue):

> I defeated Adad-idri of Damascus with 12 kings, his helpers, and laid down 29,000 of his brave fighters like reeds. The remainder of his army, I cast into the Orontes river. They fled to save their life. Adad-idri died. Hazael, son of a nobody [DUMU *la ma-ma-na*], took the throne. He mustered his large army and came against me to wage war. I fought with him and defeated him (and) took off the wall of his camp. Hazael fled to save his own life. I pursued (him) as far as Damascus, his royal city. (Yamada 2000: 188–9; cf. also Grayson 1996: 118 [A.0.102.40: i 14–35]; *ANET* 280)

The Kurba'il Statue gives some similar information but also adds data not in the other inscriptions:

> In my eighteenth regnal year, I crossed the Euphrates for the sixteenth time, Hazael of Damascus trusted in the massed might of his troops; and he mustered his army in great numbers… I decisively defeated him. I felled with the sword 16,000 of his men-of-arms. I took away from him 1,121 of his chariots, 470 of his cavalry, together with his camp. In order to save his life he ran away. I pursued after him. I confined him in Damascus, his royal city… At that time I received the tribute of the Tyrians, the Sidonians, and Jehu (*Ia-ú-a*), (the man) of Bīt-ḫumrî (Omri). (*CoS* II, 268; cf. also Grayson 1996: 60 [A.0.102.12: 21-30])

On the designation of Jehu as DUMU [m]*ḫu-um-ri-i*, often translated as 'son of Omri', see below (§4.2.3).

Shalmaneser's successor, Shamshi-Adad V (823–811), had to deal with a rebellion that had begun under Shalmaneser III, and the west of the empire was more or less abandoned during his reign. As will be seen below, this left the opportunity for Damascus to have a free hand against its neighbours. (It is widely thought that Šamši-Adad and his mother formed the basis of the Nimrod and Semiramis legend [Grabbe 2003b: 122–5].) The next king, Adad-Narari III (810–783), had a long reign with important campaigns to both the east and the west.

He renewed campaigns to Syria and the Mediterranean (ca. 805–796), though the number of campaigns is uncertain. According to the el-Rimah inscription,

> In one year I subdued the entire lands Amurru (and) Ḫatti. I imposed upon them tax (and) tribute forever. I (text 'he') received 2000 talents of silver, 1000 talents of copper, 2000 talents of iron, 3000 linen garments with multi-coloured trim – the tribute from Mari, the Damascene. I (text 'he') received the tribute of Joash (*Iu'asu*), the Samaritan, (and) of the people of Tyre (and) Sidon. (Grayson 1996: 211 [A.0.104.7.4-8]; cf. Page 1968: 143; *ANET* 281–2)

'Iu-'a-su of Samaria (*Sa-me-ri-na-a-a*) [var. land of Omri (*ḫu-um-ri-i*)]' is almost certainly Joash of Israel (M. Weippert 1978, which corrects the view expressed by McCarter [1974] that *Iuasu* should be taken as Jehu). More difficult is Mari of Damascus. *Mari* can be simply the Aramaic title, 'my lord' rather than a personal name. It has been suggested that the Assyrians referred to the Aramaean leader by this term because they were uncertain as to who he was (Lipiński 2000: 390–1). The Arslan Tash ivory might suggest that this was Hazael: '[]xx *'m'* to our lord (*mr'n*) Hazael in the year [of the tak]ing of Ḥ[]' (Puech 1981: 544–62). A similar message is found on the Hazael booty inscriptions which seems to read something along the line of the following: 'That which Hadad (?) gave to our lord (*mr'n*) Hazael from Umeq in the year that our lord crossed over the river' (Eph'al and Naveh 1989: 192–200; also Lipiński 2000: 388). The name in the Eretria horse-blinder inscription seems to have a *b* as the last letter of the name, though this could be a scribal idiosyncracy. Others, however, would identify Mari with Bar-Hadad son of Hazael (Pitard 1987: 165–6; Millard and Tadmor 1973: 63 n. 22; Kuan 1995: 81 n. 46).

The next 40 years (782–745 BCE) are rather obscure in Assyrian history. The period seems to be characterized by weak rulers and strong officials. Military campaigns were not always led by the king, and there were non-campaign years. It was basically a time of contracting borders and major problems with Urartu, with the Assyrians losing their hold on the west. However, the *tartanu* (vice-regent) Šamši-Ilu was an important figure in the region. The Maras Museum inscription describes how he took tribute from Damascus in the time of Shalmaneser IV (782–773 BCE):

> When Šamši-ilu, the field marshal, marched to Damascus, the tribute of Ḫadiiāni, the Damascene – silver, gold, copper, his royal bed, his royal couch, his daughter with her extensive dowry, the property of his palace without number – I received from him (Ḫadiiāni). On my return (from Damascus) I gave this boundary stone to Ušpilulume, king of the Kummuḫites. (Grayson 1996: 240 [A.0.105.1.4-13])

Tiglath-pileser III (744–727 BCE) was probably a usurper. Little building activity seems to have taken place because of the extensive campaigns. The three-fold system of vassalage was perfected under Tiglath-pileser. Campaigns to the west took place in 743, 738 and through the period 734–732. Annals 19* (lines 9–11) mention the rebellion of Azriyau in 738 BCE:

> 19 districts of Hamath together with the cities of their environs, which are on the seacoast of the west, which in rebellion were seized for Azriyau, I annexed to Assyria. I placed two of my eunuchs over them as governors. (Tadmor 1994: 62–3)

This Azriyau was early identified with Azariah (= Uzziah) of Judah (2 Kgs 15.1-7), partly based on the mistaken assumption that another Assyrian inscription referred to 'Azriyau of Yaudi' (Tadmor 1961; 1994: 273–4). This identification has been largely abandoned, partly because Azriyau's country is not known and partly because the coalition led by Azriyau seems to be made up of states in the area of central and northern Syria (Kuan 1995: 149 n. 57).

Tiglath-pileser III's tribute list in the Calah Annals 13* and 14* tells of the tribute collected about 738–737 BCE (Annal 13*, line 10, to 14*, line 5):

> The tribute of Kushtashpi of Kummuh, Rezin (Rahianu) of Damascus, Menahem of Samaria, Hiram of Tyre, Sibittibi'il of Byblos, Urikki of Que, Pisiris of Carchemish, Eni-il of Hamath, Panammu of Sam'al…I received. (Tadmor 1994: 69–71)

Summary Inscription 4 (lines 7–20) describes the final destruction of Damascus and the change of king in Israel (ca. 732 BCE):

> The ent[ire] wide land of [Bit-Haza'i]li (Aram) I annexed to Assyria. [I plac]ed [x eunuchs over them] as governors. Hanunu of Gaza, [who] fle[d before] my weapons, (and) escaped [to] Egypt – Gaza [...his royal city, I conquered/entered] his property (and) his gods [I despoiled/seized. A (statue) bearing the image of the gods my lo]rds and my (own) royal image [out of gold I fashioned.] In the palace [of Gaza] I set (it) up (and) I counted it among the gods of their land; [their…] I established. As for [him (i.e. Hanunu), the fear of my majesty] overwhelmed him and like a bird he flew (back) [from Egypt] […] I returned him to his position and his […I turned into an Assyrian emporium. Gold,] silver, multi-coloured garments, linen garments, large [horses,]… […] I received. The land of Bit-Humria (Israel), […its] 'auxiliary army', […] all of its people, […] I carried off [to] Assyria.

> Peqah, their king [I/they killed] and I installed Hoshea [as king] over them. 10 talents of gold, x talents of silver, [with] their [property] I received from them and [to Assyria I car]ried them. As for Samsi, the queen of the Arabs, at Mount Saqurri I de[feated 9,400] (of her people). (Tadmor 1994: 138–41)

The actual siege of Damascus is described in Tiglath-pileser III's Calah Annals 23. Summary Inscription 7 also tells us that Jehoahaz king of Judah (^{m}*Ia-ú-ha-zi* ^{kur}*Ia-ú-da-a+a*) paid tribute about this time (reverse, lines 10′–12′):

> 10′ [Ma]tanbi'il of Arvad, Sanipu of Ammon, Salamanu of Moab, [......]
> 11′ [Mi]tinti of Ashkelon, Jehoahaz of Judah, Qaushmalaka of Edom, Muṣ... [...of......]
> 12′ (and) Hanunu of Gaza... (Tadmor 1994: 170–1)

The fall of Samaria is actually claimed by two kings. First is Shalmaneser V (726–722 BCE) who apparently as crown prince had acted as chief administrator while his father was campaigning. Little is known of him apart from his siege of Samaria, as recorded in *Babylonian Chronicle 1* (i 27–31):

> On the twenty-fifth day of the month Tebet Shalmaneser (V) ascended the throne in Assyria <and Akkad>. He ravaged *Samaria.* The fifth year: Shalmaneser (V) died in the month Tebet. For five years Shalmaneser (V) ruled Akkad and Assyria. On the twelfth day of the month Tebet Sargon (II) ascended the throne in Assyria. (Grayson 1975: 73)

The editor has put 'Samaria' in italics, but it seems to be agreed by consensus that the ^{uru}*Šá-ma/ba-ra-'-in* of the text should be so read. However, Sargon II claims in his *Annals* to have conquered Samaria:

> In the begin[ning of my reign when I took (my) seat on the royal throne and was crowned with a lordly crown, the Sama]rians, [who agreed with (another) hostile king not to continue their slavery and not to deliver tribute and who started hostility in the strength of......who b]ring about my triumph, [I fought] w[ith them and completed their defeat. 27280 (or 27290) people, who lived therein, with their chariots, I] carried off (as) spoil. 50 chariots (for) my royal bodyguard [I mustered from among them and the rest of them I settled in the midst of Assyria (= Assyria proper). The city of Samaria I re]settled and made it greater than before. People of the lands conque[red by my own hand (= by myself) I brought there. My courtier I placed over them as governor and duties and] tax I imposed upon them as on Assyrians. (Tadmor 1958b: 34)

The Nimrud Prism, which is better preserved, is parallel and gives similar information (Tadmor 1958b: 34).

4.1.6 Phoenician History of Menander of Ephesus

Unfortunately, we have little historical material on Phoenicia, and what little there is comes mainly from classical writers. Menander of Ephesus is alleged to have written a *Phoenician History* using ancient records. A relevant passage for purposes of this paper is the following:

> This rainless time is also mentioned by Menander in his account of the acts of Ithōbalos, the king of Tyre, in these words: 'There was a drought in his reign, which lasted from the month of Hyperberetaios until the month of Hyperberetaios in the following year. But he made supplication to the gods, whereupon a heavy thunderstorm broke out. He it was who founded the city of Botrys in Phoenicia, and Auza in Libya.' This, then, is what Menander wrote, referring to the drought which came in Achab's reign, for it was in his time that Ithōbalos was king of Tyre. (Quoted by Josephus, *Ant.* 8.13.2 §324.)

There are many questions. What was his source? Was it a genuine Phoenician one or simply another Greek writer? Was the source (if there was one) in Greek or Phoenician? Who made the connection with the father of Jezebel, Josephus or his source?

A Phoenician sarcophagus inscription from Byblos may have some useful information: 'The sarcophagus that 'Ittoba'l, son of 'Ahirom, the king of Byblos, made for 'Ahirom, his father, when he placed him in eternity' (*CoS* II, 181 [text 2.55]). Exactly when to date this can only be guessed. The name of the son is the same as the father of Jezebel, but was this only a common name for Phoenician kings? This individual is king of Byblos, not Tyre, though Sidon may have been a general term for 'Phoenician' by outside writers at the time.

4.1.7 Biblical Text

Unlike Chapters 2 and 3 where large amounts of text are covered, only a few chapters are involved here; therefore, a more detailed outline of contents is presented. Because the books of Chronicles focus on Judah, parallels in 2 Chronicles to the Ahab story are only sporadic. They are listed where they occur, but this is not very often. (See further Grabbe 2016.)

4.1.7.1 1 Kings 16.15–2 Kings 17.41 (2 Chronicles 18–28): Outline of the Contents

1 Kgs 16.15-28: The reign of Omri.

16.15-20: Zimri reigns seven days in Tirzeh after a coup but is defeated by the army commander Omri and commits suicide.

16.21-22: The people are split between Omri and Tibni, but Omri defeats and kills the latter.

16.23-24: Omri reigns 12 years, buys a hill and founds the city of Samaria.

16.25-28: Omri's reign is given a theological summary without additional information.

1 Kgs 16.29-34: A theologizing summary of Ahab's reign.

16.29-33: Ahab reigns 22 years, marries Jezebel and worships Baal, building a temple to Baal in Samaria.

16.34: Hiel builds Jericho at the expense of his first born and youngest sons.

1 Kgs 17–19: Various tales centring on Elijah the prophet/man of God.

17.1-6: Elijah declares a famine to Ahab, then hides where he is fed by ravens.

17.7-16: Elijah lives with a widow where they are fed miraculously.

17.17-24: Elijah heals/raises to life the son of the widow.

18.1-46: Elijah's contest with the prophets of Baal and the end of the drought.

19.1-14: Elijah flees to Horeb from the wrath of Jezebel.

19.15-18: Elijah is sent to anoint Hazael, Jehu and Elisha.

19.19-21: Elisha leaves his farming to follow Elijah.

1 Kgs 20: Ahab and the attack of the Aramaeans.

20.1-21: Ben-Hadad threatens Ahab but is defeated by Israel at the word of a prophet.

20.22-30: The prophet warns of a second invasion, but the Aramaeans are defeated at the word of a man of God.

20.31-34: Ben-Hadad surrenders to Ahab who spares his life; Ben-Hadad promises to return the towns taken from Ahab's father by his father, and to let Israel set up bazaars in Damascus as his father did in Samaria.

20.35-43: A prophet has himself wounded and appears to Ahab as a sign of his error in releasing Ben-Hadad.

1 Kgs 21: Ahab and Naboth's vineyard.

21.1-16: Ahab takes Naboth's vineyard.

21.17-26: Elijah prophesies against Ahab and his house.

21.27-29: Ahab repents and the prophecy against him is postponed to his son's time.

1 Kgs 22//2 Chron. 18: Story of Ahab's death.

22.1-5//18.1-4: Ahab asks Jehoshaphat for help in retaking Ramothgilead.

22.6-28//18.5-27: Prophets are consulted, including Micaiah who prophesies defeat for Ahab.

22.29-38//18.28-34: Ahab is killed in battle, fulfilling Yhwh's word.

22.39-40: Summary of Ahab's reign, including the 'ivory house' that he built.

22.41-51//20.31–21.3: Summary of Jehoshaphat's reign, including his 'righteousness' and his failed plan to send ships of Tarshish to Ophir for gold.

22.52-54: Ahaziah son of Ahab becomes king and reigns two years.

2 Kgs 1: Ahaziah dies at the word of Elijah for enquiring of Baal-Zebub (most of the chapter concerns the efforts to get Elijah to come and visit the king on his sick bed).

2 Kgs 2: Elijah is taken to heaven and Elisha assumes his mantle.

2 Kgs 3: Coalition of kings attack Moab.

3.1-3: Jehoram becomes king over Israel.

3.4-9: Mesha the king of Moab rebels against Jehoram who assembles a coalition of Israel, Judah and Edom.

3.9-20: The kings are delivered from lack of water by Elisha.

3.21-27: Moab is defeated but Israel withdraws after Mesha sacrifices the crown prince.

2 Kgs 4.1–8.15: tales about Elisha.

4.1-44: Various tales of Elisha.

5.1-27: Elisha heals Naaman the Aramaean commander.

6.1-7: Elisha makes an axehead float.

6.8-23: Elisha delivers the Aramaean army into the king of Israel's hand, and the Aramaeans stop invading the land of Israel.

6.24–7.20: Ben-Hadad besieges Samaria, but the Aramaeans flee and the city is delivered through Elisha.

8.1-6: Elisha helps the woman whose son he had revived.

8.7-15: Elisha prophesies that Hazael will replace the ill Ben-Hadad, and the former assassinates the latter.

2 Kgs 8.16-24//2 Chron. 21.4-11; 21.20–22.1: Summary of the reign of Joram son of Jehoshaphat over Judah: he marries Athaliah, daughter of Ahab; Edom gains its independence at this time.

2 Kgs 8.25-29//2 Chron. 22.2-6: Joram of Judah dies and his son Ahaziah reigns; Joram of Israel fights alongside Ahaziah against Hazael and the Aramaeans at Ramoth-Gilead and is wounded.

2 Kgs 9–10: Jehu stages a coup and takes the throne.

9.1-14: Elisha sends a disciple to anoint Jehu king in Ramoth-Gilead.

9.15-29//22.7-9: Jehu kills Joram of Israel and Ahaziah of Judah.

9.30-37: Jehu kills Jezebel.

10.1-11: Jehu causes Ahab's offspring to be killed.
10.12-14: Relatives of Ahaziah are killed.
10.15-17: Jehu takes Jehonadab the Rechabite to witness his slaughter of the rest of Ahab's house.
10.18-28: Jehu slaughters the worshippers of Baal and removes Baal worship from Israel.
10.29-31: Yet Jehu does not follow the Torah or remove worship at Bethel and Dan.
10.32-33: Hazael takes Israelite land east of the Jordan.
10.34-36: Summary of Jehu's reign.

2 Kgs 11–12//2 Chron. 22.10-24.14: Coup of Joash and his reign over Judah.
11.1-20//22.10–23.21: Execution of Athaliah and the installation of Joash on the throne in Jerusalem.
12.1-17//24.1-14: Joash has money collected to repair Yhwh's house.
12.18-19: Hazael of Aram comes against Jerusalem, but Joash buys him off.
12.20-22: Joash's death and summary of his reign.

2 Kgs 13.1-9: Reign of Jehoahaz son of Jehu.
13.1-2: Summary of Jehoahaz's reign.
13.3: Israel afflicted by Hazael and Ben-Hadad of Aram.
13.4-6: Israel gains freedom from Aram despite remaining in the sins of Jeroboam.
13.7: Jehoahaz had been left with only a small military force.
13.8-9: Jehoahaz's death and summary of his reign.
2 Kgs 13.10-25: Reign of Jehoash of Israel.
13.10-13: Summary of Jehoash's reign.
13.14-19: Elisha on his death bed offers to Jehoash a sign of defeat of Aram.
13.20-21: Death of Elisha and resurrection of corpse by his bones.
13.22-25: Jehoash son of Jehoahaz begins to recover territory from Ben-Hadad.

2 Kgs 14.1-22//2 Chron. 25.1–26.2: Reign of Amaziah of Judah.
14.1-6//25.1-4: How he was righteous (though he did not remove the country shrines).
14.7//25.5-16: Defeat of the Edomites (version in 2 Chronicles is greatly expanded, with anecdotes about prophets).
14.8-14//25.17-24: Challenges Jehoash of Israel to battle and is defeated and Jerusalem sacked.
14.15-16: Death of Jehoash of Israel and summary of his reign.
14.17-20//25.25-28: Amaziah is assassinated in a conspiracy; summary of his reign.
14.21-22//26.1-2: Azariah (Uzziah) made king of Judah; restores Elath (Eloth) to Judah.

2 Kgs 14.23-29: Jeroboam becomes king of Israel; restores territory from Lebo-Hamath to the sea of Arabah, including Damascus and Hamath, according to the word of Jonah.
2 Kgs 15.1-7//26.3-23: Reign of Azariah (Uzziah) who is righteous but becomes a leper.
2 Kgs 15.8-12: Zechariah becomes king of Israel but is assassinated, as last of Jehu dynasty.
2 Kgs 15.13-15: Shallum reigns one month.
2 Kgs 15.16-22: Menahem is king over Israel; Pul of Assyria invades and Menahem gives him 10,000 talents.
2 Kgs 15.23-26: Reign of Pekahiah of Israel.
2 Kgs 15.27-31: Reign of Pekah of Israel; Tiglath-pileser invades and takes northern Israel.
2 Kgs 15.32-38//2 Chron. 27.1-9: Reign of Jotham of Judah; attacked by Rezin of Aram and Pekah.
2 Kgs 16//2 Chron. 28: Reign of Ahaz of Judah.
    16.1-4//28.1-4: Theologizing summary of Ahaz's reign.
    16.5-9//28.5-19: Syro-Ephraimite war.
    16.10-16//28.20-27: Ahaz makes an altar like the one of Tiglath-pileser in Damascus.
2 Kgs 17: Fall of Samaria.

4.1.7.2 Analysis

Any modern historians worth their salt would immediately recognize that not all the material in the biblical text is of the same quality. First, leaving aside for the moment the long tradition of source and redaction criticism among biblical scholars, a careful reading of this lengthy stretch of text will still detect that along with narratives giving the impression of describing unfolding events are other sorts of material that look distinctly legendary. This especially applies to stories in which the chief protagonist is a prophet. Thus, whereas the reign of Omri is described succinctly and with the prima facie appearance of factuality, the reign of Ahab is dominated by stories about the prophets Elijah and Elisha. A second point that would be obvious to a modern historian is that here and there are theological summaries and that the overall perspective is one of theological judgment (e.g., the success and failure of kings is according to whether they have been 'righteous' or 'wicked' according to the religious code of the writer). Moral judgment on rulers is not in itself unusual in ancient writings, including the Greek historians. Nevertheless, it would be noticeable to a modern historian and would need to be taken account of (see further Grabbe 2001b).

In fact, if we look carefully at the material stretching from 1 Kings 16 to 2 Kings 17, we see few passages of any length that seem to be staight-forward narratives. On the contrary, the whole section is dominated by prophetic stories or theological interests. For example, an entire chapter is devoted to the reign of Joash of Judah (2 Kgs 12), yet most of the space concerns how money was collected for the repair of the house of Yhwh. There is little from 1 Kings 17 to 2 Kings 9 that does not relate to Elijah and Elisha. Much of this long section of 15 chapters is a series of prophetic stories and anecdotes. Some of these relate to national events, but a good deal is purely focused on the doings of the prophet.

We have one new development, however, which is very important for the question of historicity. Beginning with the narrative of the 'divided monarchy' the DtrH seems to make use of a new source: a 'Chronicle of the Kings of Judah' (Grabbe 2006b). Considering the widespread evidence for such chronicles in the ancient Near East, it seems unlikely that the author was inventing fictitious sources. The 'Chronicle of the Kings of Judah' seems to have provided the framework for the 'divided monarchy', but it was supplemented by much other material. The data that might have come from a chronicle are not extensive and could be explained as coming from a fairly concise chronicle such as we find in Mesopotamia.

The text refers to both the 'Chronicle of the Kings of Israel' and the 'Chronicle of the Kings of Judah', and it has usually been assumed that the author used two sources, which he synchronized himself. I have proposed that it is not necessary to assume two chronicles since all the chronicle data in 1 and 2 Kings could have come from a single chronicle, the 'Chronicle of the Kings of Judah'. The synchronic data about the kings of Israel would have been present in the 'Chronicle of the Kings of Judah'. This chronicle had several characteristics:

- Basic accession data but also including the name of the king's mother.
- Data on its main neighbour and rival, the kingdom of Israel, including the synchronic data.
- Brief notes on major events in the king's reign. These were not necessarily stereotyped but could include a wide variety of data relating to the military, politics, building activities, personal matters relating to the king (e.g., major illnesses) and the cult. This was not according to a rigid formula.

As will be seen, some of the other sources may sometimes have contained reliable historical data, but most of the data in the text confirmed by external data as reliable could have come from such a chronicle. This means that the bulk of the DtrH's text is not of great value for historical events, though it can be of use for sociological study and of course for literary, theological and other non-historical disciplines of the Hebrew Bible. The use of stereotyped and formulaic language is not unusual in chronicles, but it is a way of organizing data, not necessarily of distorting it. So far, there is good evidence that the chronicle-type material in 1 and 2 Kings is fairly reliable (see further at §4.3).

4.2 Analysis

4.2.1 Dividing of the Kingdom (1 Kings 12–14)

The death of Solomon and the ascension of Rehoboam to the throne marks a major watershed in the narrative of the Israelite monarchy. According to the surface picture of the biblical story, a single nation of Israel split into two rival nations. More careful consideration of the geo-political facts, as well as a number of biblical passages that are easily overlooked, shows that the union of two ethnic groups under David was an artificial one (§3.2.4.2). Judah had originally been separate from the other tribes and was only temporarily united into one nation with Israel under David. Thus, rather than a split as such, this was really a reversion to an older situation. Perhaps the surprising fact is that they stayed together for so long. The two nations of course shared a good deal of culture and history, but they were not naturally one nation and did not stay that way for long.

Whatever his faults, Solomon managed to keep the country together throughout his monarchy. Thus, although there had not been a United Monarchy as depicted in the biblical text, a union of sorts had been effected by David and kept in place by his successor. Yet Solomon had evidently got the backs up of many people because of his administrative burdens; one can assume that heavy taxes was one of these. We know about these tensions from the demands made by the people to Rehoboam, 'Your father made harsh our yoke: now if you lighten your father's hard service and the heavy yoke that he imposed on us, we shall serve you' (1 Kgs 12.4). According to the biblical story, Rehoboam ignored the advice of the elders, which was to accommodate the reasonable demands of the people, and followed the advice of his young advisors who wanted him to give a brutal reply to them. Although we cannot be confident of the details, the split of the kingdom back into Judah and Israel after Solomon's death seems to be correctly remembered by the text. The rule of Solomon's son Rehoboam was accepted by Judah, but Israel chose to go with Jeroboam as ruler: he is represented as having been in charge of corvée labour during part of Solomon's reign. (On Jeroboam, see Grabbe forthcoming.)

4.2.2 Rulers of Judah and Israel to Omri (1 Kings 15.1–16.20)

Under the rule of Abijam, son of Rehoboam, in Jerusalem, the war with Jeroboam, begun under his father, continued. Otherwise, much of his rule is a blank. We do not even know whether his successor Asa was his son or his brother: 1 Kgs 15.8 says Asa was Abijam's son, but his mother was the same as Abijam's (1 Kgs 15.10; the words for 'father' [*'āv*] and 'brother' [*'āḥ*] are similar in Hebrew).

The short description of Asa's reign focuses on his righteousness, but the question is how much of the data might have come from an official chronicle, as opposed to the contribution of the Deuteronomist who was interpreting any information from a source and also making theological statements and judgments. The following *could* have come from an official annal, because they are the sort of things that a court chronicle might well record:

- Deposed the queen mother (Maacah who was his mother or possibly his grandmother).
- Deposited his father's and his own votive objects in the temple.
- Bribed the Aramaean Bar-Hadad son of Tabrimmon son of Hezion to attack Israel (so Baasha would cease to build Ramah that blocked movement from Judah to the north).
- Built Geba and Mizpah of Benjamin.
- Had an ailment in his feet.

The removal of the queen mother is a unique event in biblical history, partly because it is the only passage talking about a queen mother. If the queen mother had an official function in the Judahite monarchy, we have no information on it. According to the Deuteronomist's theological interpretation, she was removed from office because she made a cult object for Asherah. This appears prima facie unlikely, since it has recently become acknowledged that according to Israelite belief Yhwh had a female consort Asherah (§4.2.8). This female 'partner' was eventually dropped, but that apparently did not happen until the seventh century, several centuries after Asa. Thus, the statement that the queen mother was removed because of making an Asherah cult object is likely to be a Deuteronomistic interpretation rather than information from a chronicle. The same judgment applies to Asa's removing the *qᵉdēšîm* from the land. This term has often been translated as 'male cult prostitute', but this is now generally rejected: there is little or no evidence of cult prostitution (whether male or female) in Canaanite religion, as was once assumed. (On these points relating to religion, see further at §4.2.8.)

The information on bribing Bar-Hadad looks more authentic. The question is whether Israelite territory extended this far north at that time. Thus, the Deuteronomist might have had useful information, but it is also possible that he is creating a scenario from knowledge of Israelite territory at a later time. Our problem is that our knowledge of the Aramaean kingdoms that dominated Syrian history in the first millennium BCE is defective, which often makes difficult judging biblical statements on the question. There is also the matter of Asa's defeating Zerah the Cushite ('Ethiopian'), though this episode is found only in 2 Chron. 14.8-14 and is absent from 1 Kings. Some have tried to defend this as authentic even though the DtrH of Kings knows nothing about it. It was once suggested that 'Zerah' was a reflex of the name of Pharaoh Osorkon I who lived about this time, but Egyptian philologists now refute any connection between the names. The name is neither Nubian nor Egyptian but biblical: Gen. 36.17; Josh. 7.1; 1 Chron. 1.37; Neh. 11.24. The Egyptologist B. U. Schipper examined the story in the light of biblical and Egyptian considerations and concluded that 2 Chron. 14.8-14 is 'in no way a historical document from the ninth century but an example of Old Testament theology from the post-exilic period' (1999: 133–9, my translation from p. 139).

Several short-lived rulers of the Northern Kingdom filled in the time between Jeroboam and Omri: Nadab, Baasha, and Elah. Elah's chariot commander Zimri killed him while he was drinking in the capital Tirzah. But Zimri lasted only seven days, because the army chose their commander Omri who then besieged Zimri in Tirzah, and the latter committed suicide (1 Kgs 16.15-20). Omri consolidated his rule by defeating a rival Tibni who also had a following among the people (1 Kgs 16.21-22). Thus, Omri became king only 50 years after the death of Solomon, if the figures of the MT can be trusted.

Omri purchased the hill of Shemer and founded a new capital for the Northern Kingdom, Samaria. Otherwise, he is simply dismissed as wicked. Yet we know from Assyrian texts that Omri was a significant individual who gave his name to his kingdom: the Assyrians long called it *Bit-Ḫumri* ('House of Omri'). The Assyrian records thus confirm the existence and importance of Omri, though they say nothing further about him. Yet we also find a reference to Omri in the stela left by Mesha, the king of Moab, about 800 BCE (§§4.1.4; 4.2.4), which states that Omri 'oppressed' Moab for his lifetime and half the lifetime of his son, 40 years, before Mesha threw off the Israelite yoke. In this case, there is a remarkable coincidence between the biblical and the extra-biblical data.

4.2.3 Ahab

With Omri and especially with his son Ahab we start to find extra-biblical references that supplement the biblical data. Far from removing problems and difficulties, however, such extra-biblical sources often only raise new ones, especially when it comes to reconciling the biblical text with the primary sources. Also, much of the biblical text is taken up with the prophetic legend of Elijah the prophet. We begin the story with the battle of Qarqar in 853 BCE. The battle is described in an Assyrian text (see the quote at §4.1.5) in which Ahab is part of a coalition against the Assyrians. This is very surprising on the surface, since he is here allied with the Aramaeans, yet the biblical text makes the Aramaeans a major enemy of Ahab. We know that several decades later, Aram was an enemy because its king Hazael fought Johoram (or Joram), Ahab's son, and wounded him (2 Kgs 8.28-29).

The question is, what happened between Ahab's coalition with Hadadezer and the oppression of Israel by Hazael? According to the biblical text Ahab fought the Aramaeans. This seems to go contrary to the Assyrian inscriptions and M. Astour (1971), for example, argued that Jehoram was recovering from wounds received fighting against the Assyrians rather than the Aramaeans when Jehu's coup took place. Astour interprets Jehu's revolt as a move by a pro-Assyrian faction. N. Na'aman (2007b: 410–11) argues that Ahab was killed fighting the Assyrians. But some have been willing to argue that the biblical picture is not entirely wrong. That is, Ahab's alliance with the Aramaeans was a matter of necessity before a common enemy, but this did not prevent national concerns from taking over when the Assyrians were not threatening. Thus, the biblical representation of Ahab as fighting the Aramaeans toward the end of his reign is correct according to several interpreters (Bright [1980: 247] argued this). Basing himself on the Tel Dan inscription, Lipiński (2000: 373–80) has recently argued that not only had Ahab already fallen out with Hadadezer but that Jehoram and Ahaziah were slain by Hazael, not Jehu. As already noted above, however, the reconstruction of the Tel Dan inscription is not as certain as this interpretation implies. Others are willing to believe that the Israelites and Aramaeans fell out late in the reign of Jehoram, and that the latter was indeed wounded fighting with Hazael over possession of Ramoth-Gilead (2 Kgs 9.14-15: Kuan 1995: 55–9).

Thus, according to the Assyrian records Ahab was an ally of the Aramaeans and an enemy of the Assyrians, whereas the biblical text makes Ahab an enemy of the Aramaeans and does not even mention the

Assyrians at all. Most historians believe that the biblical writer has given us a false picture, perhaps because of a misreading of his sources (for a detailed discussion, see Grabbe 2012). The biblical text implies that the alliance with the Phoenicians was important to Ahab, with Ahab's marriage to Jezebel no doubt a means of sealing the alliance. This alliance is not directly attested in the non-biblical sources, but a number of the extra-biblical sources imply such a relationship. First, the name of Jezebel's father Ethbaal (*Ittobaal*) seems to have been mentioned in the sources used by Menander of Ephesus (§4.1.6). Second, in the Kurkh Monolith Tyre and Sidon are not mentioned, either as paying tribute to Shalmaneser III or as members of the alliance of twelve kings. This would be explained if their armies were counted along with Israel's.

One of the areas often discussed is the number of chariots possessed by Ahab. The text clearly reads '2,000 chariots' (2 LIM GIŠ.GIGIR.MEŠ), so the problems of trying to read a damaged text do not apply here. Yet the text is often emended. For example, D. Wiseman's translation in 1958 reads '200 chariots' without so much as a footnote or comment to indicate that the text has been emended (1958: 47). Perhaps the best defence of the view that '2,000' should be emended to '200' has been given by N. Na'aman, the main argument being that such a large force could not have been sustained by the Israelite economy (Na'aman 1976). However, this argument is not decisive for at least two reasons. The first is that the resources needed to maintain a large force of horses is not the precise equivalent of the economic support needed for manufacturing and supplying a modern tank regiment. Two thousand chariots would need a large herd of horses, but these would not necessarily have been kept permanently in stalls. Grassland unsuitable for crops could still provide good grazing for horses kept in reserve until a national emergency arose. A second point to consider is that this force may not have been supplied by the kingdom of Israel alone (Kuan 1995: 39–47). Here the biblical text may be useful. 1 Kings 22.4 suggests that Judah was subordinate to Israel, perhaps being a vassal, as was Moab. Also as noted above, Tyre and Sidon are not mentioned in Shalmaneser's inscription, either as opposing his advance or as paying tribute. Since Tyre and Sidon are often listed as paying tribute in Assyrian inscriptions, it would be surprising if they were omitted by accident. However, if they were allies of Israel (as indeed they are so presented by the biblical text), they would be neither paying tribute to Assyria nor listed separately in the inscription. Much has been made by some writers about the designation of Jehu as 'son of Omri', as some translations render it. One explanation is that the writer of the inscription did not know that Jehu was not a son of Omri but a usurper to the throne.

However, the other inscriptions of Shalmaneser show that the Sumerogram DUMU 'son of' is used in a number of cases simply to designate a citizen of a particular country (hence, the translation 'man of'), though the person so designated usually happens to be the king. See the designation of Adramu king of Hamath as DUMU *A-gu-ú-si*, Aḫunu king of Adini as DUMU *A-di-ni* and Ḫaiiānu king of Gabbari as DUMU *Gab-ba-ri* in the Kurkh Monolith (Grayson 1996: 17–18 [A.0.102.2: 15, 24, 27]) (also the discussion in Tadmor 1973: 149; Kuan 1995: 52–3 n. 167).

An important question is what type of kingdom Ahab ruled. M. H. Niemann has argued that Omri and Ahab's state was a military administration, with them as the war leaders (1993). Providing support for this interpretation are the Samarian ostraca (§4.1.2), which show attempts by the rulers to integrate the traditional tribal links into their personal power network. They did this by having the elite members of the clans reside as 'honoured guests' in Samaria for shorter or longer periods of time. Wine and oil were sent from their local constituents to the clan members residing in Samaria, and these ostraca were receipts for the goods. This practice served to stabilize political links between the Samarian king or warlord and the surrounding clans. As for Judah's relationship to the Northern Kingdom, leadership had passed to the Kingdom of Israel which had the greater concentration of natural resources and wealth potential. The rise of the Omri dynasty established the kingdom of Israel as the dominant power in the region and led to a true Israelite state. Whether Judah was its vassal, as a number have suggested (cf. 1 Kgs 22.4; also Knauf 2007), or just its junior partner, as Na'aman has recently argued (2013: 258–61), probably makes little difference. What is important is the positive effect that the Omride Israel had on Judah (even if the Bible sees it differently). This was recently discussed by O. Sergi (2013) who notes that the Omrides allied themselves with the House of David. It was this that led to the expansion of Judah south into the Negev and west into the Shephelah and aided its political development.

The focus of the biblical text is (not surprisingly) on the religious question, with Jezebel as the clear villain of the situation. This probably misrepresents things on all sides. On the question of Baal, we have to keep in mind that the writer/editor is a later Judahite writer with a particular view of worship. At the time of Ahab both Israel and Judah were polytheistic societies. Also, the House of Baal was apparently built for Jezebel as a private royal chapel, since she herself was a Phoenician and considered Baal as her chief deity. Finally, Ahab was himself a worshipper of Yhwh. His chief palace overseer Obadiah was a devoted Yhwh worshipper, and Ahab could hardly have been ignorant of that (1 Kgs 17.3). Furthermore, his two sons had theophoric names that contained a form of the divine name Yhwh (Ahaziah [1 Kgs 22.40] and Jehoram [2 Kgs 1.17]), which would hardly have been the case if he had been a Baal worshipper.

4.2.4 Israel and Moab

According to 2 Kings (1.1; 3.4-5) Moab was under the dominion of Israel but managed to break free after Ahab's death. No suggestion is made as to who subjugated Moab in the first place. The Mesha Stela states that Omri 'oppressed' Moab for his lifetime and half the lifetime of his son, 40 years, before Mesha threw off the Israelite yoke. There is a remarkable coincidence between the biblical and the extra-biblical data, as was noticed when the Moabite stone was first discovered. However, there are some discrepancies that either cannot be reconciled or at least call for an explanation.

The first query concerns the name of Omri in the Mesha Stela. It has normally been taken as the name of a contemporary king of Israel. However, a new interpretation has recently been given by Thomas Thompson and Niels Peter Lemche. Lemche gives a cautious discussion, noting the absence of Ahab, the 'mythical' figure of 40 years, the reference to Jehu as the 'son' of Omri (in the Assyrian inscriptions), and suggesting that the 'mentioning of King Omri may therefore in this inscription not be solid evidence of the existence of a king of this name but simply a reference to the apical founder of the kingdom of Israel... the dynastic name of the state of Israel' (Lemche 1998b: 44–6). If so, his 'son' could be any king of Israel down to the fall of Samaria. Thompson is more dogmatic:

> Omri 'dwelling in Moab' is not a person doing anything in Transjordan. It is a character of story, an eponym, a personification of the state, *Bit Humri*'s political power and the presence of its army in eastern Palestine. We have a text. Therefore we are dealing with the literary, not the historical. From the historical name of *Bit Humri*, the Bible's story of a King Omri as builder of Samaria and founder of its dynasty grew just as much as had the story of King David and his forty kings. These sprang from the eponymic function of a truly historical *Byt dwd.* (Thompson 2000: 325)

Of course, the Mesha Stela gives a story, but so do *all* the inscriptions we are dealing with, including the Assyrian ones. To what extent a story is historical has to be resolved on grounds other than genre. Is there evidence that Omri was a real person or only a personification of the state *Bit ḫumri*? That question cannot be answered directly because the two sources treating Omri as a person are the biblical text – which we are trying to test – and the Moabite stone – which is in question at the moment as a source. The only way to approach the question is to ask whether there are helpful analogies to this situation. There are in fact some good analogies in the person of Guš, the king of Yaḫan, an Aramaean state around Lake Gabbūl in northern Syria. We know he was an actual individual because he paid tribute to Ashurnasirpal II ca. 870 BCE (Grayson 1996: 218, lines 77–78 [text A.0.101.1]). Guš was apparently considered the founder of the state and dynasty. In 858 a 'Hadram son of Guš' paid tribute to Shalmaneser III (Grayson 1996: 17 [text A.0.102.2 ii 12]: ᵐ*a-ra-me* DUMU *gu-ú-si*; also p. 25 [A.0.102.3 96-97]). The reading of the name as 'Hadrām' (ᵐ*ad-ra-me*) follows E. Lipiński (2000: 196 n. 12; 212) who has based this interpretation on other inscriptional material. The Zakkur Inscription lists a 'Bar-Gush' among the kings arrayed against Zakkur (A 6). Other inscriptions refer to the state or dynasty as 'house of Guš' (*Bīt-Gūsi/Bīt-Agūsi* in Assyrian [Lipiński 2000: 196 and nn. 11-12]; *byt gš* in Aramaic [*KAI* 223B: 10]). Similarly, Hazael is clearly attested as king of Damascus in a number of Assyrian inscriptions, but after his death the land of Damascus is sometimes referred to as *Bit Hazael* in Assyrian inscriptions (§4.1.5).

What these two examples illustrate is that a known historical individual (e.g., Guš, Hazael) can be taken as the founder or eponym of a dynasty, with the dynasty named after the person ('house of X') and the descendants even referred to as 'son of X'. Thus, the expression *Bīt-Ḫumri* as a reference to the state/royal house of Israel does not rule out Omri as a historical personage. The question now is how to interpret the Moabite stone. Does the text suggest a eponymous ancestor when it mentions Omri or does it have in mind an actual king? First, the text refers to 'Omri' twice (lines 4–5, 7) but never to 'house of Omri'. Second, there is no reference to 'son of Omri' as we have in some of the Assyrian inscriptions, where 'DUMU/*mar* PN' seem to be the equivalent of 'king/man of (the house of) PN'. Instead, we have 'his son' (*bnh*: lines 6, 8), with a reference back to Omri alone (though *bn* probably means 'grandson' in this context; see next paragraph). This expression is not the same as that where an eponymous ancestor is used to designate an individual. The language of the Mesha Stela looks like a straightforward reference to an actual king of Israel, not just a mythical eponym of the Israelite royal house.

A second problem is the dating of Moab's vassalage to Israel. A period of 40 years is mentioned, obviously a round number. Omri is associated with the conquest of Moab; however, it is rather curious that Ahab is not mentioned at all, though the expression 'his son' might have been taken as a derogatory reference by not actually naming Ahab. We should not automatically assume that the Mesha inscription gives a correct account of the situation, since it clearly has its own biases; nevertheless, it is a near contemporary of the events, while the biblical account of Mesha is embedded in a prophetic legend and seems to have been written down or at least edited long after the events. This is not the whole story, however, because both accounts have to be treated critically. It is interesting that the length of the reigns of Omri and Ahab together total 34 years according to the biblical text (1 Kgs 16.23, 29), not far from 40 years. It may be that the reigns of Omri and Ahab have been telescoped – after all, the Moabite scribe was making a general point, not giving a blow-by-blow historical narrative – and 'half the reign of his son' could be a reference to Jehoram rather than Ahab ('son' being used generically for a more remote descendant, 'grandson' in this case). Moab rebelled in the reign of Jehoram according to 1 Kgs 1.1. Jehoram reigned 12 years, and if we add 6 of these to the 34 of Omri and Ahab, we have 40. This could just be coincidence, but it is not too improbable that the Moabite scribe was adding up the years of the reigns in similar fashion. If so, the two accounts in the Moabite stone and the Bible would in fact be quite close.

The reason for suggesting this interpretation is an obvious one: it seems unlikely that Moab could have rebelled under Ahab, considering the latter's strength according to the Assyrian inscriptions. The logical time to have rebelled was after Ahab's death, when a less experienced and weaker son was on the throne. Although the precise interpretation of the statement in the Mesha Stela is uncertain, it seems prima facie likely that the rebellion of Mesha took place after Ahab's death – as the biblical text states – but it may also be that the Mesha Stela can be reconciled with this view, as just described.

4.2.5 The Aramaeans

The Aramaeans were very important for the history of the ancient Near East (Lipiński 2000; Dion 1997; Pitard 1987; O'Callaghan 1948). Their main impact was their language, which dominated the whole region from the Mediterranean Sea to Bactria from the Assyrian empire to the coming of Islam. They formed a number of small kingdoms, the kingdom of Damascus being especially prominent, but many of the others make little impact while we know little about them. The Aramaeans first appear for certain about 1100 BCE, in a tablet of Tiglath-pileser I (Lipiński 2000: 35–40). Some are known to have settled in Mesopotamia, even in the cities, but others seem to have carried on a nomadic or semi-nomadic lifestyle in the region of Syria. They had the greatest impact on Israel during the ninth and eighth centuries BCE, especially the kingdom of

Damascus. It is even suggested that Israel might have been a vassal to the king of Damascus, in the ninth century though this is not certain (Knauf 2007).

One of the problems in the historical reconstruction of Aramaic history for this period is the tendency to multiply 'Ben-Hadad's. Some writers count up to four individuals, numbering Bar-Hadad I–IV (Dearman and Miller 1983). The reason for such a large number of individuals is that the biblical text has simply been harmonized with external sources, so that wherever 'Ben-Hadad' has been mentioned in the biblical text, it has been taken at face value (e.g., Bright 1980: 243; Dearman in Dearman and Miller 1983). This 'duplex' method of writing history is not convincing (on the question, see Grabbe 1997c: 64–5). This tendency has been resisted in more critical writers, and one recent book gives only two figures, a Bar-Hadad I and Bar-Hadad II (Miller in Dearman and Miller 1983 and Lipiński 2000: 407, who give only Bar-Hadad I and II as kings of Damascus). 1 Kings 21 refers to a 'Ben-Hadad' who was active in the time of Ahab, yet we know that the king of Damascus at this time was Hadadezer. An explanation of the biblical picture has become widely accepted in scholarship: 1 Kings 20–22 contains material from the later Jehu dynasty (e.g., 2 Kgs 13) which has been mistakenly assigned to the reign of Ahab. The hypothesis has been championed by J. M. Miller, first in an unpublished PhD thesis, and then in a series of articles (Miller 1966, 1967, 1968; see also Pitard 1987: 114–25; Kuan 1995: 36–9). Part of the theory is that the original stories had only the titles 'king of Israel' and 'king of Judah', without the personal names, which made it easy to insert them wherever the editor thought fit. This hypothesis is cogent and fits the data well, which is why it has become so widely accepted in recent years. However, all it does is explain how the final text arose. The text as it presently stands is completely misleading, and the correct understanding (assuming one accepts the hypothesis) was possible only when extra-biblical sources became available.

The Assyrian inscriptions indicate that Ahab was an ally of Hadadezer. What, then, are we to make of the biblical passages that Ahab fought with 'Ben-Hadad' (1 Kgs 20–22)? The biblical writer is of course confused over the name of the king of Damascus during Ahab's rule and, as just suggested, the stories making Ahab fight the Aramaeans might have been transferred from the later history of the Jehu dynasty. But some have been willing to argue that while Ahab's alliance with the Aramaeans was a matter of necessity before a common enemy, this did not prevent hostilities from resuming when the Assyrians were not threatening. Thus, the biblical representation of Ahab fighting the Aramaeans toward the end of his reign is correct according to several interpreters (e.g., Lipiński 2000: 373–80). This is of course possible, but it should be noted that Assyria was in a continual struggle with Hadadezer's coalition from his sixth year until at least the fourteenth year. Ahab is unlikely to have left the coalition during this time; it is only in the eighteenth year that a new king of Israel is mentioned, and the coalition under Hadadezer is defeated. If Ahab fought the Aramaeans, it would have been early in his reign, not in the last few years when he was part of the coalition organized by Hadadezer. It was only when Ahab was out of the way that the coalition was defeated.

Once the coalition assembled by Hadadezer had broken up, Hazael alone stood against the Assyrians. Campaigns against him are mentioned for Shalmaneser III's eighteenth (841 BCE) and twenty-first years (838 BCE). Then the Assyrians became occupied with troubles at home and ignored their empire in the west for several decades. This left Hazael and his son Ben-Hadad (Bar-Hadad) to cause problems for Israel, in agreement with the biblical text. It is not attested directly because of the lack of Assyrian inscriptions, but the state of affairs is presupposed when the Assyrians once again intervened in the west under Adad-Nirari III. A coalition including Bar-Hadad, son of Hazael, attacked Zakkur of Hamath (Zakkur Inscription) and apparently went on to challenge the Assyrians. Not only does the biblical text have the sequence Hazael, followed by Bar-Hadad (Hebrew: Ben-Hadad), but the 'saviour' of 2 Kgs 13.5 is probably a reference to the Assyrian help. The Zakkur Inscription probably alludes to this same anti-Assyrian coalition, whereas Zakkur is pro-Assyrian and seems to have been delivered by Assyrian intervention. The Joash of Israel who is being relieved of the oppression from Bar-Hadad is mentioned in the el-Rimah Assyrian inscription (§4.1.5) as paying tribute to the Assyrians. Finally, the fall of Damascus (ca. 802 BCE: for the possible dates, see Kuan 1995: 93–106), as described in the el-Rimah and other inscriptions, would have taken the pressure off Israel and others who were under the yoke of Damascus. About 780–775 BCE Shamshi-ilu the Assyrian commander for the region collected tribute from Ḫadiiāni. This would suggest that Damascus was not able to do just anything it wished. Thus, although the biblical text cannot be confirmed in detail, the general picture given fits the situation in the last part of the ninth century as we know it from extra-biblical sources.

An important figure in the region and a significant opponent of the Assyrians was Rezin of Damascus (the Akkadian is variously ^{m}*Ra-hi-a-nu* ^{kur}*Šá-imēri-šú-a+a* [Annal 13*, line 10 = Tadmor 1994: 68] and ^{m}*Ra-qi-a-nu* ^{kur}*Šá-imēri-šú-a+a* [*Stela* IIIA, line 4 = Tadmor 1994: 106], apparently reflecting Aramaic *Raḍyan*). Although the 'Syro-Ephraimite war' (2 Kgs 15.29; 16.5-9; Isa. 7) is not described as such in the Assyrian annals, it is compatible with everything so far known. In the end, though, both Rezin and his alleged ally Pekah lost out. Tiglath-pileser III took Damascus about 732 BCE (whether he killed Rezin is not preserved) and exiled many of the Aramaeans (Tadmor 1994: 138 [*Summary Inscription 4,* 7′–8′], 186 [*Summary Inscription* 9, reverse 3–4]).

4.2.6 From Jehu to the End of the Northern Kingdom (2 Kings 9–16)

The kings of both Israel and Judah died at the same time, whether their death is ascribed to Jehu (so the biblical text [2 Kgs 9]) or Hazael, as a number of recent scholars argue (e.g., Lipiński 2000: 373–80). Indeed, some think that Hazael instigated or approved their deaths through his vassal Jehu. Once again, we know of Jehu through the Assyrian inscriptions (§4.1.5), even though the biblical text does not so much as mention Assyria with regard to him. As mentioned above (§4.2.5), the Assyrians ceased marching to the west for a number of decades, which left Damascus free rein to dominate Israel. Thus, the picture of Hazael and his son Bar-Hadad (called Ben-Hadad in the biblical text) as causing trouble for Israel is a realistic one (2 Kgs 10.32-33; 12.18-19; 13.3-6).

The next major episode concerned the attempted coup of Athaliah (2 Kgs 11). As the daughter of Omri (or possibly Ahab), Athialiah had been married to Jehoram son of Jehoshaphat king of Judah (2 Kgs 8.18, 26). She was the mother to Jehoram's son Ahaziah (who was assassinated by Jehu), and she seized the throne of Judah after Ahaziah's death (2 Kgs 11.1-3). Jehoram's young son Joash was hidden away, however, to prevent his being killed by Athaliah, according to the text. After the passage of several years, the high priest Jehoiada arranged to have Joash crowned king, at which point Athaliah was herself taken out and executed. Whether things happened exactly as the text suggests is a question, but the basic scenario looks credible: such attempted coups and rivalry over the throne are widely attested in history. The main episode related about Joash is that he ordered money to be collected and used to repair the temple (2 Kgs 12). After his coronation, the high priest supposedly had a temple to Baal torn down and its priest slain (2 Kgs 11.18). Although this might be possible, one must ask, when was this temple to Baal built and by whom, since Jezebel's temple to Baal had been destroyed by Jehu? One suspects a literary creation in which Jehu's destruction of Baal's temple has been duplicated here.

The next two kings of Israel were part of the Jehu dynasty. First was Jehu's son Jehoahaz under whom Israel was harassed and its territory diminished by Hazael the Aramaean (2 Kgs 13.1-9). It is the small size of his army and other details that make some scholars think that some material in the Ahab cycle actually belongs to Jehoahaz but was taken over (by accident or design) into the Ahab account (§4.2.3). He was followed by his son Jehoash or Joash.

In Judah Amaziah succeeded his father Joash (2 Kgs 14). A number of scholars have suggested that he was co-regent with his father for 15 years; however, N. Na'aman argues that a scribe misread a reference to Amaziah's father Joash (who was king of Judah) in 2 Kgs 14.17 as a reference to Joash the king of Israel (2013: 250–2). This would make Amaziah rule 15 years after the death of his father Joash. Whether Amaziah defeated the Edomites as alleged in the text cannot be comfirmed (there are some major problems with interpreting the archaeology of Edom [§3.2.3]), but Na'aman suggests that his alleged activity in Edom was related to the copper trade (2013: 255–8). Amaziah challenged Jehoash king of Israel but was soundly defeated.

He was succeeded by Azariah (2 Kgs 15.1-7; called Uzziah in 2 Chron. 26) who is held up as a model of the righteous king. Yet for all his righteousness Azariah was stricken with leprosy. 2 Chronicles 26.16-21 gives a theological explanation: Uzziah attempted to offer incense in breach of the law. Yet the fact is that under the monarchy the king was the chief cultic figure and had every right to make offerings (as the biblical text admits for both David and Solomon [§4.2.8; Grabbe 1995: Chapter 2]). This text appears to show a post-monarchial priestly bias. Jeroboam II, Jehoash's son, was the next king of Israel and a successful ruler, even though the biblical text makes light of his reign because it judged him as wicked. Yet even the text recognizes that Jeroboam restored the northern part of Israel at the expense of the Aramaeans: 2 Kgs 14.26-27 is almost apologetic that this recovery was allowed to happen! The suggestion is that much of Syria was taken, but this is unlikely. The important historical point, though, is that Jeroboam II reversed the ascendancy of Damascus over Israel; however, it should be noted that the reason is primarily that Assyria had returned to the west and was putting unstoppable pressure on the Aramaeans (cf. Grayson 1996: 211 [A.0.104.7: 4-8]; *ANET* 281–2). Jeroboam took advantage of the Assyrian attack to open another front against Bar-Hadad ruler of Damascus.

Jeroboam's son Zechariah lasted only six months before being assassinated by Shallum, who was in turn immediately removed by Menahem (2 Kgs 15.8-22). The main event under Menahem's rule was that Tiglath-pileser III (here called Pul) of Assyria came against Israel and required a tribute of a thousand silver talents. Menahem raised the funds by requiring

50 shekels from all the 'men of substance' in the kingdom. Since there are usually 3000 shekels in a talent, this suggests 60,000 'men of substance' (whatever that phrase exactly means). This sounds exaggerated, but did all the tribute come from their contribution? Are these figures even accurate? Tiglath-pileser's tribute list in the Calah Annals names Menahem of Samaria as one who paid tribute to him (Tadmor 1994: 69–71), though the amount is not given.

In Judah, Uzziah's son Jotham is said to have been righteous; nevertheless, Rezin (Aramaic *Raḍyan*; see §4.2.5) of Damascus and Pekah of Israel began an assault on Judah (the so-called 'Syro-Ephramite war'). However, the main attack on Judah came under Jotham's son Ahaz (according to both 2 Kgs 16.5-9 and Isa. 7). They did not succeed in overcoming Judah because Ahaz sent a bribe to Tiglath-pileser III (that is, he made himself a vassal of Assyria, which meant that he was now required to pay an annual tribute). See the next section (§4.2.7) for details. The main part of the account is about Ahaz's supposed religious apostasy in building another altar in the temple, alongside the original. As so often, religious matters are given a disproportionate treatment in the text, which is a good indication that the author is not attempting to write history as we understand the term in modern times.

4.2.7 Fall of Samaria

Menahem's son was Pekahiah, as the next king of Israel, but he was assassinated by his aide Pekah who seized the throne. At some point, Pekah apparently allied with Rezin the Aramaean (discussed in the previous section [§4.2.6]) and attacked Judah. Although the 'Syro-Ephraimite war' (2 Kgs 15.29; 16.5-9; Isa. 7) is not described as such in the Assyrian annals, it is compatible with everything so far known. In the end, though, both Rezin and his alleged ally Pekah lost out. Tiglath-pileser III took Damascus about 732 BCE, killed Rezin and exiled many of the Aramaeans (Tadmor 1994: 138 [*Summary Inscription 4*, 7′–8′], 186 [*Summary Inscription 9*, reverse 3-4]). In what is an unusually detailed episode for comparative purposes, *Summary Inscription* 4 tells about how Tiglath-pileser had Pekah removed for disloyalty and replaced by Hoshea (Tadmor 1994: 140 [*Summary Inscription* 4, 15′–19′], 188 [*Summary Inscription* 9, 9–11]). This is remarkably close to 2 Kgs 15.30. Perhaps the one discrepancy is whether Tiglath-pileser or Hoshea deposed Pekah, but this is probably a matter of wording. The removal of Pekah is not likely to have happened without Tiglath-pileser's ultimate say-so, and one suspects that Hoshea acted only when he knew that he had Assyrian backing.

When we come to the siege and capture of Samaria and the deportation of many Israelites, there are some questions, even when we look at the Mesopotamian sources. First, there is the curious statement that Hoshea was caught out by the Assyrians for withholding tribute and sending messengers to 'So king of Egypt' for assistance (2 Kgs 17.4), which was the cause of the siege of Samaria. But who was this So king of Egypt, and is the story credible? The question has been much debated (see Day 1992), but when the historical context, the biblical text and the Egyptian philology are taken into account, the Hebrew name 'So' seems to be a version of the Egyptian name *Wsrkn*, better known as Osorkon IV (Schipper 1998; Kitchen 1986: 372–5, 551). At this time there were several minor rulers in the Egyptian Delta region, but the eastern area was controlled by Osorkon. In the end, though, Osorkon gave no help to Hoshea, and the latter was besieged by the Assyrians. A particular question is, what part did Shalmaneser V play and what hand did Sargon II have in the matter? Sargon II claims to have conquered Samaria, and some scholars have accepted these claims; however, the account in 2 Kgs 17.3-6 that this siege and capture of the city took place in the time of Shalmaneser V is supported by the *Babylonian Chronicles* (§4.1.5). The argument that the various sources can be reconciled is probably correct, though more than one solution is possible. B. Becking argued that there were two conquests of Samaria, one by Shalmaneser V in 723 BCE and another by Sargon II in 720 BCE in response to a rebellion of Ilu-bi'di of Hamath (1992, 2002). Following Becking (and Tadmor 1958b: 33–40), R. E. Tappy (2001: 558–75) argues similarly for two campaigns; however, M. C. Tetley (2002) has argued against the two-invasion hypothesis.

It seems likely that both Shalmaneser V and Sargon II were in some way both involved in the end of Samaria. Yet there is no evidence in the archaeology that the city was destroyed. Perhaps the biblical text does not clearly envisage a destruction of the city, but the archaeological evidence also seems to be against a wholesale deportation of the population (though a small portion does seem to have been removed and replaced by outside settlers [§4.1.1]). As to the question of whether the Israelites were really taken to the places alleged in 2 Kgs 17.6 and of whether peoples from the places listed in 2 Kgs 17.24 were actually brought in, there is now some evidence that some movement of populations between the two regions actually took place (Becking 2002; 1992: 61–104; Na'aman and Zadok 2000; Oded 1979: 69–71; 2000: 91–9; Cogan and Tadmor 1988: 197, 209–10). But whether the extent of the deportation was as great as described in the biblical text is definitely to be queried.

4.2.8 Development of Religion

This section attempts to deal with the developments of Israelite and Judahite religion throughout the Iron Age. It is appropriate to do so in this chapter since the biblical text suggests a religious crisis under Ahab. The Bible pictures the Israelite religion as pure, monotheistic and different from the false worship of all other nations and peoples. This is the surface image, at least, and causes us little surprise. On the other hand, if one takes a broader view (including the evidence of archaeology), Israelite worship looks very much at home among the other Semitic religions, especially those of the Northwest Semitic region. This is not to deny that Israelite worship developed unique characteristics and came to establish strong boundaries against other religions, but this took a long time to develop (Albertz 1978, 1994; M. S. Smith 2001, 2002; Keel and Uehlinger 1998; Becking et al. 2001; Day 2000; Edelman [ed.] 1995b; Dietrich and Klopfenstein [eds] 1994; Nakhai 2001; Dever 2005; Gnuse 1997; *DDD*).

4.2.8.1 The God Yhwh

The deity most frequently and strongly associated with ancient Israel is Yhwh. The precise pronunciation is not known, though it is often reconstructed as *Yahweh* based on its appearance as *Iaō* (Ἰάω) in later Greek and Latin texts (e.g., Diodorus Siculus 1.94.2; Varro, apud Lydus, *De Mensibus* 4.53, pp. 110–11) and on the form of the name as it occurs in theophorous names in Masoretic vocalization in the biblical text (*-yāhû*). Apart from the biblical text, the name Yhwh is clearly attested first in the Moabite stone or Mesha Stela from the ninth century BCE (§4.1.4): Mesha took Nebo from Israel and dedicated the 'vessels of Yhwh' (כלי יהוה *kly Yhwh*) to his god Chemosh. Among the Khirbet Beit Lei inscriptions (about 600 BCE; Gogel 1998: #6.1.11; G. I. Davies 1991: #15.005) is a reference to a Yhwh who is apparently the god of Jerusalem (the words 'Yhwh god of' [יהוה אלהי *Yhwh 'lhy*] and 'Jerusalem' are clearly visible). The name is also found in a seal from the early eighth century (Avigad and Sass 1997: #27), allegedly found in Jerusalem, which reads 'Miqneyaw servant of Yhwh' (מקניו עבד יהוה *Mqnyw 'bd Yhwh*). The ostraca from Arad (Aharoni 1981) dated to about 600 BCE contain a number of blessings and invocations in the name of Yhwh (16.3; 18.2; 21.2, 4; 40.3). There is also a reference to the 'house of Yhwh' (בית יהוה *byt Yhwh*) which is probably the local temple (18.9). The Lachish ostraca (Gogel 1998: #6.1.15; *TSSI* #12), also evidently from the last days of the kingdom of Judah, contain a number of invocations using the name of Yhwh ('may Yhwh give health/good news'; 'as Yhwh lives'; see, e.g., Lachish 2.1-2, 5; 3.2-3, 9; 4.1; 5.1, 7; 6.1, 12).

The linguistic data attesting worship of Yhwh come from what were both the Northern Kingdom and the Southern Kingdom. Yhwh appears to have been a national or ethnic god, much as Chemosh was the god of the Moabites, Qaus the god of the Edomites and so on (cf. 1 Kgs 11.33). This does not mean that Yhwh was the only god worshipped in these kingdoms, but he seems to have been the main object of devotion. His is the name most widely attested. Where did Yhwh originate? This has been a matter of intense debate over many decades, with various claims to have found the name in Ugarit, Mesopotamia and even Ebla. None of these has so far withstood scrutiny to general satisfaction. However, some Egyptian inscriptions of LB mention what may be a geographical name Yhwh, with reference to 'the land of the Shasu Yahu' (§2.2.1.4). Although the name *Yhw* seems to be geographical, it is possible that there is a connection with the divinity Yhwh, perhaps the region giving its name to the god worshipped there, or even possibly the deity giving the name to the region. However, arguments have been advanced from several quarters that Yhwh arose out of the context of El worship (see next section); this does not rule out a geographical origin (since the two theories could be combined), but it illustrates the difficulties.

The etymology of the name Yhwh has been much discussed. It would be impossible to survey and comment on the various suggestions made over the past two centuries, but two current theories need to be explored. Several biblical passages connect it with the verb *hyy/hwy* 'to be' (see below), and a number of scholars accept this and make the name a form of 'to be', but even if this etymology is accepted, there is still a controversy. Some take the name as a simple assertion ('he is'/'he exists'), but others (especially from the Albright school) have argued that there was once a common epithet of El as follows: 'El who creates (heavenly) armies' *'il ḏū yahwī ṣaba'ōt*). This verbal form developed into a name, the name of a separate deity. This makes the verb a causative of 'to be' ('he causes to be' = 'he creates' [Cross 1973: 60–75]). The difficulty in knowing the exact vocalization and form of the name makes deciding between these theories a problem; even taking the name as 'Yahweh' does not solve the question since this is potentially a base form of the verb (*Qal*) or a causative (*Hiphil*). On the other hand, it has been argued that a derivation from 'to be' is excluded but that it comes from *hwy* 'to blow' (e.g., Knauf 1984), reflecting Yhwh's original function as a storm deity. If this is correct, the connection with 'to be' in biblical passages would be a folk (or even scribal) etymology. Deciding one's stance on the etymology of the name can have major implications for any theory about the origin of the Yhwh cult.

When we turn to the biblical text, the data may well represent different periods of time, and whether any of it can be projected back to the period before the Israelite monarchy is a major question. From the first chapter of Genesis the Bible abounds in the name Yhwh. It occurs frequently in the early chapters of Genesis, in the patriarchal narratives and is the name by which the God of Israel reveals himself to Moses in Exodus. Yet a closer examination indicates some anomalies:

First, a great many personal names are theophorous, containing divine elements in them such as *'El* 'God' (including such names as *'Ab* 'Father', *'Aḥ* 'Brother' and the like which are now thought to refer to the deity, perhaps conceived of as a divine father, brother, etc., or even a reference to a literal deceased relative now conceived of as deified). Yet no name is compounded with Yhwh before the narrative of Moses. The earliest name is Joshua (whose name was actually changed from Hoshea [Num. 13.16]). None of the Genesis genealogies contain names with Yhwh, and none of Moses' contemporaries are said to have such names. The name Yhwh appears in names in the biblical text only during the later life of Moses.

Second, the text of Exodus suggests that Yhwh was first revealed to Moses and not before his time. In Exod. 3.6 (usually assigned to the E source according to the Documentary Hypothesis), the God who appears to Moses identifies himself with the ancestral god of Abraham, Isaac and Jacob. The text goes on to say that this God is called 'I am' (אהיה *'ehyeh*), and immediately connects this name with 'Yhwh the God of your fathers, the God of Abraham, the God of Isaac, and the God of Jacob' (Exod. 3.13-16). Exodus 6.3 (usually assigned to the P source) states that God appeared to Abraham, Isaac and Jacob under the name of El Shaddai but was not known to them by his name Yhwh. Thus, if these passages have any weight, they suggest that the name of Yhwh was not known in Israel before the time of Moses. It was these passages, among others, that A. Alt used to develop his theory of the 'god of the fathers' (1966). Yhwh is indeed the 'god of the fathers' in these passages, but most of Alt's thesis does not stand in the light of more recent discoveries (Cross 1973: 3–43).

This is only a simple analysis – even a simplistic one – of the biblical text and ignores the whole question of Moses' existence and the relationship of the biblical traditions to the actual settlement of the Israelite people in the land. However, we can still note two points: it does conform with extra-biblical data and it suggests memory of a time when Yhwh was not known to the Israelites but was introduced to them for the first time. For a writer to dream up a period when Yhwh was not known would be very surprising indeed, if everyone assumed that Yhwh had been in Israelite possession from the beginning. Thus, to the best of our current knowledge Yhwh originated in Palestine and his worship was confined to the peoples of Palestine. There is considerable – if not universal – support for the view that the early Egyptian inscriptions mentioning *Yhw* do in fact refer to the name Yhwh and that worship of Yhwh did not originate with Israel but was picked up sometime during the pre-settlement or settlement period (Blenkinsopp 2008).

However, evidence has more recently been found for Yhwh worship in the area of Syria in a text from Hamath (Dalley 1990). Based on this text, it has even been suggested that Yhwh was not unique to Israel/Judah but rather a deity common to a large part of Syro-Palestine (Thompson 1995a: 119 n. 13). The reference seems to be certain, but there is no supporting evidence that Yhwh was part of general worship over the region. Rather, it looks more likely that Yhwh worship had been transplanted from Palestine in some way, perhaps by a royal family which had also moved from the Palestinian region or by some other means, but remained isolated or confined to a minority. In all the inscriptions and linguistic data from the surrounding region, there is nothing to indicate that Yhwh was worshipped generally over the entire region (Grabbe 2010b).

4.2.8.2 Other Deities and Worship

The references to the God of Israel in the biblical text do not just contain the name Yhwh. Many other names and titles occur, though often translated in Bible translations as epithets or descriptions rather than rendered as names. For example, the name *'El* is used of the Israelite God but can also mean just 'god' in a generic sense. This is in line with much Northwest Semitic usage in which *'el* (or the earlier form *'ilu*) could stand both for the head of the pantheon (the god El) and for the word 'god, divinity' in general). The name El Shaddai (or just Shaddai alone) is also used in a number of passages in Genesis (17.1; 28.3; 35.11; 48.3; 49.25). It is also the divine name found through most of the poem of Job and seems to be the prime divinity for the original composer of the book's core (the name Yhwh occurs in Job only in the framework). Genesis 14.18 attests the deity El Elyon, not known anywhere else. (Some scholars doubt the accuracy of the text here, though the name Elyon by itself also occurs in Num. 24.16, Deut. 32.8 and Isa. 14.14, while the Ugaritic equivalent [*ly*] is applied to Baal [*KTU* 1.16.3.6, 8].)

Other biblical texts also suggest a time when Yhwh was not only a deity alongside other deities but perhaps even a subordinate of El. Scholars had long wondered whether the reading of the Hebrew text of Deut. 32.8 was not due to a later editing because of the Septuagint text which seemed to presuppose a different Hebrew original: the god Elyon 'established the boundaries of the nations according to the number of the angels of God'. The suggestion of another more original Hebrew reading seems now to have been confirmed by a Hebrew manuscript from Qumran (4QDeut[j] = 4Q37) which reads '[according to the number of] the sons of God' (בני אלהים *bny 'lhym*). The passage goes on to say that Jacob is Yhwh's portion (32.9). All of these data suggest that the passage originally read something along the lines of the following:

When Elyon gave the inheritance of the nations,
When he divided the sons of Adam (or man),
He established the boundaries of the peoples
According to the number of the sons of El.
For Yhwh's lot is his people
And Jacob his inherited portion.

This suggests that Yhwh (as one of these sons of El) inherited Israel as his particular portion.

Such a situation in which Yhwh is merely one among the sons of El in the divine assembly is found in Ps. 89.7-8 which reads literally:

For who in heaven compares to Yhwh?
Who is like Yhwh among the sons of the Elim (gods)?
El creates awe in the council of the Holy Ones.
He is great and strikes fear in all about him.

Here Yhwh is a son of El, among other sons, even if he is said to be incomparable to his fellow sons of El. Similarly, Ps. 82.1 speaks of God judging among the gods.

The concept of the divine assembly or divine council is one widespread among Semitic pantheons. Perhaps one of the clearest examples of Yhwh himself having a divine council is 1 Kgs 22.19-22 in which he presides over the 'host of heaven' (צבא השמים *ṣĕbā' haššāmayim*). In later times this divine council was interpreted as consisting of angels who surrounded Yhwh, but angels have only a minor place in Israelite tradition until the post-exilic period. The Hebrew word for 'angel' is מלאך *mal'ak*, meaning 'messenger' and may be used of human messengers as well as heavenly ones. Studies of the Northwest Semitic pantheons have shown that the gods had various ranks, the lowest being the messenger gods (Handy 1994). These messengers spoke for the gods sending them. Similarly, angels in the Bible speak for Yhwh; for example, Exod. 3.2-5 mentions that 'the *mal'ak Yhwh*' appeared to Moses, but then the rest of the passage goes on to say that 'Yhwh said'. Thus, the messenger gods of the original

Northwest Semitic pantheon (and perhaps other divinities as well) became reduced to angels in later Judaism, but the outlines of the original polytheistic divine council are still retained despite the monotheistic views of the final editors of the tradition.

A number of other passages also give a mythical picture of Yhwh not found in most biblical texts (Day 1985). They remind one of myths about Baal known from the Ugaritic texts and even have overtones of Marduk's defeat of Tiamat from whose body he created the heavens and the earth in the Babylonian creation epic *Enuma Elish.* Unlike Genesis 1, these passages suggest that God created by defeating various monsters of chaos who appear as supernatural beings. For example, in Isa. 27.1 Yhwh takes his sword and defeats 'Leviathan (לויתן *lwytn*) the piercing (ברח *brḥ*) serpent, even Leviathan the slippery (עקלתון *'qltwn*) serpent, and he will slay the Tannin (תנין *tnyn*) in the sea'. This can be compared with Ugaritic texts which allege that Baal defeated such monsters. One prominent Baal myth describes Baal's defeat of the sea god Yamm (*KTU* 1.2). Another passage alludes to battles which so far have not come to light in detailed texts. *KTU* 1.3.3.37–42 tells of other monsters of chaos defeated by Baal:

> Did I not destroy Yamm the darling of El,
> did I not make an end of Nahar the great god?
> Was not the dragon (*tnn*) captured and vanquished?
> I did destroy the wriggling (*qltn*) serpent,
> the tyrant with seven heads.

Similarly, *KTU* 1.5.1.1–3 states:

> For all that you smote Leviathan the slippery serpent (*ltn.bṯn.brḥ*) and made an end of the wriggling (*qltn*) serpent…, the tyrant with seven heads?

Cf. also *KTU* 1.5.1.27–30. The Hebrew and Ugaritic texts are not only similar in theme but even share some of the same basic vocabulary.

These various passages are isolated survivals of older beliefs which had been obliterated or reinterpreted by the dominant monotheistic view of Yhwh that controlled the final shaping of the biblical text. A few verses escaped editing, however, confirming what we now know from inscriptions: Yhwh was originally conceived as one god among many, perhaps even subordinate to and a son of El. He created by fighting and defeating various monsters of chaos, such as Leviathan, Tannin and Rahab, much as Baal did in the Ugaritic texts. When monotheism became the dominant view, these older views were simply expunged or, in some cases, they were reinterpreted so as not to be an embarrassment to monotheistic views.

Biblical names also suggest a plethora of deities. The names with El are too numerous to mention (Israel, Elijah, Elisha, Samuel and so on); more significant are Shaddai (e.g., Num. 1.5-6: Shedeur, Zurishaddai; Num. 1.12: Ammishaddai). But perhaps most interesting are the names with Baal. Considering the biblical polemic against Baal, one might have expected not to see such names, but they are found in surprising contexts. One of Saul's sons has a name compounded with Baal: Eshbaal ('man of Baal'), and Jonathan's son was Meribbaal. These names are often overlooked because the Samuel texts actually substitute surrogate names compounded with the word 'shame' (Ishbosheth [2 Sam. 2.8]; Mephibosheth [2 Sam. 21.7]), but they are correctly preserved in 1 Chronicles (8.33-34; 9.39-40).

Should we be surprised at all this since, after all, does not the biblical text show that Israel had a penchant for 'falling away' from true worship into paganism, idolatry and worship of other gods? To balance this, one might well point to the opposition to Baal worship in the time of Elijah. However, it is not entirely clear that this is as simple as it looks, for the 'Baal' of Jezebel was most likely a Phoenician god – and thus a foreign cult – introduced into Israel. It was symbolic of a foreign queen and would have been opposed by certain traditionalists. The fact that all the Baal worshippers could supposedly fit into the small Baal temple (2 Kgs 10.18-28) is evidence that this was not a widespread alternative to Yhwh worship. Further indication is found in the names of Ahab's family and associates. His chief minister was named Obadiah ('servant of Yhwh': 1 Kgs 18.3) and his two sons had Yhwh names (Ahaziah and Jehoram); the prophets he consulted were prophets of Yhwh (1 Kgs 22.5-28). Although the text accuses him of Baal worship (1 Kgs 16.31-32), we see no actual evidence that he promoted Baal worship beyond the royal cult specifically established for his wife. The opposition of Elijah and others was probably political opposition to Jezebel, even if disguised as religious piety. Ahab himself, by all accounts, was a Yhwh worshipper.

The ostraca found during the excavation of Samaria give a similarly mixed picture (§4.1.2). A variety of theophorous names are found in the texts known so far; of these eleven are compounded with Yhwh while six have Baal. There is no way to see any social distinction in the names: one has the impression that these were common, ordinary names about which people would not have thought very much except perhaps in a cultic context. It would appear that Baal and Yhwh were worshipped happily side by side.

Recent finds have been even more revealing. An inscription found in 1975–76 at Kuntillet Ajrud in the Negev (dated about the eighth century BCE) is conventionally read, 'I blessed you by Yhwh of Samaria and by his Asherah' (Gogel 1998: #6.1.14; G. I. Davies 1991: #8.017, #8.021). Similarly, in Khirbet el-Qôm near Hebron, another inscription has been found and dated to the seventh century (Dever 1970; Gogel 1998: #6.1.12; G. I. Davies 1991: #25.003). It is very difficult to read – partly, because it seems to have some of the letters duplicated – and a number of readings have been given (Zevit 2001: 359–70): the original editor A. Lemaire translated it as: 'Blessed be Uriah by Yhwh and <by his Asherah>, from his enemies he has saved him'. The epigrapher Joseph Naveh read it: 'May Uriyahu be blessed by Yahweh my guardian and by his Asherah'. Ziony Zevit interpreted it as: 'I blessed Uryahu to YHWH / to wit, from his enemies…for the sake of Asheratah save him / by Abiyahu'.

These finds have created a great deal of debate because this is the first time that any direct evidence of goddess worship had turned up (even the Samaria ostraca had no goddess names). There was naturally some question as to whether the 'Asherah' was a reference to a cult object or to a goddess. It partly hinges on the grammatical question of whether one can put a pronominal suffix on a proper name in the Northwest Semitic languages. Some have suggested alternative interpretations (e.g., that the final letter - *h* is not 'his' but a so-called locative *hē* or perhaps even a vowel letter), but others argue that the grammatical problems with a pronominal suffix can be overcome (Zevit 2001: 363–6). After considerable disagreement, the consensus is moving definitely in the direction of seeing a consort with Yhwh, a female divinity called Asherah (even if not everyone agrees, e.g., Keel and Uehlinger 1998: 281–2). If so, this would be quite parallel to Ugarit in which El the head of the pantheon has Athirat (cognate with Hebrew Asherah) as his consort.

The biblical text itself suggests goddess worship in several passages: it refers to 'Asherah', though at times this seems to designate a cult object, especially when appearing in the masculine plural ('Asherim'). Yet a number of passages seem definitely to refer to a goddess. 1 Kings 15.13 mentions the cult object made for Asherah. This was presumably in the temple; indeed, 2 Kgs 23.4, 7 mentions vessels of Asherah (among others) and cult personnel dedicated to Asherah in the Jerusalem temple, and 2 Kgs 21.7 also speaks of an image of Asherah in the temple. 1 Kings 18.19 designates 'the prophets of Asherah', alongside the prophets of Baal, which can only be a reference to a goddess. Thus, the biblical text itself preserves evidence that Asherah was worshipped – even in the Jerusalem temple – most likely as a consort of Yhwh. Worship of the 'host of heaven', referred to in 2 Kgs 17.16; 21.3; 23.4-5, is confirmed by solar symbols found on a number of Israelite seals (Keel and Uehlinger 1998: 282–309). Jeremiah (44.17–19, 25) mentions worship of the 'Queen of Heaven' who is likely to have been Asherah or Anat or perhaps even an amalgam of the two goddesses. Yet even though the text presents these as acts of apostasy, there is no hint that such worship was criticized or opposed at the time. If there was criticism, it was likely to have come from a minority movement, perhaps a 'Yhwh-alone movement' (as argued by Morton Smith 1971).

One other indication is an inscription of Sargon II relating to the fall of Samaria about 722 BCE. The Nimrud Prism states as follow (4.29–33, minor restorations not indicated):

> 29) With the power of the great gods, my lords,
> 30) against them I fought.
> 31) 27,280 persons with their chariots
> 32) and the gods in whom they trusted, as spoil
> 33) I counted.

It was quite normal for the Assyrians to remove the divine images of the people they conquered, often melting them down for the metal. The most reasonable interpretation in the context is that these referred to images of the Samarian gods. That is, the temple(s) of the Samarians contained images of more than one god, and the Assyrians took these away as spoil as was their custom.

Finally, the Jewish military colony at Elephantine was almost certainly pre-Persian, probably being established during the Neo-Babylonian or possibly even in the Assyrian period before the fall of Jerusalem in 587/586 BCE. The community had its own temple to *Yhw* (probably pronounced Yahu or Yaho) until it was destroyed by some of the local Egyptians (*TAD* A4.7–9 = *AP* 30–32), later being rebuilt by Persian authority. However, a list of contributors to the cult indicates that other divinities also had a place. Specifically listed are Eshem-Bethel and Anat-Bethel (*TAD* C3.15:127–8 = *AP* #22:124–5) and Anat-Yahu (*TAD* B7.3:3 = *AP* #44:3). It has been suggested that these were actually only hypostases of Yhwh (cf. Porten 1968: 179). This is a difficult matter to resolve, partly because these names occur only here – as if they had ceased to have much of a function in the Elephantine religion. They no doubt originated as goddess figures, but they may have developed in other ways (see further Grabbe 2004a: 241–2). Perhaps we are witnessing an evolution toward monotheism in this late period (see further below).

Archaeology has also given a good deal of information which confirms this textual picture (Nakhai 2001; Dever 2005: 110–75; Vriezen 2001). Only some brief references can be given here, though some have been discussed elsewhere (e.g., the Arad altar [§5.1.1]). Just to give a couple of examples, one of the most striking objects is the Taanach altar, usually dated to the tenth century and found at what seems to be a *bamah* or open air cult site (Lapp 1969: 42–4). The goddess Asherah seems to have a prominent place on it. Another striking object is the bronze bull of the 'Bull Site' (A. Mazar 1982). Again, it was found as the focal point of a cult site. It is not always possible to tell who used a particular cult site or the god represented (is the bull Yhwh or Baal?), but the archaeology amply demonstrates the variety of worship that texts have delineated.

4.2.8.3 Temple Religion versus 'Popular'/'Folk'/'Family' Religion

There are some problems with using the term 'popular' or 'folk' or 'family' religion. First, this might imply that such religion is less important or even less religion. Such is not the case: popular/folk/family religion is as legitimate and as much religion as any other. A second problem is a tendency to see this type of religion in a different category from other types of religion. This is erroneous: while perhaps having its own social and practical characteristics, it does not differ from any other type of religion. In the ancient Near East we can perhaps talk about three spheres of religion: the cult of the ruler, the national cult or cult of the national god (which might be the same as the ruler cult but not necessarily), and local or family or 'popular' cults. In Israel and Judah the distance between the temple cults and family cults might not have been that great. Yhwh worship seems to have been widespread, and with a multitude of altars it was common for ordinary people to attend worship in a temple (cf. 1 Sam. 1). What tends to characterize popular religion is the devotion to a particular deity for personal concerns and favours and the practice of the 'esoteric arts' for personal benefit: cults (including underworld cults) relating to the dead, healing, curses/blessings, magic, divination (Grabbe 1995: 119–51).

Temple religion came to be perhaps the main manifestation of Israelite religion before it became a book religion, but both these were probably post-exilic developments. That is, temples existed in pre-exilic times, including in Jerusalem, but it was probably only in the Persian period that the Jerusalem temple became the only one in many people's eyes (though there still existed temples on Gerizim, at Elephantine, in Leontopolis and possibly at Iraq al-Amir in Transjordan). As for Judaism as a 'religion of the book', I have argued that it was a development only toward the end of the Second Temple period (Grabbe 2000a: 317–18). The centre of temple religion was the sacrificial cult (Grabbe 1993a: 29–43; Nakhai 2001). Although the book of Leviticus is a late writing, it is likely that the cult described there had continued in broad outline for many centuries (Grabbe 1993a). The book of Leviticus is not a handbook for priests as some have suggested (Grabbe 2004b). The priestly knowledge was most likely passed down by word of mouth and through apprenticeship training without being committed formally to writing (at least, until very late). But we seem to have some knowledge of the cult and priesthood in the Persian period (Grabbe 2004a: 216–37; Schaper 2000) which can, with suitable caution, be projected back into the period of the monarchy. One of the differences was that during the monarchy the king was the chief religious figure – the chief priest, you could even say (Grabbe 1995: 20–40).

A cult of the dead was evidently a widespread phenomenon in ancient Israel, attested both from the text and archaeology (Bloch-Smith 1992; Grabbe 1995: 141–5) – and, incidentally, another indication of polytheism. A cult of the dead can take many forms and have many connotations, but one type is to treat the deceased ancestors as joining the Rephaim and becoming deified. Although the biblical text treats the Rephaim as early inhabitants of Canaan in some passages, texts from Ugarit and Phoenicia and even the Bible (Job 26.5; Ps. 88.11-13; Isa. 26.14, 19; Prov. 9.18) indicate the Rephaim are associated with the dead. Necromancy was evidently quite widely practised in ancient Israel (cf. Deut. 18.9-14; 1 Sam. 15.22-23; 28; Ezek. 21.26-27). The text in its present form naturally condemns such practices, but it equally attests its popularity. Another cult associated with the dead and the underworld is Molek worship. Whether Molek is a deity or only a sacrifice is still debated (cf. Heider 1985; Day 1989; Smelik 1995), but in any case, it seems to have been a chthonic cult associated with the underworld and with a cult of the dead. How widespread this cult was in Palestine is debatable, but it certainly existed, even in Jerusalem. It may also have involved child sacrifice, a subject still controversial to debate (2 Kgs 16.3; 17.17, 31; 21.6; Jer. 7.31-32; Day 1989; Smelik 1995). Finally, there are the teraphim mentioned in a number of passages (1 Sam. 15.22-23; 2 Kgs 23.24; Ezek. 21.26-27; Hos. 3.4; Zech. 10.2). Recent study of the teraphim argues that they were a common shrine to the ancestors kept in the home (Toorn 1990). Even the future king David had one, which his wife placed in his bed to deceive Saul's men so that he could escape (1 Sam. 19).

A subject of considerable controversy is that of cultic prostitution. According to some of the Greek writers, worship in Babylonian temples required all women to prostitute themselves at one time in their lives

(Herodotus 1.199). We also have some evidence of 'sacred marriage' rites in Mesopotamia, which might have involved the king and queen or the king and a priestess in ritual sex (Kramer 1969), though this is now disputed (Lapinkivi 2004). Among the cult personnel at Ugarit are those called *qdšm*, which some have proposed were male cultic prostitutes. This idea is now best rejected; there is no evidence for ritual prostitution – male or female – at Ugarit (Tarragon 1980: 138–41; Soden 1970). The biblical text (and subsequent Jewish and Christian religious traditions) asserts decadent sexual practices in 'pagan' worship, especially among the so-called Canaanites. It was therefore easy to believe in 'abominations' such as sexual orgies, prostitution, sodomy and the like as a constituent part of the cults which Israel was to eradicate (cf. Yamauchi 1973). As already suggested above, recent study has now called into question many of the assumptions about the 'Canaanite' cults and other worship in Israel's environment, as well as the biblical version of the development of Israelite religion. Most of the biblical references can be interpreted as symbolic language for religious straying, and there is really little support for the oft-repeated assertion that cultic prostitution formed a part of the non-Yahwistic cults (Barstad 1984: 21–33; Goodfriend and Toorn 1992; Grabbe 2015).

4.2.8.4 Development of Monotheism

How early monotheism developed is very much a point of dispute, though the general view today is that it was fairly late. The final form of the text in most books bears the stamp of those who were apparently monotheistic. In the biblical text Yhwh is clearly equated with El and with other divine names. Since Asherah is most often a consort of El in Northwest Semitic texts, a number of recent scholars have suggested that this equation is not fortuitous but represents the actual origin of Yhwh, that is, that the latter developed in the context of El worship (§4.2.8.1). In any case, it would not be surprising for El and Yhwh to be assimilated over time even if they were once separate deities. The various other male deities are equated with Yhwh (except for Baal who is depicted as being in a life-or-death struggle with Yhwh). This is a part of the process of moving toward monotheism. Many would argue that we find monotheism already in Second Isaiah with his denial of the existence of other gods (e.g., Albertz 1994: 417–18; M. S. Smith 2001: 179–94; 2002: 191–9; Becking et al. 2001: 191–2; contrast Thompson [1995a: 113] who states that Second Isaiah is an example of 'inclusive monotheism'): Yhwh alone is without beginning or end, uniquely divine and God alone, the creator of the cosmos and there is nothing like him (Isa. 46.9; 48.12-13).

The book of Deuteronomy has some statements that express similar ideas (e.g., Deut. 4.35, 39), but these exist alongside others that seem to accept the existence of other gods (Deut. 5.7; 6.4 [cf. M. S. Smith 2001: 153]). This could be explained by an editing process in which the monotheistic statements were later additions to the text. Thus, many scholars see the development of monotheism – in some circles, anyway – during the seventh to sixth centuries BCE. For example, it has been pointed out that astral imagery of the late eighth and seventh centuries had disappeared from seals and seal impressions of the Jerusalem elite by the early sixth and also the blessing and salvation functions of Yhwh's 'Asherah', known from several inscriptions, had been absorbed by Yhwh by the time of the Lachish and Arad ostraca (Uehlinger 1995, 2005). This has been interpreted as indirect evidence of Josiah's reform and a move in the direction of monotheism.

A topic closely associated with the issue of monotheism is the question of whether the worship of the Israelite god was aniconic. A number of biblical texts forbid the use of images in worship, such as the second commandment (Exod. 20.4; Deut. 5.8) and images are ridiculed (Isa. 40.18-20; 44.9-20; 46.1-2; Jer. 10.2-10). We know from later Jewish texts that the use of images or living forms of any kind was considered abhorrent and strongly rejected (Wis. 13–15; *Liber Antiquitatum Biblicarum* 44; *Testament of Job* 2–5; *Apocalypse of Abraham* 1–8; see also the quote from Hecataeus below). Some have argued that the worship of Yhwh was aniconic from the beginning; that is, that the non-use of images was a characteristic of Yhwh worship in the earlier period. Yet there are a number of indications that images were used in divine worship in Israel and Judah. The quotation from Sargon II above (§4.2.8.2) is already one indication. The many 'Astarte' images found by archaeologists all over Palestine is another (Moorey 2001; Stern 2001: 205–11). These by themselves do not prove that idols were used to represent Yhwh since the passages just mentioned could be referring to other deities, but the possibility that an image of Yhwh was to be found in the Jerusalem temple at one stage is a reasonable inference from the data just presented.

Apart from the biblical text, whose interpretation some dispute, one of the first and best indications of monotheistic, aniconic worship is found in Hecataeus of Abdera, a Greek writing from about 300 BCE. He describes the Jews in Palestine in a long paragraph which was then picked up and quoted by Diodorus of Sicily (40.3.4). The significant passage states:

> But he [Moses] had no images whatsoever of the gods made for them, being of the opinion that God is not in human form; rather the Heaven that surrounds the earth is alone divine, and rules the universe.

4.3 Synthesis

By the ninth century we seem to have reached a period where there is more agreement about the general outline of history in Palestine. There seems to be general agreement that Omri and Ahab ruled over some sort of state, even if the exact nature of that state is still debated (H. M. Niemann [2007], for example, refers to Omri as the war leader of a military administration). Judah was also a separate entity, but whether it is called a state is more controversial: it might have been a vassal of Israel, which in turn was a vassal of Damascus part of the time, though not under Omri (Knauf 2007). Jerusalem could well have been much what it was in the Amarna period, perhaps more of a city-state than anything else. Most seem to agree, though, that sometime in the eighth century Judah had become a territorial state.

In the ninth century the brief hiatus of freedom from the major powers, which Palestine had enjoyed since Egypt withdrew, came to an end. Shoshenq seems to have conducted some sort of excursion(s) into Palestine, though the extent and the effects are currently moot, but in any case he did not stay. But then in the early ninth century Assyria began to make excursions to the west, and in the middle of the century are the repeated clashes between Shalmaneser III and a coalition of twelve kings from the Syro-Palestinian region, led by Damascus but with Ahab an important ally. According to the Assyrian inscriptions the coalition remained intact up to Shalmaneser's fourteenth year (845 BCE). Between then and the eighteenth year (841 BCE) things must have fallen apart, for in 841 the coalition was defeated, and with Hadadezer now dead Damascus, under a new king Hazael, alone faced the Assyrian army. In the same year the new king of Israel, Jehu, submitted to Assyria, putting it on the opposite side from the Aramaeans. The Assyrians continued to cause problems for Hazael for another three years, until Shalmaneser's twenty-first year, but then Assyria ceased to concern itself with the western part of its empire for the next 30 years. This left Damascus a free hand to dominate the region, including Israel, first under the leadership of Hazael and then under his son Bar-Hadad. This is exactly the picture of the biblical text (2 Kgs 10.34-36; 12.18-19; 13.3, 22-25).

After the events around 800 BCE, there is not a lot of further extra-biblical information for the next half century until the reign of Tiglath-pileser III. The biblical text assigns a good deal of important activity to Jeroboam II, but this individual is not mentioned by any extra-biblical sources. About 780–775 BCE Shamshi-ilu the Assyrian commander for the region collected tribute from Ḫadiiāni. This would suggest that Damascus was not able to do just anything it wished. The next king of Israel mentioned is Menahem, in Tiglath-pileser's *Annals* and in the Iran Stele III (ca. 738). For the first time in the Assyrian annals, we also find a mention of the kingdom of Judah, in Tiglath-pileser's *Summary Inscription* 7. According to *Summary Inscription* 4, the Assyrian king also annexed Gilead, Galilee and other areas of northern Israel (cf. 2 Kgs 15.29).

The Syro-Ephraimite war in 734–732 BCE is not mentioned as such in the Assyrian records, but it is indirectly attested. The exact cause of Damascus and Israel ganging up on Judah still escapes us, but a number of biblical passages presuppose it. It also brought Judah into Assyria's sphere, though this was likely to have happened shortly, anyway. It presaged the final fall of the Northern Kingdom. Here again the original sources give more than one picture. Was Samaria captured by Shalmaneser V or Sargon II? The proposal that it was taken twice – in 722 and again in 720 BCE – has merit, but there are other explanations, such as Sargon claiming to capture the city when all he did was deport its inhabitants. But the basic picture of the biblical text seems to be in harmony with the Assyrian sources, even if the details are not always reliable.

We can now summarize the results of this chapter as far as history is concerned. In doing so, it is difficult to indicate graphically the relative importance of the points listed below.

4.3.1 Biblical Data Confirmed

- A number of the Israelite kings and their approximate dates are confirmed: Omri, Ahab, Jehu, Joash, Menahem, Pekah, Hoshea, as well as probably Jehoram. Of the kings of Judah, Jehoahaz and possibly Ahaziah are correctly remembered.
- Mesha king of Moab is correctly remembered and his breaking away from Israelite rule (though some of the details remain questionable).
- Of the Aramaean rulers, Hazael of Damascus, his son Ben-Hadad, and Rezin are given correctly.
- Strength of Hazael over Israel and the region.
- Strength of Ben-Hadad, son of Hazael, and his loss of power over Israel (the Assyrian intervention is not mentioned explicitly, though it may be alluded to).
- Menahem's payment of tribute.
- Pekah's defeat and death.
- Assyrian defeat of Rezin of Damascus.

- Hoshea of Israel as replacement for Pekah.
- Jehoahaz (also called just Ahaz) of Judah's interaction with Tiglathpileser III.
- Fall of Samaria to Shalmaneser V.

4.3.2 Biblical Data Not Confirmed, Though They May Be Correct

- Ahab may have fought the Aramaeans during part of his reign, though not at the end.
- Whether any of the stories about Elijah and Elisha preserve data about the doings of actual individuals is hard to say. It would not be surprising if such individuals actually lived, but it would be very unlikely that the details of their lives could be verified. Of course, most of us would discount miraculous happenings and prescient knowledge.
- Jehu's revolt and coup.
- Rule of Athaliah.
- Reign of Jeroboam II.
- Syro-Ephraimite War.
- The other kings of Judah (in addition to Ahaz and perhaps Ahaziah).
- 'Minor kings' of Israel, such as Zechariah and Pekahiah.
- Hoshea may indeed have sought to gain help from a king of Egypt against the Assyrians (2 Kgs 17.4)

4.3.3 Biblical Picture Incorrect

- Ahab is presented as weak militarily.
- The Aramaeans are the main enemy.
- The king of Aram is wrongly given as Ben-Hadad in the time of Ahab.
- Asa's defeat of Zerah the Cushite (found only in 2 Chron. 14.8-14) looks completely invented (including the name Zerah).

4.3.4 Biblical Picture Omits/has Gaps

- The Assyrians are strangely absent from the picture until the time of Tiglath-pileser. It is possible that the biblical writer had no knowledge of the Assyrians in the time of Ahab, but if he did, he has suppressed this information. If material from the later Jehu dynasty is found in 1 Kings 20 and 22, as many scholars now believe, the biblical writer may have placed it in the present position by mistake.

The alternative – that the editor/compiler knew the true nature of the material but deliberately misused it – is by no means impossible, but the ignorant use of the material is more likely.

- Jehu's submission to Shalmaneser III, along with his payment of tribute, is not mentioned in the Bible.
- The submission of Joash of Israel to the Assyrians.

Chapter 5

IRON IIC (720–539 BCE): PEAK AND DECLINE OF JUDAH

The end of the eighth century marked a major watershed in the history of Israel. The Kingdom of Israel came to an end by about 720 BCE, leaving only Judah as a semi-independent kingdom. This might seem to have removed a major rival for Judah, but the kingdom was now an Assyrian vassal, and Assyria was now in close proximity in the form of the Assyrian provinces to Judah's north: Samerina, Megiddo and Dor. Then came Sennacherib's invasion in 701 BCE, which was by any reckoning a crucial event in Judah's history. In many ways, the period of Judah's history between Sennacherib's and Nebuchanezzar's invasions is the subject of this chapter.

5.1 Sources

5.1.1 Archaeology

This period in Judah's history began with the invasion of Sennacherib, which left Judah devastated (see the survey in Grabbe [ed.] 2003: 3–20). Only Jerusalem and a few other (mostly northern) sites (e.g., Mizpah [Tell en-Nasbeh] and Gezer) escaped the Assyrian wrath. Major sites destroyed included Ramat-Rahel, Timnah (Tell Batash), Beth-Shemesh, Tell Judeidah, Tel 'Erani, Tell Beit Mirsim, Tell Halif (Tell Khuweilifeh), Khirbet Rabud (Debir/Kiriath-Sepher) and Arad. Beersheba is often thought to have been destroyed by Sennacherib, but E. A. Knauf now argues against this (2002). Of 354 Judaean settlements in existence in the late eighth century and destroyed, only 39 are presently known to have been rebuilt in the seventh (Stern 2001: 142; cf. Finkelstein 1994a).

Central to determining Sennacherib's destruction have been two factors: (1) the stratigraphy of Lachish and (2) the 1,200+ *lmlk* seal impressions found on storage jars in Jerusalem, Lachish and elsewhere. It has now been determined that Sennacherib's siege and destruction of Lachish is found in stratum III (see references in Grabbe [ed.] 2003: 6–8). Curiously, the siege and fall of Lachish are not mentioned in Sennacherib's inscriptions. As for the *lmlk* seals, their use was likely to have been over a rather short period of time because of the seal impressions of named officials on them and because *lmlk* jars were found in some sites (e.g., in Philistia) that did not come under Judah's control until Hezekiah's reign. If their production and use was thus over a very narrow time frame, they can be used to date particular events in the context of Hezekiah's rebellion and subsequent Assyrian attack (for information on the *lmlk* seals, see §5.1.2.6).

One of the central questions has been the way in which Sennacherib shut up Hezekiah 'like a bird in a cage'. Was this by the standard siege methods of surrounding the city by a siege mound? The difficulty has been excavation work in Jerusalem that found evidence of this period. A. van der Kooij (1986) examined two issues: (1) whether the Assyrian statements imply a siege and (b) whether there is any evidence for such a siege. Not strictly based on the archaeology, van der Kooij's argument involved the question of how to interpret the statements in the Assyrian inscriptions. He concluded that the wording of the Assyrian inscriptions did not envisage an actual siege. H. Tadmor (1985) also argued that Jerusalem did not come under siege; indeed, the Assyrian text also implies that it did not. More recently W. Mayer (1995, 2003) has similarly argued that the Assyrian army did not in fact set up siege works around Jerusalem directly. Yet just 4 km southwest of Jerusalem, Ramat Raḥel (*ḫirbet ṣāliḥ*) seems to show evidence of a destruction of level VB which has 170 *lmlk* jar handles associated with it (Dessel 1997; Vaughn 1999a: 102–5).

The seventh century saw great changes, yet some were positive. Stern sums up things in this way:

> The overall picture emerging from the excavations at the sites along the Judaean Hill ridge appears to corroborate that in other parts of the Judaean monarchy: a severe destruction followed Sennacherib's 701 BCE campaign at almost all sites, excluding Jerusalem. Between that date and the arrival of the Babylonians, the country enjoyed a period of rebuilding and relative prosperity. (Stern 2001: 163)

According to Stern (2001: 130–1), despite the widespread destruction by Sennacherib, the rebuilding process was quite rapid. A number of archaeologists put specific times on developments in the seventh century; however, such a precise dating of events from archaeology can be disputed: 'Archaeologically, it is not easy to distinguish the finds of the early seventh century from those of the second half of that century' (Finkelstein and Silberman 2001: 265; cf. also 345–6). Being able to distinguish the archaeology from Manasseh's reign, as opposed to Josiah's, is not easy, though a number of finds go together to suggest that the main recovery of prosperity occurred early in the century (Finkelstein and Silberman 2001: 265–9; Stern 2001: 130–1).

Throughout the seventh century Jerusalem had no rivals, because most of those urban areas that approached it in size and importance in the eighth century had been destroyed by the Assyrians and had not been rebuilt (Tatum 1991: 141–2; Steiner 2001: 285; 2003a: 76–7). Even Lachish, which had its fortifications repaired, was only sparsely inhabited. There seems to be general agreement that in the Judaean heartland the settlement area in general increased in the seventh century, though it was mainly in rural areas (including the desert fringe) or new towns or fortresses (Tatum 1991: 142; Finkelstein 1994a: 174–80). The increase in settlement area has been explained as the accommodation of those who were forced to leave the Shephelah when the Assyrians took it from Judaean control. The situation varied somewhat in different parts of the country, as did the situation in the eighth century in comparison with that in the seventh. Not all of the country was devastated by the Assyrian army. The old area of Benjamin (now a part of Judah north of Jerusalem) had prospered in the late eighth century and continued to do so in the seventh, apparently having escaped (at least to some extent) the ravages of Sennacherib (Ofer 2001: 29).

The result was that Jerusalem was left as the only real urban centre in Judah in the seventh century (on the archaeology of Jerusalem, see in particular the essays in Vaughn and Killebrew [eds] 2003). Yet there is little evidence of the city's being an administrative centre: no public buildings were built in the seventh century, and the city seems mainly residential (Steiner 2001: 284). It may be that the city functioned primarily as a commercial and trading centre. This period also saw a huge expansion of Jerusalem, though exactly how early that began is disputed. Since the excavations in the Jewish Quarter in the 1970s, it is now widely accepted that this growth took in the western hill (Geva 2003). The expansion is thought by some to be a result of Sennacherib's invasion, but many now think that it began earlier, in the late eighth century BCE (Geva 2003: 203–7; Reich and Shukron 2003; Finkelstein 1994a: 175). One explanation for this unprecedented growth is that it was at least in part due to immigration from the Northern Kingdom after the conquest of Samaria and from the Shephelah after 701 BCE when a large part of it was removed from Judaean control (Broshi 1974). The Broad Wall was built about this time, apparently to protect this new western quarter. This growth is also evidenced by a new quarter on the eastern slope, in which a number of luxurious houses were constructed together with a new section of the city wall to the east to enclose this section within the fortifications. About this time there was also apparently expansion of settlement to the north, into an unfortified section of the city.

Conventional estimates put the size of all Jerusalem about 600 BCE at 600 dunams or a minimum of 6,000–7,000 inhabitants (Geva 2003: 206), but G. Barkay (as cited in Lipschits 2003: 327) thinks it was 900–1,000 dunams in size, which could mean a population of up to a maximum of 25,000 persons; however, such an estimate would take in even farms on the edge of the built-up area (Lipschits 2003: 327 n. 14). It has been argued that residential parts of the city to the north were damaged in Sennacherib's siege and remained deserted (Geva 2003: 207), but it seems unlikely that the Assyrian army actually encamped at Jerusalem or laid siege to the city in traditional fashion (cf. Grabbe [ed.] 2003: 8–10). Nevertheless, both the eastern extension and the northern expansion seem to have been abandoned before the fall of Jerusalem to the Babylonians, while the settlement on the western hill appears to have withdrawn to within the wall (Geva 2003: 207; Reich and Shukron 2003: 217).

One site has become controversial in recent years. 2 Kings 20.20 states that Hezekiah made the 'pool' (הברכה) and the 'conduit' (התעלה) and brought water into the city. The Siloam tunnel has long been thought to provide the evidence for the truth of this verse. J. Rogerson and P. R. Davies (1996) challenged this consensus and sought to redate the tunnel and its inscription to the time of the Maccabees. This identification has been widely rejected (e.g., Hendel 1996; Norin 1998); however, E. A. Knauf (2001b) has now argued for the reign of Manasseh as the time of its building. Thus, the question of whether the Siloam tunnel belongs to Hezekiah's time is far from settled, but it well fits other trends in the seventh century and would fall logically in the reign of Manasseh.

In the Judaean hills south of Jerusalem, Ramat Raḥel was a major centre. The site, with its citadel, was probably destroyed at the time of Sennacherib's invasion. A new citadel was built in the seventh century (stratum VA) and shows some Assyrian influence. It has often been interpreted as a royal palace, but why would the Judaean kings build a palace so close to Jerusalem? N. Na'aman (2001) argues that it was Assyrian policy to construct emporia and centres of government near the capitals of vassal kingdoms. Ramat Raḥel would be much better explained as an Assyrian building used as an administrative centre (though Judaeans would have been conscripted to do the actual work). As supporting evidence, the presence of Assyrian officials can be proposed for a number of vassal kingdoms at this time, including Byblos, Tyre, Ashdod and Gaza.

According to this interpretation, economic considerations were a major factor, with Assyria actually competing with its vassals for revenues. No wonder anti-Assyrian rebellions broke out periodically! Assyria's relentless imperialism was severely damaging to its subjects. No exact dating for the destruction of the fortress is possible, and 587 is only one possibility. It may have been abandoned by the withdrawing Assyrians, or even destroyed by them as they left. Yet, other interpretations are possible. E. A. Knauf (2005a: 170–1) argues that such building projects were often undertaken as propaganda for the ruling dynasty. It was not as if a royal palace so close to Jerusalem was *needed* but simply that it proclaimed the splendour of the king.

The Judaean hills cover the general area from just south of Jerusalem on the north to Beersheba valley in the south, and from the Judaean desert on the east to the descent to the coastal plain on the west, an area of approximately 900 km^2. The question of the population in the seventh century compared to the eighth is controversial (cf. Finkelstein 1994a: 174–5). The Judaean hills survey (by A. Ofer; cf. Ofer 2001) found that from the mid-eleventh to the eighth century the population nearly doubled in each century, but the seventh century showed a decline compared to the eighth. Although the number of settlements was similar (86 in the seventh, compared to 88 in the eighth), the settled area was much less (70 hectares in the seventh, versus 90 in the eighth). This meant a decline in population from about 23,000 to about 17,000. Even if one slightly reinterprets the data for less of a contrast (from 84 to 74 hectares, or 21,000 to 18,500 inhabitants), there was still a marked fall off. This could be due to a variety of causes, but one obvious possibility is Sennacherib's invasion of 701 BCE.

I. Finkelstein, however, is not convinced of the contrast between the density of population in the Judaean highlands between the eighth and seventh centuries (Finkelstein 1994a: 174–5). He notes that 'all major excavated sites in the Judaean highlands were occupied in both the eighth and seventh centuries BCE' (1994a: 174). He makes several points (in addition to the one about the occupation of all major excavated sites in both the eighth and seventh centuries): that in the seventh century, possibly Tell en-Nasbeh and Gibeon, and certainly Ramat Rahel reached their peak, that a group of forts was established around Jerusalem, that a system of farmhouses was established around Jerusalem and Bethlehem, and that the Judahite population spread to nearby arid zones (Judaean desert and Negev). Finkelstein argues that there may be reasons why the survey shows some differences between the two centuries, but he assumes that the Judaean hills south of Jerusalem were as densely populated in the seventh as the eighth century.

Sennacherib's invasion was hard on the Shephelah: the city of Lachish was one of the major cities besieged by the Assyrians (Uehlinger 2003), but others destroyed were Tell Beit Mirsim and Beth-Shemesh. Afterwards, the Assyrians appear to have removed a good portion of the Shephelah from Judaean control. The late seventh and early sixth century saw a decrease of 70 per cent in built-up areas, mostly in unwalled villages and farmsteads and mostly in the eastern part of the region (Finkelstein 1994a: 172–4). About 85 per cent of the eighth-century sites were not resettled in the seventh. Archaeologists disagree about the case of Tell Beit Mirsim. E. Stern (2001: 149) states that the town was certainly rebuilt in the seventh century, before being destroyed by the Babylonians. However, R. Greenberg (1993: I, 180) notes: 'There is slight ceramic and stratigraphic evidence for a partial reoccupation of the site in the seventh or early sixth century BCE'. The only site that grew was Tell Miqne (usually identified with ancient Ekron), but this area had generally been outside Judah. Tell Batash (Timnah) was also apparently outside Judah but likely under the control of Ekron (the pottery is mixed but Philistine predominates).

One of the interesting phenomena of the seventh century was the growth in settlement in the arid regions: the Negev and the eastern deserts. En-Gedi may have been settled in the eighth. In any event, both it and Jericho grew considerably in the second half of the seventh century, with an unprecedented amount of settlement (59 sites) between the two sites (Lipschits 2003: 338–9). Beersheba was abandoned at this time, but new sites were also established at Tel Masos, Ḥorvat 'Uza, Ḥorvat Radom, Tel 'Ira and Aroer (Finkelstein 1994a: 175–6).

Arad has often been discussed in connection with the reign of Josiah, but it is a site about which prominent archaeologists have come to some significantly different conclusions, mainly because the excavator Y. Aharoni was not able to publish a full report before his death (see especially the summary in Manor and Heron 1992). The original interpretation was that a shrine persisted through layers XI–IX, consisting of a courtyard with a large altar, a broadroom and a small inner room apparently with a stela (מצבה) and two incense altars. Some alterations were made over time, but in stratum VIII some significant changes were made in the temple area: it was dismantled and much of it covered in a metre-thick layer of earth. This activity has been associated with the cult reforms of Hezekiah. Nevertheless, the stratigraphy, the dating of the strata, and the possible historical events with which they are to be associated are all disputed. D. Ussishkin (1988), for example, interpreted matters rather differently (though depending on the preliminary publications and interviews with some of the excavators). He noted (with others) that the homogeneity of the pottery from strata X–VIII suggests a relatively short period of time, and these layers may represent only different stages of a single building phase. The shrine, which some had dated even as early as stratum XI, was in fact not built until stratum VII.

Now, a new complete stratigraphical examination conducted in 1995–96 has led to a re-evaluation, with differences from that of the original excavator and the many studies built on it (Herzog 2001: 156–78; cf. Uehlinger 2005). There were particular problems in relating the temple complex to the stratigraphy by the earlier excavators, partly because of the 'biblical archaeology' paradigm embraced by the excavation team (among whom Herzog includes himself). Stratum VII elsewhere in the site was 2.5 m above the temple floor, showing that the temple was earlier than that (contra Ussishkin). The temple began in stratum X (not XI, as widely believed) or the eighth century, with a second phase of construction in stratum IX. The temple was not destroyed by fire but was dismantled in stratum VIII (late eighth century), which Herzog attributes to Hezekiah. The question is, though, whether the dismantling was done to destroy the temple or, on the contrary, to protect the pillars and so on, for future use (cf. Uehlinger 2005: 287–92; Niehr 1995: 35; Ussishkin 1988).

This settlement in the eastern and southern arid regions was short-lived for the most part, however, collapsing at the end of the Iron Age (Lipschits 2003: 334–7). In the eastern desert sites, there is no evidence of physical destruction but gradual abandonment. In the Negev, a number of the fortresses show signs of destruction (including Ḥorvat 'Uza and Arad and the settlement sites of Tel 'Ira and Tel Malḥata). Other sites appear to have been abandoned (e.g., Ḥorvat Radum). It seems that the decline came about primarily because the areas of Judah which the arid regions depended on for military and economic support had themselves been destroyed by the Babylonians. The inhabitants of the settlements gradually withdrew because they had no other choice.

The archaeology also provides data about aspects of the economy, though this often has to be put together with other data. The Edomite plateau gained a significant population at this time, and there are indications of contact with Arabia (Finkelstein 1994a: 177–80; Finkelstein and Silberman 2001: 267–9). This could suggest the place of Judah in a trade route from Arabia. We know from Assyrian sources that Gaza was an important trading centre for the Assyrians. The seventh-century forts at Qadesh-Barnea and Ḥaṣeva (both probably outside Judah; see below) may have been built with the protection of this trade in mind. There is also evidence of a major olive-oil production centre at Tel Miqne (Ekron). This was an old Philistine city and not part of Judah; however, the olives could not be grown locally, which leads to the inference that they would most likely have been imported from the Samarian and Judaean highlands.

One feature of the archaeological data that particularly stands out is the sudden increase in the quantity of written objects preserved from the seventh century: seals/bullae, ostraca and inscribed weights (Finkelstein and Silberman 2001: 270, 281, 284; Stern 2001: 169–200). This phenomenon is apparently not found in the neighbouring Assyrian provinces or vassal states. It thus appears to be a genuine increase in the production of written objects in Judah at the time and not just an impression created by the accidents of discovery. A number of conclusions have been drawn from this fact, not all of them justified (§§3.2.5; 5.2.4).

Attempts have been made to determine the borders of Judah from archaeological data. Several sites have been put forward as an indication of an expansion of the territory of Judah during the reign of Josiah. The arguments are only in part based on archaeology, but the archaeology of the sites is important: Megiddo, Meṣad Ḥashavyahu, Ḥaṣeva and Qadesh-Barnea. With regard to Megiddo, no Judaean artifacts have been found from the seventh century (stratum II). A consideration of the historical situation suggests that it was more likely under Egyptian control (cf. Na'aman 1991: 51–2), but no Egyptian artifacts have been found, either (Finkelstein and Silberman 2001: 350). This might be the case if the occupation was brief, whether by Josiah or the Egyptians, but the fact is that nothing in the archaeology connects Megiddo with Josiah. With regard to the fortresses at Ḥaṣeva and Qadesh-Barnea (cf. Cohen and Yisrael 1995; Cohen 1981, 1997), the archaeology is ambiguous. They seem to be of Assyrian construction (Na'aman 1991: 48). Although Judaean artifacts have been found at Qadesh-Barnea (Judaean inscribed weights, pottery vessels, Hebrew ostraca), the material culture is mixed (Kletter 1999: 42). A number of ostraca were found at Qadesh-Barnea, including two with Hebrew writing, some written in Egyptian hieratic, and at least two with a mixture of Hebrew and Egyptian. Once again, the connection with Josiah comes primarily from considerations other than the archaeology. Na'aman (1991: 48–9), on the other hand, suggests that the best way to explain the archaeology is that as the Assyrians withdrew, the Egyptians took over.

Based on an ostracon, as well as the pottery, Meṣad Ḥashavyahu has been a prime part of the argument for Josiah's expansion, since it is not only well outside the traditional territory of Judah but also on the coast, which could suggest an effort by Judah to obtain its own outlet to the sea. The excavations of this settlement on the coast have only recently been published (Fantalkin 2001). The settlement was very short-lived, only a couple of decades or so. From archaeological evidence alone, it was either late seventh century or early sixth. There is actually no direct evidence for supposing it to be linked with Josiah. A large amount of eastern Greek pottery has suggested that a large portion of the population was Greek, but the names in the published ostracon are Hebrew, three with the name Yahu and one with Baal (Gogel 1998: 423–4). One theory suggests that it was a Greek trading colony, but the location and the finds do not support this. It is more likely that it was a settlement of Greek mercenaries, though also with some Judaeans in various capacities (Na'aman 1991: 44–6; Fantalkin 2001: 139–47; Finkelstein and Silberman 2001: 350–1). If so, they were probably in Egyptian service (Psammetichus I or possibly even Necho II). The Egyptians controlled this area between the withdrawal of the Assyrians and the coming of the Babylonians. For it to be settled by mercenaries in the service of Judah is not very credible. Judaean control is even less likely if the date of Meṣad Ḥashavyahu is lowered to 600 BCE (Kletter 1999: 42). Stern (2001: 140–2) objects, pointing to the lack of Egyptian remains; however, the site also lacks characteristic Judaean remains (e.g., rosette seal impressions), and the short time of occupation might have left no characteristic Egyptian remains (though one cooking-pot lid is possibly Egyptian). The site could have been destroyed by the Babylonians in 604 BCE, along with Ashkelon and other areas on the coast.

Also as an indication of borders, a number of artifacts have been considered as of potential help (Kletter 1999). These include the following: (1) 'Judaean pillar figurines'. Most of these are from the eighth and seventh centuries. They show differences from pillar figurines of other areas (such as Israel and Transjordan). It has been suggested that these represent Asherah, though any direct proof is lacking, and little evidence exists of a relation to the cult. But none was apparently broken deliberately. (2) Inscribed scale weights. The main period of use was the seventh century, though some are as early as the eighth. They are thus not an invention of Josiah. Most likely common weights rather than royal, they may represent private trade relations rather than public administration. (3) Horse and rider figurines. Most of these are from the eighth century, but some are dated to the seventh. Of the five types, the first type is definitely Judaean, while types 3 and 4 are Phoenician and Transjordanian, which means that the Judaean type is easily distinguishable from neighbouring areas. (4) The rosette stamps (on these, see §5.1.2.6). Their distribution leaves no doubt of their Judaean identification, but since hardly any are found in the central hill country of Negev, it makes it hard to use them for political borders.

Kletter (1999: 40–3) comes to several conclusions about the artifacts in relation to Judah's possible borders. He notes that the overwhelming majority of artifacts are found in the Judaean heartland: 96 per cent of Judaean pillar figures, 98 per cent of the horse and rider figures, 96 per cent of the rosette seal impressions and 75 per cent of the Judaean inscribed weights. Various explanations have been given for those outside the heartland, such as trade, but only the western Shephelah shows a meaningful concentration of Judaean artifacts. Archaeology cannot pinpoint accurate borders nor establish the political affiliation of single sites. But the finds fit more or less with the Judaean heartland and do not indicate large-scale expansion. They cannot prove or refute the possibility that Josiah or another king lost or gained small areas for short durations. Nevertheless, artifacts are varied and also of general value for political borders: some relate to trade, some to religious beliefs.

O. Lipschits (2005: esp. 185–271) has provided the definitive account of the archaeology of Judah in the sixth century BCE. The local pottery assemblages show an unbroken material cultural tradition in Judah from the end of the Iron Age into the Persian period. The settlement continuity from Babylonian to Persian rule has made it quite difficult to distinguish these periods. The distinction between Lachish strata 3 and 2 provides the chronological and stratigraphic key. It is only in the mid-fifth century that the pottery repertoires begin to include types and forms considered typical of the Persian-period local culture. To date all destruction layers to 587/586 in Judah is to depend on the text, not archaeology: the notion of a demographic and material-culture gap in the sixth century BCE goes too far. We find considerable variation across the region. In Judah there was a sharp decline in urban life but continuity in rural settlements in the highlands, particularly between Hebron and Benjamin. As we might expect from the text, Jerusalem and the cities of the west were destroyed, following which we have a collapse in the east (the Judaean desert, the Jordan Valley, the Dead Sea region) and south (the south Shephelah and the Negev). Benjamin and the Judaean highland, which apparently escaped the Babylonian destruction, contained most of the population. As for Jerusalem itself, signs of the Babylonian destruction are found throughout the city. Surprisingly, there is no evidence of settlement from then until the middle of the Persian period: Jerusalem seems to have been uninhabited during the four decades or so of the 'exilic period'. The capital had apparently been moved to Tell en-Nasbeh (Mizpah), and Benjamin was where most people in the province now lived.

5.1.1.1 Conclusions with Regard to Archaeology

1. The two important horizons in the stratigraphy of this time are the destructions by Sennacherib and Nebuchadnezzar. They are helpful in defining the layers relating to the seventh and early sixth century. The stratigraphy and dating at Lachish is extremely important, and much of the interpretation of other sites depends on their relation to the finds at Lachish.
2. It is difficult, however, to distinguish between the early seventh century and the second half of the century. Very specific dating by archaeology alone is not necessarily possible. This means that assertions about developments in the reign of Manasseh versus that of Josiah or later kings (some quoted in the discussion above) need to be looked at carefully.
3. The area of Judah where the *lmlk* seals are found and where destruction seems to have taken place in relation to the events of 701 BCE is a fairly well-defined area (see especially Na'aman 1986a). The main cities of defence were those in the Judaean hill country and the Shephelah, with Hebron as the main hub. Most of them show evidence both of the stamped jar handles and attack by the Assyrians. The distribution of finds also has interesting affinities with the list of fortified cities in 2 Chron. 11.5-10, though the exact relationship has been much debated (Na'aman 1986a, 1988a; Garfinkel 1988; Hobbs 1994; Ben Zvi 1997).
4. There is so far no archaeological or other evidence that Jerusalem was invested by the Assyrian army in the sense of being surrounded by a siege mound and having an Assyrian army camped outside its wall. It was 'shut up' by having the various communication routes blocked, but the nearest evidence of the Assyrian army is presently at Ramat Raḥel, 4 km from Jerusalem.
5. Jerusalem's position was considerably enhanced in the seventh century. Although the question of whether some of the main eighth-century sites were settled seems to be answered differently by different interpreters, the size and dominance of Jerusalem appears to have been many times greater than any other cities. The expansion had already begun in the eighth century, but because Sennacherib destroyed most other towns in Judah, Jerusalem was left without a rival. This dominance does not appear to have come about because of greater centralization of the administration, however, since the character of Jerusalem is that of a residential city. The Siloam tunnel, usually assumed to have been built during the time of Hezekiah, may well belong to the time of Manasseh.

6. The borders of Judah do not appear to have enlarged under Josiah's rule as is sometimes alleged. On the contrary, at the beginning of the seventh century, there was an immediate loss of territory in that much of the Shephelah was taken away. Perhaps to make up for this loss, evidence exists that settlements extended into some of the arid zones of the east and the south. There is some indication of a boundary as far north as Bethel, but the areas of Samaria, the Galilee, the coastal plain or Transjordan do not show any signs of Judaean expansion (Na'aman 1991). Allegations that the borders of Judah took in areas as far as Meṣad Ḥashavyahu and even Megiddo do not appear to have much support in the archaeological record and would have been brief, if at all. Despite claims to the contrary, there seems little archaeological evidence of either political or religious centralization in the seventh century. The evidence of cult suppression claimed for Arad is ambiguous.
7. The archaeology provides some evidence of economic developments. Population growth in the Negev area, objects allegedly inscribed with Old South Arabian inscriptions (though Professor Knauf has pointed out to me that the South Arabian connection is uncertain) and forts in the south of the country (such as Qadesh-Barnea) may be evidence of trade through the region of Judah. There is also evidence of olive-oil production on a major scale at Ekron (Tel Miqre), though the olives themselves would have had to come from elsewhere, including the Judaean highlands.
8. The much greater number of ostraca, inscribed seals and other written objects seems to be evidence of the development of the bureaucracy. Whether it indicates anything else, such as an increase in literacy, is a matter of debate (§3.2.5).
9. The Babylonian destruction of Jerusalem and the surrounding area caused a collapse further afield, in the east and south. But Benjamin had not suffered from the Babylonian invasion and became the centre of the province for the next century. All the evidence suggests that Jerusalem itself remained uninhabited from 587/586 to the beginning of Persian rule.

5.1.2 Palestinian Inscriptions

5.1.2.1 The Adon Papyrus

The date and the sender of this document have not been preserved; however, a Demotic notation on the back of the document has been interpreted as a reference to Ekron (*CoS* III, 132–3). The papyrus is generally dated to the late seventh century, but this is only an educated guess. In it

Adon, king of a site now lost from the manuscript, calls on the Pharaoh for help.

5.1.2.2 Meṣad Ḥashavyahu

The following translation of ostracon 1 is from Gogel:

> 1 May the official, my lord, hear
> 2 the plea of his servant. Your servant
> 3 is working at the harvest…
> 6 When your [se]rvant had finished his reaping and had stored
> 7 it a few days ago, Hoshayahu ben Shabay came
> 8 and took your servant's garment. When I had finished
> 9 my reaping, at that time, a few days ago, he took your servant's garment.
> 10 All my companions will testify for me, all who were reaping with me in the heat of
> 11 the sun – they will testify for me that this is true. I am guiltless of an
> 12 in[fraction. (So) please return] my garment. If the official does (= you do) not consider it an obligation to retur[n]
> 13 [your] ser[vant's garment, then hav]e pi[ty] upon him
> 14 [and re]turn your [se]rvant's [garment]. You must not remain silent.
> (Gogel 1998: 423–4)

5.1.2.3 Arad Ostraca

The Arad archive is associated with a man named Eliashib who seems to have been commander of the fortress. Ten of the ostraca speak about the 'Kittim', often with regard to distributing rations to them (## 1, 2, 4, 5, 7, 8, 10, 11, 14, 17). These are usually interpreted as Greek mercenaries, but which king they served is still a moot point. The following quotation is from Arad 18:

> 1 To my lord Elyashib.
> 2 May Yhwh concern
> 3 himself with your well-being. And now,
> 4 give Shemaryahu
> 5 one *letek*-measure, and to the Qerosite
> 6 give one *homer*-measure. Regarding
> 7 the matter about which you
> 8 gave me orders: everything is fine:
> 9 he is staying in
> 10 the house (temple) of Yhwh. (Gogel 1998: 390–1)

5.1.2.4 Lachish Letters

An important collection of ostraca was found at Lachish. Some of these seem to have been correspondence (perhaps military) in the period not long before the capture of Jerusalem in 587/586. Lachish 4 says:

> 1 May Yhw[h] cause my [lord] to hear
> 2 good tidings at this time!...
> 9 For if he [co]me[s around] during the morning tour
> 10 he will know that we
> 11 are watching the Lachish (fire-)signals, according to all the signs which my lord
> 12 gave us, for we cannot see
> 13 Azeqah. (Gogel 1998: 417)

5.1.2.5 The Ashyahu Ostracon

An ostracon published in 1996 has been associated with the reign of Josiah (Bordreuil, Israel and Pardee 1996, 1998). The ostracon was obtained on the antiquities market and is of unknown provenance. More recently I. Eph'al and J. Naveh (1998) have outlined their reasons for 'hesitations regarding the authenticity' of this document (plus another ostracon published at the same time).

5.1.2.6 Seals and Bullae

One of the valuable sources of information for the eighth and seventh centuries BCE is the seal impressions (and occasionally the actual seals themselves) from both public officials and private individuals. A number of these have been found in proper archaeological contexts, but many were obtained on the antiquities market. This always leaves open the possibility that some of the seals and impressions cited in scholarly literature are counterfeits (§1.2.4.8). Fortunately, we have a number of provenanced seal impressions.

5.1.2.6.1 Lmlk *and Rosette Seals and Impressions*

The *lmlk* seal impressions get their name because they all have the Hebrew word *lmlk* ('to/for the king'), either by itself or with one or more names (Ussishkin 1977; Na'aman 1979, 1986a; Tushingham 1992; Barkay and Vaughn 1996; Vaughn 1999a). The large number found makes them important; furthermore, there has been considerable controversy in the past few years about them among archaeologists. More than 1,200 *lmlk* seal impressions have been found on storage jars in Jerusalem, Lachish and elsewhere. They tended to be present on the four-handled jars with certain physical characteristics in common, and to occur associated with one of two particular emblems: a four-winged type (in two varieties) and a two-winged type. In some cases, 'private seals' are found on jars which also have the *lmlk* seal impressions. On various of the *lmlk* seal impressions are found four names which seem to be place names: Hebron, *mmšt*, Socoh and Ziph. The jars all seem to have been produced in a single pottery centre (Mommsen, Perlman and Yellin 1984; Na'aman 1986a: 16–17), and examples of the four-winged seal impressions have been found in the same sealed destruction layer as the two-winged (Aharoni 1979: 394–400; 1982: 254–64; Ussishkin 1977: 54–7; Na'aman 1979: 70–1).

The older conclusion was that the jars were produced by Hezekiah as a storage unit important in trade but also ideal for stockpiling liquid foodstuffs (especially wine) in anticipation of invasion (Vaughn 1999a: 152–7). Their use was likely to have been over a rather short period of time because of the seal impressions of named officials on them, which would not have been used for more than a few decades, and because *lmlk* jars were found in some sites (e.g., in Philistia) that did not come under Judah's control until Hezekiah's reign. One view was that they continued to be used to the fall of the kingdom of Judah, but other interpreters have seen them as confined to the reign of Hezekiah. A. Mazar (1993: 455–8) and more recently E. Stern (2001: 174–8) have argued, however, that a few continued to be used for some decades after Hezekiah's death.

O. Lipschits and his colleagues have recently proposed a new thesis about the development of *lmlk* and related seal use (Lipschits, Sergi and Koch 2010, 2011; Sergi et al. 2012). They put forward the following four-stage evolution of use (summary based on Finkelstein 2012: 75; Na'aman 2016: 111–12):

1. early *lmlk* impressions in use in the last quarter of the eighth century BCE; found especially in the Shephelah and the highlands;
2. late *lmlk* impressions of the first half of the seventh century BCE, found mainly in the highlands;
3. concentric incisions that gradually replaced the *lmlk* stamps during the mid-seventh century BCE (about half on late *lmlk* handles); and
4. rosette impressions that were current in the late seventh–early sixth centuries BCE

This position was attacked by Ussishkin, who defended the position that the *lmlk* handles could be mainly dated to the period before 701 BCE and Sennacherib's intervention, while the rosette handles dated to the time shortly before 587/586 and the Babylonian siege and conquest of Jerusalem (Ussishkin 2011, 2012; reply by Lipschits 2012). Finkelstein

(2012) entered the fray with some methodological observations, but he argued against Lipschits and colleagues that there was a more significant recovery of Judah from Sennacherib's devastations under Manasseh than they had allowed, and the transition to the rosette pattern came at this time, earlier than they had argued. Na'aman has also recently commented on the question, arguing that although the *lmlk* system, including the four- and two-winged symbols, was under royal warrant, estate owners began marking the royal jars with their private seals as well. This ended with the invasion of 701 BCE. After Sennacherib withdrew, employment of private seals ceased. The two-winged symbol continued in use but the four-winged version was dropped.

It seems to be generally accepted that the rosette seal and the concentric circles are developed stylized forms of the four-winged and two-winged seal impressions (Na'aman 1991: 31–3; Stern 2001: 176–8). The presence of these is an indication of a seventh-century archaeological layer, much as the *lmlk* seals are of the late eighth. Some want to date the rosette seal impressions specifically to the reign of Josiah or Jehoiakim, but as Kletter (1999: 34–8) argues, there is no reason for such a narrow dating. It often seems to be taken for granted that they are royal, but the rosette motif was widespread in the ancient Near East, and there are many examples of non-royal use. Unlike the *lmlk* seal, which is dominant in the eighth, the rosette is only one of a number of types in the seventh century.

5.1.2.6.2 Other Seals and Seal Impressions

This section gives a somewhat abbreviated summary; for more details, see Grabbe (2006a). The bullae in Y. Shiloh's excavations in Jerusalem (Shiloh 1986; Shiloh and Tarler 1986; Shoham 1994, 2000; Avigad and Sass 1997; Mykytiuk 2004: 139–47) were found in stratum 10B which appears to cover the last few decades of the kingdom of Judah and ends in 587/586.

- 'Gemaryahu son of Shaphan' (לגמריהו בן שפן: see the discussion in Mykytiuk 2004: 139–47), which the stratigraphy would date to about 630–586 BCE, a dating not contradicted by the epigraphy. This is the same name as Gemariah son of Shaphan the scribe who has a chamber in the temple precincts (Jer. 36.10) and is an official in the palace (Jer. 36.12). The name Gemariah occurs in six other provenanced inscriptions but Shaphan in only one (Mykytiuk 2004: 142 n. 133). The one missing ingredient in the seal inscription is the title 'scribe' or something similar; nevertheless, the possibility of identification of the individual in this seal with one in Jeremiah is relatively high (Myktiuk 2004: 146).

- 'Gedalyahu who is over the house' (לגדליהו אשר על הבית [Gogel 1998: 487 (Lachish seal 6); *AHI*: 100.149; Becking 1997: 75–8]). This has been widely identified with the Gedaliah who was made governor (king?) of Judah after the destruction of Jerusalem in 587/586; however, this identification has been labelled as 'disqualified' because if the script is dated to the mid-seventh century (as some do), it would be too early for the individual in Jeremiah 40–41 (Mykytiuk 2004: 235). Whether the alleged palaeographical dating is so accurate as to rule out the early sixth century is a question (cf. Vaughn 1999b), but the existence of another official called Gedaliah son of Pashhur (Jer. 38.61) shows that the name was a relatively common one. Another seal with a similar inscription (לגדליהו עבד המלך 'Gedalyahu the servant of the king') is in identical script but was obtained as part of the 'Burnt Archive' published by Avigad (1986: 24–5). The lack of a proper provenance is a major difficulty. Thus, one has to conclude with B. Becking (1997: 78) that the possibility that this is from a seal belonging to the Gedaliah of Jeremiah 40–41 is relatively low.
- 'Milkomor the servant of Baalisha' (למלכמער עבד בעלישע: Herr 1985; Becking 1993, 1997). The name 'Baalis' (בעליס) was unique to Jer. 40.14 until this seal impression was found. Since a king of Ammonites with a name of this sort is so rare, I agree with Becking (1997: 82) that the possibility of an identification is high, despite the differences between the names.
- 'Jaazaniah the servant of the king' (יאזניה עבד המלך: *AHI*: 100.069; Avigad and Sass 1997: #8). As well as the inscription, it contains the image of a fighting cockerel. A Jaazaniah son of the Maachite (יאזניהו בן־המעכתי) was associated with Gedaliah at Mizpah after the fall of Jerusalem (2 Kgs 25.23). The chances are that he was some sort of royal official before the Babylonian siege. I would consider the identification as of moderate probability.
- Finally, a seal found in the Shiloh excavations in Jerusalem has the name 'Azariah son of Hilkiah' (לעזריהו בן חלקיהו: Gogel 1998: 485 [Jerusalem Bulla 27]; *AHI*: 100.827; Mykytiuk 2004: 149–52). The high priest Hilkiah (2 Kgs 22.4-14; 23.4) had a son named Azariah (1 Chron. 6.13; 9.11; Ezra 7.1). I would put the identification as moderately high.
- 'Belonging to Eliaqim servant of Yochan'; on the seal impressions with this inscription, see §1.2.3.6.

We now come to the unprovenanced bullae. One set is that published by N. Avigad as ‘remnants of a burnt archive from the time of Jeremiah’. Unfortunately, they were obtained on the antiquities market and are of unknown provenance. Avigad asserted that there ‘was no reason to suspect their authenticity, and I seriously doubt whether it would be possible to forge such burnt and damaged bullae’ (1986: 13). The question of forgery cannot be so lightly dismissed: no scientific tests appear to have been applied to these bullae. If they are authentic, the biblical parallels are striking – which is precisely why their authenticity needs to be scrutinized. In some ways, these seal impressions in the ‘Burnt Archive’ are superficially more interesting than those excavated by Shiloh and other archaeologists because of their biblical parallels; however, this greater incidence of biblical names in itself might arouse some suspicions: are they ‘too good to be true’? It illustrates the problems of working with material bought on the antiquities market.

- ‘Berekyahu son of Neriah the scribe’ (לברכיהו בן נריהו הספר: Avigad 1978; 1986: 28–9; Avigad and Sass 1997: #417; Mykytiuk 2004: 188–90). If the seal impression is authentic, the parallel to the biblical Baruch would be impressive, but the seal is probably not authentic, as the recent investigation by Goren and Arie (2014) concludes, which seems now to settle the question.
- ‘Jerahmeel son of the king’ (לירחמאל בן המלך: Avigad 1978; 1986: 27–8; Avigad and Sass 1997: #414; Mykytiuk 2004: 191–6). According to Jer. 36.26 an individual with this name and title was one of the officials sent by Jehoiakim to arrest Jeremiah and Baruch.
- ‘Elishama servant of the king’ (לאלשמע עבד המלך). Elishama the scribe is one of the king’s officials giving a hearing to Jeremiah’s prophecies (Jer. 36.12); he could also be designated as ‘servant of the king’ because of his office.
- ‘Ishmael son of the king’ (לישמעאל בן המלך: Barkay 1993; Becking 1997: 78–80). The dating to about 600 BCE is said to be consistent with the palaeography, but there is no confirmation from an archaeological context. As A. G. Vaughn’s detailed investigation has shown, the palaeographic dating of seals is far from precise, with only half a dozen letters being diagnostic (1999b). The title ‘son of the king’ is found on a number of seals and impressions. Whether it is a literal son of the king or only a ‘title of an official’ is not certain (see Mykytiuk [2004: 194 n. 109] for a bibliography of discussion on the subject). Ishmael was apparently in some way a member of

> the royal family (2 Kgs 25.25; Jer. 41.1). Becking's estimation is that this had a moderate probability of being authentically identified with the figure of Jeremiah 40 (on a scale of 1 to 10, he puts it at 5. Similarly, Mykytiuk rates it a 2 on a scale of 1 to 3 or 'reasonable but uncertain' [2004: 235]). I might put it a bit lower because the name was not infrequent, but I think this evaluation is reasonable (though the question of authenticity has not been seriously investigated, as far as I know).

An important question is the relationship of the iconic to the aniconic seals. It was observed several decades ago that there seems to have been a move from iconic to aniconic seals (or seals with only a small amount of ornamental decoration) in Judah between the eighth and seventh centuries (Uehlinger 1993: 278–81 conveniently catalogues some of the past discussion; see also Keel and Uehlinger 1998: Chapter 8, esp. 354–60). This trend toward aniconic seals does seem to be genuine, as far as extant seals are concerned, though Uehlinger (1993: 287–8) has shown that the matter is more complicated than sometimes represented. Even though there are other possible factors (e.g., increasing literacy), the influence of a growing 'Deuteronomistic movement' is plausible. Perhaps more significant is the loss of astral images. The coming of the Assyrians in the eighth and seventh centuries saw a major increase in the use of Aramaean-influenced astral imagery on seals (see Uehlinger 1995: 65–7; 2005; Keel and Uehlinger 1998: Chapter 8). The change on Judaean seals is not so apparent, but when they are seen in the context of other seals in the region, the astralization of the iconography is readily identified. This imagery disappears from Judahite seals by the late seventh century.

5.1.3 Assyrian Sources

We are fortunate in the amount of Assyrian material we possess which is one of the main sources for the history of the ancient Near East at this time. The relevant inscriptions are catalogued below under the particular Assyrian king who was responsible for them.

5.1.3.1 Sargon II (721–705 BCE)

The most significant inscriptions of Sargon II are those that suggest he conquered Jerusalem and exiled its inhabitants (Tadmor 1958b: 33–40). Then in 716 he settled a colony of Assyrians on 'the brook of Egypt', the Egyptian border (Tadmor 1958b: 35, 77–8). In 713–712 Ashdod revolted and was conquered and turned into a colony (1958b: 79–80; *ANET* 286–7). The biblical text suggests that Egypt was the instigator of this revolt (Isa. 18), and Judah may even have been tempted to join (Isa. 20). Wisely, though, she seems to have remained aloof and did not revolt until Sennacherib came to the throne.

5.1.3.2 Sennacherib (705–681 BCE)

The recent excavations at Lachish have not only established a good deal about the history of Lachish but, together with the remarkable reliefs from Sennacherib's palace, provide a unique insight into an ancient historical event (Ussishkin [ed.] 2004; Ussishkin 1980a, 1982). The pictorial depiction of the siege and conquest of Lachish is found in Sennacherib's palace in the new capital of Assyria at Nineveh. These wall reliefs were already found and described in the early days of Assyriology (Layard 1853a, 1853b).

Scholarly work on the Sennacherib inscriptions has made an important contribution to progress in historical understanding (Levine 1983). The various inscriptions were collected in an edition with English translation by A. K. Grayson and J. Novotny (2012, 2014).

One of the significant recent additions to the textual repertory was made by N. Na'aman (1974, 1979), who demonstrated that fragments already known actually belonged together. A recent study is that of E. Frahm (1997), while W. Mayer (2003) has now rechecked the inscriptions and produced an edition and English translation. A study of the reliefs, with impressive drawings by Judith Dekel, was made by D. Ussishkin (1982). A critique of Ussishkin and others, with an extensive new interpretation of the reliefs, has been given by C. Uehlinger (2003). These and the archaeology confirm the savage attack on and destruction of Lachish hinted at in 2 Kgs 18.14, 17.

5.1.3.3 Esarhaddon (681–669 BCE)

Sennacherib was assassinated in 681 BCE and was succeeded by the crown prince Esarhaddon. Most of the royal inscriptions for this ruler have been collected in Leichty (2011, in transliteration and English translation).

> I called up the kings of the country Hatti and (of the region) on the other side of the river (Euphrates) (to wit): Ba'lu, king of Tyre, Manasseh (*Me-na-si-i*), king of Judah (*Ia-ú-di*) Qaushgabri, king of Edom, Musuri, king of Moab, Sil-Bel, king of Gaza, Metinti, king of Ashkelon, Ikausu, king of Ekron, Milkiashapa, king of Byblos, Matanba'al, king of Arvad, Abiba'al, king of Samsimuruna, Puduil, king of Beth-Ammon, Ahimilki, king of Ashdod – 12 kings from the seacoast…10 kings from Cyprus (*Iadnana*) amidst the sea, together 22 kings of Hatti, the seashore and the islands; all these I sent out

and made them transport under terrible difficulties, to Nineveh, the town (where I exercise) my rulership, as building material for my palace: big logs, long beams (and) thin boards from cedar and pine trees, products of the Sirara and Lebanon (*Lab-na-na*) mountains, which had grown for a long time into tall and strong timber, (also) from their quarries (lit.: place of creation) in the mountains, statues of protective deities (lit.: of Lamassû and Shêdu). (*ANET* 291)

5.1.3.4 Ashurbanipal (669–627 BCE)

Ashurbanipal's reign was in many ways the height of the Assyrian empire, but it had come to the edge of a precipice. The internal chronology of his reign is one of the most uncertain in Assyrian history: the last of the annals cease about 639, which leaves a gap in information until the *Nabopolassor Chronicle* takes up about 626 BCE.

In my first campaign I marched against Egypt (Magan) and Ethiopia (Meluhha). Tirhakah (*Tarqû*), king of Egypt (*Muṣur*) and Nubia (*Kûsu*), whom Esarhaddon, king of Assyria, my own father, had defeated and in whose country he (Esarhaddon) had ruled, this (same) Tirhakah forgot the might of Ashur, Ishtar and the (other) great gods, my lords, and put his trust upon his own power. He turned against the kings (and) regents whom my own father had appointed in Egypt… (Then) I called up my mighty armed forces which Ashur and Ishtar have entrusted to me and took the shortest (lit.: straight) road to Egypt (*Muṣur*) and Nubia. During my march (to Egypt) 22 kings from the seashore, the islands and the mainland…

Ba'al, king of Tyre, Manasseh (*Mi-in-si-e*), king of Judah (*Ia-ú-di*), Qaushgabri, king of Edom…together 12 kings from the seashore, the islands and the mainland; servants who belong to me, brought heavy gifts (*tâmartu*) to me and kissed my feet. I made these kings accompany my army over the land – as well as (over) the sea-route with their armed forces and their ships (respectively)… Afterwards, (however), all the kings whom I had appointed broke the oaths (sworn to) me, did not keep the agreements sworn by the great gods, forgot that I had treated them mildly and conceived an evil (plot)… They continued to scheme against the Assyrian army, the forces (upon which) my rule (was based), (and) which I had stationed (in Egypt) for their own support. (But) my officers heard about these matters, seized their mounted messengers with their messages and (thus) learned about their rebellious doings. They arrested these kings and put their hands and feet in iron cuffs and fetters. The (consequences of the broken) oaths (sworn) by Ashur, the king of the gods, befell them. I called to account those who had sinned against the oath (sworn by) the great gods (and those) whom I had treated (before) with clemency… Those kings who had repeatedly schemed, they brought alive to me to Nineveh. From all of them, I had only mercy upon Necho and granted him life. I made (a treaty) with him (protected by) oaths which greatly surpassed (those of the former treaty)… I returned to him Sais as residence (the place) where my own father had appointed him king. (*ANET* 294–5)

Two minas of gold from the inhabitants of Bit-Ammon ([mat]*Bît-Am-man-na-a-a*); one mina of gold from the inhabitants of Moab ([mat]*Mu-'-ba-a-a*); ten minas of silver from the inhabitants of Judah ([mat]*Ia-ú-da-a-a*); […mi]nas of silver from the inhabitants of [Edom] ([mat][*U-du-ma*]*-a-a*). (*ANET* 301)

5.1.4 Babylonian Sources

The fall of Assyria happened quickly and for unknown reasons since the data are missing at important points. Sin-sharra-ishkun was king for much of the time from 627–612 when Nineveh succumbed to a coalition of Babylonians and Medes under Nabopolassar. A remnant of the empire continued in the west for a few more years under Ashur-uballit II who ruled in Harran.

5.1.4.1 Nabopolassar (626–605 BCE)

He was the ruler of Babylon who allied with the Medes to bring down the Assyrian empire and was founder of the short-lived Neo-Babylonian empire. We know a good deal about him because of the *Nabopolassar Chronicle.*

[The fourteenth year]: The king of Akkad mustered his army [and marched to…] The king of Umman-manda [*marched*] towards the king of Akkad […]…they met one another. [40] [The k]ing of Akkad…[…Cy]axares… brought across and they marched along the bank of the Tigris. […they encamp]ed against Nineveh. From the month Sivan until the month Ab – for three [months –…]…they subjected the city to a heavy siege. [On the Nth day] of the month Ab […] they inflicted a major [defeat upon a g]reat [*people*]. At that time Sin-sharra-ishkun, king of Assyria, [*died*]…[…]… [45] They carried off the vast booty of the city and the temple (and) [turned] the city into a ruin heap… [On the Nth day of the] month [*…Ashuruballit (II)*] [50] ascended the throne in Harran to rule Assyria. (Grayson 1975: 94–5 = *Chronicle* 3: 38)

5.1.4.2 Nebuchadnezzar II (605–562 BCE)

This was one of the great kings in history, even if the biblical portrait has made him notorious. Unfortunately, we have little information after 594 BCE when *Babylonian Chronicle 2* (*Nabopolasser Chronicle*) comes to an end and royal inscriptions become undatable. Here is some information from the *Babylonian Chronicles*:

> [The twenty-first year]: The king of Akkad stayed home (while) Nebuchadnezzar (II), his eldest son (and) the crown prince, mustered [the army of Akkad]. He took his army's lead and marched to Carchemish which is on the bank of the Euphrates. He crossed the river [*to encounter the army of Egypt*] which was encamped at Carchemish. [...] They did battle together. The army of Egypt retreated before him. [5] He inflicted a [defeat] upon them (and) finished them off completely... For twenty-one years Nabopolassar ruled Babylon. [10] On the eighth day of the month Ab he died. In the month Elul Nebuchadnezzar (II) returned to Babylon and on the first day of the month Elul he ascended the royal throne in Babylon. In (his) accession year Nebuchadnezzar (II) returned to Hattu. (Grayson 1975: 99–100 = *Chronicle* 5 Obverse: 1)

> The fourth year: The king of Akkad mustered his army and marched to Hattu. [He marched about victoriously] in Hattu. In the month Kislev he took his army's lead and marched to Egypt. (When) the king of Egypt heard (the news) he *m*[*ustered*] his army. They fought one another in the battlefield and both sides suffered severe losses (lit. they inflicted a major defeat upon one another). The king of Akkad and his army turned and [went back] to Babylon. The fifth year: The king of Akkad stayed home (and) refitted his numerous horses and chariotry. The sixth year: In the month Kislev the king of Akkad mustered his army and marched to Hattu. He despatched his army from Hattu and [10] they went off to the desert. They plundered extensively the possessions, animals, and gods of the numerous Arabs. In the month Adar the king went home. The seventh year: In the month Kislev the king of Akkad mustered his army and marched to Hattu. He encamped against the city of Judah and on the second day of the month Adar he captured the city (and) seized (its) king. A king of his own choice he appointed in the city (and) taking the vast tribute he brought it into Babylon. (Grayson 1975: 101–2 = *Chronicle 5* Reverse: 5)

Berossus, *History of Chaldaea* 3 (*apud* Josephus, *Ant.* 10.11.1 §§220–26) also mentions the death of Nabopolassar and how Nebuchadnezzar marched across the desert to reach Babylon quickly and assert his claim to the throne.

The later Neo-Babylonian kings are discussed at §5.2.11.

5.1.4.3 Jehoiachin Documents

Tablets from Babylon are generally believed to mention Jehoiachin who was in captivity:

> (*a*) To Ya'u-kīn, king [of the land of Yahudu].
> (*b*) ½ (PI) for Ya'u kīnu, king of the land of Ya[hu-du]
> 2½ *sila* for the fi[ve]sons of the king of the land of Yahudu

> 4 *sila* for eight men, Judaeans [each] ½ [sila]
> (*c*) ½ (PI) for Ya'u [-kīnu]
> 2½ *sila* for the five sons.......
> ½ (PI) for Yakū-kinu, son of the king of the land of Yakudu
> 2½ *sila* for the five sons of the king of Yakundu by the hand of Kanama.
> (*d*) ......Ya]'u-kīnu, king of the land of Yahudu
> [......the five sons of the king] of the land of Yahudu by the hand of Kanama.
> (Weidner 1939; *DOTT*: 84–6)

5.1.4.4 Texts from āl-Yāhūdu and Našar

A preliminary report has recently been made on an archive in private hands that was obtained on the antiquities market (Pearce 2006; 2015). The tablets range in date from Nebuchadnezzar (year 33, ca. 572 BCE) to Xerxes (year 13, ca. 473 BCE). Of the almost one hundred tablets, a third each was composed at āl-Yāhūdu and Našar, with the final third composed at Babylon and other sites. The city āl-Yāhūdu had only recently come to light, in some texts from the Persian period (Joannès and Lemaire 1999). It means 'city of Judah', but the forms URU šá LÚ *ia-a-ḫu-du-a-a* 'city of the Judahite' and *ālu šá* [LU]*Yaḫūdāia* 'city of the Jews' also appear. These all suggest that the city was originally named after the first inhabitants, that is, deportees from Judah. The city seems to have been a neighbour of Našar and in the region of Borsippa and Babylon. Of the 600 individuals named in the text, about 120 have Yahwistic names. The texts are typical of those one might expect to find in an archive of this nature: receipts for sales of various sorts, promissory notes and notes of indebtedness, and leases of property or labour. Unfortunately, there is little information about the social status of the community members, since the profession of individuals in the texts is seldom recorded.

5.1.5 Egyptian Source: Psammetichus Inscription

> In the fourth regnal year of Pharaoh Psamtek Neferibre they sent to the great temples of Upper and Lower Egypt, saying, 'Pharaoh (Life, Prosperity, Health) is going to the Land of Palestine. Let the priests come with the bouquets of the gods of Egypt to take them to the Land of Palestine.' And they sent to Teudjoy saying: 'Let a priest come with the bouquet of Amun, in order to go to the Land of Palestine with Pharaoh'. And the priests agreed and said to Pediese, the son of Essamtowy, 'you are the one who, it is agreed, ought to go to the Land of Palestine with Pharaoh. There is no one here in the town who is able to go to the Land of Palestine except you. Behold, you must do it, you, a scribe of the House of Life; there is nothing they can ask you and you not be able to answer it, for you are a priest of Amun. It is only the priests of the great gods of Egypt that are going to the

> Land of Palestine with Pharaoh.' And they persuaded Pediese to go to the Land of Palestine with Pharaoh and he made his preparations. So Pediese, son of Essamtowy, went to the Land of Palestine, and no one was with him save his servant and an hour-priest of Isis named Osirmose. (Inscription of Psammetichus II = Griffith 1909: II, 95–6)

5.1.6 The Biblical Story: 2 Kings 21–25 and Parallels

NB: Only passages specifically mentioning the period are considered here. Other passages may well be from this time (e.g., the town lists of Josh. 15, 18 and 19) but are omitted here.

5.1.6.1 2 Kings//2 Chronicles (a dash marks omissions in the parallel writing)

21.1-18//33.1-20: Reign of Manasseh.

- 21.1//33.1: Manasseh begins to reign at age 12 and reigns 55 years.
- 21.2-9//33.2-9: He does what is evil by building altars to Baal and an Asherah, worshipping the host of heaven, making his son to pass through the fire, practising divination.
- —//33.10-13: Manasseh taken captive to Babylon, where he repents and turns to Yhwh.
- —//33.14-17: Manasseh builds Jerusalem's wall and removes the religious abominations.
- 21.10-15//—: Yhwh speaks against Manasseh through prophets, promising disaster on Jerusalem and to deliver the remnant of the people to their enemies.
- 21.16//—: Manasseh puts the innocent to death and fills Jerusalem with blood.
- 21.17//33.18: The other events of Manasseh's reign are found in the annals of the kings of Judah.
- —//33.19: Words of Hozai recording Manasseh's sins and his prayer of repentance.
- 21.18//33.20: Manasseh dies and is buried.

21.19-26//33.21-25: Reign of Amon.

- 21.19//33.21: Begins reign at age 22 and reigns 2 years.
- 21.20-22//33.22-23: Wicked like his father.
- 21.23-26//33.24-25: Assassinated in a conspiracy.

22.1–23.30//34.1–35.27: Reign of Josiah.

- 22.1//34.1: Begins reign at age 8 and reigns 22 years.
- 22.2//34.2: Is righteous like David.
- —//34.3-7: Begins purge of shrines and cults in his 12th year.
- 22.3-7//34.8-13: Josiah orders the cleansing of the temple in his 18th year.
- 22.8-10//34.14-18: Finding of scroll and reading of it to Josiah.

22.11-20//34.19-28: Prophetess Huldah is consulted about the contents of the scroll.
23.1-3//34.29-32: Josiah makes a covenant with the people to keep the laws of the scroll.
23.4-7//—: Cleansing of the temple and the removal of the *kemarim* from the shrines.
23.8-9//—: Priests of the high places brought to Jerusalem.
23.10-14//—: Other cults and objects removed from the temple and city.
23.15-18//—: Bethel purified, including destruction of Jeroboam's altar.
23.19-20//—: Rest of Samaria purified of its cult places and priests.
—//34.33: Summary of Josiah's reign.
23.21-23//35.1-19: Passover kept.
23.24//—: Divination eliminated.
23.25-27//—: Prophecy of Judah's destruction postponed because of Josiah's righteousness.
23.28-30//35.20-27: Josiah's death at the hands of Necho.

23.30-34//36.1-4: Reign of Jehoahaz.

23.31//36.2: Begins reign at age of 23 and reigns 3 months.
23.32//—: Is wicked like his fathers.
23.33-34//36.3: Removed by Pharaoh Necho and taken to Egypt, and tribute imposed.

23.34–24.7//36.4-8: Reign of Jehoiakim.

23.35//—: Jehoiakim collects money for tribute.
23.36//36.5: Begins reign at age 25 and reigns 11 years.
23.37//36.5: Wicked like his fathers.
24.1-2//—: Vassal of Nebuchadnezzar 3 years and then rebels; raids against Judah.
24.3-4//—: Happens because Jehoiakim sheds innocent blood.
—//36.6-7: Nebuchadnezzar takes Jehoiakim captive to Babylon.
24.5-6//36.8: Death of Jehoiakim.
24.7//—: King of Babylon had taken all land to borders of Egypt.

24.8-16//36.8-10: Reign of Jehoiachin.

24.8//36.9: Begins to reign at age 18 and reigns 3 months.
24.9//36.9: Wicked like his father.
24.10-17//36.10: Nebuchadnezzar takes the city and deports Jehoiachin and family to Babylon.

24.17–25.21//36.10-21: Reign of Zedekiah.

24.18//36.11: Begins reign at age 21 and rules for 11 years.
24.19-20//36.12: Wicked like Jehoiakim.
25.1-21//36.13-21: Rebels and Jerusalem taken by Nebuchadnezzar; king and people exiled.

5.1.6.2 Jeremiah

22.18-19: Prophecy that Jehoiakim would have the 'burial of an ass'.
25.1: 1st year of Nebuchadnezzar is the 4th of Jehoiakim.
32.1-2: Babylonian army besieging Jerusalem in the 10th year of Zedekiah, which is the 18th of Nebuchadnezzar.
34.7: Only Lachish and Azekah of the fortified cities holding out against besieging Babylonians.
37.11: The Chaldaean army lifts the siege of Jerusalem because of the Egyptian army.
39.1: Nebuchadnezzar besieges Jerusalem in the 9th year of Zedekiah, the 10th month.
39.2: Jerusalem falls in the 11th year of Zedekiah, 9th day of 4th month.
39.3: Babylonian officers set up quarters.
39.4-7: Zedekiah taken prisoner.
39.8-10: Exile of those left in the city.
43.8-13: Prediction that Nebuchadnezzar would conquer Egypt.
44.30: Prediction that Pharaoh Hophrah would be delivered into the hands of his enemies (Nebuchadnezzar?).
46–47: Prophecy of Nebuchadnezzar's destruction of Egypt.
46.2: Egyptian army of Necho defeated at Carchemish by the Babylonians in the 4th year of Jehoiakim.
52.1: Zedekiah aged 21 when he became king and reigned 11 years.
52.3-4: Jerusalem besieged in the 9th year, the 10th day of the 10th month, by Nebuchadnezzar.
52.5-7: City falls in the 11th year, the 9th day of the 4th month.
52.8-11: Zedekiah taken prisoner to Babylon.
52.12-14: Jerusalem razed by Nebuzaradan in Nebuchadnezzar's 19th year, 10th day of the 5th month.
52.15-16: Those left in the city exiled.
52.28-30: Captivities in 7th, 18th and 23rd year of Nebuchadnezzar.

5.1.6.3 Ezekiel

26–27: Prophecy against Tyre.
26.7: Nebuchadnezzar will come against Tyre and destroy it.
29–30: Prophecy against Egypt.
29.8-16: Egypt to be ruined and desolate 40 years, then to become the lowest of the kingdoms.
29.17-20: Having failed to take Tyre, Nebuchadnezzar will be given Egypt as a reward.
30.20-26: The king of Babylon will break the arms of the king of Egypt.

5.1.6.4 Ezra

4.1-4: The enemies of Judah and Benjamin – 'the people of the land' – were brought to the region by Esarhaddon.
4.9-10: Men of Erech, Babylon, Susa and others had been settled in Samaria and elsewhere in Ebir-Nari by Osnappar (Ashurbanipal?).

5.1.6.5 Daniel

1.1-2: Nebuchadnezzar besieges and takes Jerusalem in the 3rd year of Jehoiakim.
4.1-34: Nebuchadnezzar's 'madness'.
5.1-30: Belshazzar, king of Babylon.

5.1.6.6 Analysis of the Text

The account of the seventh century in 2 Kings is part of the DtrH (§3.1.6.2). Most of the text of 2 Chronicles and some parts of Jeremiah parallel the narrative of 2 Kings. The relationship of Jeremiah to 2 Kings is not immediately apparent, but it seems plain that 2 Chronicles is mainly derived from 2 Kings; however, here and there are significant deviations. The main ones are the following:

- Manasseh's alleged captivity in Babylon and subsequent repentance is given in 2 Chron. 33.10-17 but completely absent from 2 Kings.
- 2 Chronicles (33.14), but not 2 Kings, states that Manasseh built the outer wall around part of Jerusalem.
- According to 2 Chron. 34.3-7 Josiah began the purge of 'foreign' cults in his twelfth year.
- Whereas 2 Kgs 22.21-23 mentions briefly Josiah's Passover, 2 Chron. 35.1-19 goes into great detail about how it was celebrated.
- According to 2 Chron. 35.20-27 Josiah was killed in a battle with Pharaoh Necho, but 2 Kgs 23.28-30 is unspecific and does not at all imply a battle.
- According to 2 Chron. 36.6-7 Jehoiakim was taken captive to Babylon, along with the temple vessels. On the other hand, according to Jeremiah he was to have 'the burial of an ass', cast outside Jerusalem unburied (Jer. 22.18-19).
- In spite of Josiah's far-reaching reform programme described in 2 Kings and 2 Chronicles, Jeremiah seems strangely silent about it.

On the stories in Daniel, see §5.2.6; §5.2.11.

5.2 Analysis

The following section is in part organized around the names of Judaean kings. The reason is that this particular study is asking specifically about the bibical data: What could we regard as reliable if we had only the Bible? Therefore, it makes sense to shape the question broadly around the Judaean kings.

5.2.1 Hezekiah

Although we have more information about Hezekiah than many other Judahite kings, there are considerable questions about when he began and ended his reign, as well as events within his reign (see especially the essays in Grabbe [ed.] 2003). The account of Hezekiah's reign begins with a religious and cultic reform (2 Kgs 18.3-6). This reform had been widely accepted in scholarship (e.g., Albertz 1994: I, 180–6), but it is now also widely questioned (e.g., Na'aman 1995a). The problem is that it looks very much like the reform later ascribed to Josiah. Did Josiah try to revive what failed under Hezekiah, or did the biblical writer borrow from Josiah's story to improve Hezekiah's piety by literary invention? K. A. Swanson (2002) has suggested that what lies behind the story is Hezekiah's shift from Egyptian religious symbolism, which had been widespread, to aniconism and the rosette. Since the rosette was an Assyrian symbol, at least some of the change can be ascribed to Hezekiah's acceptance of Assyrian subjugation.

On the question of cult reforms, there is also considerable controversy. L. S. Fried (2002) argued that the archaeology of the *bāmôt* does not support the alleged cult reforms of the text. In a more recent study, Na'aman (2002a) looked at the abandonment of cult places as a result of alleged cult reforms, with special emphasis on Arad and Beersheba; he concluded that these represented an attempt to consolidate royal power. Z. Herzog, however, has argued that the cancelling of the temples at Arad and Beersheba supports the story of Hezekiah's reform (2001: 165–7) and continues to do so in his latest study (Herzog 2010). His is mainly a critique of Na'aman, claiming that the latter has completely misunderstood the archaeology. However, he does not really respond to Knauf's restructuring and redating of the archaeology that places the dismantling of the temples under Manasseh (see below). It should also be kept in mind that David Ussishkin (1988) redated the sanctuary to the seventh century and put the cancellation of it to the sixth century BCE. Herzog made the curious statement:

> The suggestion to interpret finds related to remains of cult at Arad and Tel Beer-sheba as evidence of cultic reform in general, and the reform of King Hezekiah in particular, has won the support of archaeologists and – at the same time – the sharp criticism mainly of Historians and Biblical scholars. (Herzog 2010: 179)

However, apart from the fact that there are archaeologists (already noted above) who do not agree with Herzog, it should not be overlooked that Herzog dismisses the event of a religious reform under Josiah, which seems even more radical than dismissing a reform under Hezekiah! The analysis of the biblical narrative has been an important part of the discussion relating to historicity. On the invasion of Sennacherib, more than a century ago B. Stade (1886) produced a basic analysis that has continued to dominate the literary discussion. He noted that 18.14-16 had already been recognized as an insertion from a good source that was early. He then argued that 18.13, 17 to 19.9a was parallel to 19.9b-37. Neither of these narratives could be considered trustworthy historical sources but were both 'legendary', even if here and there they contained a correct historical datum. B. Childs (1967) refined Stade's analysis, with the following terms:

> Account A: 2 Kgs 18.13-16.
> Account B_1: 2 Kgs 18.17–19.9a, 36-37//Isa. 36.1–37.9a
> Account B_2: 2 Kgs 19.9b-35//Isa. 37.9b-36

Attempts to rationalize the various narratives in the biblical text already began in the infancy of Assyriology. In 1864 George Rawlinson first suggested that Sennacherib had invaded twice (1864: II, 30–46), the events of 2 Kgs 18.17–19.37 relating to this second invasion. This conclusion was not made on the basis of the Assyrian inscriptions but the requirements of the biblical text, as he admitted (1864: II, 439 n. 4). Thus, the idea of reconciling the two sets of texts by postulating more than one invasion was already present not long after the Assyrian inscriptions had begun to give new understanding to the events of Sennacherib's reign. The question continued to be debated until the present, with eminent scholars for more than one invasion (J. Jeremias, R. W. Rogers, L. L. Honor, W. F. Albright, J. Bright) and others against it (J. Wellhausen, E. Schrader, E. Meyer, J. A. Montgomery, J. Meinhold, A. Alt, M. Noth, A. Parrot, A. T. Olmstead, J. Gray, H. H. Rowley) (see the survey in Grabbe [ed.] 2003: 20–34). It was W. H. Shea (1985) who advanced well beyond Bright with a lengthy circumstantial argument that Sennacherib had conducted a second invasion after 689 BCE; however, Shea's argument was refuted point by point by Frank Yurco (1991).

The Egyptian data were crucial to the question: When did Taharqa take the throne and what was his age in 701 BCE? K. A. Kitchen argued that the Egyptian inscriptions allowed only one invasion (1983; 1986: 154–61, 552–9). A. Rainey (1976), Yurco (1980: 222–3) and Kitchen (1986: 164–70) asserted that new grammatical studies and improved readings of the text made it now clear that Taharqa was at least 20 years old in 701 BCE and fully capable of leading a military campaign as crown prince. However, it should be noted that not all Egyptologists agree on this interpretation. D. Redford (1992a: 351–3, esp. n. 163) still read the relevant inscription as saying that Taharqa was only 20 when he came from Nubia to Egypt in 690, while J. von Beckerath argued that Taharqa came to Egypt in 700 BCE at the earliest and probably later (1992: 7). Most recently, though, a new inscription has been assigned to the reign of Taharqa (Redford 1993), and Shea (1997, 1999) has argued that this inscription is to be connected to an invasion of Sennacherib, though not the one in 701 BCE but a postulated 'second invasion'. M. Cogan, however, has dismissed this argument, pointing out that those deported by the Egyptians could not have been the Assyrian army and that subsequent Assyrian rule has no place for such a defeat of the Assyrian army (2001; on the chronology of the Twenty-Fifth Dynasty, see Redford 1999). We can sum up the situation by noting that as long as detailed information on Sennacherib's reign after 689 BCE remains undiscovered, we cannot absolutely rule out a second Assyrian invasion of Judah; however, all the available evidence presently known is against this scenario.

So how reliable are the accounts in 2 Kings 18–20? Noth gave an interpretation that depended almost entirely on 2 Kgs 18.16-19 (along with the Assyrian inscriptions); the rest of the biblical account was largely ignored (1960: 266–9). This was essentially the consensus of the discussion by the European Seminar in Historical Methodology (Grabbe [ed.] 2003: 308–23): Account A was the most widely accepted as reliable but Accounts B_1 and B_2 were thought to be much later and unreliable compositions. N. Na'aman (2003) argued that B_1 was probably written in the mid-seventh century. B_2 was modelled on B_1 but was rather later, probably in the late Neo-Babylonian period. E. Ben Zvi (2003) put the final composition of 2 Kings 18–20 in the post-exilic period, the purpose being to contrast Hezekiah's experience with Zedekiah's and explain why Jerusalem was conquered by the Babylonians. Going against the consensus, C. R. Seitz (1993) doubted whether the Annals of Sennacherib can be said to confirm

2 Kgs 18.14-16 and concluded that, whatever its basis in fact, Account A must still be interpreted in the larger redactional context of 2 Kings; it may even be intended to tone down the otherwise positive account of Hezekiah. K. Smelik (1992) argued that historical reconstruction must be based on 18.13-16 and Assyrian sources, which can be reconciled 'in all essentials'. The narratives were written as a reaction to the destruction of the Jerusalem temple, retrojecting current problems into the past; thus, they cannot be used for historical reconstruction of 701 but rather of 586.

W. R. Gallagher's study (1999) 'most closely adheres' to the approach that uses all sources and assumes that they are largely reliable and comes to some quite conservative conclusions about it. He accepts that Account A is from a separate source but rejects the division of Account B into two separate sources and the idea that they form two accounts of the same events. The B account as a whole is by and large reliable. He would excise the name 'Tirhakah' from 19.9 but accept an Egyptian–Cushite force of some sort. The interpretation of 19.35 as referring to a plague is looked at sympathetically but seen as uncertain. His reconstruction of events is thus heavily influenced by the biblical Account B read as a sequential narrative (Account A is seen essentially as an overall summary). Yet C. Hardmeier (1989) also took up Childs' challenge. His solution was to dismiss any association of 2 Kings 18–19 with Sennacherib but to connect it with events shortly before the fall of Jerusalem. Instead of describing the siege of Jerusalem by Sennacherib, these chapters were a fictional creation to support those nationalists who wanted to resist the Babylonians. Written in 588 BCE, with the same background as described in Jeremiah 37–40 (but from the opposite perspective), they held up Sennacherib's invasion as an exemplar of how God would intervene to save his people. When this did not happen, the narratives were re-interpreted as an actual description of events in the time of Hezekiah. He thus rejects the consensus that the A narrative is an actual report of what happened. Hardmeier's is a major challenge to much previous thinking. Although others are willing to argue that parts of the Hezekiah narrative (particularly the B narrative) are even later than Hardmeier proposes (e.g., Na'aman 2003), his argument that the entire narrative is a fictive creation goes further than most are willing to go.

In an important study, S. Parpola (1980) showed that the name of Sennacherib's assassin had been wrongly interpreted for many years. It should be read as Arda-Mulišši of which the biblical Adrammelech (2 Kgs 19.37) is a corrupt but recognizable form. A question is how to take the visit of Merodach-baladan to Jerusalem. Because a king of Babylon, Marduk-apla-dan actually existed, some have wanted to suggest that this is a plausible story: the Babylonian king, who was rebelling against the Assyrians, was seeking support and allies. This might seem to be a valid argument until one considers the distance that Judah lay from Babylon and the lack of any possibility of giving help. The story looks more like an explanation of why Jerusalem fell to the Babylonians.

One of Childs' main contributions to the debate was the comparison of the Rabshakeh's speech with that of an Assyrian document, leading Childs to argue that the B_2 biblical account reflected historical reality (1967: 78–93; Saggs 1955a, 1955b, 1956). This view seems to have gone unchallenged until 1990 when an article by Ehud Ben Zvi undermined the whole basis of the argument by showing that the alleged parallels were made up of common biblical language, and the reference to Hezekiah's reform shows Deuteronomic features (1990). Following on this are studies by Klaas Smelik (1992), who considers the speeches free compositions by the author, and D. Rudman (2000), who points out the resemblance of the Rabshakeh's speech to biblical prophetic language. However, W. R. Gallagher (1999) has recently argued that both this passage and Isa. 10.5-19 were written close to the time of the alleged speech and are summaries of it.

The 'fourteenth year' (2 Kgs 18.13) has been a major difficulty since the Assyrian inscriptions showed that Sennacherib's invasion was in 701 BCE. According to 2 Kgs 18.1, Hezekiah became king in Hoshea's third year, while Samaria fell in Hezekiah's fourth year. If so, the events of 701 would have taken place about Hezekiah's twenty-fifth year, not the 'fourteenth'. Rawlinson simply emended the text to 'twenty-seventh', without giving any justification for this change except to try to reconcile the biblical and Assyrian accounts (1864: II, 434 n. 12). J. A. Montgomery (1951: 483) also emended, to the 'twenty-fourth year', but he expressed the view that the synchronism with Hoshea's reign was an error. Several other solutions have been advanced in the past few decades. One was by A. K. Jenkins (1976) who argued that the 'fourteenth year' refers to the invasion under Sargon II about 713–711 (Isa. 20). According to this explanation the original account had an anonymous Assyrian king, but this king was later identified with Sennacherib. This interpretation depends on the 'high chronology' which makes Hezekiah's reign about 727–698 BCE. Very recently a similar explanation was given by J. Goldberg (1999) who argued for a 'limited invasion' of Palestine by Sargon II in 712 BCE, referred to in 18.13-16 and later confused with the 701 invasion. Hayim Tadmor and Michael Cogan (1982) put forward the case that the 'fourteenth year' was a reference to Hezekiah's illness, an incident that originally preceded the account of Sennacherib's invasion. Since

Hezekiah's life was extended for 15 years after his illness, this gave the 29-year total of his reign.

In 1994 Na'aman surveyed the arguments on both sides and proposed that, though not conclusive, the balance of evidence favoured taking the fourteenth year as correct and dating Hezekiah's reign ca. 715–686 (1994a). Sennacherib's inscriptions continued to be revised by scribes at least until 691, yet Hezekiah's death is not mentioned, making it unlikely that he died in 698 as some have thought. The problem created with regard to Manasseh's reign by this dating is resolved by assuming a ten-year co-regency between Hezekiah and his son. B. Becking (1992, 2002, 2003) also addressed some of the questions of chronology. He has argued for the dating of the fall of Samaria to 723 BCE, a year earlier than the conventional 722. He accepts that the synchronism made by the Deuteronomic editor between the reigns of Hoshea and Hezekiah (2 Kgs 18.9-10) is based on Judaean archives. This means that the fourteenth year of Hezekiah has to be either spring 715 to spring 714 or autumn 716 to autumn 715. At that time Sargon II dispatched an expedition to Palestine that was relatively peaceful. This may have been led by the crown prince Sennacherib. This was the 'first campaign' of Sennacherib, dated to the summer of 715 BCE. Becking thus hypothesizes two campaigns of Sennacherib, but his schema differs from the conventional one in that the 701 invasion was his second campaign. (For further on Becking's chronology, see §4.2.7.)

The current situation can be stated succinctly as follows. The firmest datum we have at the end of the eighth century is the invasion of Sennacherib. It can be precisely calculated to 701 BCE. We have detailed descriptions in the Assyrian sources, including mention of local Palestinian rulers by name (e.g., Hezekiah), and the widespread destruction left a distinct mark in the archaeological record. There is substantial agreement that reliable memory of this is found in 2 Kgs 18.13-16, and rather less reliable memory in various other parts of 2 Kings 18–20 (Grabbe [ed.] 2003). The 'two-invasion' hypothesis, although once widely accepted, looks now to be in tatters. The main extra-biblical support has collapsed. Although Sennacherib's reign is poorly documented after 689 BCE, there does not seem to be any room for another campaign to Palestine.

Although still debated, the weight of opinion seems to be that Taharqa was capable of leading a military expedition against the Assyrians in 701 BCE, although he did not take the throne until a decade later (690 BCE). Whether he did or not is naturally still a matter of debate, but the reason for his mention in 2 Kgs 19.9 probably derives from his later image as the great Egyptian (Nubian) king who stood up to Assyria (Schipper 1999: 210–28; Dion 1988). However, the chronology of Hezekiah's reign remains disputed, and the way in which Jerusalem avoided a siege is considerably debated. How much longer Hezekiah ruled after 701 and what events took place in his reign are not matters of agreement. Our only information is from the biblical text, and even the sequence of events of the original story is thought to be disturbed, making it that much more difficult to ask questions about their basis in historical reality. For a continuation of the debate, see Grabbe ([ed.] 2003: esp. 308–23). As for Hezekiah's cult reform, there is still considerable question whether such took place, though the story might reflect some sorts of events during Hezekiah's reign.

5.2.2 Manasseh

What emerges from recent study is the importance of the reign of Manasseh. Far from being a time of depravity and fear, many think it represents a remarkable recovery from the devastations of Sennacherib. It must have given many Judaeans a return to some sort of prosperity and hope for the future. Of course, the name of Manasseh is one of the blackest in the biblical text. He is perhaps equalled – but not surpassed – only by Ahab and Jezebel. This suggests that the long reign ascribed to him is likely to be a firm part of the tradition and thus to have some basis in fact. Manasseh's existence is well attested in the Assyrian inscriptions. He is named as an apparently loyal subject paying the required tribute to both Esarhaddon and Ashurbanipal (though it has been pointed out that Manasseh's tribute is smaller than that of his neighbours [Finkelstein and Silberman 2001: 265]). He also supplied military assistance for Ashurbanipal's attack on Egypt.

What the archaeology suggests is that Judah made a significant recovery from the disaster of 701 (Finkelstein 1994a; Finkelstein and Silberman 2001: 264–74). The important agricultural region of the Shephelah remained sparsely populated, probably the larger part of it having been removed from Judahite control. Elsewhere, though, settlements were re-established in destroyed southern areas, possibly with even a population increase. Settlements were also pushed into the marginal desert areas to make use of all possible land for agricultural purposes. Although dating is not easy, the suggestion is that this happened under Manasseh's leadership. Manasseh seems to have been responsible for building a city wall (2 Chron. 33.15), which could be the one dating from the seventh century discovered on the eastern slope of Jerusalem's southeastern hill (Tatum 2003: 300). It has also been proposed by E. A. Knauf that Manasseh built some prestige projects, including the Siloam tunnel (Knauf 2001b) and a palace at Ramat Rahel (Knauf 2005a: 170).

There is also some evidence of the part played by Judah in the economy of the Assyrian empire, a role that would have benefited the inhabitants of Judah. The territory of Judah formed a significant link in the caravan trade from Arabia, which the Assyrians would have controlled. The Idumaean plateau gained a significant population at this time, with the trade route leading through the valley of Beersheba and the southern coastal plain to Gaza. There are indications of contact with South Arabia, and the seventh-century forts at Qadesh-Barnea and Haseva might have been built with the protection of this trade in mind. A major olive-oil production centre existed at Tel Miqne (usually identified with ancient Ekron); however, the olives were not grown locally but would most likely have been imported from the Samarian and Judaean highlands.

Of particular interest is the apparent increase in written material. The finds indicate a greater quantity of written objects preserved from the seventh century: seals/bullae, ostraca and inscribed weights (Finkelstein and Silberman 2001: 270, 280–1; Stern 2001: 169–200). This 'explosion of writing' has been explained as evidence of an increase in the bureaucracy (Finkelstein and Silberman 2001: 270; Stern 2001: 169) and even that Judah had become a fully developed state by this time (Finkelstein and Silberman 2001: 281, 284). These conclusions seem quite reasonable ones. The sorts of written objects catalogued here do look like the type of written material that would be the product of the bureaucracy and state administration. Whether they are evidence of greater general literacy, however, is another issue (§§3.2.5; 5.2.4).

The question of an imposed Assyrian cult has been much debated in recent years. From the early days of cuneiform study it was argued that the Assyrians imposed their god Ashur on conquered peoples (interestingly, apparently first proposed by George Rawlinson [McKay 1973: 1–4]). This consensus was challenged by two works that appeared about the same time. First, J. McKay (1973) argued that there are no indications of Assyrian cults in any of the accounts of the kings under Assyrian rule: Ahaz, Hezekiah, Manasseh, Josiah. McKay also pointed out the importance of astral cults in the biblical account, which he ascribed to Canaanite practices rather than Assyrian. A telling point made by McKay is that the description of the cults set up under Manasseh and removed by Josiah indicates they were Syro-Phoenician, not Assyrian. Independently of McKay, M. Cogan (1974) also argued against an imposed Assyrian cult, his focus being on the cuneiform texts to try to determine Assyrian practice. He noted that the Assyrians made good use of the concept of divine abandonment by the gods. Although the Assyrians occasionally destroyed images and temples of recalcitrant peoples, their normal practice was to take the images of native gods to Assyrian territories. The treaties with conquered peoples invoked Ashur, and the Assyrians certainly understood submission to Assyria as submission to Ashur, yet this does not imply cultic obligations. Regions which were turned into Assyrian provinces, however, were considered Assyrian and their peoples Assyrian citizens; in such cases an Assyrian cult was established (before 'Ashur's weapon', the symbol of Assyrian rule) though native cults were not prohibited. Then Hermann Spieckermann (1982) replied to both monographs, though most of his arguments related more to Cogan's work. Cogan (1993) eventually replied to Spieckermann and, not surprisingly, reaffirmed the view that there was no evidence for imposed cults and that those described in the Bible seem to be indigenous ones. This is unlikely to be the last word on the subject, but although Manasseh seems to have been a loyal vassal, the cults in existence under his rule were more likely to be old indigenous ones rather than those imposed from the outside. Finkelstein and Silberman (2001: 265) think that there was a return to popular religion by the people of the countryside after Hezekiah's failed cultic reform (assuming there was such a reform). Others would argue that nothing innovative from a religious point of view happened under Manasseh; rather, he was just blamed for what had been the traditional religion among the people for many centuries. This does not, though, rule out foreign influence, such as from Assyro-Aramaic astral cults (§5.2.4).

One of the most curious episodes related in the Bible is about Manasseh's deportation to and imprisonment in Babylon, followed by a return to Jerusalem and his throne and by repentance for his wicked deeds. This story is found in only one passage, significantly in Chronicles (2 Chron. 33.10–17), but not a hint is found in 2 Kgs 21.1–18. Furthermore, other biblical passages know nothing of Manasseh's repentance: Jer. 15.4 speaks of Manasseh's wickedness; 2 Kgs 23.12 says that Josiah – not Manasseh – removed the abominations; and even 2 Chron. 33.22 says that Amon was wicked like Manasseh. If Manasseh actually did all this, why would the Deuteronomist omit it? He was either ignorant of the information or he deliberately suppressed it. It is difficult to believe that if such an incident took place he had no information, so we must assume that he knew of Manasseh's repentance but purposefully ignored it. Is this likely? Yes, perhaps if the idea of an act of repentance on Manasseh's part created problems with his underlying pattern of presentation, but this would be a serious reflection on the claim made by some that the Deuteronomist was writing history.

Yet there is an interesting parallel which suggests that what is alleged to have happened to Manasseh was not unlikely in and of itself. During Ashurbanipal's invasion of Egypt, some of his allies plotted to rebel. When he discovered the plot, he removed them all from office except Necho II who was allowed to remain on the throne (*ANET* 294–5). It is possible that Manasseh was also plotting to rebel (Elat 1975b: 67). If so, he might have been allowed to regain his throne after appropriate punishment, just as Necho was. However, it must be admitted that this is entirely speculation – there is no evidence that Manasseh plotted to rebel or that he was punished by either of the Assyrian kings under whom he was vassal; on the contrary, of the rebels apparently only Necho was pardoned.

As has been pointed out, having Manasseh repent would fit the Chronicler's purpose very well: because Manasseh lived so long, he could have done so only if he repented of his evil deeds. To the Chronicler's way of thinking, length of life was a reward for obedience. Yet is it likely that the Chronicler invented the story out of whole cloth? It is always possible, but it seems more likely that he had knowledge – however tenuous – of some incident involving Manasseh, which is indeed indicated by his citation of the 'words of Hozai'. The events under Ashurbanipal, in which Manasseh and others had to accompany the Assyrian king in his invasion of Egypt, might well be such a pretext. In sum, though, the story of Manasseh's having been arrested and taken 'with hooks and bound in bronze fetters' to Babylon is unlikely.

5.2.3 Amon

We have no data on him other than what is in the Bible. He is unlikely to have been invented. It was unusual for a king to be assassinated, and there is nothing about Amon to give this a literary significance. Thus, it is likely to have happened. However, the figures given for his age look suspect: although it is theoretically possible that he had a child at age 16, this seems highly improbable. Possibly the problem is with the age of Josiah (see next section), though in cases of the sudden death of a king a minor child might well take the throne.

5.2.4 Josiah

Josiah is known only from the biblical text, in spite of his important role in the history of seventh-century Judah. Furthermore, many past reconstructions have depended on the picture in 2 Chronicles, even in those aspects which differ at significant points from those in 2 Kings. Neither the surviving Babylonian nor Egyptian records contain any reference to him. We are left with archaeology and the biblical text with which to make sense of his reign, though the Egyptian material and the Babylonian chronicles provide useful background and contextual information.

One theory that has held considerable sway for a number of decades is that Josiah was attempting to create a 'greater Israel', perhaps on the model of the Davidic kingdom. There are many obvious parallels between Josiah and David, though one could put these down to literary creation rather than actual activity of the ruler. The 'righteousness' of both kings is the most obvious contact, but the conquest of territory is another that many scholars have managed to glean from the biblical material: the attempt to return to a 'greater Israel' and a recovery of former glory. It has been argued that, although Josiah's reform was indeed religious, the basis of it was economic (Claburn 1973). Na'aman (1991: 33–41; 2005: 210–17) has argued, however, that there was no political vacuum which gave Josiah room to try to found a new Davidic 'empire'. Rather, the declining Assyrian power in the west was matched by the growing power of Egypt; indeed, there may have been an orderly transfer of territorial control by mutual agreement (Na'aman 1991: 40). Miller and Hayes (1986: 383–90) had already argued that Josiah was an Egyptian vassal his entire reign. Na'aman has gone on to create a picture of Judah as a vassal state during the entirety of Josiah's reign, first under the Assyrians and then under the Egyptians. This gave only very limited scope for expansion of territory. There is some evidence of shifting the border as far north as Bethel. However, the expansion further north into the Galilee or west into the area of Philistia is unjustified from either archaeology or the text.

A further potential source of information about Judah's boundaries are the town lists of Joshua (15.21-62; 18.21-28; 19.2-8, 40-46). It was argued by A. Alt that the lists of the southern tribes actually reflected Josiah's kingdom, and the question has now been investigated at length by Na'aman (1991, 2005). It is impossible to summarize the detailed textual analysis here, but the lists of Judah and Benjamin are the main ones in question. The northern border should be set along the Bethel–Ophrah line, which was north of the traditional border of the kingdom of Judah (Josh. 18.21-28); Jericho is also included, though it had previously been an Israelite town. If Josh. 21.45-47 is deleted as an addition by the editor, the list includes the eastern Shephelah. 2 Kings 23.8 makes reference to the territory 'from Geba to Beersheba', which is likely to be an indication of Judah's actual extent under Josiah. Therefore, the reference to Qadesh-Barnea (if this is indeed the site indicated in Josh. 15.23) is probably to be seen as an addition to the list, but most of the sites are no further south than Beersheba. The main point made by Na'aman is the extent to which archaeology (e.g., the rosette seal impressions) and other sources of data fit with these lists in Joshua.

The ostraca from Mesad Hashavyahu do not seem to show a Judaean outpost, as often alleged, but probably an Egyptian one with some Judaean soldiers (Fantalkin 2001: 139–47; Na'aman 1991: 44–6; 2005: 220–2). Other names in the texts are Phoenician, for example. Neither does the text of Ostracon 1 provide evidence of Josiah's religious reform. The sender of the ostracon appeals to the humanity of the recipient, not to the law of the king or the Torah. Similarly, the Arad ostraca indicate a contingent of Greek mercenaries in that area, which was probably in the employ of the Egyptians.

With regard to borders, R. Kletter (1999: 40–3) considers the question in the light of several types of artifacts. He argues that archaeology cannot pinpoint accurate borders nor establish the political affiliation of single sites. The overwhelming majority of the artifacts considered by him fit more or less with the Judaean heartland and do not indicate large-scale expansion. Various explanations have been given for those finds of artifacts outside the heartland; however, only the western Shephelah shows much of a concentration. Although Judaean artifacts have been found at Qadesh-Barnea and Meṣad Ḥashavyahu (Judaean inscribed weights, pottery vessels, Hebrew ostraca), the material culture of both sites is mixed, as is that of the area bounded by Ekron–Gezer–Tel Batash; perhaps a similar phenomenon occurred in the Negev. According to Kletter, they could show a mixed population or a temporary Judaean domination; in any case, they cannot help in defining Judah's borders because they are isolated sites outside any sequence of Judaean settlements. They thus cannot prove or refute the possibility that Josiah expanded his territory for a short duration, though the few finds outside Judah are best explained by trade or exchange.

The significant increase in written artifacts (seals, seal impressions, ostraca, inscribed weights) has been interpreted as demonstrating a greater degree of literacy in Judah under Josiah. This seems to me to be doubtful; see further the discussion under §3.2.5.

It was once conventional to accept Josiah's reform at face value, but the question is currently much debated (Albertz 1994: 198–201; 2005; Lohfink 1995; P. R. Davies 2005; Knauf 2005a). We have no direct evidence outside the biblical text, which makes us at least ask whether it is an invention of the Deuteronomist. The alleged absence of any reference to this reform in Jeremiah has always been a major puzzle. Some have found allusions here and there, but one has to admit that they are surprisingly obscure. Considering Jeremiah's overall message and position, he should have embraced such a reform and made copious comments about it. Some have seen evidence in the material remains (e.g., Uehlinger 1995, 2005), but others have argued against it (e.g., Niehr 1995). The central passage is 2 Kings 22–23, however. It is widely agreed that this passage has been the subject of Deuteronomistic editing, leaving the question of how much might be Deuteronomistic invention. C. Hardmeier (2005) and C. Uehlinger (2005) argue that at the heart of 2 Kings 22–23 is a simple list of reform measures affecting mainly Jerusalem and perhaps Bethel, to which the Deuteronomistic editors have added an extensive superstructure that makes the reform much more extensive in scope and geography than the original list. Uehlinger argues that the original list – but not the much-expanded present text – is supported by the archaeology and iconography. Knauf, however, argues against any 'core' from the time of Josiah (2005a: 166–8).

2 Chronicles 34.3-7 also states that Josiah began to purge the country of the various shrines and cults in his twelfth year (i.e., at age 20). This does not accord with 2 Kgs 22.3-7 which has the reform follow the discovery of the law book in the temple. This is not an easy issue to address because the description in 2 Kings 22–23 is an idealized one: the only question is how idealized. This is perhaps why a significant number of scholars have accepted the statement in 2 Chron. 34.3-7 that Josiah began his reform six years before the finding of the law book. Yet as Na'aman (1991: 38), among others, has pointed out, the theological motives of the writer of Chronicles have had their way here as elsewhere. He notes that when Josiah reached the age of majority at 20, it would have been 'unthinkable' in the theological world of the Chronicler that he would have done nothing about the 'pagan' shrines for another six years. Thus, it was theologically desirable that Josiah begin his reform in his twelfth year rather than wait until his eighteenth. Na'aman has also connected the dating of the reform (which he puts in 622 BCE) with the height of the crisis in Assyria during the revolt of Babylon in 626–623 BCE. It may be that the Assyrian ruler Sin-shar-ishkun's problems were sufficient to give Josiah confidence to initiate his reforms without being in danger of attracting Assyrian disapproval, while the Egyptians who replaced them may not have been particularly concerned.

Until recently it was seldom if ever questioned that Josiah died in a pitched battle (2 Chron. 35.20-24). This seems unlikely, however, since Judah as an Egyptian vassal state is not likely to have been in a military position to challenge the Egyptian army. On the other hand, a vassal king would have been expected to appear before the new ruler (Necho II [610–595 BCE] in this case) to pay homage and swear allegiance. Doubts have been expressed about the fate of Josiah for some considerable period of time (Na'aman 1991: 51–5, with earlier literature). 2 Kings is clearly reticent to tell what happened, but Na'aman's argument that Necho had Josiah executed for suspected disloyalty of some sort makes the most sense, not only from the general historical situation but also from a close reading of the text in 2 Kings.

5.2.5 Jehoahaz

Beyond the biblical account (2 Kgs 23.30-34) nothing is known of him, though he has only the brief reign of three months. What does fit is that he would have been removed from the throne by the Egyptians who were probably in control of the region at this time (as discussed under §5.2.4 above).

5.2.6 Jehoiakim

The reign of Jehoiakim illustrates the external politics of the ancient Near East at this time and fits in well with them (2 Kgs 23.34–24.6). Judah was clearly an Egyptian vassal, since it was the Egyptians who put Jehoiakim on the throne. But in Jehoiakim's fourth year Nebuchadnezzar gained control of the region after the battle of Carchemish, and Judah became the vassal of the Babylonians. He then rebelled after three years. Why? The answer is that in 601 BCE Nebuchadnezzar fought a costly battle with Necho II which inflicted considerable damage on both armies; indeed, it took the Babylonians several years to recover, as indicated by *Babylonian Chronicle* 5 (§5.1.4.2). It was after this battle that Jehoiakim rebelled. It was not until two years later that Nebuchadnezzar retaliated by fostering raids against Judah, and it was not until late in 598 that he sent an army against Jerusalem. 2 Chronicles 36.6 states that Nebuchadnezzar besieged Jerusalem and took Jehoiakim captive to Babylon, while Jer. 22.18-19 predicts that he would have the 'burial of an ass' (i.e., his carcass would be dragged outside Jerusalem and left exposed and unburied). Neither appears to be what happened: from 2 Kings 24 it looks as if Jehoiakim died a natural death only a couple of months or so before Nebuchadnezzar set siege to Jerusalem, and it was his son who paid the price for his rebellion. As for Dan. 1.1-2, it is completely confused, most likely based on a misreading of the narrative in 2 Kings and 2 Chronicles (Grabbe 1987: 138–40).

5.2.7 Jehoiachin

Jehoiachin is well attested in both biblical and extra-biblical sources. Even though he reigned only briefly, he became a symbol to many Judahites as their last king. In the biblical writings his name is mentioned not only in 2 Kings and 2 Chronicles but also in Jeremiah (22.24, 28; 27.20; 28.4; 29.2; 37.1; 52.31), Ezekiel (1.2) and Esther (2.6). Jehoiachin is known (though not by name) from the *Babylonian Chronicles* which tell of Nebuchadnezzar's taking of Jerusalem and his carrying of the Judaean king into captivity. Jehoiachin's name has also been preserved in the Jehoiachin tablets from Babylon (§5.1.4.3). Thus, this young ephemeral ruler is better known from extra-biblical sources than the famous Josiah.

5.2.8 Zedekiah

Although many Judahites apparently considered the last legitimate king to be Jehoiachin, the last official king of Judah is known from the *Babylonian Chronicles* as the king placed on the throne by Nebuchadnezzar after his conquest of Jerusalem in early 597 BCE (§5.1.4.3). Zedekiah's name is known only from the biblical text, however, since the Babylonian sources do not give his name. We have no Mesopotamian historical sources after 594 when the *Babylonian Chronicles* come to an end. Yet the inscription of Psammetichus II (595–589 BCE) describing a tour of Palestine fits a situation in which the king of Judah was constantly looking for ways to free himself from the overlordship of Nebuchadnezzar (§5.1.5). The book of Jeremiah describes a number of episodes involving the king or courtiers (see below). The rebellion and final siege and capture of Jerusalem are, unfortunately, not known from any Mesopotamian source. Yet in view of the detailed information confirmed for 2 Kings in the period before this, the reasonableness (for the most part) of the picture in 2 Kings and the general background situation in the ancient Near East, it does not take much of a leap of faith to accept the general picture and the approximate date for the destruction of Jerusalem.

The Egyptians were supposed to have assisted Zedekiah temporarily by sending an army, which caused the Babylonians to lift their siege, but the Egyptians withdrew, and the Babylonian siege was resumed (Jer. 37.4-11). We know nothing of this from either Babylonian or Egyptian sources. The pharaoh at the time was Apries (589–570 BCE, called Hofrah in the biblical text [Jer. 44.30]), yet our knowledge of Pharaoh Apries from native Egyptian sources is deficient. However, we have some information from Greek sources that has generally been accepted by Egyptologists (Herodotus 2.161-69; Diodorus Siculus 1.68.1-6). According to these sources, Apries brought Phoenicia into submission. Jeremiah 27.3

indicates that Tyre and Sidon supported Zedekiah's rebellion. Apries' actions seem to fit into this context. Although we do not know for certain whether Jerusalem fell in 587 or 586 BCE, the overall description in 2 Kings and Jeremiah is probably reasonably accurate.

5.2.9 The Case of Jeremiah

In spite of R. P. Carroll (1986) and the problems of reading the text of Jeremiah as a contemporary, dispassionate biography, there are a number of statements in Jeremiah about external events that could be based only on contemporary knowledge (Grabbe 2006a). These involve the activities of Nebuchadnezzar and their dating. The writer knows about the battle of Carchemish and its correct dating (Jer. 26.2). He is aware of the siege of Lachish and Azekah (Jer. 34.6-7), a situation which has appeared in a remarkable way in Lachish Letter #4. Only some of the statements about Nebuchadnezzar can be checked with Mesopotamian sources, but the exact recital of events in particular years of the king have the look of authenticity.

In addition, Jeremiah describes the prophet's interaction with the Judaean kings (especially Zedekiah) and various members of the court and temple. A whole network of supporters, opponents and relatives appears in the book. We are unlikely to find confirmation of this information outside the Bible. However, data from other texts – which do not seem to be the author's sources – may give some independent support to the reliability of this information for the most part (cf. Long 1982). Yet the find of a seal of 'Baruch son of Neriah the scribe' does not prove that Jeremiah had a scribe named Baruch (cf. Carroll 1997: 96–100), even if the seal is authentic (which it probably is not [§5.1.2.6.2]). An authentic seal could help to confirm the existence of Baruch the scribe, but the question would still remain as to whether a high government official – as this Baruch would seem to be – would have had the interest and leisure to serve as Jeremiah's private scribe. As for the prophecies about Jehoiakim's having the 'burial of an ass' and Nebuchadnezzar's conquest of Egypt, these seem to be mistaken. Perhaps they were genuine prophecies – that failed!

The book of Jeremiah contains a variety of material; I think most would admit to that even if they did not subscribe to the specific analysis of S. Mowinckel (1914) or others. Carroll's sharp observations have called into question the amount of personal material from Jeremiah himself (Carroll 1981), yet he did not explain adequately some of the material in the book. It seems likely that some of the data there can be explained best as coming from a contemporary writer. Unlike 2 Kings, however, the information is not likely to come from a chronicle. Although it refers to international events on occasion, a lot of it is highly individual to Jeremiah or those around him. The best explanation seems to be that a contemporary of Jeremiah's did write some sort of 'biography' of the prophet. If this suggestion does not commend itself, any alternative theory has to take account of how the book has some statements that match what we know of the wider history of the ancient Near East at the time.

5.2.10 The Case of Nebuchadnezzar

One of the most interesting points that has arisen out of this study is the number of statements about Nebuchadnezzar in 2 Kings and Jeremiah that accord with the contemporary sources. The rules of Jehoiakim, Jehoiachin and Zedekiah are tied closely to Nebuchadnezzar's reign. The battle of Carchemish is known and given the correct chronological position. Although Jehoiakim's rebellion is not explained in the biblical text, both the reason for it and the timing make sense in the light of Nebuchadnezzar's stand-off with Egypt in 601 BCE. The biblical account of the Babylonian king's taking of Jerusalem in 597 BCE fits with everything we know from Mesopotamian sources. The Jehoiachin tablets (§5.1.4.3) confirm the presence of Jehoiachin in Babylon, along with his sons and other Judahites. Not every reference to contemporary history is accurate (e.g., whether Nebuchadnezzar ever conquered Egypt), but the amount of specific information is remarkable.

When it comes to Ezekiel, however, the information is much more doubtful. It may be that Nebuchadnezzar besieged Tyre, since Ezekiel's original prophecy is 'corrected' later on. But there is no evidence for a 40-year period of desolation for Egypt, as predicted. 2 Chronicles seems to be dependent on 2 Kings, and none of the additional passages is proved to have reliable information, with the possible exception of the city wall. The one specifically relating to Nebuchadnezzar is Jehoiakim's Babylonian captivity, and this goes contrary not only to 2 Kings but also the *Babylonian Chronicles*. As for Daniel, the writer seems to know of Nebuchadnezzar only through the biblical text. The siege of Jerusalem in Jehoiakim's third year is based on a partial misunderstanding of 2 Chronicles. The other stories in Daniel about Nebuchadnezzar seem at least in part based on legends rising out of the reign of Nabonidus. This was first recognized by W. von Soden (1935) but confirmed in a startling way by the discovery of 4Q Prayer of Nabonidus (see further the discussion in Grabbe 1987).

5.2.11 The 'Exile'

The 'exile' has been seen as a seminal period in Israel's history, though interpreted in widely different ways (Grabbe [ed.] 1998; Scott [ed.] 1997). It now seems to be agreed that a good deal of literary production went on during this time. The Deuteronomic History may have been compiled during this time or, according to some, had a second edition issued in that period (§3.1.6.2). What one thinks occurred depends a good deal on how one responds to the 'myth of the empty land' (Carroll 1992; Barstad 1996). Some have objected to this designation and insisted that the biblical text is correct: the land was basically empty (Oded 2003). Yet although O. Lipschits (e.g., 2005: 187 n. 11; 190 nn. 22–3) is sometimes critical of Barstad, he takes a definite stand against the 'myth of the empty land' (2004). Jerusalem itself was uninhabited (§5.1.1), but there was a thriving settlement in the Benjamin area and also settlements here and there in the area of Judah.

Most of our knowledge of Judah is based on archaeology, but we have knowledge of the Neo-Babylonian kings. Most of their actions do not appear to have had a direct effect on the people of Judah. One biblical tradition, however, has to be considered. This is the story of Belshazzar in Daniel 5. We know a lot about the reign of Nabonidus, the last king of the Neo-Babylonian empire, and his son Belshazzar (Beaulieu 1989). Although acting for his father while the latter was in Tema, Belshazzar was nevertheless never declared king. In any case, Nabonidus had returned to the city by the time of the Persian siege. Belshazzar is not mentioned in the account of the fall of Babylon (though Nabonidus is) and may not even have been alive at that point. Daniel 5 is an exciting drama but no more than that.

For Judah during the Persian period, see Grabbe 2004a.

5.3 Synthesis

Because of the nature of the sources and the study of history in the period of this chapter, a synthesis was already given above under §5.2 and will not be repeated here. Thus, all that needs to be done at this point is to indicate how the biblical text matches with the critical history of the period.

5.3.1 Biblical Data Confirmed

- In broad terms, Hezekiah's existence and revolt and Sennacherib's destructive invasion of Judah are supported by the Assyrian records and by archaeology, especially relative to the city of Lachish.
- Manasseh's existence and name are attested by the inscriptions of both Esarhaddon and Ashurbanipal.
- The one datum about Manasseh's reign found in Chronicles, but not in Kings, that is likely to be correct concerns his building of a city wall (2 Chron. 33.14): something very like this was found down the eastern slope of the southeastern hill by K. Kenyon.
- Although some of the data from seals are problematic, because of either problems of interpretation or questions of authenticity, some are supportive of the biblical data, to a lesser or greater extent. Perhaps one of the most likely is the one reading 'Gemaryahu son of Shaphan' (cf. Jer. 36.10, 12); another is the reference to an official of 'Baalisha', king of Ammon (cf. Jer. 40.14). Moderately high in probability is 'Azariah son of Hilkiah' (cf. 2 Kgs 22–23; 1 Chron. 6.13; 9.11; Ezra 7.1). Of more moderate probability is the one reading 'Jaazaniah the servant of the king' (cf. 2 Kgs 25.23).
- Josiah's religious reforms – the aspect of his reign, and of the seventh century, of most interest to many modern scholars – are difficult to establish in any direct way. (There are some cogent arguments from textual analysis that a modest list of cult measures lies at the heart of 2 Kgs 22–23 [Uehlinger 2005], but my concern here is not primarily with inner-biblical analysis.) But the disappearance of Yhwh's consort and astral symbols from the iconography suggest a significant religious change. This does not by itself establish Josiah's reforms but combines with other considerations to make the general biblical account (not necessarily the details) plausible.
- Pharaoh Necho (II) and his support of the Assyrians against the Babylonians are confirmed by Egyptian sources and especially the *Babylonian Chronicles*.
- Jeremiah's references to the battle of Carchemish and other activities of Nebuchadnezzar (II) are remarkably accurate, suggesting they would have been based on contemporary or near contemporary information.
- Jehoiakim's rebellion in Nebuchadnezzar's fourth year fits the events described in the *Babylonian Chronicles*, even though Judah is not specifically mentioned in the entry for that year.

- Nebuchadnezzar's attack on Jerusalem of 597, and the deposition of one king and the replacement with another, is given substance by the *Babylonian Chronicles.* Although the name of Jehoiachin is not found in the *Babylonian Chronicles*, it seems confirmed by the reference in the Jehoiachin tablets.
- One of the Lachish ostraca mentions the siege of Lachish and Azekah (cf. Jer. 34.6-7).

5.3.2 Biblical Data Not Confirmed, Though They May Be Correct

- Amon's assassination is not likely to have been made up, especially since he seems to have made so little impact in the history of Judah.
- Surprisingly, nothing of Josiah's reign can be directly confirmed from extra-biblical sources, not only his cultic reform but even his existence, since he is not mentioned in any Assyrian or Egyptian sources so far discovered.
- The statement of 2 Chron. 34.3-7 that Josiah began his religious purge already in his twelfth year may be true, and many scholars have accepted it. However, it seems unlikely; otherwise, why was there such a reaction to finding the law book in the temple? (This consideration is apart from the arguments of those who maintain that the cultic reform was not a part of Josiah's reign.)
- Ezra 4.2 refers to a deportation to Palestine under Esarhaddon, but the exact place is not specified. Ezra 4.9-10 mentions various peoples brought to Samaria by 'Osnappar', a name unknown in Assyrian history, though some think it is a corruption of Ashurbanipal or possibly Esarhaddon. In addition to the problems with the two passages just noted, no such deportation is known under either Esarhaddon or Ashurbanipal. One can only say that it is possible in the present state of our knowledge.
- The names and actions of the various palace and temple officials with whom Jeremiah interacts may be correctly recorded. As noted above, there are internal data that suggest the plausibility of some of them. There are no external data except possibly some seal inscriptions in a few cases.
- The destruction of Jerusalem by Nebuchadnezzar in 587/586 is likely to be correct, given the general accuracy of such data in this section of 2 Kings.
- Nebuchadnezzar may have besieged Tyre. The fact that Ezekiel first says he would conquer it and then admits that he did not is an indication of prophecies contemporary with the events.

5.3.3 Biblical Picture is Most Likely Incorrect

- 2 Kings has Judah throw off the Assyrian yoke under Hezekiah, and no hint of an imposition until after the death of Josiah. This is an omission, but it goes further: it seems to be a deliberate attempt by the compiler to mask the fact that Josiah was a vassal, probably first of the Assyrians and then of the Egyptians.
- 2 Chronicles 33.10-17 has Manasseh being taken captive to Babylon. Although some event might lie behind this (§5.2.2), it is contradicted by the silence in 2 Kings, the general image of Manasseh in the Assyrian inscriptions (such as the lack of any indication of rebellion) and the unlikelihood that he would have been taken to Babylon if he had been taken captive.
- Although it is not impossible, Amon is unlikely to have had a child at age 16.
- The picture in 2 Chron. 35.20-27 that Josiah fought a pitched battle with Pharaoh Necho and was mortally wounded by an arrow is contradicted by 2 Kgs 23.28-30 and looks like a literary topos.
- The 2 Chron. 36.6-7 statement that Jehoiakim was taken captive to Babylon fits neither the picture in 2 Kings nor that in the *Babylonian Chronicles*.
- The statement in Jer. 22.18-19 that Jehoiakim would have 'the burial of an ass' by being thrown out without a proper burial is contradicted by the statements in 2 Kgs 24.6 that Jehoiakim simply 'slept with his fathers' – which usually means a peaceful death and burial.
- The prophecies of Jeremiah and Ezekiel that Nebuchadnezzar would conquer Egypt and that it would remain desolate for 40 years are contradicted by what we know of both Nebuchadnezzar's reign and of Egyptian history.
- Daniel seems to have known little or nothing about this period except what the author read in the biblical text or had received in the form of very legendary material. Jerusalem was not besieged by Nebuchadnezzar in Jehoiakim's third year. Nebuchadnezzar was not mad (or whatever word one wishes to use) for seven years. Belshazzar was not king of Babylon when the Persians captured it.

5.3.4 Biblical Picture Omits/Has Gaps

- The truly devastating effects of Hezekiah's rebellion on the cities and villages of Judah are only hinted at; the text is at pains to establish Hezekiah's faithfulness to Yhwh in his rebellion against Assyria rather than the suffering he caused to his country and people. Also, as noted above, Judah remained an Assyrian vassal throughout the reigns of Hezekiah, Manasseh and Amon, and the first part of Josiah's reign.

- The real achievements of Manasseh's reign from a political, economic and social point of view (as attested especially in the archaeology) are completely ignored.
- The text is coy about giving the real reason for Josiah's death. The thesis that he was executed by Necho is plausible, though not certain, but it is unlikely he was killed in battle.

Part III

CONCLUSIONS

Chapter 6

'The End of the Matter': What Can We Say about Israelite and Judahite History?

We now return to consider our original aim: we set out to investigate what we can know about the history of Israel and Judah, keeping in mind questions of sources, method and current debates. This has been *prolegomena* to a history, not the history itself. It has attempted to address those issues and questions that have to be considered and answered before any history can be written. Just to remind ourselves, here is a brief summary of the principles of historical method used throughout this book (§1.3.3):

- All potential sources should be considered.
- Preference should be given to original sources.
- The *longue durée* needs always to be kept in mind.
- Each episode or event has to be judged on its own merits.
- All reconstructions are provisional.
- All reconstructions have to be argued for.

Among the sources – and questions – considered in each chapter has been the biblical text: To what extent is the Bible reliable – to what extent can we use it in writing our history? Confirmed minimalists and hardened maximalists already know the answer, it seems (though they generally claim to be open to the facts), but most scholars do not pitch their tents at these extreme ends of the spectrum. For those who do not immediately embrace or reject the text, no easy answer arises from our pages: we cannot say that the biblical text is reliable or unreliable, because it all depends on which episode or text one has in mind.

Some cannot understand why the biblical text seems to have been so 'vilified', as they would see it, but the answer is simple: the fundamental historical principle of distinguishing between primary and secondary (tertiary, etc.) sources. Primary sources are those contemporary (or nearly so) with the events they describe and usually have some other direct connection (eyewitness report, compilation from eyewitness reports or other good sources, proximity to the events or those involved in the events). Secondary sources are those further removed in time and space from the original events. The Bible is not being attacked or vilified, but it is, unfortunately, almost always a secondary source because of the long history of writing, compilation and editing. The complicated history of the biblical text has been partially worked out in the past two centuries, but there is still much unknown and much on which there is disagreement. Primary sources are not always trustworthy, and secondary sources may sometimes contain reliable information, and no two sources agree entirely. Thus, the historian has to make a critical investigation of all data, whatever the source. Yet the basic principle has to be maintained: primary sources normally take precedent, and secondary sources normally need some sort of confirmation.

We began with the *longue durée* (§1.2.2). The history of Palestine is heavily shaped by the landscape and climate. The land is divided between the fertile, more congenial north; the drier, less productive south; the desert margins in the south and east. There is great variation between the northern valleys, the central hill country, the Shephelah, the coastal plain and the Negev. One cannot write a history in a vacuum, nor should one advance scenarios that depend on improbable population and material resources. The topography and similar factors resulted in many of the same urban sites being inhabited throughout the second and first millennium BCE. Jerusalem was important not because of great wealth or rich resources of Judah but because the rugged terrain gave it natural defences and made it generally not worth the effort to attack. There was also a cycle of alternation between agrarian settlement and pastoralism over the centuries, going up and down according to climatic, economic and other factors. Finally, Palestine lay between great powers to the south and north whose expansion and conflicts affected the situation of the whole Syro-Palestinian region.

The history of Israel begins in the second millennium BCE. We do not know when the name 'Israel' or an entity called Israel came into existence, but we have the first reference to both these just before 1200 BCE. Yet texts, as well as archaeology, take us further back into the second millennium BCE. Texts from Egypt mention a number of sites, well-known from the first millennium BCE, that already existed centuries earlier, including Jerusalem, Shechem, Megiddo, Akko, Lachish, Gaza, Ashkelon and Laish. We find, for example, that the cities (city-states) of Shechem and Jerusalem seem to have dominated the Palestinian highlands in the fourteenth century, according to the Amarna letters. This does not mean that Jerusalem was a major urban area: it could have been little more than a citadel or country manor (insufficient archaeological remains have been found to tell us), but it certainly existed as the seat of the region's ruler. We next hear of Jerusalem as a Jebusite stronghold which the Israelites could capture but from which they could not expel the inhabitants (Grabbe 2003a).

In early Iron I, settlements in the highlands suddenly blossomed. About the same time, the coastal plain was settled by a group whose material culture seems strongly influenced by Aegean and Cypriot forms (§3.2.2). Egyptian texts refer to the Sea Peoples who seem to have settled along the Palestinian coast. The much later biblical text refers to a variety of groups who inhabited the interior of Palestine, as well as the Israelites who are associated with the highlands in some passages. Although the biblical references are sometimes garbled or improbable, a number of the names coincide with peoples from Syria and Asia Minor (the Amorites, Hittites, Hurrians [Horites], Hivites, Girgashites), as well as the (indigenous?) Canaanites (§§2.2.1.2; 2.2.1.5). On the whole, the biblical text is problematic for Iron I (and the earlier periods). Its picture of a massive exodus and rapid unitary conquest do not match either written records or archaeology, nor can much be found in the book of Judges that can be supported, even though the general scenario of a multitude of individual, (semi-)independent groups, each doing its own thing, seems to coincide broadly with what we know from other sources.

When 'Israel' next occurs in original sources (about the mid-ninth century BCE), it is now a kingdom in the northern part of Palestine, allied with the Aramaean king of Damascus and others against the expanding Assyrian empire (§4.2.1). Later Assyrian inscriptions make clear that alongside Israel to the south was another kingdom, that of Judah. What happened between the first mention of 'Israel' about 1200 BCE and the second mention some 350 years later? We have no information from primary written sources, only archaeology, plus we have the secondary source of the Bible which gives a detailed picture of the rise of a unified state under Saul, David and Solomon, followed by a split into the two kingdoms of Israel and Judah. Does this answer our question? Unfortunately, just as the exodus and conquest are contradicted by the primary sources, the biblical picture of the united monarchy has some problems associated with it.

The archaeology suggests that the inhabitants of the coastal plain were likely to be stronger in population and resources than those in the hill country. There is also the question of whether they would have felt the need to expand into the highlands at this stage. It is intrinsically unlikely that the highlanders would have conquered the Philistines at this point. The extensive conquests of David and the empire of Solomon from the 'river of Egypt' to the Euphrates are not supported by the archaeology, the international context or the resources available. The visit of the 'queen of Sheba' simply has no support in the sources. The archaeology in Jerusalem so far does not corroborate a massive capital city with monumental architecture. There is still hope on the part of some that such will be discovered, but it seems unlikely that anything like the city envisaged in the Bible is going to be found. Archaeology is very important in all this, but the debate over the LC and ^{14}C dating means that there is even less agreement than usual over what can be inferred from the material culture.

Some argue for a 'united monarchy' on a much reduced scale, with David perhaps more like a chieftain or the ruler of an archaic state of some sort. The arguments sometimes hinge on seeing David as an exceptional individual who was able to achieve this rule in spite of the expectations that the north would achieve statehood before Judah. Much also depends on being convinced that the biblical writer did not just invent it all – that some sort of historical scenario lies behind the text even if the compiler has relied on legendary material or exaggerated thinking. All this is, of course, possible. In 1998 I gave an address that made some predictions about the future of historical study (Grabbe 2000b). At that time, I suggested that the 'united monarchy' might not survive but did not predict that it would fall. Getting toward two decades later, the question still remains. The issue remains fiercely debated, but there is little new evidence. What seems overwhelmingly the case is that no one's idea of the 'united monarchy' bears much resemblance to the biblical description.

Although archaeology helps us bridge the gap between 1200 and 850 BCE, there is still much debate over how to interpret it and, therefore, much debate over how much of the text we can accept. But from early in the 'divided monarchy', we suddenly find aspects of the text supported fairly consistently by external sources: the names of Israelite and (later) Judahite kings, their relative time and order of reign, some of their deeds. The data confirmed tend to be those in portions of the text belonging to a particular literary formula that has long been associated with a court or temple chronicle. Sometimes two such chronicles (one from Israel and one from Judah) have been assumed, but I argue that the most parsimonious thesis is to hypothesize a single 'Chronicle of the Kings of Judah' (Grabbe 2006b). In some cases, in 1 and 2 Kings much of the king's reign seems to be drawn from such a chronicle, but in other cases (e.g., Ahab) we have other, more legendary, material taken from other sources (such as prophetic legends, in the case of Ahab).

The first kingdom for which we have solid evidence is the Northern Kingdom, the state founded by Omri. This fits what we would expect from the *longue durée*; if there was an earlier state, we have no direct information on it except perhaps some memory in the biblical text. This does not mean that nothing existed before Omri in either the north or the south, but what was there was probably not a state as such. In any case, Israel is soon caught between the great empires to the north and south. Hardly has Omri passed from the scene before the Assyrians are threatening. In not much over a century, his kingdom had become an Assyrian province. Judah seems to have been the younger brother throughout their history and only came to flourish when Israel disappeared as a kingdom. But Judah, too, came under the Assyrian thumb even before Samaria fell. The seventh century was marked first by Assyrian domination, then Egyptian, then Babylonian.

As for our knowledge of Judah, we have the same type of records preserved that helped us with the Northern Kingdom: the same mixture of chronicle data, oral tales, legends and other material marks the descriptions of the reigns of kings until the fall of Jerusalem. In some cases, material has clearly been inserted for theological reasons, such as the accusations against Manasseh designed to blacken his name, and the claims that Josiah reformed the cult even as far as Samaria. Yet there is a gradual increase in reliability the later the narrative progresses. In the last years of the kings of Judah, when there are times that we know what was happening year by year, the biblical text can be remarkably accurate, and in the last few years (after 594 BCE) when our external sources cease, we can still have reasonable confidence that the basic narrative is correct. Yet plenty of inaccurate biblical text can also be found, such as the book of Daniel, which means that it must always be subject to critical analysis.

After Jerusalem fell in 587/586 BCE, there was no 'empty land' as was once proposed, but the settlement varied greatly. The population overall had been considerably reduced and was now concentrated to the north of Jerusalem in Benjamin, and Mizpah (Tell el-Nasbeh) seems to have been designated the administrative centre of the province by the Babylonians. Jerusalem appears to have been uninhabited or almost so during the four decades or so from the fall of Jerusalem until Persian rule.

This investigation has drawn attention to a number of broader points or themes relating to writing a history of Israel. By way of a conclusion to the study – and without repeating the general historical principles used throughout this study (§1.3.3) – here they are:

1. Writing the history of ancient Israel and Judah is no different from writing any other history. The data available and the problems involved may be different, but this is true of writing the history of any period or entity – each has certain unique problems and unique features. The problems with a history of the 'united monarchy' are very similar to those of a history of the Trojan War. The basic principle of giving preference to primary sources (as noted above) only goes so far, because much of what we want to know is not available in primary sources. Secondary sources (the biblical text and the Homeric poems) have to be considered.
2. The minimalist argument that the biblical text cannot be used except where there is external confirmation has often been supported in our investigation; however, as a working principle it is inadequate. The biblical text should always be considered: it is one of the sources for the history of ancient Israel and needs to be treated like any other source, being neither privileged nor rejected a priori, but handled straightforwardly and critically. Unfortunately, the Bible is not an 'ancient Near Eastern text' *tout court*: we know the biblical text solely from the versions (of which there are usually several) attested only in later copies. In some cases, these copies are mediaeval, though we are in the happy position that recent discoveries have allowed us to obtain versions of part of the text going back to the later centuries before the Common Era. Yet these finds show that the text was still developing, being edited and growing until the first century CE.
3. Particular sorts of information are more likely to be trustworthy than others: wherever an Israelite or Judahite ruler is mentioned in an external source, the biblical text is shown to have the genuine name, the correct sequence of rule and the approximate time of the person's rule in every case where there are sufficient external comparative sources to make a determination. Material likely to have been taken from or based on a court or temple chronicle has, prima facie, a much greater chance of having usable data. Prophetic stories, for example, do not generally make good historical sources. The main point here, however, is that the biblical text was not written as a record of the past nor for purely antiquarian reasons. Its purpose was a theological and religious one, as indicated already simply by the contents of the text. There is still a gulf between the concerns of the biblical writers and those of the historians beginning already with the ancient Greeks (cf. Grabbe 2001b). In general, though, the later a passage is in the history of Israel, the more reliable it is likely to be.

4. The most fruitful method is the multiple-source approach. Although preference should be given to archaeological and inscriptional sources, the use of a variety of data – archaeological, inscriptional, contemporary textual, biblical – has turned out to give us a reasonable grasp of some portions of the history of Israel, especially the later part of the monarchy. It is important to study each source independently in the initial stages of the investigation, lest one 'contaminate' the evidence by circular interpretation of one against the other. Nevertheless, once the groundwork has been done and the nature of the different sources has been understood, then they can and should be synthesized in a rigorous way to work toward an understanding of the history of this period.
5. The social sciences can sometimes provide important models for and approaches to understanding the data. These models – theories – must always be critically tested against the data and not imposed on them. But they can be valuable in interrogating the textual and artifactual data available and suggesting new ways of interpreting them. The application of social anthropology to archaeology revolutionized things in the 1970s and 1980s, but texts may similarly acquire new significance by adding social scientific data and theoretical understanding to the intellectual process.

Bibliography

Aharoni, Yohanan

1967 'Forerunners of the Limes: Iron Age Fortresses in the Negev', *IEJ* 17: 1–17.

1979 *The Land of the Bible: A Historical Geography* (trans. and ed. A. F. Rainey; London: Burns & Oates; Philadelphia: Westminster Press, 2nd edn).

1981 *Arad Inscriptions* (in co-operation with Joseph Naveh; Jerusalem: Israel Exploration Society).

1982 *The Archaeology of the Land of Israel* (trans. A. F. Rainey; Philadelphia: Westminster Press).

Ahituv, Shmuel

1984 *Canaanite Toponyms in Ancient Egyptian Documents* (Jerusalem: Magnes Press).

Ahlström, Gösta W.

1986 *Who Were the Israelites?* (Winona Lake, IN: Eisenbrauns).

1991 'The Role of Archaeological and Literary Remains in Reconstructing Israel's History', in Diana V. Edelman (ed.), *The Fabric of History: Text, Artifact and Israel's Past* (JSOTSup, 127; Sheffield: Sheffield Academic Press): 116–41.

1993a *The History of Ancient Palestine from the Palaeolithic Period to Alexander's Conquest* (JSOTSup, 146; Sheffield Academic Press).

1993b 'Pharaoh Shoshenq's Campaign to Palestine', in André Lemaire and Benedikt Otzen (eds), *History and Traditions of Early Israel: Studies Presented to Eduard Nielsen, May 8th 1993* (VTSup, 50; Leiden: Brill): 1–16.

Ahlström, Gösta W., and Diana Edelman

1985 'Merneptah's Israel', *JNES* 44: 59–61.

Albertz, Rainer

1978 *Persönliche Frömmigkeit und offizielle Religion: Religionsinterner Pluralismus in Israel und Babylon* (Calwer Theologische Monographien, A 9; Stuttgart: Calwer).

1994 *A History of Israelite Religion in the Old Testament Period.* Vol. I: *From the Beginnings to the End of the Monarchy.* Vol. II: *From the Exile to the Maccabees* (London: SCM Press); ET of *Geschichte der israelitischen Religion* (2 vols; Das Alte Testament Deutsch Ergänzungsreihe 8; Göttingen: Vandenhoeck & Ruprecht, 1992).

2003 *Israel in Exile: The History and Literature of the Sixth Century B.C.E.* (trans. David Green; SBLSBL, 3; Atlanta, GA: Society of Biblical Literature); ET of *Die Exilszeit: 6. Jahrhundert v. Chr.* (Biblische Enzyklopädie, 7; Stuttgart: Kohlhammer, 2001).

2005 'Why a Reform Like Josiah's Must Have Happened', in Lester L. Grabbe (ed.), *Good Kings and Bad Kings: The Kingdom of Judah in the Seventh Century BCE* (JSOTSup, 393; ESHM, 5: London/New York: T&T Clark International): 27–46.

Albright, William F.

1932 *The Excavation of Tell Beit Mirsim in Palestine I: The Pottery of the First Three Campaigns* (AASOR, 12; Boston, MA: American Schools of Oriental Research).

1961 'Abram the Hebrew: A New Archaeological Interpretation', *BASOR* 163: 36–54.

Alt, G. Albrecht

1966 *'The God of the Fathers': Essays on Old Testament History and Religion* (Oxford: Blackwell): 1–77; ET of *Der Gott der Väter: Ein Beitrag zur Vorgeschichte der israelitischen Religion* (BWANT, 48; Stuttgart: Kohlhammer, 1929).

Anbar, Moshé

1991 *Les tribus amurrites de Mari* (OBO, 108; Freiburg [Schweiz]: Universitätsverlag; Göttingen: Vandenhoeck & Ruprecht).

Appleby, Joyce, Lynn Hunt, and Margaret Jacob

1994 *Telling the Truth about History* (New York and London: W. W. Norton).

Ash, Paul S.

1999 *David, Solomon and Egypt: A Reassessment* (JSOTSup, 297; Sheffield: Sheffield Academic Press).

Assmann, Jan

2015 'Exodus and Memory', in Thomas E. Levy, Thomas Schneider, and William H. C. Propp (eds), *Israel's Exodus in Transdisciplinary Perspective: Text, Archaeology, Culture, and Geoscience* (Quantitative Methods in the Humanities and Social Sciences; Cham, Switzerland: Springer): 3–15.

Astour, Michael C.

1971 '841 B.C.: The First Assyrian Invasion of Israel', *JAOS* 91: 383–9.

Athas, George

2003 *The Tel Dan Inscription: A Reappraisal and a New Interpretation* (JSOTSup, 360; Copenhagen International Seminar, 12; Sheffield: Sheffield Academic Press).

Avigad, Nahman

1978 'Baruch the Scribe and Jerahmeel the King's Son', *IEJ* 28: 52–6.

1986 *Hebrew Bullae from the Time of Jeremiah: Remnants of a Burnt Archive* (Jerusalem: Israel Exploration Society).

Avigad, Nahman, revised and completed by Benjamin Sass

1997 *Corpus of West Semitic Stamp Seals* (Jerusalem: Israel Academy of Sciences and Humanities/Israel Exploration Society).

Avigad, Nahman, and Hillel Geva
2000 *Jewish Quarter Excavations in the Old City of Jerusalem conducted by Nahman Avigad, 1969–1982* (ed. Hillel Geva; 2 vols; Jerusalem: Israel Exploration Society/Institute of Archaeology, Hebrew University).
Avioz, Michael
2005 'The Book of Kings in Recent Research (Part I)', *CBR* 4: 11–55.
Avishur, Yitzhak
2000 *Phoenician Inscriptions and the Bible: Select Inscriptions and Studies in Stylistic and Literary Devices Common to the Phoenician Inscriptions and the Bible* (Tel Aviv and Jaffa: Archaeological Center Publication).
Avi-Yonah, Michael, and Ephraim Stern (eds)
1975–78 *Encyclopedia of Archaeological Excavations in the Holy Land* (Oxford: Oxford University Press).
Baines, John
1982 'Interpreting *Sinuhe*', *JEA* 68: 31–44.
Barako, Tristan J.
2013 'Philistines and Egyptians in Southern Coastal Canaan during the Early Iron Age', in Ann E. Killebrew and Gunnar Lehmann (eds), *The Philistines and Other 'Sea Peoples' in Text and Archaeology* (SBLABS, 15; Atlanta, GA: Society of Biblical Literature): 37–51.
Barfield, Thomas J.
1990 'Tribe and State Relations: The Inner Asian Perspective', in Philip S. Khoury and Joseph Kostiner (eds), *Tribes and State Formation in the Middle East* (Berkeley: University of California Press): 153–82.
Barkay, Gabriel
1992 'The Iron Age II–III', in Amnon Ben-Tor (ed.), *The Archaeology of Ancient Israel* (trans. R. Greenberg; New Haven, CT: Yale University Press): 302–73.
1993 'A Bulla of Ishmael, the King's Son', *BASOR* 290–1: 109–14.
Barkay, Gabriel, and Andrew G. Vaughn
1996 '*Lmlk* and Official Seal Impressions from Tel Lachish', *TA* 23: 61–74.
Barr, James
1961 *Semantics of Biblical Language* (Oxford: Clarendon Press).
1977 *Fundamentalism* (London: SCM Press).
2000 *History and Ideology in the Old Testament: Biblical Studies at the End of a Millennium* (Hensley Henson Lectures for 1997; Oxford: Oxford University Press).
Barstad, Hans M.
1984 *The Religious Polemics of Amos: Studies in the Preaching of Am 2,7B-8; 4,1-13; 5,1-27; 6,4-7; 8,14* (VTSup, 34; Leiden: Brill).
1996 *The Myth of the Empty Land: A Study in the History and Archaeology of Judah during the 'Exilic' Period* (Symbolae Osloenses, 28; Oslo and Cambridge, MA: Scandinavian University Press).
1998 'The Strange Fear of the Bible: Some Reflections on the "Bibliophobia" in Recent Ancient Israelite Historiography', in Lester L. Grabbe (ed.), *Leading Captivity Captive: 'The Exile' as History and Ideology* (JSOTSup, 278; ESHM, 2; Sheffield: Sheffield Academic Press): 120–7.

Barth, Frederik

1969 'Introduction', in Frederik Barth (ed.), *Ethnic Groups and Boundaries: The Social Organization of Culture Difference* (Boston: Little, Brown & Company): 1–38.

Barth, Frederik (ed.)

1969 *Ethnic Groups and Boundaries: The Social Organization of Culture Difference* (Boston: Little, Brown & Company).

Bates, Daniel G.

1980 'Yoruk Settlement in Southeast Turkey', in Philip Carl Salzman (ed.), *When Nomads Settle: Processes of Sedentarization as Adaptation and Response* (New York: Praeger): 124–39.

Beaulieu, Paul-Alain

1989 *The Reign of Nabonidus, King of Babylon 556–539 B.C.* (Yale Near Eastern Researches, 10; New Haven, CT: Yale University Press).

Beckerath, J. von

1992 'Ägypten und der Feldzug Sanheribs im Jahre 701 v.Chr.', *UF* 24: 3–8.

Becking, Bob

1992 *The Fall of Samaria: An Historical and Archaeological Study* (SHANE, 2; Leiden: Brill); ET and updating of Chapter 2 of the doctoral thesis, *De ondergang van Samaria: Historische, exegetische en theologische opmerkingen bij II Koningen 17* (ThD, Utrecht Fakulteit de Godgeleerheit, 1985).

1993 'Baalis, the King of the Ammonites: An Epigraphical Note on Jeremiah 40:14', *JSS* 38: 15–24.

1996 'The Second Danite Inscription: Some Remarks', *BN* 81: 21–9.

1997 'Inscribed Seals as Evidence for Biblical Israel? Jeremiah 40.7–41.15 *Par Exemple* in Lester L. Grabbe (ed.), *Can a 'History of Israel' Be Written?* (JSOTSup, 245; ESHM, 1; Sheffield: Sheffield Academic Press): 65–83.

1999 'Did Jehu Write the Tel Dan Inscription?', *SJOT* 13: 187–201.

2002 'West Semites at Tell Šēḫ Ḥamad: Evidence for the Israelite Exile?', in Ulrich Hübner and Ernest Axel Knauf (eds), *Kein Land für sich allein: Studien zum Kulturkontakt in Kanaan, Israel/Palästina und Ebirnâri für Manfred Weippert zum 65. Geburtstag* (OBO, 186: Freiburg [Schweiz]: Universitätsverlag; Göttingen: Vandenhoeck & Ruprecht): 153–66.

2003 'Chronology: A Skeleton without Flesh? Sennacherib's Campaign as a Case-Study', in Lester L. Grabbe (ed.), *'Like a Bird in a Cage': The Invasion of Sennacherib in 701 BCE* (JSOTSup, 363; ESHM, 4; Sheffield: Sheffield Academic Press): 46–72.

Becking, Bob, Meindert Dijkstra, Marjo C. A. Korpel, and Karel J. H. Vriezen

2001 *Only One God? Monotheism in Ancient Israel and the Veneration of the Goddess Asherah* (Biblical Seminar, 77; Sheffield: Sheffield Academic Press); ET of *Één God aleen…? Over monotheïsme in Oud-Israël en de verering van de godin Asjera* (Kampen: Kok Pharos, 1998).

Ben-Ami, Doron

2001 'The Iron Age I at Tel Hazor in Light of the Renewed Excavations', *IEJ* 51: 148–70.

2014 'Notes on the Iron IIA Settlement in Jerusalem in Light of Excavations in the Northwest of the City of David', *TA* 41: 3–19.

Ben-Tor, Amnon

1998 'The Fall of Canaanite Hazor – The "Who" and "When" Questions', in Seymour Gitin, Amihai Mazar and Ephraim Stern (eds), *Mediterranean Peoples in Transition: Thirteenth to Early Tenth Centuries BCE, in Honor of Professor Trude Dothan* (Jerusalem: Israel Exploration Society): 456–67.

2000 'Hazor and the Chronology of Northern Israel: A Reply to Israel Finkelstein', *BASOR* 317: 9–15.

Ben-Yosef, Erez

2012 'Environmental Constraints on Ancient Copper Production in the Aravah Vallley: Implications of the Newly Discovered Site of Khirbet Mana'iyah in Southern Jordan', *TA* 39: 186–202.

Ben-Yosef, Erez, Thomas E. Levy, Thomas Higham, Mohammad Najjar, and Lisa Tauxe

2010 'The Beginning of Iron Age Copper Production in the Southern Levant: New Evidence from Khirbat al-Jariya, Faynan, Jordan', *Antiquity* 84: 724–46.

Ben-Yosef, Erez, Ron Shaar, Lisa Tauxe, and Hagai Ron

2012 'A New Chronological Framework for Iron Age Copper Production at Timna (Israel)', *BASOR* 367: 31–71.

Ben Zvi, Ehud

1990 'Who Wrote the Speech of Rabshakeh and When?', *JBL* 109: 79–92.

1997 'The Chronicler as a Historian: Building Texts', in M. Patrick Graham, Kenneth G. Hoglund and Steven L. McKenzie (eds), *The Chronicler as Historian* (JSOTSup, 238; Sheffield: Sheffield Academic Press): 132–49.

2003 'Malleability and its Limits: Sennacherib's Campaign against Judah as a Case-Study', in Lester L. Grabbe (ed.), *'Like a Bird in a Cage': The Invasion of Sennacherib in 701 BCE* (JSOTSup, 363; ESHM, 4; Sheffield: Sheffield Academic Press): 73–105.

Berner, Christoph

2015 'The Exodus Narrative between History and Literary Fiction: The Portrayal of the Egyptian Burden as a Test Case', in Thomas E. Levy, Thomas Schneider, and William H. C. Propp (eds), *Israel's Exodus in Transdisciplinary Perspective: Text, Archaeology, Culture, and Geoscience* (Quantitative Methods in the Humanities and Social Sciences; Cham, Switzerland: Springer): 285–92.

Betancourt, Philip P.

1997 'Relations between the Aegean and the Hyksos at the End of the Middle Bronze Age', in Eliezer D. Oren (ed.), *The Hyksos: New Historical and Archaeological Perspectives* (University Museum Monograph, 96; University Museum Symposium Series, 8; Philadelphia: University of Pennsylvania, The University Museum): 429–32.

Bienkowski, Piotr

1990 'Umm el-Biyara, Tawilan and Buseirah in Retrospect', *Levant* 22: 91–109.

1992a 'The Beginning of the Iron Age in Southern Jordan: A Framework', in Piotr Bienkowski (ed.), *Early Edom and Moab: The Beginning of the Iron Age in Southern Jordan* (Sheffield Archaeological Monographs, 7; Sheffield: J. R. Collis Publications): 1–12.

1992b 'The Date of Sedentary Occupation in Edom: Evidence from Umm el-Biyara, Tawilan and Buseirah', in Piotr Bienkowski (ed.), *Early Edom and Moab: The Beginning of the Iron Age in Southern Jordan* (Sheffield Archaeological Monographs, 7; Sheffield: J. R. Collis Publications): 99–112.

1992c 'The Beginning of the Iron Age in Edom: A Reply to Finkelstein', *Levant* 24: 167–9.

1995 'The Edomites: The Archaeological Evidence from Transjordan', in Diana Vikander Edelman (ed.), *You Shall Not Abhor an Edomite for He Is Your Brother: Edom and Seir in History and Tradition* (SBLABS, 3; Atlanta, GA: Scholars Press): 41–92.

Bienkowski, Piotr (ed.)

1992 *Early Edom and Moab: The Beginning of the Iron Age in Southern Jordan* (Sheffield Archaeological Monographs, 7; Sheffield: J. R. Collis Publications).

Bienkowski, Piotr, Christopher Mee, and Elizabeth Slater (eds)

2005 *Writing and Ancient Near Eastern Society: Papers in Honour of Alan R. Millard* (LHBOTS, 426; London/New York: T&T Clark International).

Bienkowski, Piotr, and Eveline van der Steen

2001 'Tribes, Trade, and Towns: A New Framework for the Late Iron Age in Southern Jordan and the Negev', *BASOR* 323: 21–47.

Bietak, Manfred

1987 'Comments on the "Exodus"', in Anson F. Rainey (ed.), *Egypt, Israel, Sinai: Archaeological and Historical Relationships in the Biblical Period* (Tel Aviv University Kaplan Project on the History of Israel and Egypt; Tel Aviv: Tel Aviv University): 163–71.

1997 'Avaris, Capital of the Hyksos Kingdom: New Results of Excavations', in Eliezer D. Oren (ed.), *The Hyksos: New Historical and Archaeological Perspectives* (University Museum Monograph, 96; University Museum Symposium Series, 8; Philadelphia: University of Pennsylvania, The University Museum): 87–139.

Bimson, John J.

1981 *Redating the Exodus and Conquest* (JSOTSup, 5; Sheffield: Sheffield Academic Press, 2nd edn).

1991 'Merneptah's Israel and Recent Theories of Israelite Origins', *JSOT* 49: 3–29.

Biran, Avraham, and Joseph Naveh

1993 'An Aramaic Stele Fragment from Tel Dan', *IEJ* 43: 81–98.

1995 'The Tel Dan Inscription: A New Fragment', *IEJ* 45: 1–18.

Blenkinsopp, Joseph

2008 'The Midianite-Kenite Hypothesis Revisited and the Origins of Judah', *JSOT* 33: 131–53.

Bloch-Smith, Elizabeth

1992 *Judahite Burial Practices and Beliefs about the Dead* (JSOTSup, 123; JSOT ASOR Monograph Series, 7; Sheffield: JSOT Press).

2003 'Israelite Ethnicity in Iron I: Archaeology Preserves What Is Remembered and What Is Forgotten In Israel's History', *JBL* 122: 401–25.

Bloch-Smith, Elizabeth, and Beth Alpert Nakhai

1999 'A Landscape Comes to Life: The Iron I Period', *NEA* 62: 62–92, 101–27.

Boer, Roland (ed.)
2002 *Tracking* The Tribes of Yahweh*: On the Trail of a Classic* (JSOTSup, 351; Sheffield: Sheffield Academic Press).
Bordreuil, Pierre, Felice Israel, and Dennis Pardee
1996 'Deux ostraca paléo-hébreux de la Collection Sh. Moussaïeff', *Semitica* 46: 49–76.
1998 'King's Command and Widow's Plea: Two New Hebrew Ostraca of the Biblical Period', *NEA* 61: 2–13.
Borger, Rykele
1967 *Die Inschriften Esarhaddons Königs von Assyrien* (AfO Beiheft, 9; Osnabrück: Biblio Verlage, 2nd edn).
1979 *Babylonisch-assyrische Lesestücke* (Rome: Biblical Institute Press, 2nd edn).
Braudel, Fernand
1980 *On History* (trans. Sarah Matthews; London: Weidenfeld & Nicolson); ET of *Écrits sur l'histoire* (Paris: Flammarion, 1969).
Brett, Mark G. (ed.)
1996 *Ethnicity and the Bible* (BIS, 19; Leiden: Brill).
Brettler, Marc Zvi
1995 *The Creation of History in Ancient Israel* (London/New York: Routledge).
Bright, John
1959 *A History of Israel* (Philadelphia: Westminster Press; London: SCM Press).
1980 *A History of Israel* (Philadelphia: Westminster Press, 3rd edn).
Broshi, Magen
1974 'The Expansion of Jerusalem in the Reigns of Hezekiah and Manasseh', *IEJ* 24: 21–6.
2001 'Estimating the Population of Ancient Jerusalem', in Magen Broshi, *Bread, Wine, Walls and Scrolls* (JSPSup, 36; Sheffield: Sheffield Academic Press): 110–20; earlier publication (in French) *RB* 82 (1975): 5–14; (in English) *BAR* 4.3 (June 1978): 10–15.
Broshi, Magen, and Israel Finkelstein
1992 'The Population of Palestine in Iron Age II', *BASOR* 287: 47–60.
Buccellati, Giorgio
1966 *The Amorites of the Ur III Period* (Pubblicazioni del Seminario di Semitistica a cura di G. Garbini, Richerche, 1; Naples: Istituto Orientale di Napoli).
1997 'Amorites', *OEANE* I, 107–11.
Bunimovitz, Shlomo
1990 'Problems in the "Ethnic" Identity of the Philistine Material Culture', *TA* 17: 210–22.
1998 'On the Edge of Empires – Late Bronze Age (1500–1200 BCE)', in Thomas E. Levy (ed.), *The Archaeology of Society in the Holy Land* (New Approaches in Anthropological Archaeology; London: Leicester University Press, 2nd edn): 320–31.
Bunimovitz, Shlomo, and Avraham Faust
2001 'Chronological Separation, Geographical Segregation, or Ethnic Demarcation? Ethnography and the Iron Age Low Chronology', *BASOR* 322: 1–10.

2003 'Building Identity: The Four Room House and the Israelite Mind', in William G. Dever and Seymour Gitin (eds), *Symbiosis, Symbolism, and the Power of the Past: Canaan, Ancient Israel, and their Neighbors from the Late Bronze Age through Roman Palaestina: Proceedings of the Centennial Symposium W. F. Albright Institute of Archaeological Research and the American Schools of Oriental Research Jerusalem, May 29–31, 2000* (Winona Lake, IN: Eisenbrauns): 411–23.

Bunimovitz, Shlomo, and Zvi Ledermann

2001 'The Iron Age Fortifications of Tel Beth Shemesh: A 1990–2000 Perspective', *IEJ* 51: 121–47.

2008 'A Border Case: Beth-Shemesh and the Rise of Ancient Israel', in Lester L. Grabbe (ed.), *Israel in Transition: From Late Bronze II to Iron IIA (c. 1250–850 BCE)*. Vol. I: *The Archaeology* (LHBOTS, 491; ESHM, 7; London/New York: T&T Clark International): 21–31.

Bunimovitz, Shlomo, and A. Yasur-Landau

1996 'Philistine and Israelite Pottery: A Comparative Approach to the Question of Pots and People', *TA* 23: 88–101.

Cahill, Jane M.

2003 'Jerusalem at the Time of the United Monarchy: The Archaeological Evidence', in Andrew G. Vaughn and Ann E. Killebrew (eds), *Jerusalem in Bible and Archaeology: The First Temple Period* (SBLSymS, 18; Atlanta, GA: Society of Biblical Literature): 13–80.

2004 'Jerusalem in David and Solomon's Time', *BAR* 30.6: 20–31, 62–3.

Campbell, Anthony F., S.J.

1975 *The Ark Narrative (1 Sam 46; 2 Sam 6): A Form-Critical and Traditio-Historical Study* (SBLDS, 16; Missoula, MT: Scholars Press).

Campbell, Anthony F., and Mark A. O'Brien

2000 *Unfolding the Deuteronomistic History: Origins, Upgrades, Present Text* (Minneapolis: Fortress Press).

Carroll, Robert P.

1981 *From Chaos to Covenant* (London: SCM Press).

1986 *Jeremiah: A Commentary* (OTL; London: SCM Press).

1992 'The Myth of the Empty Land', in David Jobling and T. Pippin (eds), *Ideological Criticism of Biblical Texts* (Semeia, 59; Atlanta, GA: Scholars Press): 79–93.

1997 'Madonna of Silences: Clio and the Bible', in Lester L. Grabbe (ed.), *Can a 'History of Israel' Be Written?* (JSOTSup, 245; ESHM, 1; Sheffield: Sheffield Academic Press): 84–103.

Caton, Steven C.

1990 'Anthropological Theories of Tribe and State Formation in the Middle East: Ideology and the Semiotics of Power', in Philip S. Khoury and Joseph Kostiner (eds), *Tribes and State Formation in the Middle East* (Berkeley: University of California Press): 74–108.

Chaney, Marvin L.

1983 'Ancient Palestinian Peasant Movements and the Formation of Premonarchic Israel', in David Noel Freedman and D. F. Graf (eds), *Palestine in Transition: The Emergence of Ancient Israel* (SWBA, 2; Sheffield: Sheffield Academic Press): 39–90.

Chatty, Dawn

1980 'The Pastoral Family and the Truck', in Philip Carl Salzman (ed.), *When Nomads Settle: Processes of Sedentarization as Adaptation and Response* (New York: Praeger): 80–94.

Childs, Brevard S.

1967 *Isaiah and the Assyrian Crisis* (SBT, second series, 3; London: SCM Press).

Claburn, W. E.

1973 'The Fiscal Basis of Josiah's Reforms', *JBL* 92: 11–22.

Clark, W. Malcolm

1977 'The Patriarchal Traditions: The Biblical Traditions', in John H. Hayes and J. Maxwell Miller (eds), *Israelite and Judaean History* (OTL; Philadelphia: Westminster Press): 120–48.

Clements, Ronald E.

1974 *''abhrāhām', TDOT* I, 52–8.

Cline, Eric H.

2014 *1177 B.C.: The Year Civilization Collapsed* (Turning Points in Ancient History; Princeton, NJ/Oxford: Princeton University Press).

Cogan, Mordechai [Morton]

1974 *Imperialism and Religion: Assyria, Judah and Israel in the Eighth and Seventh Centuries B.C.E.* (SBLMS, 19; Missoula, MT: Society of Biblical Literature).

1993 'Judah Under Assyrian Hegemony: A Re-examination of Imperialism and Religion', *JBL* 112: 403–14.

2001 'Sennacherib's Siege of Jerusalem', *BAR* 27.1 (Jan./Feb.): 40–5, 69.

Cogan, Mordechai, and Hayim Tadmor

1988 *II Kings: A New Translation with Introduction and Commentary* (AB, 11; Garden City, NY: Doubleday).

Cohen, Rudolf

1981 'Excavations at Kadesh-barnea 1976–1978', *BA* 44: 93–107.

1997 'Qadesh-barnea', in Eric M. Meyers (ed.), *The Oxford Encyclopedia of Archaeology in the Near East* (Oxford: Oxford University Press), IV, 365–7.

Cohen, Rudolph, and Yigal Yisrael

1995 'The Iron Age Fortresses at 'En Ḥaṣeva', *BA* 58: 223–35.

Coldstream, Nicolas

2003 'Some Aegean Reactions to the Chronological Debate in the Southern Levant', *TA* 30: 247–58.

Cook, Edward M.

2005 'The Forgery Indictments and *BAR*: Learning from Hindsight', *SBL Forum*. Online: http://www.sbl-site.org/Article.aspx?ArticleId=371: 1–4.

Coote, Robert, and Keith W. Whitelam

1987 *The Emergence of Early Israel in Historical Perspective* (SWBA, 5; Sheffield: Sheffield Academic Press).

Craig Jr, Kenneth M.

2003 'Judges in Recent Research', *CBR* 1.2: 159–85.

Crenshaw, James L.
1985 'Education in Ancient Israel', *JBL* 104: 601–15.
1998 *Education in Ancient Israel: Across the Deadening Silence* (Anchor Bible Reference Library; New York: Doubleday).
Cross Jr, Frank M.
1969 'Judean Stamps', *EI* 9: 20–7.
1973 *Canaanite Myth and Hebrew Epic* (Cambridge, MA: Harvard University Press).
Cross Jr, Frank M., and David Noel Freedman
1955 'The Song of Miriam', *JNES* 14: 237–50.
Cryer, Frederick H.
1994 'On the Recently-Discovered "House of David" Inscription', *SJOT* 8: 3–19.
1995a 'A "Betdawd" Miscellany: Dwd, Dwd' or Dwdh?', *SJOT* 9: 52–8.
1995b 'King Hadad', *SJOT* 9: 223–35.
Dagan, Yehuda
2004 'Results of the Survey: Settlement Patterns in the Lachish Regions', in David Ussishkin (ed.), *The Renewed Archaeological Excavations at Lachish (1973–1994)* (vols 1–5; Tel Aviv University Ronia and Marco Nadler Institute of Archaeology, Monograph Series, 22; Tel Aviv: Emery and Claire Yass Publications in Archaeology): 2672–90.
2009 'Khirbet Qeiyafa in the Judean Shephelah: Some Considerations', *TA* 36: 68–81.
Dalley, Stephanie
1990 'Yahweh in Hamath in the 8th Century BC: Cuneiform Material and Historical Deductions', *VT* 40: 21–32.
Davies, Graham I.
1990 'The Wilderness Itineraries and Recent Archaeological Research', in J. A. Emerton (ed.), *Studies in the Pentateuch* (VTSup, 41; Leiden: Brill): 161–75.
1991 *Ancient Hebrew Inscriptions: Corpus and Concordance* (Cambridge: Cambridge University Press).
2004 'Was There an Exodus?', in John Day (ed.), *In Search of Pre-exilic Israel: Proceedings of the Oxford Old Testament Seminar* (JSOTSup, 406; Old Testament Studies; London/New York: T&T Clark International): 23–40.
Davies, Philip R.
1992 *In Search of 'Ancient Israel'* (JSOTSup, 148; Sheffield: Sheffield Academic Press).
1995 'Method and Madness: Some Remarks on Doing History with the Bible', *JBL* 114: 699–705.
2005 'Josiah and the Law Book', in Lester L. Grabbe (ed.), *Good Kings and Bad Kings: The Kingdom of Judah in the Seventh Century BCE* (JSOTSup, 393; ESHM, 5: London/New York: T&T Clark International): 65–77.
Davis, Brent, Aren M. Maeir, and Louise A. Hitchcock
2015 'Disentangling Entangled Objects: Iron Age Inscriptions from Philistia as a Reflection of Cultural Processes', *IEJ* 65: 140–66.

Day, John

1985 *God's Conflict with the Dragon and the Sea* (Cambridge: Cambridge University Press).

1989 *Molech: A God of Human Sacrifice in the Old Testament* (University of Cambridge Oriental Publications, 41; Cambridge: Cambridge University Press).

1992 'The Problem of "So, King of Egypt" in 2 Kings XVII 4', *VT* 42: 289–301.

2000 *Yahweh and the Gods and Goddesses of Canaan* (JSOTSup, 265; Sheffield: Sheffield Academic Press).

Dearman, J. Andrew

1992 'Settlement Patterns and the Beginning of the Iron Age in Moab', in Piotr Bienkowski (ed.), *Early Edom and Moab: The Beginning of the Iron Age in Southern Jordan* (Sheffield Archaeological Monographs, 7; Sheffield: J. R. Collis Publications): 65–75.

Dearman, J. Andrew, and J. Maxwell Miller

1983 'The Melqart Stele and the Ben Hadads of Damascus: Two Studies', *PEQ* 115: 95–101.

Demsky, Aaron

1973 'Geba, Gibeah, and Gibeon – An Historico-Geographic Riddle', *BASOR* 212: 26–31.

Dessel, J. P.

1997 'Ramat Raḥel', *OEANE* IV, 402–4.

Deutsch, Robert, and Michael Heltzer

1994 *Forty New Ancient West Semitic Inscriptions* (Tel Aviv and Jaffa: Archaeological Center Publications).

Dever, William G.

1970 'Iron Age Epigraphic Material from the Area of Khirbet el-Kôm', *HUCA* 40–41: 139–205.

1977 'The Patriarchal Traditions: Palestine in the Second Millennium BCE: The Archaeological Picture', in John H. Hayes and J. Maxwell Miller (eds), *Israelite and Judaean History* (OTL; Philadelphia: Westminster Press): 70–120.

1981 'The Impact of the "New Archaeology" on Syro-Palestinian Archaeology', *BASOR* 242: 15–29.

1982 'Monumental Architecture in Ancient Israel in the Period of the United Monarchy', in T. Ishida (ed.), *Studies in the Period of David and Solomon and Other Essays* (Winona Lake, IN: Eisenbrauns): 269–306.

1984 'Asherah, Consort of Yahweh? New Evidence from Kuntillet 'Ajrûd', *BASOR* 255: 21–37.

1985 'Syro-Palestinian and Biblical Archaeology', in Douglas A. Knight and Gene M. Tucker (eds), *The Hebrew Bible and Its Modern Interpreters* (SBLBMI, 1; Atlanta, GA: Scholars Press): 31–74.

1987 'The Middle Bronze Age – The Zenith of the Urban Canaanite Era', *BA* 50: 148–77.

1990 '"Hyksos", Egyptian Destructions, and the End of the Palestinian Middle Bronze Age', *Levant* 22: 75–81.

1992a 'How to Tell a Canaanite from an Israelite', in Hershel Shanks (ed.), *The Rise of Ancient Israel: Symposium at the Smithsonian Institution, October 26, 1991* (Smithsonian Resident Associate Program; Washington, DC: Biblical Archaeology Society): 27–60 (plus reply to responses, pp. 79–85).

1992b 'Israel, History of (Archaeology and the Israelite "Conquest")', *ABD* III, 545–58.

1993 'Cultural Continuity, Ethnicity in the Archaeological Record and the Question of Israelite Origins', in Shmuel Ahituv and B. A. Levine (eds), *Avraham Malamat Volume* (*EI*, 24; Jerusalem: Israel Exploration Society): 22*–33*.

1995a Review of A. Ben-Tor, *The Archaeology of Ancient Israel*, *JBL* 114: 122.

1995b 'Ceramics, Ethnicity, and the Question of Israel's Origins', *BA* 58: 200–213.

1996 'Revisionist Israel Revisited: A Rejoinder to Niels Peter Lemche', *CRBS* 4: 35–50.

1997a 'Is There Any Archaeological Evidence for the Exodus?', in Ernest S. Frerichs and Leonard H. Lesko (eds), *Exodus: The Egyptian Evidence* (Winona Lake, IN: Eisenbrauns): 67–86.

1997b 'Archaeology, Urbanism, and the Rise of the Israelite State', in Walter E. Aufrecht, Neil A. Mirau and Steven W. Gauley (eds), *Urbanism in Antiquity, from Mesopotamia to Crete* (JSOTSup, 244; Sheffield: Sheffield Academic Press): 172–93.

1998a 'Israelite Origins and the "Nomadic Ideal": Can Archaeology Separate Fact from Fiction?', in Seymour Gitin, Amihai Mazar and Ephraim Stern (eds), *Mediterranean Peoples in Transition: Thirteenth to Early Tenth Centuries BCE, in Honor of Professor Trude Dothan* (Jerusalem: Israel Exploration Society): 220–37.

1998b 'Social Structure in Palestine in the Iron II Period on the Eve of Destruction', in Thomas E. Levy (ed.), *The Archaeology of Society in the Holy Land* (New Approaches in Anthropological Archaeology; London: Leicester University Press, 2nd edn): 416–31.

2001 *What Did the Biblical Writers Know and When Did They Know It? What Archaeology Can Tell Us about the Reality of Ancient Israel* (Grand Rapids, MI: Eerdmans).

2003a *Who Were the Early Israelites and Where Did They Come From?* (Grand Rapids, MI: Eerdmans).

2003b 'Syro-Palestinian and Biblical Archaeology: Into the Next Millennium', in William G. Dever and Gitin Seymour (eds), *Symbiosis, Symbolism, and the Power of the Past: Canaan, Ancient Israel, and their Neighbors from the Late Bronze Age through Roman Palaestina: Proceedings of the Centennial Symposium W. F. Albright Institute of Archaeological Research and the American Schools of Oriental Research Jerusalem, May 29–31, 2000* (Winona Lake, IN: Eisenbrauns): 513–27.

2003c 'Visiting the Real Gezer: A Reply to Israel Finkelstein', *TA* 30: 259–82.

2005 *Did God Have a Wife? Archaeology and Folk Religion in Ancient Israel* (Grand Rapids, MI: Eerdmans).

2009 'Merenptah's "Israel", the Bible's, and Ours', in J. David Schloen (ed.), *Exploring the* Longue Durée: *Essays in Honor of Lawrence E. Stager* (Winona Lake, IN: Eisenbrauns): 89–96.

2014 *Excavations at the Early Bronze IV Sites of Jebel Qa'aqir and Be'er Resisim* (Studies in the Archaeology and History of the Levant, 6; Winona Lake, IN: Eisenbrauns).

2015 'The Exodus and the Bible: What Was Known; What Was Remembered; What Was Forgotten?', in Thomas E. Levy, Thomas Schneider, and William H. C. Propp (eds), *Israel's Exodus in Transdisciplinary Perspective: Text, Archaeology, Culture, and Geoscience* (Quantitative Methods in the Humanities and Social Sciences; Cham, Switzerland: Springer): 399–408.

Dever, William G., and Seymour Gitin (eds)

2003 *Symbiosis, Symbolism, and the Power of the Past: Canaan, Ancient Israel, and their Neighbors from the Late Bronze Age through Roman Palaestina: Proceedings of the Centennial Symposium W. F. Albright Institute of Archaeological Research and the American Schools of Oriental Research Jerusalem, May 29–31, 2000* (Winona Lake, IN: Eisenbrauns).

Dever, William, Niels Peter Lemche, P. Kyle McCarter Jr, and Thomas Thompson

1997 'Face to Face: Biblical Minimalists Meet their Challengers', *BAR* 23.4 (July/August): 26–42, 66.

Diebner, B.-J.

1995 'Wann sang Deborah ihr Lied? Überlegungen zu zwei der ältesten Texte des TNK (Ri 4 und 5)', *ACEBT* 14: 106–30.

Dietrich, Manfried, Oswald Loretz, and Joaquín Sanmartín (eds)

2013 *Die keilalphabetischen Texte aus Ugarit, Ras Ibn Hani und anderen Orten/The Cuneiform Alphabetic Texts from Ugarit, Ras Ibn Hani and Other Places (KTU: Second, Enlarged Edition)* (AOAT, 360/1; Münster: Ugarit-Verlag).

Dietrich, Walter

2007 *The Early Monarchy in Israel: The Tenth Century B.C.E.* (Society of Biblical Literature Biblical Encyclopedia, 3; trans. Joachim Vette; Atlanta, GA: Society of Biblical Literature); revised and expanded from *Die frühe Königszeit in Israel: 10. Jahrhundert v. Chr.* (Biblische Enzyklopädie, 3; Stuttgart: Kohlhammer, 1997).

2011 *1 Samuel: Teilband 1: 1 Sam 1–12* (BKAT, 8/1; Neukirchen-Vluyn: Neukirchener Theologie, 2011).

2012 'David and the Philistines: Literature and History', in Gershon Galil, Ayelet Gilboa, Aren M. Maeir, and Dan'el Kahn (eds), *The Ancient Near East in the 12th–10th Centuries BCE: Culture and History: Proceedings of the International Conference Held at the University of Haifa, 2–5 May, 2010* (AOAT, 392; Münster: Ugarit-Verlag): 79–98.

Dietrich, Walter, and Martin A. Klopfenstein (eds)

1994 *Ein Gott allein? JHWH-Verehrung und biblischer Monotheismus im Kontext der israelitischen und altorientalischen Religionsgeschichte* (OBO, 139; Freiburg [Schweiz]: Universitätsverlag; Göttingen: Vandenhoeck & Ruprecht).

Dijkstra, Meindert

2011 'Origins of Israel between History and Ideology', in Bob Becking and Lester L. Grabbe (eds), *Between Evidence and Ideology: Essays on the History of Ancient Israel read at the Joint Meeting of the Society for Old Testament Study and the Oud Testamentisch Werkgezelschap Lincoln, July 2009* (OTS, 59; Leiden: Brill): 41–82.

2017 'Canaan in the Transition from the Late Bronze to the Early Iron Age from an Egyptian Perspective', in Lester L. Grabbe (ed.), *The Land of Canaan in the Late Bronze Age* (LHBOTS, 636; ESHM, 10; London/New York: Bloomsbury T&T Clark).

Dijkstra, Meindert, and Karel J. H. Vriezen

2015 'Swords or Ploughshares? The Transition from the Late Bronze to the Early Iron Age in Northern Jordan', in Marjo C. A. Korpel and Lester L. Grabbe (eds), *Open-Mindedness in the Bible and Beyond: A Volume of Studies in Honour of Bob Becking* (LHBOTS, 616; London: Bloomsbury T&T Clark): 69–95.

Dion, Paul E.

1988 'Sennacherib's Expedition to Palestine', *Bulletin of the Canadian Society of Biblical Literature* 48: 3–25.

1995 'Syro-Palestinian Resistance to Shalmaneser III in the Light of New Documents', *ZAW* 107: 482–9.

1997 *Les Araméens à l'âge du fer: histoire politique et structures sociales* (Etudes bibliques, nouvelle série, 34; Paris: Librairie Lecoffre, Gabalda).

Donner, Herbert

1969 'Adoption oder Legitimation? Erwägungen zur Adoption im Alten Testament auf dem Hintergrund der altorientalischen Rechte', *Oriens Antiquus* 8: 87–119.

1984 *Teil 1: Von den Anfängen bis zur Staatenbildungszeit* (Grundrisse zum Alten Testament; ATD Ergänzungsreihe, 4/1; Göttingen: Vandenhoeck & Ruprecht).

1986 *Teil 2: Von der Königszeit bis zu Alexander dem Großen, mit einem Ausblick auf die Geschichte des Judentums bis Bar Kochba;* (Grundrisse zum Alten Testament; ATD Ergänzungsreihe, 4/2; Göttingen: Vandenhoeck & Ruprecht).

Dothan, Trude, and David Ben-Shlomo

2013 'Mycenaean IIIC:1 Pottery in Philistia: Four Decades of Research', in Ann E. Killebrew and Gunnar Lehmann (eds), *The Philistines and Other 'Sea Peoples' in Text and Archaeology* (SBLABS, 15; Atlanta, GA: Society of Biblical Literature), 29–35.

Dothan, Trude, and Alexander Zukerman

2004 'A Preliminary Study of the Mycenaean IIIC:1 Pottery Assemblages from Tel Miqne-Ekron and Ashdod', *BASOR* 333: 1–54.

Draper, Jonathan A. (ed.)

2004 *Orality, Literacy, and Colonialism in Antiquity* (SemeiaSt, 47; Atlanta, GA: Society of Biblical Literature).

Drews, Robert

1993 *The End of the Bronze Age: Changes in Warfare and the Catastrophe ca. 1200 B.C.* (Princeton, NJ: Princeton University Press).

1998 'Canaanites and Philistines', *JSOT* 81: 39–61.

Dubovský, P., Dominik Markl, and J.-P. Sonnet (eds)

2016 *The Fall of Jerusalem and the Rise of the Torah: Conference Held at the Pontifical Biblical Insititute, Rome, 27–28 March 2015, Co-Sponsored by Georgetown University, Washington, DC* (FAT, 107; Tübingen: Mohr Siebeck).

Earle, Timothy (ed.)

1991 *Chiefdoms: Power, Economy, and Ideology* (School of American Research Advanced Seminar Series; Cambridge: Cambridge University Press).

Edelman, Diana

1986 'Saul's Battle Against Amaleq (1 Sam. 15)', *JSOT* 35: 71–84.

1991 *King Saul in the Historiography of Judah* (JSOTSup, 121; Sheffield: Sheffield Academic Press).

1996a 'Saul ben Kish in History and Tradition', in Volkmar Fritz and Philip R. Davies (eds), *The Origins of the Ancient Israelite States* (JSOTSup, 228; Sheffield: Sheffield Academic Press): 142–59.

1996b 'Ethnicity and Early Israel', in Mark G. Brett (ed.), *Ethnicity and the Bible* (BIS 19; Leiden: Brill): 42–7.

1997 'Foreword', in Lowell K. Handy (ed.), *The Age of Solomon: Scholarship at the Turn of the Millennium* (SHCANE, 11; Leiden: Brill).

Edelman, Diana V. (ed.)

1995a *You Shall Not Abhor an Edomite for He Is Your Brother: Edom and Seir in History and Tradition* (SBLABS, 3; Atlanta, GA: Scholars Press).

1995b *The Triumph of Elohim: From Yahwisms to Judaisms* (CBET, 13; Kampen: Kok Pharos; Grand Rapids, MI: Eerdmans).

Ehrlich, Carl S.

1996 *The Philistines in Transition: A History from ca. 1000–730 B.C.E.* (SHCANE, 10; Leiden: Brill).

Eichler, B. L.

1977 'Another Look at the Nuzi Sistership Contracts', in Maria de Jong Ellis (ed.), *Essays on the Ancient Near East in Memory of Jacob Joel Finkelstein* (Memoirs of the Connecticut Academy of Arts and Sciences, 19; Hamden, CT: Archon Books): 45–59.

Eissfeldt, Otto

1965 *Palestine in the Time of the New Kingdom: The Exodus and Wanderings.* Fascicle for *CAH* II.

Elat, Moshe

1975a 'The Campaigns of Shalmaneser III against Aram and Israel', *IEJ* 25: 25–35.

1975b 'The Political Status of the Kingdom of Judah within the Assyrian Empire in the 7th Century B.C.E.', in Yohanan Aharoni (ed.), *Investigations at Lachish: The Sanctuary and the Residency (Lachish V)* (Tel Aviv University, Publications of the Institute of Archaeology, 4; Tel Aviv: Gateway Publishers): 61–70.

Eliyahu-Behar, Adi, Naama Yahalom-Mack, Sana Shilstein, Alexander Zukerman, Cynthia Shafer-Elliott, Aren M. Maeir, Elisabetta Boaretto, Israel Finkelstein, and Steve Weiner

2012 'Iron and Bronze Production in Iron Age IIA Philistia: New Evidence from Tell es-Safi/Gath, Israel', *Journal of Archaeological Science* 39: 255–67.

Engel, Helmut

1979 'Die Siegesstele des Merneptah: Kritischer Überblick über die verschiedenen Versuche historischer Auswertung des Schlussabschnitts', *Biblica* 60: 373–99.

Eph'al, Israel, and Joseph Naveh

1989 'Hazael's Booty Inscription', *IEJ* 39: 192–200.

1998 'Remarks on the Recently Published Moussaieff Ostraca', *IEJ* 48: 269–73.

Evans, Richard J.

1997 *In Defence of History* (London: Granta Books).

Fantalkin, Alexander

2001 'Meẓad Ḥashavyahu: Its Material Culture and Historical Background', *TA* 28: 1–165.

Fantalkin, Alexander, and Israel Finkelstein

2006 'The Sheshonq I Campaign and the 8th-Century BCE Earthquake – More on the Archaeology and History of the South in the Iron I–IIA', *TA* 33: 18–42.

Faust, Avraham

2002 'Accessibility, Defence and Town Planning in Iron Age Israel', *TA* 29: 297–317.

2006 *Israel's Ethnogenesis: Settlement, Interaction, Expansion and Resistance* (Approaches to Anthropological Archaeology; London: Equinox).

Faust, Avraham, and Shlomo Bunimovitz

2003 'The Four Room House: Embodying Iron Age Israelite Society', *NEA* 66: 22–61.

Feinman, Gary M., and Joyce Marcus (eds)

1998 *Archaic States* (School of American Research Advanced Seminar Series; Santa Fe, NM: School of American Research Press).

Finkelstein, Israel

1981 'The Date of Gezer's Outer Wall', *TA* 8: 136–45.

1988 *The Archaeology of the Israelite Settlement* (Jerusalem: Israel Exploration Society).

1988–89 'The Land of Ephraim Survey 1980–1987: Preliminary Report', *TA* 15–16: 117–83.

1992a 'Edom in the Iron I', *Levant* 24: 159–66.

1992b 'Stratigraphy, Pottery and Parallels: A Reply to Bienkowsky', *Levant* 24: 171–2.

1993 'The Sociopolitical Organization of the Central Hill Country in the Second Millennium B.C.E.', in Avraham Biran and Joseph Aviram (eds), *Biblical Archaeology Today, 1990: Proceedings of the Second International Congress on Biblical Archaeology.* Supplement: *Pre-Congress Symposium: Population, Production and Power, Jerusalem, June 1990* (Jerusalem: Israel Exploration Society): 110–31.

1994a 'The Archaeology of the Days of Manasseh', in Michael D. Coogan, Cheryl J. Exum, and Lawrence E. Stager (eds), *Scripture and Other Artifacts: Essays on the Bible and Archaeology in Honor of Philip J. King* (Louisville, KY: Westminster John Knox): 169–87.

1994b 'Penelope's Shroud Unravelled: Iron II Date of Gezer's Outer Wall Established', *TA* 21: 276–82.

1995a *Living on the Fringe: The Archaeology and History of the Negev, Sinai and Neighbouring Regions in the Bronze and Iron Ages* (Monographs in Mediterranean Archaeology, 6; Sheffield: Sheffield Academic Press).

1995b 'The Date of the Settlement of the Philistines in Canaan', *TA* 22: 213–39.

1996a 'The Archaeology of the United Monarchy: An Alternative View', *Levant* 28: 177–87.

1996b 'The Philistine Countryside', *IEJ* 46: 225–42.

1996c 'The Territorial-Political System of Canaan in the Late Bronze Age', *UF* 28: 1–32.

1997 'Pots and People Revised: Ethnic Boundaries in the Iron Age I', in Neil A. Silberman and David B. Small (eds), *The Archaeology of Israel: Constructing the Past, Interpreting the Present* (JSOTSup, 239; Sheffield: Sheffield Academic Press): 216–37.

1998a 'Bible Archaeology or Archaeology of Palestine in the Iron Age? A Rejoinder', *Levant* 30: 167–74.

1998b 'The Great Transformation: The "Conquest" of the Highlands Frontiers and the Rise of the Territorial States', in Thomas E. Levy (ed.), *The Archaeology of Society in the Holy Land* (New Approaches in Anthropological Archaeology; London: Leicester University Press, 2nd edn): 349–65.

1998c 'The Rise of Early Israel: Archaeology and Long-Term History', in Shmuel Ahituv and Eliezer D. Oren (eds), *The Origin of Early Israel – Current Debate: Biblical, Historical and Archaeological Perspectives* (Beer-Sheva, 12; Beersheba: Ben-Gurion University of the Negev Press): 7–39.

1998d 'Notes on the Stratigraphy and Chronology of Iron Age Taanach', *TA* 25: 208–18.

1998e 'From Sherds to History: Review Article', *IEJ* 48: 120–31.

1999a 'State Formation in Israel and Judah: A Contrast in Context, A Contrast in Trajectory', *NEA* 62: 35–52.

1999b 'Hazor and the North in the Iron Age: A Low Chronology Perspective', *BASOR* 314: 55–70.

2000a 'Omride Architecture', *ZDPV* 116: 114–38.

2000b 'Hazor XII-XI with an Addendum on Ben-Tor's Dating of Hazor X-VII', *TA* 27: 231–47.

2001 'The Rise of Jerusalem and Judah: the Missing Link', *Levant* 33: 105–15.

2002a 'Gezer Revisited and Revised', *TA* 29: 262–96.

2002b 'The Philistines in the Bible: A Late-Monarchic Perspective', *JSOT* 27: 131–67.

2002c 'The Campaign of Shoshenq I to Palestine: A Guide to the 10th Century BCE Polity', *ZDPV* 118: 109–35.

2003a 'City-States to States: Polity Dynamics in the 10th–9th Centuries B.C.E.', in William G. Dever and Seymour Gitin (eds), *Symbiosis, Symbolism, and the Power of the Past: Canaan, Ancient Israel, and their Neighbors from the Late Bronze Age through Roman Palaestina: Proceedings of the Centennial Symposium W. F. Albright Institute of Archaeological Research and the American Schools of Oriental Research Jerusalem, May 29–31, 2000* (Winona Lake, IN: Eisenbrauns): 75–83.

2003b 'The Rise of Jerusalem and Judah: The Missing Link', in Andrew G. Vaughn and Ann E. Killebrew (eds), *Jerusalem in Bible and Archaeology: The First Temple Period* (SBLSymS, 18; Atlanta, GA: Society of Biblical Literature): 81–101.

2005a 'A Low Chronology Update: Archaeology, History and Bible', in Thomas E. Levy and Thomas Higham (eds), *The Bible and Radiocarbon Dating: Archaeology, Text and Science* (London: Equinox): 31–42.

2005b 'High or Low: Megiddo and Reḥov', in Thomas E. Levy and Thomas Higham (eds), *The Bible and Radiocarbon Dating: Archaeology, Text and Science* (London: Equinox): 302–9.

2005c 'Khirbet en-Nahas, Edom and Biblical History', *TA* 32: 119–25.

2011 'Saul, Benjamin and the Emergence of "Biblical Israel": An Alternative View', *ZAW* 123: 348–67.

2012 'Comments on the Date of Late-Monarchic Judahite Seal Impressions', *TA* 39: 75–83.

2013 *The Forgotten Kingdom: The Archaeology and History of Northern Israel* (SBL Ancient Near East Monographs, 5; Atlanta, GA: Society of Biblical Literature).

2015 'The Wilderness Narrative and Itineraries and the Evolution of the Exodus Tradition', in Thomas E. Levy, Thomas Schneider, and William H. C. Propp (eds), *Israel's Exodus in Transdisciplinary Perspective: Text, Archaeology, Culture, and Geoscience* (Quantitative Methods in the Humanities and Social Sciences; Cham, Switzerland: Springer): 39–53.

Finkelstein, Israel, and Alexander Fantalkin

2012 'Khirbet Qeiyafa: An Unsensational Archaeological and Historical Interpretation', *TA* 39: 38–63.

Finkelstein, Israel, Ze'ev Herzog, Lily Singer-Avitz, and David Ussishkin

2007 'Has King David's Palace in Jerusalem Been Found?', *TA* 34: 142–64.

Finkelstein, Israel, and Zvi Lederman (eds)

1997 *Highlands of Many Cultures: The Southern Samaria Survey: The Sites* (2 vols; Institute of Archaeology Monograph Series, 14; Tel Aviv: Tel Aviv University).

Finkelstein, Israel, and Nadav Na'aman

2005 'Shechem of the Amarna period and the Rise of the Northern Kingdom of Israel', *IEJ* 55: 172–93.

Finkelstein, Israel, and Nadav Na'aman (eds)

1994 *From Nomadism to Monarchy: Archaeological and Historical Aspects of Early Israel* (Jerusalem: Israel Exploration Society).

Finkelstein, Israel, and Eli Piasetzky

2003 'Wrong and Right: High and Low – ^{14}C Dates from Tel Reḥov and Iron Age', *TA* 30: 283–95.

Finkelstein, Israel, and Neil Asher Silberman

2001 *The Bible Unearthed: Archaeology's New Vision of Ancient Israel and the Origin of its Sacred Texts* (New York: Free Press).

2006 *David and Solomon: In Search of the Bible's Sacred Kings and the Roots of the Western Tradition* (New York: Free Press).

Finkelstein, Israel, David Ussishkin, and Baruch Halpern (eds)
2000 *Megiddo III: The 1992–1996 Seasons* (2 vols; Tel Aviv University Institute of Archaeology Monograph Series, 18; Tel Aviv: Institute of Archaeology).

Fischer, Peter M.
2014 'The Southern Levant (Transjordan) during the Late Bronze Age', in Margreet L. Steiner and Ann E. Killebrew (eds), *The Oxford Handbook of the Archaeology of the Levant, c. 8000–332 BCE* (Oxford: Oxford University Press): 561–76.

Fohrer, Georg
1968 *Geschichte der israelitischen Religion* (Berlin: de Gruyter); ET: *A History of Israelite Religion* (trans. D. E. Green; Nashville: Abingdon; London: SPCK, 1972).

Fortes, M., and E. Evans-Pritchard
1940 *African Political Systems* (Oxford: Oxford University Press).

Frahm, E.
1997 *Einleitung in die Sanherib-Inschriften* (AfO Beiheft, 26; Horn: F. Berger & Söhne).

Franklin, Norma
2004 'Samaria: From the Bedrock to the Omride Palace', *Levant* 36: 189–202.
2005 'Correlation and Chronology: Samaria and Megiddo Redux', in Thomas E. Levy and Thomas Higham (eds), *The Bible and Radiocarbon Dating: Archaeology, Text and Science* (London: Equinox): 310–22.
2006 'Revealing Stratum V at Megiddo', *BASOR* 342: 95–111.
2008 'Jezreel: Before and after Jezebel', in Lester L. Grabbe (ed.), *Israel in Transition: From Late Bronze II to Iron IIa (c. 1250–850 BCE)*. Vol. I: *The Archaeology* (LHBOTS, 491; ESHM, 7; London/New York: T&T Clark International): 45–53.

Freedman, David Noel
1978 'The Real Story of the Ebla Tablets: Ebla and the Cities of the Plain', *BA* 41.6: 143–64.

Freedman, David Noel, and D. F. Graf (eds)
1983 *Palestine in Transition: The Emergence of Ancient Israel* (SWBA, 2; Sheffield: Sheffield Academic Press).

Frerichs, Ernest S., and Leonard H. Lesko (eds)
1997 *Exodus: The Egyptian Evidence* (Winona Lake, IN: Eisenbrauns).

Frevel, Christian
2016 *Geschichte Israels* (Kohlhammer Studienbücher Theologie; Stuttgart: Kohlhammer).

Frick, Frank S.
1985 *The Formation of the State in Ancient Israel: A Survey of Models and Methods* (SWBA, 4; Sheffield: Almond).

Fried, Lisbeth E.
2002 'The High Places (*BĀMÔT*) and the Reforms of Hezekiah and Josiah: An Archaeological Investigation', *JAOS* 122: 437–65.

Fried, Morton H.
1968 'On the Concepts of "Tribe" and "Tribal Society"', in June Helm (ed.), *Essays on the Problem of Tribe: Proceedings of the 1967 Annual Spring Meeting of the American Ethnological Society* (Seattle and London: University of Washington Press): 3–20.
1975 *The Notion of Tribe* (Menlo Park, CA: Cummings Publishing Company).

Fritz, Volkmar
1980 'Die kulturhistorische Bedeutung der früheisenzeitlichen Siedlung auf der *ḫirbet el-Mšāš* und das Problem der Landnahme', *ZDPV* 96: 121–35.
1981 'The Israelite "Conquest" in the Light of Recent Excavations at Khirbet el-Meshâsh', *BASOR* 214: 61–73 [ET of Volkmar 1980].
1987 'Conquest or Settlement? The Early Iron Age in Palestine', *BA* 50: 84–100.

Fritz, Volkmar, and Philip R. Davies (eds)
1996 *The Origins of the Ancient Israelite States* (JSOTSup, 228; Sheffield: Sheffield Academic Press).

Fritz, Volkmar, and Aharon Kempinski (eds)
1983 *Ergebnisse der Ausgrabungen auf der* Ḫirbet el-Mšāš (Tel Māśoś) *1972–1975: Teil I: Textband; Teil II: Tafelband; Teil III: Pläne* (Abhandlungen des Deutschen Palästinavereins; Wiesbaden: Harrassowitz).

Gal, Zvi
1992 *Lower Galilee during the Iron Age* (trans. M. Reines Josephy; ASOR Dissertation Series, 8; Winona Lake, IN: Eisenbrauns).

Galil, Gershon
2009 'The Hebrew Inscription from Khirbet Qeiyafa/Neṭa'im: Script, Language, Literature and History', *UF* 41: 193–242.

Gallagher, W. R.
1999 *Sennacherib's Campaign to Judah* (SHCANE, 18; Leiden: Brill).

Galling, Kurt
1966 'Goliath und seine Rüstung', in *Volume du Congrès: Genève 1965* (VTSup, 15; Leiden: Brill): 150–69.

Garbini, Giovanni
1986 *Storia e Ideologia nell'Israele Antico* (Rome: Paideia).
1988 *History and Society in Ancient Israel* (London: SCM Press; New York: Crossroad) [ET of Garbini 1986].
2004 *Myth and History in the Bible* (JSOTSup, 362; London/New York: Continuum).

Gardiner, Alan H.
1933 'Tanis and Pi-Ra'messe: A Retraction', *JEA* 19: 122–8.

Garfinkel, Yosef
1988 '2 Chronicles 11:5-10 Fortified Cities List and the *lmlk* Stamps – Reply to Nadav Na'aman', *BASOR* 271: 69–73.
1990 'The *Eliakim Na'ar Yokan* Seal Impressions: Sixty Years of Confusion in Biblical Archaeological Research', *BA* 53: 74–9.
2011 'The Davidic Kingdom in Light of the Finds at Khirbet Qeiyafa', *City of David Studies of Ancient Jerusalem* 6: 14*–35*.

Garfinkel, Yosef, Saar Ganor, and Michael G. Hasel
2012a 'The Iron Age City of Khirbet Qeiyafa after Four Seasons of Excavations', in Gershon Galil, Ayelet Gilboa, Aren M. Maeir, and Dan'el Kahn (eds), *The Ancient Near East in the 12th–10th Centuries BCE: Culture and History* (AOAT, 392; Münster: Ugarit-Verlag): 149–74.
2012b 'Khirbat Qeiyafa 2010–2011', *Hadashot Arkheologiyot* 124 (19/4/2012): 1–12.
Garfinkel, Yosef, Mitka R. Golub, Haggai Misgav, and Saar Ganor
2015 'The ʾIšbaʿal Inscription from Khirbet Qeiyafa', *BASOR* 373: 217–33.
Garfinkel, Yosef, and Hoo-Goo Kang
2011 'The Relative and Absolute Chronology of Khirbet Qeiyafa: Very Late Iron Age I or Very Early Iron Age IIA?', *IEJ* 61: 171–83.
Garfinkel, Yosef, Katharina Streit, Saar Ganor, and Michael G. Hasel
2012 'State Formation in Judah: Biblical Tradition, Modern Historical: Theories, and Radiometric Dates at Khirbet Qeiyafa', *Radiocarbon* 54: 359–69.
Garfinkel, Yosef, Katharina Streit, Saar Ganor, and Paula J. Reimer
2015 'King David's City at Khirbet Qeiyafa: Results of the Second Radiocarbon Dating Project', *Radiocarbon* 57: 881–90.
Geertz, Clifford
1973 *The Interpretation of Cultures* (New York: Basic Books).
Gelb, Ignace J.
1961 'The Early History of the West Semitic Peoples', *JCS* 15: 27–47.
1980 *Computer-Aided Analysis of Amorite* (Assyriological Studies, 21; Chicago: Oriental Institute of the University of Chicago).
Gellner, Ernest
1981 'Cohesion and Identity: The Magreb from Ibn Khaldun to Emile Durkheim', in *Idem, Muslim Society* (Cambridge: Cambridge University Press).
Geraty, Lawrence T., and Øystein Sakala LaBianca (eds)
1987–98 *Hesban* (vols 1–10; Berrien Springs, MI: Andrews University Press).
Geus, C. H. J. de
1976 *The Tribes of Israel: An Investigation into Some of the Presuppositions of Martin Noth's Amphictyony Hypothesis* (Studia Semitica Neerlandica, 18; Assen and Amsterdam: Van Gorcum).
Geva, Hillel
2003 'Western Jerusalem at the End of the First Temple Period in Light of the Excavations in the Jewish Quarter', in Andrew G. Vaughn and Ann E. Killebrew (eds), *Jerusalem in Bible and Archaeology: The First Temple Period* (SBLSymS, 18; Atlanta, GA: Society of Biblical Literature): 183–208.
2014 'Jerusalem's Population in Antiquity: A Minimalist View', *TA* 41: 131–60.
Gibson, John C. L.
1973 *Textbook of Syrian Semitic Inscriptions.* Vol. I: *Hebrew and Moabite Inscriptions* (Oxford: Clarendon, corrected edn).
1975 *Textbook of Syrian Semitic Inscriptions.* Vol. II: *Aramaic Inscriptions, including Inscriptions in the Dialect of Zenjirli* (Oxford: Clarendon).

1978 *Canaanite Myths and Legends* (originally edited by G. R. Driver; Edinburgh: T. & T. Clark, 2nd edn).

1982 *Textbook of Syrian Semitic Inscriptions*. Vol. III: *Phoenician Inscriptions, including the Inscriptions in the Mixed Dialect of Arslan Tash* (Oxford: Clarendon).

Gibson, Shimon

2001 'Agricultural Terraces and Settlement Expansion in the Highlands of Early Iron Age Palestine: Is There Any Correlation between the Two?', in Amihai Mazar (ed.), *Studies in the Archaeology of the Iron Age in Israel and Jordan* (JSOTSup, 331; Sheffield: Sheffield Academic Press): 113–46.

Gilboa, Ayelet

2005 'Sea Peoples and Phoenicians along the Southern Phoenician Coast – A Reconciliation: An Interpretation of Šikila (*SKL*) Material Culture', *BASOR* 337: 47–78.

Gilboa, Ayelet, and Ilan Sharon

2003 'An Archaeological Contribution to the Early Iron Age Chronological Debate: Alternative Chronologies for Phoenicia and their Effects on the Levant, Cyprus, and Greece', *BASOR* 332: 7–80.

Gilboa, Ayelet, Ilan Sharon, and Jeffrey Zorn

2004 'Dor and Iron Age Chronology: Scarabs, Ceramic Sequence and ^{14}C', *TA* 31: 32–59.

Gitin, Seymour, Trude Dothan, and Joseph Naveh

1997 'A Royal Dedicatory Inscription from Ekron', *IEJ* 47: 1–16.

Giveon, Raphael

1971 *Les bédouins Shosou des documents égyptiens* (Documenta et Monumenta, 199; Orientis Antiqui, 22; Leiden: Brill).

Glueck, Nelson

1934–51 *Explorations in Eastern Palestine* (4 vols; Annual of the American Schools of Oriental Research, 14, 15, 18/19, 25/28; New Haven: American Schools of Oriental Research).

1970 *The Other Side of the Jordan* (Cambridge, MA: American Schools of Oriental Research).

Gnuse, Robert Karl

1997 *No Other Gods: Emergent Monotheism in Israel* (JSOTSup, 241; Sheffield: Sheffield Academic Press).

Godelier, Maurice

1986 *The Making of Great Men: Male Domination and Power among the New Guinea Baruya* (trans. Rupert Sawyer; Cambridge Studies in Social Anthropology, 56; Cambridge: Cambridge University Press).

Goedicke, Hans

1968 'The Capture of Joppa', *Chronique d'Egypte* 43: 219–33.

Gogel, Sandra Landis

1998 *A Grammar of Epigraphic Hebrew* (Society of Biblical Literature Resources for Biblical Study, 23; Atlanta, GA: Scholars Press).

Goldberg, Jeremy

1999 'Two Assyrian Campaigns against Hezekiah and Later Eighth Century Biblical Chronology', *Biblica* 80: 360–90.

Goldschmidt, Walter

1980 'Career Reorientation and Institutional Adaptation in the Process of Natural Sedentarization', in Philip Carl Salzman (ed.), *When Nomads Settle: Processes of Sedentarization as Adaptation and Response* (New York: Praeger): 48–61.

Goodfriend, Elaine Adler, and Karel van der Toorn

1992 'Prostitution', *ABD* V, 505–13.

Gordon, Cyrus H.

1958 'Abraham and the Merchants of Ura', *JNES* 17: 28–31.

1963 'Abraham of Ur', in D. W. Thomas and W. D. McHardy (eds), *Hebrew and Semitic Studies* (Oxford: Clarendon Press): 77–84.

Gordon, Daniel

1999 'Capital Punishment for Murderous Theorists?', *History and Theory* 38: 378–88.

Goren, Yuval

2005 'The Jerusalem Syndrome in Biblical Archaeology', *SBL Forum*. Online: http://www.sbl-site.org/Article.aspx? Articleld=374: 1–8.

Goren, Yuval, and Eran Arie

2014 'The Authenticity of the Bullae of Berekhyahu Son of Neriyahu the Scribe', *BASOR* 372: 147–58.

Goren, Yuval, Avner Ayalon, Miryam Bar-Matthews, and Bettina Schilman

2004 'Authenticity Examination of the Jehoash Inscription', *TA* 31: 3–16.

Goren, Yuval, Israel Finkelstein, and Nadav Na'aman

2002 'The Seat of Three Disputed Canaanite Rulers According to Petrographic Investigation of the Amarna Tablets', *TA* 29: 221–37.

Görg, Manfred

2001 'Israel in Hierglyphen', *BN* 46: 7–12; reprinted in Manfred Görg, *Mythos und Mythologie: Studien zur Religionsgeschichte und Theologie* (Ägypten und Altes Testament, 70; Wiesbaden: Harrassowitz, 2010): 251–58.

Gosden, Chris

1999 'The Organization of Society', in Graeme Barker (ed.), *Companion Encyclopedia of Archaeology* (London/New York: Routledge): 470–504.

Gottlieb, Yulia

2010 'The Advent of the Age of Iron in the Land of Israel: A Review and Reassessment', *TA* 37: 89–110.

Gottwald, Norman K.

1979 *The Tribes of Yahweh: A Sociology of the Religion of Liberated Israel, 1250–1050 B.C.E.* (Maryknoll, NY: Orbis; reprinted with new Preface: Biblical Seminar, 66; Sheffield: Sheffield Academic Press, 1999).

1993 'Recent Studies of the Social World of Premonarchic Israel', *CRBS* 1: 163–89.

Grabbe, Lester L.

1987 'Fundamentalism and Scholarship: The Case of Daniel', in B. P. Thompson (ed.), *Scripture: Method and Meaning: Essays Presented to Anthony Tyrrell Hanson for his Seventieth Birthday* (Hull: Hull University Press): 133–52.

1988 'Another Look at the *Gestalt* of "Darius the Mede"', *CBQ* 50: 198–213.

1991 'Reconstructing History from the Book of Ezra', in Philip R. Davies (ed.), *Second Temple Studies: The Persian Period* (JSOTSup, 117; Sheffield: Sheffield: JSOT Press): 98–107.

1993a *Leviticus* (Society for Old Testament Study, Old Testament Guides; Sheffield: Sheffield Academic Press).

1993b 'Comparative Philology and Exodus 15, 8: Did the Egyptians Die in a Storm?', *SJOT* 7: 263–9.

1994a 'What Was Ezra's Mission?', in T. C. Eskenazi and K. H. Richards (eds), *Second Temple Studies: 2. Temple Community in the Persian Period* (JSOTSup, 175; Sheffield: JSOT Press): 286–99.

1994b '"Canaanite": Some Methodological Observations in Relation to Biblical Study', in G. J. Brooke et al. (eds), *Ugarit and the Bible: Proceedings of the International Symposium on Ugarit and the Bible, Manchester, September 1992* (Ugaritisch-Biblische Literatur, 11; Münster: Ugarit-Verlag): 113–22.

1995 *Priests, Prophets, Diviners, Sages: A Socio-historical Study of Religious Specialists in Ancient Israel* (Valley Forge, PA: Trinity Press International).

1997a 'Are Historians of Ancient Palestine Fellow Creatures – Or Different Animals?', in Lester L. Grabbe (ed.), *Can a 'History of Israel' Be Written?* (JSOTSup, 245; ESHM, 1; Sheffield: Sheffield Academic Press): 19–36.

1997b 'The Book of Leviticus', *CRBS* 5: 91–110.

1997c 'The Current State of the Dead Sea Scrolls: Are There More Answers than Questions?', in Stanley E. Porter and Craig A. Evans (eds), *The Scrolls and the Scriptures: Qumran Fifty Years After* (Roehampton Institute London Papers, 3; JSPSup, 26; Sheffield: Sheffield Academic Press): 54–67.

1998a *Ezra and Nehemiah* (Readings; London: Routledge).

1998b '"The Exile" under the Theodolite: Historiography as Triangulation', in Lester L. Grabbe (ed.), *Leading Captivity Captive: 'The Exile' as History and Ideology* (JSOTSup, 278; ESHM, 2; Sheffield: Sheffield Academic Press): 80–100.

2000a *Judaic Religion in the Second Temple Period: Belief and Practice from the Exile to Yavneh* (London/New York: Routledge).

2000b 'Writing Israel's History at the End of the Twentieth Century', in André Lemaire and Magne Saebø (ed.), *Congress Volume: Oslo 1998* (VTSup, 80; Leiden: Brill): 203–18.

2000c *'Adde Praeputium Praeputio Magnus Acervus Erit*: If the Exodus and Conquest Had Really Happened…', in J. Cheryl Exum (ed.), *Virtual History and the Bible* (Biblical Interpretation, 8; Leiden: Brill): 23–32.

2000d 'Hat die Bibel doch recht? A Review of T. L. Thompson's *The Bible in History*', *SJOT* 14: 117–39.

2001a 'Jewish Historiography and Scripture in the Hellenistic Period', in Lester L. Grabbe (ed.), *Did Moses Speak Attic? Jewish Historiography and Scripture in the Hellenistic Period* (JSOTSup, 317; ESHM, 3; Sheffield: Sheffield Academic Press): 129–55.

2001b 'Who Were the First Real Historians? On the Origins of Critical Historiography', in Lester L. Grabbe (ed.), *Did Moses Speak Attic? Jewish Historiography and Scripture in the Hellenistic Period* (JSOTSup, 317; ESHM, 3; Sheffield: Sheffield Academic Press): 156–81.

2001c 'Sup-urbs or Only Hyp-urbs? Prophets and Populations in Ancient Israel and Socio-historical Method', in Lester L. Grabbe and Robert D. Haak (eds), *'Every City Shall Be Forsaken': Urbanism and Prophecy in Ancient Israel and the Near East* (JSOTSup, 330; Sheffield: Sheffield Academic Press, 2001): 93–121.

2002 'The "Comfortable Theory", "Maximal Conservativism", and Neo-fundamentalism Revisited', in Alastair G. Hunter and Philip R. Davies (eds), *Sense and Sensitivity: Essays on Reading the Bible in Memory of Robert Carroll* (JSOTSup, 348; Sheffield: Sheffield Academic Press): 174–93.

2003a 'Ethnic Groups in Jerusalem', in Thomas L. Thompson, with the collaboration of Salma Khadra Jayyusi (eds), *Jerusalem in Ancient History and Tradition* (JSOTSup, 381; Copenhagen International Seminar, 13; London/New York: T&T Clark International): 145–63.

2003b 'Of Mice and Dead Men: Herodotus 2.141 and Sennacherib's Campaign in 701 BCE', in Lester L. Grabbe (ed.), *'Like a Bird in a Cage': The Invasion of Sennacherib in 701 BCE* (JSOTSup, 363; ESHM, 4; Sheffield: Sheffield Academic Press): 119–40.

2003c 'Were the Pre-Maccabean High Priests 'Zadokites'?', in J. Cheryl Exum and H. G. M. Williamson (eds), *Reading from Right to Left: Essays on the Hebrew Bible in Honour of David J. A. Clines* (JSOTSup, 373; Sheffield: Sheffield Academic Press): 205–15.

2004a *A History of the Jews and Judaism in the Second Temple Period 1: Yehud: A History of the Persian Province of Judah* (London/New York: T&T Clark International).

2004b Review of M. Douglas, *Leviticus as Literature*, *Journal of Ritual Studies* 18: 157–61.

2004c Review of Provan, Long, and Longman, *A Biblical History of Israel*, *RBL* 8: 1–4.

2005 'The Kingdom of Judah from Sennacherib's Invasion to the Fall of Jerusalem: If We Had Only the Bible…', in Lester L. Grabbe (ed.), *Good Kings and Bad Kings: The Kingdom of Judah in the Seventh Century BCE* (JSOTSup, 393; ESHM, 5: London/New York: T&T Clark International): 78–122.

2006a '"The Lying Pen of the Scribes"? Jeremiah and History', in Yairah Amit, Ehud Ben Zvi, Israel Finkelstein, and Oded Lipschits (eds), *Essays on Ancient Israel in Its Near Eastern Context: A Tribute to Nadav Na'aman* (Winona Lake, IN: Eisenbrauns): 189–204.

2006b 'Mighty Oaks from (Genetically Manipulated?) Acorns Grow: The Chronicle of the Kings of Judah as a Source of the Deuteronomistic History', in R. Rezetko, T. H. Lim, and W. B. Aucker (eds), *Reflection and Refraction: Studies in Biblical Historiography in Honour of A. Graeme Auld* (VTSup, 113; Leiden: Brill): 154–73.

2006c 'The Law, the Prophets, and the Rest: the State of the Bible in Pre-Maccabean Times', *DSD* 13: 319–38.

2007a *Ancient Israel: What Do We Know and How Do We Know It?* (London/ New York: T&T Clark International).

2007b 'The Kingdom of Israel from Omri to the Fall of Samaria: If We Had Only the Bible…', in Lester L. Grabbe (ed.), *Ahab Agonistes: The Rise and Fall of the Omri Dynasty* (LHBOTS, 421; ESHM, 6; London/New York: T&T Clark International): 54–99.

2010a 'From Merneptah to Shoshenq: If We Had Only the Bible…', in Lester L. Grabbe (ed.), *Israel in Transition: From Late Bronze II to Iron IIA (c. 1250–850 BCE)*. Vol. II: *The Text* (LHBOTS, 521; ESHM, 8; London/ New York: T&T Clark International): 62–129.

2010b '"Many Nations Will Be Joined to Yhwh in That Day": The Question of Yhwh Outside Judah', in Francesca Stavrakopoulou and John Barton (eds), *Religious Diversity in Ancient Israel and Judah* (London/New York: T&T Clark International): 175–87.

2011a 'The Case of the Corrupting Consensus', in Bob Becking and Lester L. Grabbe (eds), *Between Evidence and Ideology: Essays on the History of Ancient Israel read at the Joint Meeting of the Society for Old Testament Study and the Oud Testamentisch Werkgezelschap Lincoln, July 2009* (OTS, 59; Leiden: Brill): 83–92.

2011b 'Review of Provan, Long, Longman, *A Biblical History of Israel'*, in Lester L. Grabbe (ed.), *Enquire of the Former Age: Ancient Historiography and Writing the History of Israel* (LHBOTS, 554; ESHM, 9; London/New York: T&T Clark International): 215–34.

2011c 'Alberto Soggin's *Storia d'Israele*: Exemplifying Twenty Years of Debate and Changing Trends in Thinking', in Lester L. Grabbe (ed.), *Enquire of the Former Age: Ancient Historiography and Writing the History of Israel* (LHBOTS, 554; ESHM, 9; London/New York: T&T Clark International): 253–60.

2013 'Elephantine and the Torah', in Alejandro F. Botta (ed.), *In the Shadow of Bezalel: Aramaic, Biblical, and Ancient Near Eastern Studies in Honor of Bezalel Porten* (CHANE, 60; Leiden/Boston: Brill): 125–35.

2014 'The Exodus and Historicity', in Thomas B. Dozeman, Craig A. Evans, and Joel N. Lohr (eds), *The Book of Exodus: Composition, Reception, and Interpretation* (VTSup, 164; Leiden: Brill): 61–87.

2015 'The Use and Abuse of Herodotus by Biblical Scholars', in Anne Fitzpatrick-McKinley (ed.), *Assessing Biblical and Classical Sources for the Reconstruction of Persian Influence, History and Culture* (Classica et Orientalia, 10; Wiesbaden: Harrassowitz): 49–72.

2016 'The Last Days of Judah and the Roots of the Pentateuch: What Does History Tell Us?', in P. Dubovský, Dominik Markl, and J.-P. Sonnet (eds), *The Fall of Jerusalem and the Rise of the Torah* (FAT, 107; Tübingen: Mohr Siebeck): 19–45.

2017 *1 and 2 Kings: History and Story in Ancient Israel: An Introduction and Study Guide* (T&T Clark Study Guides to the Old Testament; London/ New York: Bloomsbury T&T Clark).

Forthcoming 'Jeroboam I? Jeroboam II? or Jeroboam 0? Jeroboam in History and Tradition', in Oded Lipschits et al. (eds), *Festschrift for Israel Finkelstein* (Winona Lake, IN: Eisenbrauns).

Grabbe, Lester L. (ed.)
1997 *Can a "History of Israel" Be Written?* (JSOTSup, 245; ESHM, 1; Sheffield: Sheffield Academic Press).
1998 *Leading Captivity Captive: 'The Exile' as History and Ideology* (JSOTSup, 278; ESHM, 2; Sheffield: Sheffield Academic Press).
2001 *Did Moses Speak Attic? Jewish Historiography and Scripture in the Hellenistic Period* (JSOTSup, 317; ESHM, 3; Sheffield: Sheffield Academic Press).
2003 *'Like a Bird in a Cage': The Invasion of Sennacherib in 701 BCE* (JSOTSup, 363; ESHM, 4; Sheffield: Sheffield Academic Press).
2005 *Good Kings and Bad Kings: The Kingdom of Judah in the Seventh Century BCE* (JSOTSup, 393; ESHM, 5; London/New York: T&T Clark International).
2007 *Ahab Agonistes: The Rise and Fall of the Omri Dynasty* (LHBOTS, 421; ESHM, 6; London/New York: T&T Clark International).
2008 *Israel in Transition: From Late Bronze II to Iron IIA (c. 1250–850 BCE): The Archaeology* (LHBOTS, 491; ESHM, 7; London/New York: T&T Clark International).
2010 *Israel in Transition: From Late Bronze II to Iron IIA (c. 1250–850 BCE): The Texts* (LHBOTS, 521; ESHM, 8; London/New York: T&T Clark International).
2011 *Enquire of the Former Age: Ancient Historiography and Writing the History of Israel* (LHBOTS, 554; ESHM, 9; London/New York: T&T Clark International).
2017 *The Land of Canaan in the Late Bronze Age* (LHBOTS, 636; ESHM, 10; London/New York: Bloomsbury T&T Clark).
Forthcoming *Not Even God Can Alter the Past: Reflections on 16 Years of the European Seminar in Historical Methodology* (LHBOTS; ESHM, 11; London/New York: Bloomsbury T&T Clark).

Grayson, A. K.
1975 *Assyrian and Babylonian Chronicles* (Texts from Cuneiform Sources, 5; Locust Valley, NY: J. J. Augustin).
1991a 'Chapter 23. Assyria: Sennacherib and Esarhaddon (704–669 B.C.)', *CAH* III/2: 103–41.
1991b 'Chapter 24. Assyria 668–635 B.C.: The Reign of Ashurbanipal', *CAH* III/2: 142–61.
1996 *Assyrian Rulers of the Early First Millennium BC II (858–745 BC)* (RIMA, 3; Toronto: University of Toronto Press).

Grayson, A. Kirk, and Jamie Novotny
2012 *The Royal Inscriptions of Sennacherib, King of Assyria (704–681 BC), Part 1* (The Royal Inscriptions of the Neo-Assyrian Period, 3/1; Winona Lake, IN: Eisenbrauns).
2014 *The Royal Inscriptions of Sennacherib, King of Assyria (704–681 BC), Part 2* (The Royal Inscriptions of the Neo-Assyrian Period, 3/2; Winona Lake, IN: Eisenbrauns).

Greenberg, Moshe
1955 *The ḫab/piru* (American Oriental Series, 39; New Haven, CT: American Oriental Society).

Greenberg, Raphael
1993 'Beit Mirsim, Tell', *NEAEHL* I, 177–80.
Greengus, Samuel
1975 'Sisterhood Adoption at Nuzi and the "Wife-Sister" in Genesis', *HUCA* 46: 5–31.
Greenstein, Edward L.
2012 'Methodological Principles in Determining that the So-Called Jehoash Inscription Is Inauthentic', in Marilyn J. Lundberg, Steven Fine, and Wayne T. Pitard (eds), *Puzzling Out the Past: Studies in Northwest Semitic Languages and Literature in Honor of Bruce Zuckerman* (CHANE, 55; Leiden and Boston: Brill): 83–92.
Griffith, F. L. (ed.)
1909 *Catalogue of the Demotic Papyri in the John Rylands Library* (3 vols; Manchester: Manchester University Press).
Guest, P. Deryn
1998 'Can Judges Survive without Sources? Challenging the Consensus', *JSOT* 78: 43–61.
Gugler, Werner
1996 *Jehu und seine Revolution* (Kampen: Kok Pharos).
Hackett, Jo Ann, Frank Moore Cross, P. Kyle McCarter Jr, Ada Yardeni, André Lemaire, Esther Eshel, and Avi Hurvitz
1997 'Defusing Pseudo-Scholarship: The Siloam Inscription Ain't Hasmonean', *BAR* 23.2 (March/April): 41–50, 68.
Hallo, William W.
1980 'Biblical History in its Near Eastern Setting: The Contextual Approach', in Carl D. Evans, William W. Hallo and John B. White (eds), *Scripture in Context: Essays on the Comparative Method* (Pittsburgh Theological Monograph Series, 34; Pittsburgh, PA: Pickwick Press): 1–26.
2005 'The Kitchen Debate: A Context for the Biblical Account', *BAR* 31.4 (July–Aug.): 50–1.
Hallo, William W. (ed.)
1997 *The Context of Scripture.* Vol. I: *Canonical Compositions from the Biblical World* (Leiden: Brill).
2000 *The Context of Scripture.* Vol. II: *Monumental Inscriptions from the Biblical World* (Leiden: Brill).
2002 *The Context of Scripture.* Vol. III: *Archival Documents from the Biblical World* (Leiden: Brill).
Halpern, Baruch
1988 *The First Historians: The Hebrew Bible and History* (San Francisco: Harper & Row).
1993 'The Exodus and the Israelite Historians', *EI* 24: 89*–96*.
2001 *David's Secret Demons: Messiah, Murderer, Traitor, King* (Grand Rapids, MI: Eerdmans).
Handy, Lowell K.
1994 *Among the Host of Heaven: The Syro-Palestinian Pantheon as Bureaucracy* (Winona Lake, IN: Eisenbrauns).
Handy, Lowell K. (ed.)
1997 *The Age of Solomon: Scholarship at the Turn of the Millennium* (SHCANE, 11; Leiden: Brill).

Haran, Menahem
1967 'The Rise and Decline of the Empire of Jeroboam ben Joash', *VT* 17: 266–97.
1976 'Exodus, The', *IDBSup* 304–10.
1988 'On the Diffusion of Schools and Literacy', in J. A. Emerton (ed.), *Congress Volume: Jerusalem 1986* (VTSup, 40; Leiden: Brill): 81–95.

Hardmeier, Christoph
1989 *Prophetie im Streit vor dem Untergang Judas: Erzählkommunikative Studien zur Entstehungssituation der Jesaja- und Jeremiaerzählungen in II Reg 18–20 und Jer 37–40* (BZAW, 187; Berlin: de Gruyter).
2005 'King Josiah in the Climax of DtrH (2 Kgs 22–23) and the Pre-Dtr Document of a Cult Reform at the Place of Residence (23.4-15*): Criticism of Sources, Reconstruction of Earlier Texts and the History of Theology of 2 Kgs 22–23', in Lester L. Grabbe (ed.), *Good Kings and Bad Kings: The Kingdom of Judah in the Seventh Century BCE* (LHBOTS, 393; ESHM, 5: London/New York: T&T Clark International): 123–63.

Harris, Mark
2015 'The Thera Theroies: Science and the Modern Reception History of the Exodus', in Thomas E. Levy, Thomas Schneider, and William H. C. Propp (eds), *Israel's Exodus in Transdisciplinary Perspective: Text, Archaeology, Culture, and Geoscience* (Quantitative Methods in the Humanities and Social Sciences; Cham, Switzerland: Springer): 91–9.

Harris, William V.
1989 *Ancient Literacy* (Cambridge, MA: Harvard University Press).

Harrison, Timothy P., and Celeste Barlow
2005 'Mesha, the Mishor, and the Chronology of Iron Age Mādāba', in Thomas E. Levy and Thomas Higham (eds), *The Bible and Radiocarbon Dating: Archaeology, Text and Science* (London: Equinox): 179–90.

Hart, Stephen
1992 'Iron Age Settlement in the Land of Edom', in Piotr Bienkowski (ed.), *Early Edom and Moab: The Beginning of the Iron Age in Southern Jordan* (Sheffield Archaeological Monographs, 7; Sheffield: J. R. Collis Publications): 93–8.

Hasel, Michael G.
1998 *Domination and Resistance: Egyptian Military Activity in the Southern Levant, ca. 1300–1185 BC* (PdÄ, 11; Leiden: Brill).
2003 'Merenptah's Inscription and Reliefs and the Origin of Israel', in Beth Alpert Nakhai (ed.), *The Near East in the South west: Essays in Honor of William G. Dever* (AASOR, 58; Boston: American Schools of Oriental Research): 19–44.
2009 'Pa-Canaan in the Egyptian New Kingdom: Canaan or Gaza?', *Journal of Ancient Egyptian Interconnections* 1.1: 8–17.

Hayes, John H., and Jeffrey Kah-Jin Kuan
1991 'The Final Years of Samaria (730–720 BC)', *Biblica* 72: 153–81.

Hayes, John H., and J. Maxwell Miller (eds)
1977 *Israelite and Judaean History* (OTL; Philadelphia: Westminster Press).

Heider, George C.
1985 *The Cult of Molek: A Reassessment* (JSOTSup, 43; Sheffield: JSOT Press).
Heimpel, Wolfgang
2003 *Letters to the King of Mari: A New Translation, with Historical Introduction, Notes, and Commentary* (Mesopotamian Civilizations, 12; Winona Lake, IN: Eisenbrauns).
Helck, Wolfgang
1965 'Tkw und die Rameses-Stadt', *VT* 15: 35–48.
1971 *Die Beziehungen Ägyptens zu Vorderasien im 3. und 2. Jahrtausend v. Chr.* (Ägyptololgische Abhandlungen, 5; Wiesbaden: Harrassowitz, 2nd ed.).
1986 'Wenamun', *LdÄ* VI: 1215–17.
Helck, Wolfgang, Eberhard Otto, and Wolfhart Westendorf (eds)
1975–92 *Lexikon der Ägyptologie* (vols 1–7; Wiesbaden: Harrassowitz).
Helm, June (ed.)
1968 *Essays on the Problem of Tribe: Proceedings of the 1967 Annual Spring Meeting of the American Ethnological Society* (Seattle and London: University of Washington Press).
Hendel, Ronald S.
1996 'The Date of the Siloam Inscription: A Rejoinder to Rogerson and Davies', *BA* 59: 233–47.
2015 'The Exodus as Cultural Memory: Egyptian Bondage and the Song of the Sea', in Thomas E. Levy, Thomas Schneider, and William H. C. Propp (eds), *Israel's Exodus in Transdisciplinary Perspective: Text, Archaeology, Culture, and Geoscience* (Quantitative Methods in the Humanities and Social Sciences; Cham, Switzerland: Springer): 65–77.
Herr, Larry G.
1985 'The Servant of Baalis', *BA* 48: 169–72.
1997 'Emerging Nations: The Iron Age II Period', *BA* 60: 114–83.
2001 'The History of the Collared Pithos at Tell el-'Umeiri, Jordan', in Samuel R. Wolff (ed.), *Studies in the Archaeology of Israel and Neighboring Lands in Memory of Douglas L. Esse* (The Oriental Institute of the University of Chicago Studies in Ancient Oriental Civilization, 59; ASOR Books, 5; Chicago: Oriental Institute): 237–50.
Herr, L.G., and M. Najjar
2001 'The Iron Age', in B. MacDonald, R. Adams and P. Bienkowski (eds), *The Archaeology of Jordan* (Sheffield: Sheffield Academic Press): 323–45.
Herr, Larry G. et al. (eds)
1989–2002 *Madaba Plains Project* (vols 1–5; Berrien Springs, MI: Andrews University Press).
Herrmann, Siegfried
1975 *A History of Israel in Old Testament Times* (London: SCM; Philadelphia: Fortress Press).
Herzog, Ze'ev
1994 'The Beer-Sheba Valley: From Nomadism to Monarchy', in Israel Finkelstein and Nadav Na'aman (eds), *From Nomadism to Monarchy: Archaeological and Historical Aspects of Early Israel* (Jerusalem: Israel Exploration Society): 122–49.

1997 'Beersheba', *OEANE* I, 287–91.

2001 'The Date of the Temple of Arad: Reassessment of the Stratigraphy and the Implications for the History of Religion in Judah', in Amihai Mazar (ed.), *Studies in the Archaeology of the Iron Age in Israel and Jordan* (JSOTSup, 331; Sheffield: Sheffield Academic Press): 156–78.

2002 'The Fortress Mound at Tel Arad: An Interim Report', *TA* 29: 3–109.

2010 'Perspectives on Southern Israel's Cult Centralization: Arad and Beersheba', in R. G. Kratz and H. Spieckermann (eds), *One God, One Cult, One Nation: Archaeological and Biblical Perspectives* (BZAW 405; Berlin and New York: de Gruyter): 169–99.

Herzog, Ze'ev (ed.)

1984 *Beer-Sheba II: The Early Iron Age Settlements* (Publications of the Institute of Archaeology, 7; Tel Aviv: Tel Aviv University Institute of Archaeology).

Herzog, Ze'ev, and Lily Singer-Avitz

2004 'Redefining the Centre: The Emergence of State in Judah', *TA* 31: 209–44.

Hess, Richard S.

1998 'Occurrences of "Canaan" in Late Bronze Age Archives of the West Semitic World', in Shlomo Izre'el, Ithamar Singer and Ran Zadok (eds), *Past Links: Studies in the Languages and Cultures of the Ancient Near East* (= *IOS*, 18; Winona Lake, IN: Eisenbrauns): 365–72.

Hesse, Brian, and Paul Wapnish

1997 'Can Pig Remains Be Used for Ethnic Diagnosis in the Ancient Near East?', in Neil A. Silberman and David B. Small (eds), *The Archaeology of Israel: Constructing the Past, Interpreting the Present* (JSOTSup, 239; Sheffield: Sheffield Academic Press): 238–70.

Hezser, Catherine

2001 *Jewish Literacy in Roman Palestine* (TSAJ, 81; Tübingen: Mohr Siebeck).

Higginbotham, Carolyn R.

2000 *Egyptianization and Elite Emulation in Ramesside Palestine: Governance and Accommodation on the Imperial Periphery* (CHANE, 2; Leiden: Brill).

Higham, Thomas, Johannes van der Plicht, Christopher Bronk Ramsey, Hendrik J. Bruins, Mark A. Robinson, and Thomas E. Levy

2005 'Radiocarbon Dating of the Khirbat en-Nahas Site (Jordan) and Bayesian Modeling of the Results', in Thomas E. Levy and Thomas Higham (eds), *The Bible and Radiocarbon Dating: Archaeology, Text and Science* (London: Equinox): 164–78.

Hitchcock, Louise A., and Aren M. Maeir

2013 'Beyond Creolization and Hybridity: Entangled and Transcultural Identities in Philistia', *Archaeological Review from Cambridge* 28: 43–65.

Hjelm, Ingrid, and Thomas L. Thompson

2002 'The Victory Song of Merneptah, Israel and the People of Palestine', *JSOT* 27: 3–18.

Hobbs, T. R.

1994 'The "Fortresses of Rehoboam" Another Look', in Lewis M. Hopfe (ed.), *Uncovering Ancient Stones: Essays in Memory of H. Neil Richardson* (Winona Lake, IN: Eisenbrauns): 41–64.

Hoch, James E.
1994 *Semitic Words in Egyptian Texts of the New Kingdom and Third Intermediate Period* (Princeton, NJ: Princeton University Press).
Hodder, Ian, Michael Shanks, Alexandra Alexandri, Victor Buchli, John Carman, Jonathan Last, and Gavin Lucas (eds)
1995 *Interpreting Archaeology: Finding Meaning in the Past* (London/New York: Routledge).
Hoffmeier, James K.
1990 'Some Thoughts on William G. Dever's "'Hyksos', Egyptian Destructions, and the End of the Palestinian Middle Bronze Age"', *Levant* 22: 83–9.
1991 'James Weinstein's "Egypt and the Middle Bronze IIC/Late Bronze IA Transition": A Rejoinder', *Levant* 23: 117–24.
1997 *Israel in Egypt: The Evidence for the Authenticity of the Exodus Tradition* (Oxford: Oxford University Press).
2005 *Ancient Israel in Sinai: The Evidence for the Authenticity of the Wilderness Tradition* (Oxford: Oxford University Press).
2007 'What Is the Biblical Date for the Exodus? A Response to Bryant Wood', *JETS* 50: 225–47.
Holladay Jr, John S.
2001 'Pithom', in Donald B. Redford (ed.), *Oxford Encyclopedia of Ancient Egypt* (Oxford: Oxford University Press): 50–3.
Hort, Greta
1957 'The Plagues of Egypt', *ZAW* 69: 84–103; 70: 48–59.
Huffmon, Herbert B.
1965 *Amorite Personal Names in the Mari Texts: A Structural and Lexical Study* (Baltimore: The Johns Hopkins University Press).
Hutchinson, John, and Anthony D. Smith (eds)
1996 *Ethnicity* (Oxford Readers; Oxford: Oxford University Press).
Iggers, Georg G.
1997 *Historiography in the Twentieth Century: From Scientific Objectivity to the Postmodern Challenge* (Hanover, NH: University Press of New England).
Ilan, David
1998 'The Dawn of Internationalism – The Middle Bronze Age', in Thomas E. Levy (ed.), *The Archaeology of Society in the Holy Land* (New Approaches in Anthropological Archaeology; London: Leicester University Press, 2nd edn): 297–319.
Irons, William, and Neville Dyson-Hudson (eds)
1972 *Perspectives on Nomadism* (International Studies in Sociology and Social Anthropology, 13; Leiden: Brill).
Irvine, Stuart A.
1990 *Isaiah, Ahaz, and the Syro-Ephraimitic Crisis* (SBLDS, 123; Atlanta, GA: Scholars Press).
Jagersma, H.
1994 *A History of Israel to Bar Kochba: Part I The Old Testament Period. Part II: From Alexander the Great to Bar Kochba* (1982–85; 1-vol. repr. London: SCM Press).

James, T. G. H.
1991 'Chapter 35: Egypt: The Twenty-fifth and Twenty-sixth Dynasties', *CAH* III/2: 677–747.
2002 *Ramesses II* (Vercelli: White Star Publishers).
Jamieson-Drake, David W.
1991 *Scribes and Schools in Monarchic Judah: A Socio-Archeological Approach* (JSOTSup, 109; SWBA, 9; Sheffield: Almond Press).
Jenkins, A. K.
1976 'Hezekiah's Fourteenth Year: A New Interpretation of 2 Kings xviii 13-xix 37', *VT* 26: 284–98.
Jenkins, Keith (ed.)
1997 *The Postmodern History Reader* (London/New York: Routledge).
Joannès, F., and André Lemaire
1999 'Trois tablettes cunéiforme à onomastique ouest-sémitique (collection Sh. Moussaïeff)', *Trans* 17: 17–34.
Joffe, Alexander H.
2002 'The Rise of Secondary States in the Iron Age Levant', *JESHO* 45: 425–67.
Johnson, Allen W., and Timothy Earle
2000 *The Evolution of Human Societies: From Foraging Group to Agrarian State* (Stanford: Stanford University Press, 2nd edn).
Johnson, M. D.
1988 *The Purpose of the Biblical Genealogies* (SNTSMS, 8; Cambridge: Cambridge University Press, 2nd edn).
Jones, Siân
1997 *The Archaeology of Ethnicity: Constructing Identities in the Past and Present* (London/New York: Routledge).
Kallai, Zecharia
1995 'The Twelve-Tribe Systems of Israel', *VT* 47: 53–90.
1999 'A Note on the Twelve-Tribe Systems of Israel', *VT* 49: 125–7.
Kamp, Kathryn A., and Norman Yoffee
1980 'Ethnicity in Ancient Western Asia During the Early Second Millennium B.C.: Archaeological Assessments and Ethnoarchaeological Prospectives', *BASOR* 237: 85–104.
Kaufman, Ivan T.
1992 'Samaria Ostraca', *ABD* V, 921–6.
Keel, Othmar, and Christoph Uehlinger
1998 *Gods, Goddesses, and Images of God in Ancient Israel* (trans. Thomas H. Trapp; Minneapolis: Fortress; Edinburgh: T. & T. Clark); ET of *Göttinnen, Götter und Gottessymbole: Neue Erkenntnisse zur Religionsgeschichte Kanaans und Israels aufgrund bislang unerschlossener ikonographischer Quellen* (Quaestiones Disputatae, 134; Freiburg: Herder, 4th exp. edn).
Kenyon, Kathleen
1942 'The Stratigraphy and Building Phases', in J. W. Crowfoot, Kathleen M. Kenyon and E. L. Sukenik, *The Buildings at Samaria* (Samaria-Sebaste: Reports of the Work of the Joint Expedition in 1931–1933 and of the British Expedition in 1935, no. 1; London: Palestine Exploration Fund).
Keyes, Charles F.

1997 'Ethnic Groups, Ethnicity', in Thomas Barfield (ed.), *The Dictionary of Anthropology* (Oxford: Blackwell): 152–4.

Khazanov, A. M.

1994 *Nomads and the Outside World* (trans. Julia Crookenden; Cambridge: Cambridge University Press, 2nd rev. edn).

Khoury, Philip S., and Joseph Kostiner

1990 'Introduction: Tribes and the Complexities of State Formation in the Middle East', in Philip S. Khoury and Joseph Kostiner (eds), *Tribes and State Formation in the Middle East* (Berkeley: University of California Press): 1–22.

Khoury, Philip S., and Joseph Kostiner (eds)

1990 *Tribes and State Formation in the Middle East* (Berkeley: University of California Press).

Killebrew, Ann E.

2000 'Aegean-Style Early Philistine Pottery in Canaan during the Iron I Age: A Stylistic Analysis of Mycenaean IIIC:1b Pottery and its Associated Wares', in Eliezer D. Oren (ed.), *The Sea Peoples and their World: A Reassessment* (University Museum Monograph, 108; University Museum Symposium Series, 11; Philadelphia: University of Pennsylvania, The University Museum): 233–53.

2001 'The Collared Pithos in Context: A Typological, Technological, and Functional Reassessment', in Samuel R. Wolff (ed.), *Studies in the Archaeology of Israel and Neighboring Lands in Memory of Douglas L. Esse* (The Oriental Institute of the University of Chicago Studies in Ancient Oriental Civilization, 59; ASOR Books, 5; Chicago: Oriental Institute): 377–98.

2003 'Biblical Jerusalem: An Archaeological Assessment', in Andrew G. Vaughn and Ann E. Killebrew (eds), *Jerusalem in Bible and Archaeology: The First Temple Period* (SBLSymS, 18; Atlanta, GA: Society of Biblical Literature): 329–45.

2005 *Biblical Peoples and Ethnicity: An Archaeological Study of Egyptians, Canaanites, Philistines, and Early Israel 1300–1000 B.C.E.* (SBLABS, 9; Atlanta, GA: Society of Biblical Literature).

2006 'The Emergence of Ancient Israel: The Social Boundaries of a "Mixed Multitude" in Canaan', in Aren M. Maeir and Pierre de Miroschedji (eds), *'I Will Speak the Riddles of Ancient Times': Archaeological and Historical Studies in Honor of Amihai Mazar on the Occasion of his Sixtieth Birthday* (Winona Lake, IN: Eisenbrauns): 555–72.

2008 'Aegean-Style Pottery and Associated Assemblages in the Southern Levant: Chronological Implications Regarding the Tradition from the Late Bronze Age II to the Iron I and the Appearance of the Philistines', in Lester L. Grabbe (ed.), *Israel in Transition: From Late Bronze II to Iron IIA (c. 1250–850 BCE): The Archaeology* (LHBOTS, 491; ESHM, 7; London/New York: T&T Clark International): 54–71.

Killebrew, Ann E., and Gunnar Lehmann (eds)

2013 *The Philistines and Other 'Sea Peoples' in Text and Archaeology* (SBLABS, 15; Atlanta, GA: Society of Biblical Literature).

Kitchen, Kenneth A.
1983 'Egypt, the Levant and Assyria in 701 BC', in Manfred Görg (ed.), *Fontes atque Pontes: Eine Festgabe für Hellmut Brunner* (Ägypten und Altes testament, 5; Wiesbaden: Harrassowitz): 243–53.
1986 *The Third Intermediate Period in Egypt (1100–650 BC)* (Warminster, Wilts.: Aris & Philips, 2nd edn).
1992 'The Egyptian Evidence on Ancient Jordan', in Piotr Bienkowski (ed.), *Early Edom and Moab: The Beginning of the Iron Age in Southern Jordan* (Sheffield Archaeological Monographs, 7; Sheffield: J. R. Collis Publications): 21–34.
2004 'The Victories of Merenptah, and the Nature of their Record', *JSOT* 28: 259–72.
1997 'Sheba and Arabia', in Lowell K. Handy (ed.), *The Age of Solomon: Scholarship at the Turn of the Millennium* (SHCANE, 11; Leiden: Brill): 126–53.

Klengel, Horst
1992 *Syria 3000 to 300 B.C. A Handbook of Political History* (Berlin: Akademie Verlag).

Kletter, Raz
1999 'Pots and Polities: Material Remains of Late Iron Age Judah in Relation to its Political Borders', *BASOR* 314: 19–54.
2002 'People without Burials? The Lack of Iron I Burials in the Central Highlands of Palestine', *IEJ* 52: 28–48.
2006 'Can a Proto-Israelite Please Stand Up? Notes on the Ethnicity of Iron Age Israel and Judah', in Aren M. Maeir and Pierre de Miroschedji (eds), *'I Will Speak the Riddles of Ancient Times': Archaeological and Historical Studies in Honor of Amihai Mazar on the Occasion of his Sixtieth Birthday* (Winona Lake, IN: Eisenbrauns): 573–86.

Knauf, Ernst Axel
1984 'Yahwe', *VT* 34: 467–72.
1985 *Ismael: Untersuchungen zur Geschichte Palästinas und Nordarabiens im 1. Jahrtausend v. Chr.* (Abhandlungen des Deutschen Palästinavereins; Wiesbaden: Harrassowitz).
1988 *Midian: Untersuchungen zur Geschichte Palästinas und Nordarabiens am Ende des 2. Jahrtausends v. Chr.* (Abhandlungen des Deutschen Palästinavereins; Wiesbaden: Harrassowitz).
1991a 'From History to Interpretation', in Diana V. Edelman (ed.), *The Fabric of History: Text, Artifact and Israel's Past* (JSOTSup, 127; Sheffield: Sheffield Academic Press): 26–64.
1991b 'Eglon and Ophrah: Two Toponymic Notes on the Book of Judges', *JSOT* 51: 25–44.
1991c 'King Solomon's Copper Supply', in E. Lipiński (ed.), *Phoenicia and the Bible* (Studia Phoenicia, 11; OLA, 44; Leuven: Peeters): 167–86.
1992 'The Cultural Impact of Secondary State Formation: The Cases of the Edomites and Moabites', in Piotr Bienkowski (ed.) *Early Edom and Moab: The Beginning of the Iron Age in Southern Jordan* (Sheffield Archaeological Monographs, 7; Sheffield: Sheffield Academic Press): 47–54.

1997 'Le roi est mort, vive le roi! A Biblical Argument for the Historicity of Solomon', in Lowell K. Handy (ed.), *The Age of Solomon: Scholarship at the Turn of the Millennium* (SHCANE 11; Leiden: Brill): 81–95.

2000a 'Jerusalem in the Late Bronze and Early Iron Ages: A Proposal', *TA* 27: 75–90.

2000b 'Does "Deuteronomistic Historiography" (DH) Exist?', in Albert de Pury, Thomas Römer, and Jean-Daniel Macchi (eds), *Israel Constructs its History: Deuteronomistic Historiography in Recent Research* (JSOTSup, 306; Sheffield: Sheffield Academic Press, 2000): 388–98.

2001a 'History, Archaeology, and the Bible', *TZ* 57: 262–8.

2001b 'Hezekiah or Manasseh? A Reconsideration of the Siloam Tunnel and Inscription', *TA* 28: 281–7.

2002 'Who Destroyed Beersheba II?', in Ulrich Hübner and Ernest Axel Knauf (eds), *Kein Land für sich allein: Studien zum Kulturkontakt in Kanaan, Israel/Palästina und Ebirnâri für Manfred Weippert zum 65. Geburtstag* (OBO, 186: Freiburg [Schweiz]: Universitätsverlag; Göttingen: Vandenhoeck & Ruprecht): 181–95.

2005a 'The Glorious Days of Manasseh', in Lester L. Grabbe (ed.), *Good Kings and Bad Kings: The Kingdom of Judah in the Seventh Century BCE* (JSOTSup, 393; ESHM, 5: London/New York: T&T Clark International): 164–88.

2005b 'Deborah's Language: Judges Ch. 5 in its Hebrew and Semitic Context', in Bogdan Burtea, Josef Tropper, and Helen Younansardaroud (eds), *Studia Semitica et Semitohamitica: Festschrift für Rainer Voigt anläßlich seines 60. Geburtstages am 17. Januar 2004* (AOAT, 317; Münster: Ugarit-Verlag): 167–82; reprinted in Ernst Axel Knauf, *Data and Debates: Essays in the History and Culture of Israel and its Neighbors in Antiquity. Daten und Debatten: Aufsätze zur Kulturgeschichte des antiken Israel und seiner Nachbarn* (ed. H. M. Niemann, K. Schmid and S. Schroer; AOAT, 407; Münster: Ugarit-Verlag, 2013): 277–328.

2007 'Was Omride Israel a Sovereign State?', in Lester L. Grabbe (ed.), *Ahab Agonistes: The Rise and Fall of the Omri Dynasty* (LHBOTS, 421; ESHM, 6; London/New York: T&T Clark International): 100–103.

2008a 'From Archaeology to History, Bronze and Iron Ages with Special Regard to the Year 1200 BCE and the Tenth Century', in Lester L. Grabbe (ed.), *Israel in Transition: From Late Bronze II to Iron IIA (c. 1250–850 BCE): The Archaeology* (LHBOTS, 491; ESHM, 7; London/New York: T&T Clark International): 72–85.

2008b *Josua* (Zürcher Bibelkommentare AT, 6; Zürich: Theologischer Verlag).

2010a 'History in Joshua', in Lester L. Grabbe (ed.), *Israel in Transition: From Late Bronze II to Iron IIA (c. 1250–850 BCE)*. Vol. II: *The Text* (LHBOTS, 521; ESHM, 8; London/New York: T&T Clark International): 130–39.

2010b 'History in Judges', in Lester L. Grabbe (ed.), *Israel in Transition: From Late Bronze II to Iron IIA (c. 1250–850 BCE)*. Vol. II: *The Text* (LHBOTS, 521; ESHM, 8; London/New York: T&T Clark International): 140–49.

2010c 'Appendix: Exodus and Settlement', in Lester L. Grabbe (ed.), *Israel in Transition: From Late Bronze II to Iron IIA (c. 1250–850 BCE)*. Vol. II: (LHBOTS, 521; ESHM, 8; London/New York: T&T Clark International): 241–50.

2017 'The Impact of the Late Bronze III Period on the Origins of Israel', in Lester L. Grabbe (ed.), *The Land of Canaan in the Late Bronze Age* (LHBOTS, 636; ESHM, 10; London/New York: Bloomsbury T&T Clark).

Knauf, Ernst Axel, and Philippe Guillaume

2016 *A History of Biblical Israel: The Fate of the Tribes and Kingdoms from Merenptah to Bar Kochba* (Worlds of the Ancient Near East and Mediterranean; London: Equinox).

Knudtson, J. A.

1907–15 *Die El-Amarna Tafeln* (Vorderasiatische Bibliotek, 2; Berlin: Hinrichs).

Kooij, Arie van der

1986 'Das assyrische Heer vor den Mauern Jerusalems im Jahr 701 v. Chr.', *ZDPV* 102: 93–109.

Kottsieper, Ingo

2007 'The Tel Dan Inscription (*KAI* 310) and the Political Relations between Aram-Damascus and Israel in the First Half of the First Millennium BCE', in Lester L. Grabbe (ed.), *Ahab Agonistes: The Rise and Fall of the Omri Dynasty* (LHBOTS, 421; ESHM, 6; London/New York: T&T Clark International): 104–34.

Krahmalkov, C. R.

1994 'Exodus Itinerary Confirmed by Egyptian Evidence', *BAR* 20.5: 55–62, 79.

Kramer, Samuel Noah

1969 *The Sacred Marriage Rite: Aspects of Faith, Myth, and Ritual in Ancient Sumer* (Bloomington: University of Indiana Press).

Kuan, Jeffrey Kah-Jin

1995 *Neo-Assyrian Historical Inscriptions and Syria-Palestine: Israelite/Judean-Tyrian-Damascene Political and Commercial Relations in the Ninth-Eighth Centuries BCE* (Jian Dao Dissertation Series, 1; Bible and Literature, 1; Hong Kong: Alliance Bible Seminary).

Kuhrt, Amélie

1995 *The Ancient Near East c. 3000–300 BC* (2 vols; Routledge History of the Ancient World; London/New York: Routledge).

LaBianca, Øystein S.

1997 'Palestine in the Bronze Age', *OEANE* IV, 212–17.

LaBianca, Øystein S., and Randall W. Younker

1998 'The Kingdoms of Ammon, Moab and Edom: The Archaeology of Society in Late Bronze/Iron Age Transjordan (ca. 1400–500 BCE)', in Thomas E. Levy (ed.), *The Archaeology of Society in the Holy Land* (New Approaches in Anthropological Archaeology; London: Leicester University Press, 2nd edn): 399–415.

Lambert, W. G.

1994 'When Did Jehu Pay Tribute?', in Stanley E. Porter, Paul Joyce and David E. Orton (eds), *Crossing the Boundaries: Essays in Biblical Interpretation in Honour of Michael D. Goulder* (BIS, 8; Leiden: Brill): 51–6.

Lamon, Robert S., and Geoffrey Shipton
1939 *Megiddo I: Seasons of 1925–34, Strata I–V* (Oriental Institute Publications, 42; Chicago: University of Chicago Press).
Lapinkivi, Pirjo
2004 *The Sumerian Sacred Marriage in the Light of Comparative Evidence* (SAAS, 15; Helsinki: The Neo-Assyrian Text Corpus Project).
Lapp, Paul W.
1969 'The 1968 Excavations at Tell Ta'annek', *BASOR* 195: 2–49.
Larson, Mogens Trolle
1976 *The Old Assyrian City-State and its Colonies* (Mesopotamia: Copenhagen Studies in Assyriology, 4; Copenhagen: Akademisk Forlag).
Layard, Austen Henry
1853a *Discoveries among the Ruins of Nineveh and Babylon* (New York: G. P. Putnam).
1853b *A Second Series of the Monuments of Nineveh* (London: J. Murray).
Leahy, Anthony
2001 'Foreign Incursions', in Donald B. Redford (ed.), *Oxford Encyclopedia of Ancient Egypt* (Oxford: Oxford University Press): 548–52.
Lehmann, Gunnar
2003 'The United Monarchy in the Countryside: Jerusalem, Judah, and the Shephelah during the Tenth Century B.C.E.', in Andrew G. Vaughn and Ann E. Killebrew (eds), *Jerusalem in Bible and Archaeology: The First Temple Period* (SBLSymS, 18; Atlanta, GA: Society of Biblical Literature): 117–62.
Lehmann, Gunnar, and Hermann Michael Niemann
2014 'When Did the Shephelah Become Judahite?', *TA* 41: 77–94.
Leichty, Erle
2011 *The Royal Inscriptions of Esarhaddon, King of Assyria (680–669 BC)* (The Royal Inscriptions of the Neo-Assyrian Period, 4; Winona Lake, IN: Eisenbrauns).
Lemaire, André
1977 *Inscriptions hebraiques, Tome I Les ostraca* (Paris, Cerf).
1981 *Les écoles et la formation de la Bible dans l'ancien Israël* (OBO, 39; Freiburg [Schweiz]: Universitätsverlag; Göttingen: Vandenhoeck & Ruprecht).
1993 'Joas de Samarie, Barhadad de Dams, Zakkur de Hamat: La Syrie-Palestine vers 800 av. J.-C.', *EI* 24: 148*–57*.
1994a 'La dynastie davidique (Byt Dwd) dans deux inscriptions Ouest-Sémitique de Iè S. Av. J.-C.', *SEL* 11: 17–19.
1994b '"House of David" Restored in Moabite Inscription', *BAR* 20.3: 30–7.
2005 'Response to the Forgeries Issue', *SBL Forum*. Online: http://www.sbl-site.org/ Article.aspx?ArticleId=379: 1–3.
Lemche, Niels Peter
1977 'The Greek "Amphictyony" – Could It Be a Prototype for the Israelite Society in the Period of the Judges?', *JSOT* 4: 48–59.
1985 *Early Israel: Anthropological and Historical Studies on the Israelite Society before the Monarchy* (VTSup, 37; Leiden: Brill).
1991 *The Canaanites and their Land: The Tradition of the Canaanites* (JSOTSup, 110; Sheffield: Sheffield Academic Press).

1992a 'Ḥabiru, Ḥabiru', *ABD* III, 6–10.
1992b 'Israel, History of (Premonarchic Period)', *ABD* III, 526–45.
1996a *Die Vorgeschichte Israels: Von den Anfängen bis zum Ausgang des 13. Jahrhunderts v. Chr.* (Biblische Enzyklopädie, 1; Stuttgart, Berlin and Köln: Kohlhammer).
1996b 'Where Should We Look for Canaan? A Reply to Nadav Na'aman', *UF* 28: 767–72.
1998a *Prelude to Israel's Past: Background and Beginnings of Israelite History and Identity* (trans. E. F. Maniscalco; Peabody, MA: Hendrickson).
1998b *The Israelites in History and Tradition* (Library of Ancient Israel; Louisville, KY: Westminster John Knox; London: SPCK).
1998c 'Greater Canaan: The Implications of a Correct reading of EA 151:49–67', *BASOR* 310: 19–24.
2000 'Ideology and the History of Ancient Israel', *SJOT* 14: 165–93.

Levin, Yigal
2001 'Understanding Biblical Genealogies', *CRBS* 9: 11–46.
2010 'Sheshonq I and the Negev *Ḥăṣērîm*', *Maarav* 17: 189–215.

Levine, Louis D.
1983 'Preliminary Remarks on the Historical Inscriptions of Sennacherib', in H. Tadmor and M. Weinfeld (eds), *History, Historiography and Interpretation: Studies in Biblical and Cuneiform Literatures* (The Hebrew University of Jerusalem, The Institute for Advanced Studies; Jerusalem: Magnes Press; Leiden: Brill): 58–75.

Levy, Thomas E.
2009a 'Ethnic Identity in Biblical Edom, Israel, and Midian: Some Insights from Mortuary Contexts in the Lowlands of Edom', in J. David Schloen (ed.), *Exploring the* Longue Durée: *Essays in Honor of Lawrence E. Stager* (Winona Lake, IN: Eisenbrauns): 251–61.
2009b 'Pastoral Nomads and Iron Age Metal Production in Ancient Edom', in Jeffrey Szuchman (ed.), *Nomads, Tribes, and the State in the Ancient Near East: Cross-Disciplinary Perspectives* (University of Chicago Oriental Institute Seminars, 5; Chicago: Oriental Institute): 147–77.

Levy, Thomas E. (ed.)
1998 *The Archaeology of Society in the Holy Land* (London and Washington: Leicester University Press, 2nd edn).

Levy, Thomas E., Russell B. Adams, and Adolfo Muniz
2004 'Archaeology and the Shasu Nomads: Recent Excavations in the Jabal Hamrat Fidan, Jordan', in Richard Elliott Friedman and William H. C. Propp (eds), *Le-David Maskil: A Birthday Tribute for David Noel Freedman* (Biblical and Judaic Studies, 9; Winona Lake, IN: Eisenbrauns): 63–89.

Levy, Thomas E., Russell B. Adams, Mohammad Najjar, Andreas Hauptmann, James D. Anderson, Baruch Brandl, Mark A. Robinson and Thomas Higham
2004 'Reassessing the Chronology of Biblical Edom: New Excavations and ^{14}C Dates from Khirbat en-Nahas (Jordan)', *Antiquity* 302: 865–79.

Levy, Thomas E., and Thomas Higham (eds)
2005 *The Bible and Radiocarbon Dating: Archaeology, Text and Science* (London: Equinox).

Levy, Thomas E., Thomas Higham, and Mohammad Najjar
2005 'Response to van der Steen and Bienkowski'. Online: http://antiquity.ac.uk/ProjGall/levy/index.html.

Levy, Thomas E., and Augustin F. C. Holl
2002 'Migrations, Ethnogenesis, and Settlement Dynamics: Israelites in Iron Age Canaan and Shuwa-Arabs in the Chad Basin', *Journal of Anthropological Archaeology* 21: 83–118.

Levy, Thomas E., Mohammad Najjar, and Erez Ben-Yosef (eds)
2014 *New Insights into the Iron Age Archaeology of Edom, Southern Jordan: Surveys, Excavations, and Research from the University of California, San Diego & Department of Antiquities of Jordan, Edom Lowlands Regional Archaeology Project (ELRAP)* (2 vols; Monumenta Archaeologica, 35; Los Angeles: Cotsen Institute of Archaeology Press).

Levy, Thomas E., Mohammad Najjar and Thomas Higham
2005 'How Many Fortresses Do You Need to Write a Preliminary Report? Or Response to "Edom and the Early Iron Age: Review of a Recent Publication in *Antiquity*"'. Online: http://www.wadiarabahproject.man.ac.uk.

Levy, Thomas E., Mohammad Najjar, Johannes van der Plicht, Neil G. Smith, Hendrik J. Bruins and Thomas Higham
2005 'Lowland Edom and the High and Low Chronologies: Edomite State Formation, the Bible and Recent Archaeological Research in Southern Jordan', in Thomas E. Levy and Thomas Higham (eds), *The Bible and Radiocarbon Dating: Archaeology, Text and Science* (London: Equinox): 129–63.

Levy, Thomas E., Thomas Schneider, and William H. C. Propp (eds)
2015 *Israel's Exodus in Transdisciplinary Perspective: Text, Archaeology, Culture, and Geoscience* (Quantitative Methods in the Humanities and Social Sciences; Cham, Switzerland: Springer).

Lichtheim, Miriam
1973–80 *Ancient Egyptian Literature* (3 vols; Berkeley and Los Angeles: University of California Press).

Lindars, Barnabas
1995 *Judges 1–5: A New Translation and Commentary* (ed. A. D. H. Mayes; Edinburgh: T. & T. Clark).

Lipiński, Edward
2000 *The Aramaeans: Their Ancient History, Culture, Religion* (OLA, 100; Leuven: Peeters).

Lipschits, Oded
1999 'The History of the Benjaminite Region under Babylonian Rule', *TA* 26: 155–90.
2003 'Demographic Changes in Judah between the Seventh and the Fifth Centuries B.C.E.', in Oded Lipschits and Joseph Blenkinsopp (eds), *Judah and the Judeans in the Neo-Babylonian Period* (Winona Lake, IN: Eisenbrauns): 323–76.
2004 'The Rural Settlement in Judah in the Sixth Century B.C.E.: A Rejoinder', *PEQ* 136.2: 99–107.
2005 *The Fall and Rise of Jerusalem: Judah under Babylonian Rule* (Winona Lake, IN: Eisenbrauns).

2012 'Archaeological Facts, Historical Speculations and the Date of the *LMLK* Storage Jars: A Rejoinder to David Ussishkin', *Journal of Hebrew Scriptures* 12.4: 1–15.

Lipschits, Oded, Omer Sergi, and Ido Koch

2010 'Royal Judahite Jar Handles: Reconsidering the Chronology of the *lmlk* Stamp Impressions', *TA* 37: 3–32.

2011 'Judahite Stamped and Incised Jar Handles: A Tool for Studying the History of Late Monarchic Judah', *TA* 38: 5–41.

Liverani, Mario

2005 *Israel's History and the History of Israel* (trans. Chiara Peri and Philip R. Davies; London: Equinox).

Lohfink, Norbert

1995 'Gab es eine deuteronomistische Bewegung?', in Walter Gross (ed.), *Jeremia und die 'deuteronomistische Bewegung'* (BBB, 98; Beltz: Athenäum): 313–82.

Long, Burke O.

1982 'Social Dimensions of Prophetic Conflict', in Robert C. Culley and Thomas W. Overholt (eds), *Anthropological Perspectives on Old Testament Prophecy* (*Semeia*, 21; Chico, CA: Society of Biblical Literature): 31–53.

Loretz, Oswald

1984 *Habiru-Hebräer: Eine sozio-linguistische Studie über die Herkunft des Gentiliziums* 'ibrî *vom Appellativum* ḫabiru (BZAW, 160; Berlin and New York: de Gruyter).

Loud, Gordon

1948 *Megiddo II: Seasons of 1935–1939* (Oriental Institute Publications, 62; Chicago: University of Chicago).

Luckenbill, D. D.

1924 *The Annals of Sennacherib* (Oriental Institute Publications, 2; Chicago: University of Chicago).

McCarter Jr, P. Kyle

1974 'Yaw, Son of "Omri": A Philological Note on Israelite Chronology', *BASOR* 216: 5–7.

Macchi, Jean-Daniel

1999 *Israël et ses tribus selon Genèse 49* (OBO, 171; Freiburg [Schweiz]: Universitätsverlag; Göttingen: Vandenhoeck & Ruprecht).

McCullagh, C. Behan

1991 'Can Our Understanding of Old Texts Be Objective?', *History and Theory* 30: 302–23.

1998 *The Truth of History* (London/New York: Routledge).

McDermott, John J.

1998 *What Are They Saying about the Formation of Israel?* (Mahwah, NJ: Paulist Press).

MacDonald, Burton

1994 'Early Edom: The Relation between the Literary and Archaeological Evidence', in Michael D. Coogan, Cheryl J. Exum and Lawrence E. Stager (eds), *Scripture and Other Artifacts: Essays on the Bible and Archaeology in Honor of Philip J. King* (Louisville, KY: Westminster John Knox): 230–46.

1999 'Ammonite Territory and Sites', in Burton MacDonald and Randall W. Younker (eds), *Ancient Ammon* (SHCANE, 17; Leiden: Brill): 30–56.

2000 *'East of the Jordan': Territories and Sites of the Hebrew Scriptures* (ASOR Books, 6; Boston, MA: American Schools of Oriental Research).

MacDonald, Burton, Russell Adams, and Piotr Bienkowski (eds)

2001 *The Archaeology of Jordan* (Levantine Archaeology, 1; Sheffield: Sheffield Academic Press).

MacDonald, Burton, and Randall W. Younker (eds)

1999 *Ancient Ammon* (SHCANE, 17; Leiden: Brill).

Macdonald, M. C. A.

2005 'Literacy in an Oral Environment', in Piotr Bienkowski, Christopher Mee and Elizabeth Slater (eds), *Writing and Ancient Near Eastern Society: Papers in Honour of Alan R. Millard* (LHBOTS, 426; London/New York: T&T Clark International): 49–118.

McGovern, Patrick E., and Garman Harbottle

1997 '"Hyksos" Trade Connections between Tell el-Dab'a (Avaris) and the Levant: A Neutron Activation Study of the Canaanite Jar', in Eliezer D. Oren (ed.), *The Hyksos: New Historical and Archaeological Perspectives* (University Museum Monograph, 96; University Museum Symposium Series, 8; Philadelphia: University of Pennsylvania, The University Museum): 141–57.

McKane, William

1996 *A Critical and Exegetical Commentary on Jeremiah*. Vol. II: *Commentary on Jeremiah XXVI–LII* (ICC; Edinburgh: T. & T. Clark).

McKay, John W.

1973 *Religion in Judah under the Assyrians 732–609 BC* (SBT, second series, 26; London: SCM Press).

McKenzie, Stephen L.

2000 *King David: A Biography* (Oxford: Oxford University Press).

McNutt, Paula

1999 *Reconstructing the Society of Ancient Israel* (Library of Ancient Israel; Louisville, KY: Westminster John Knox; London: SPCK).

Maeir, Aren M.

2012a 'Insights on the Philistine Culture and Related Issues: An Overview of 15 Years of Work at Tell eṣ-Ṣafi/Gath', in Gershon Galil, Ayelet Gilboa, Aren M. Maeir, and Dan'el Kahn (eds), *The Ancient Near East in the 12th–10th Centuries BCE: Culture and History: Proceedings of the International Conference Held at the University of Haifa, 2–5 May, 2010* (AOAT, 392; Münster: Ugarit-Verlag, 2012): 345–404.

2012b 'Philistia and the Judean Shephelah after Hazael and the "Uzziah Earthquake": The Power Play between the Philistines, Judahites and Assyrians in the 8th Century BCE in Light of the Excavations at Tell eṣ-Ṣafi/Gath', in Angelika Berlejung (ed.), *Disaster and Relief Management/Katastrophen und ihre Bewältigung* (FAT, 81; Tübingen: Mohr Siebeck): 241–62.

2015 'Exodus as a *Mnemo-Narrative*: An Archaeological Perspective', in Thomas E. Levy, Thomas Schneider, and William H. C. Propp (eds), *Israel's Exodus in Transdisciplinary Perspective: Text, Archaeology, Culture, and Geoscience* (Quantitative Methods in the Humanities and Social Sciences; Cham, Switzerland: Springer): 409–18.

Maeir, Aren M. (ed.)
2012 *Tell es-Safi/Gath I: The 1996–2005 Seasons*. Part 1: *Text* (Ägypten und Altes Testament, 69; Wiesbaden: Harrassowitz).
Maeir, Aren M., Louise A. Hitchcock, and Liora Kolska Horwitz
2013 'On the Constitution and Transformation of Philistine Identity', *Oxford Journal of Archaeology* 32: 1–38.
Maeir, Aren M., and Pierre de Miroschedji (eds)
2006 *'I Will Speak the Riddles of Ancient Times': Archaeological and Historical Studies in Honor of Amihai Mazar on the Occasion of his Sixtieth Birthday* (Winona Lake, IN: Eisenbrauns).
Maeir, Aren M., and Joe Uziel
2007 'A Tale of Two Tells: A Comparative Perspective on Tel Miqne-Ekron and Tell es-Sâfi/Gath in Light of Recent Archaeological Research', in S. Crawford, A. Ben-Tor, J. P. Dessel, W. G. Dever, A. Mazar, and J. Aviram. (eds), *'Up to the Gates of Ekron': Essays on the Archaeology and History of the Eastern Mediterranean in Honor of Seymour Gitin* (Jerusalem: Israel Exploration Society): 29–42.
Maidman, M. P.
1994 *Two Hundred Nuzi Texts from the Oriental Institute of the University of Chicago, Part I* (Studies on the Civilization and Culture of Nuzi and the Hurrians, 6; Bethesda, MD: CDL Press).
Malamat, Abraham
1997 'The Exodus: Egyptian Analogies', in Ernest S. Frerichs and Leonard H. Lesko (eds), *Exodus: The Egyptian Evidence* (Winona Lake, IN: Eisenbrauns): 15–26.
1982 'A Political Look at the Kingdom of David and Solomon and its Relations with Egypt', in Tomoo Ishida (ed.), *Studies in the Period of David and Solomon and Other Essays* (Winona Lake, IN: Eisenbrauns): 189–204.
Manor, Dale W., and Gary A. Heron
1992 'Arad', *ABD* I, 331–6.
Marcus, Joyce, and Gary M. Feinman
1998 'Introduction', in Gary M. Feinman and Joyce Marcus (eds), *Archaic States* (School of American Research Advanced Seminar Series; Santa Fe, NM: School of American Research Press): 3–13.
Margalith, Othniel
1990 'On the Origin and Antiquity of the Name "Israel"', *ZAW* 102: 225–37.
Master, Daniel M.
2001 'State Formation Theory and the Kingdom of Ancient Israel', *JNES* 60: 117–31.
Mayer, Walter
1995 *Politik und Kriegskunst der Assyrer* (ALASPM, 9; Münster: Ugarit-Verlag).
2003 'Sennacherib's Campaign of 701 BCE: The Assyrian View', in Lester L. Grabbe (ed.), *'Like a Bird in a Cage': The Invasion of Sennacherib in 701 BCE* (JSOTSup, 363; ESHM, 4; Sheffield: Sheffield Academic Press): 168–200.
Mayes, A. D. H.
1974 *Israel in the Period of the Judges* (SBT, second series, 29; London: SCM Press).

Mazar, Amihai

1982 'The "Bull Site" – An Iron Age I Open Cult Place', *BASOR* 247: 27–42.

1993 *Archaeology of the Land of the Bible 10,000–586 B.C.E.* (New York: Doubleday; Cambridge: Lutterworth Press).

1994 'The Northern Shephelah in the Iron Age: Some Issues in Biblical History and Archaeology', in Michael D. Coogan, Cheryl J. Exum and Lawrence E. Stager (eds), *Scripture and Other Artifacts: Essays on the Bible and Archaeology in Honor of Philip J. King* (Louisville, KY: Westminster John Knox): 247–67.

1997 'Iron Age Chronology: A Reply to I. Finkelstein', *Levant* 29: 157–67.

2004 'Greek and Levantine Iron Age Chronology: A Rejoinder', *IEJ* 54: 24–36.

2005 'The Debate over the Chronology of the Iron Age in the Southern Levant: Its History, the Current Situation, and a Suggested Resolution', in Thomas E. Levy and Thomas Higham (eds), *The Bible and Radiocarbon Dating: Archaeology, Text and Science* (London: Equinox): 15–30.

2006 'Jerusalem in 10th Century BCE: The Glass Half Full', in Y. Amit, Ehud Ben-Zvi, Israel Finkelstein, and Oded Lipschits (eds), *Essays on Ancient Israel in its Near Eastern Context – A Tribute to Nadav Na'aman* (Winona Lake, IN: Eisenbrauns): 255–72.

2007 'The Spade and the Text: The Interaction between Archaeology and Israelite History Relating to the Tenth-Ninth Centuries BCE', in Hugh G. M. Williamson (ed.), *Understanding the History of Ancient Israel* (Proceedings of the British Academy 143; Oxford: OUP for the British Academy): 143–71.

2008 'From 1200 to 850 BCE: Remarks on Some Selected Archaeological Issues', in Lester L. Grabbe (ed.), *Israel in Transition: From Late Bronze II to Iron IIA (c. 1250–850 BCE): The Archaeology* (LHBOTS, 491; ESHM, 7; London/New York: T&T Clark International): 86–120.

Mazar, Amihai, Hendrik J. Bruins, Nava Panitz-Cohen, and Johannes van der Plicht

2005 'Ladder of Time at Tel Reḥov: Stratigraphy, Archaeological Context, Pottery and Radiocarbon Dates', in Thomas E. Levy and Thomas Higham (eds), *The Bible and Radiocarbon Dating: Archaeology, Text and Science* (London: Equinox): 193–255.

Mazar, Amihai, and Ehud Netzer

1986 'On the Israelite Fortress at Arad', *BASOR* 263: 87–91.

Mazar, Benjamin

1957 'The Campaign of Pharaoh Shishak to Palestine', in *Volume de Congrès: Strasbourg 1956* (VTSup, 4; Leiden: Brill): 57–66 = S. Ahituv and B. A. Levine (eds), *The Early Biblical Period: Historical Studies* (Jerusalem: Israel Exploration Society, 1986): 57–66.

Mazar, Eilat

2006 'Did I Find King David's Palace?', *BAR* 32.1: 16–27, 70.

2009 *The Palace of King David: Excavations at the Summit of the City of David: Preliminary Report of Seasons 2005–2007* (Jerusalem/New York: Shoham Academic Research and Publication).

2011 *Discovering the Solomonic Wall in Jerusalem: A Remarkable Archaeological Adventure* (Jerusalem: Shoham Academic Research and Publication).

Mazar, Eilat, and Benjamin Mazar
1989 *Excavations in the South of the Temple Mount: The Ophel of Biblical Jerusalem* (Qedem, 29; Jerusalem: Institute of Archaeology, Hebrew University).
Meitlis, Yitzhak
2008 'A Re-Analysis of the Archaeological Evidence for the Beginning of the Iron Age I', in Alexander Fantalkin and Assaf Yasur-Landau (eds), *Bene Israel: Studies in the Archaeology of Israel and the Levant during the Bronze and Iron Ages in Honour of Israel Finkelstein* (CHANE, 31; Leiden: Brill): 105–11.
Mendenhall, George E.
1962 'The Hebrew Conquest of Palestine', *BA* 25: 66–87.
1983 'Ancient Israel's Hyphenated History', in David Noel Freedman and D. F. Graf (eds), *Palestine in Transition: The Emergence of Ancient Israel* (SWBA, 2; Sheffield: Sheffield Academic Press): 91–103.
Merrillees, Robert S.
1986 'Political Conditions in the Eastern Mediterranean during the Late Bronze Age', *BA* 49: 42–50.
Mettinger, Tryggve N. D.
1995 *No Graven Image? Israelite Aniconism in its Ancient Near Eastern Context* (ConBOT, 42; Stockholm: Almqvist & Wiksell).
Meyers, Eric M. (editor-in-chief)
1997 *The Oxford Encyclopedia of Archaeology in the Near East* (5 vols; Oxford: Oxford University Press).
Mieroop, Marc van de
2004 *A History of the Ancient Near East, ca. 3000–323 BC* (Blackwell History of the Ancient World, 1; Oxford: Blackwell).
Millard, A. R.
1985 'An Assessment of the Evidence of Writing in Ancient Israel', *Biblical Archaeology Today: Proceedings of the International Congress of Biblical Archaeology, Jerusalem 1984* (Jerusalem: Israel Exploration Society): 301–12.
1992 'Abraham', *ABD* I, 35–41.
Millard, Alan R., and Hayim Tadmor
1973 'Adad-nirari III in Syria: Another Stele Fragment and the Dates of his Campaigns', *Iraq* 35: 57–64.
Millard, Alan R., and D. J. Wiseman (eds)
1980 *Essays on the Patriarchal Narratives* (Leicester: Inter-Varsity Press).
Miller, J. Maxwell
1966 'The Elisha Cycle and the Accounts of the Omride Wars', *JBL* 85: 441–54.
1967 'The Fall of the House of Ahab', *VT* 17: 307–24.
1968 'The Rest of the Acts of Jehoahaz (I Kings 20 $22_{1\text{-}38}$)', *ZAW* 80: 337–72.
1974 'The Moabite Stone as a Memorial Stela', *PEQ* 106: 9–18.
1975 'Geba/Gibeah of Benjamin', *VT* 25: 145–66.
1976 *The Old Testament and the Historian* (Guides to Biblical Scholarship, Old Testament; Minneapolis: Fortress Press).
1977 'Archaeology and the Israelite Conquest of Canaan: Some Methodological Observations', *PEQ* 109: 87–93.

1979 'W. F. Albright and Historical Reconstruction', *BA* 42: 37–47.

1991 'Is It Possible to Write a History of Israel without Relying on the Hebrew Bible?', in Diana V. Edelman (ed.), *The Fabric of History: Text, Artifact and Israel's Past* (JSOTSup, 127; Sheffield: Sheffield Academic Press): 93–102.

1992 'Early Monarchy in Moab?', in Piotr Bienkowski (ed.), *Early Edom and Moab: The Beginning of the Iron Age in Southern Jordan* (Sheffield Archaeological Monographs, 7; Sheffield: J. R. Collis Publications): 77–91.

1997a 'Separating the Solomon of History from the Solomon of Legend', in L. K. Handy (ed.), *The Age of Solomon: Scholarship at the Turn of the Millennium* (SHCANE, 11; Leiden: Brill): 1–24.

1997b 'Ancient Moab: Still Largely Unknown', *BA* 60: 194–204.

Miller, J. Maxwell (ed.)

1991 *Archaeological Survey of the Kerak Plateau, Conducted during 1978–1982 under the Direction of J. Maxwell Miller and Jack M. Pinkerton* (ASOR Archaeological Reports; Atlanta, GA: Scholars Press).

Miller, J. Maxwell, and John H. Hayes

1986 *A History of Ancient Israel and Judah* (Minneapolis: Fortress; London: SCM Press).

Miller II, Robert D.

2004 'Identifying Earliest Israel', *BASOR* 333: 55–68.

2005 *Chieftains of the Highland Clans: A History of Israel in the 12th and 11th Centuries B.C.* (Grand Rapids, MI: Eerdmans).

Mohammed, Abbas

1973 'The Nomadic and the Sedentary: Polar Complementaries – Not Polar Opposites', in Cynthia Nelson (ed.), *The Desert and the Sown: Nomads in the Wider Society* (Institute of International Studies; Berkeley: University of California Press): 97–12.

Mojola, Aloo Osotsi

1998 'The "Tribes" of Israel? A Bible Translator's Dilemma', *JSOT* 81: 15–29.

Mommsen, H., I. Perlman, and J. Yellin

1984 'The Provenance of the *lmlk* Jars', *IEJ* 34: 89–113.

Montgomery, James A.

1951 *A Critical and Exegetical Commentary on the Books of Kings* (ed. H. S. Gehman; ICC; Edinburgh: T. & T. Clark).

Moor, Johannes C. de

1997 *The Rise of Yahwism: The Roots of Israelite Monotheism* (BETL, 91; Leuven: Peeters/University Press, 2nd edn).

Moorey, P. R. S.

2001 *Idols of the People: Miniature Images of Clay in the Ancient Near East* (Schweich Lectures, 2001; Oxford: Oxford University Press for the British Academy).

Moran, William L.

1992 *The Amarna Letters* (Baltimore: Johns Hopkins University Press).

Morris, Ellen Fowles

2005 *The Architecture of Imperialism: Military Bases and the Evolution of Foreign Policy in Egypt's New Kingdom* (PdÄ, 22; Leiden: Brill).

Mowinckel, Sigmund
1914 *Zur Komposition des Buches Jeremia* (Kristiania: Jacob Dybwad).
Munslow, Alun
1997 *Deconstructing History* (London/New York: Routledge).
Mykytiuk, Lawrence J.
2004 *Identifying Biblical Persons in Northwest Semitic Inscriptions of 1200–539 B.C.E.* (SBL Academia Biblica, 12; Atlanta, GA: Society of Biblical Literature).
2009 'Corrections and Updates to "Identifying Biblical Persons in Northwest Semitic Inscriptions of 1200–539 B.C.E."', *Maarav* 16: 49–132.
Na'aman, Nadav
1974 'Sennacherib's "Letter to God" on his Campaign to Judah', *BASOR* 214: 25–39.
1976 'Two Notes on the Monolith Inscription of Shalmaneser III from Kurkh', *TA* 3: 89–106.
1979 'Sennacherib's Campaign to Judah and the Date of the *LMLK* Stamps', *VT* 29: 60–86.
1986a 'Hezekiah's Fortified Cities and the *LMLK* Stamps', *BASOR* 261: 5–21.
1986b 'Historical and Chronological Notes on the Kingdoms of Israel and Judah in the Eighth Century B.C.', *VT* 36: 71–92.
1986c 'ḫabiru and Hebrews: The Transfer of a Social Term to the Literary Sphere', *JNES* 45: 271–88.
1988a 'The Date of 2 Chronicles 11:5-10 – A Reply to Y. Garfinkel', *BASOR* 271: 74–7.
1988b Review of O. Loretz, *Habiru-Hebräer*, *JNES* 47: 192–4.
1990 'The Historical Background to the Conquest of Samaria (720 BC)', *Biblica* 71: 206–25.
1991 'The Kingdom of Judah under Josiah', *TA* 18: 3–71 [see also 2005 below].
1992a 'Canaanite Jerusalem and its Central Hill Country Neighbours in the Second Millennium B.C.E.', *UF* 24: 275–91.
1992b 'The Pre-Deuteronomistic Story of King Saul and its Historical Significance', *CBQ* 54: 638–58.
1992c 'Israel, Edom and Egypt in the 10th Century B.C.E.', *TA* 19: 71–93.
1993 'Azariah of Judah and Jeroboam II of Israel', *VT* 43: 227–34.
1994a 'Hezekiah and the Kings of Assyria', *TA* 21: 235–54.
1994b 'The Canaanites and their Land: A Rejoinder', *UF* 26: 397–418 = *Canaan in the Second Millennium B.C.E.: Collected Essays*, Vol. II (Winona Lake, IN: Eisenbrauns, 2005): 110–33.
1994c 'The "Conquest of Canaan" in the Book of Joshua and in History', in Israel Finkelstein and Nadav Na'aman (eds), *From Nomadism to Monarchy: Archaeological and Historical Aspects of Early Israel* (Jerusalem: Israel Exploration Society): 218–81.
1994d 'The Hurrians and the End of the Middle Bronze Age in Palestine', *Levant* 26: 175–87 = *Canaan in the Second Millennium B.C.E.: Collected Essays*, Vol. II (Winona Lake, IN: Eisenbrauns, 2005): 1–24.
1995a 'The Debated Historicity of Hezekiah's Reform in the Light of Historical and Archaeological Research', *ZAW* 107: 179–95.

1995b 'Tiglath-pileser III's Campaign against Tyre and Israel (734–732 B.C.E.)', *TA* 22: 268–78.

1995c 'Hazael of 'Amqi and Hadadezer of Beth-rehob', *UF* 27: 381–94.

1996a 'Sources and Composition in the History of David', in Volkmar Fritz and Philip R. Davies (eds), *The Origins of the Ancient Israelite States* (JSOTSup, 228; Sheffield: Sheffield Academic Press): 170–86.

1996b 'The Contribution of the Amarna Letters to the Debate on Jerusalem's Political Position in the Tenth Century B.C.E.', *BASOR* 304: 17–27.

1997a 'King Mesha and the Foundation of the Moabite Monarchy', *IEJ* 47: 83–92.

1997b 'Historical and Literary Notes on the Excavations of Tel Jezreel', *TA* 24: 122–28.

1997c 'The Network of Canaanite Late Bronze Kingdoms and the City of Ashdod', *UF* 29: 599–626 = *Canaan in the Second Millennium B.C.E.: Collected Essays*, Vol. II (Winona Lake, IN: Eisenbrauns, 2005): 145–72.

1997d 'Sources and Composition in the History of Solomon', in L. K. Handy (ed.), *The Age of Solomon: Scholarship at the Turn of the Millennium* (SHCANE, 11; Leiden: Brill): 57–80.

1998a 'Two Notes on the History of Ashkelon and Ekron in the Late Eighth-Seventh Centuries B.C.E.', *TA* 25: 219–27.

1998b 'Jehu Son of Omri: Legitimizing a Loyal Vassal by his Overlord', *IEJ* 48: 236–8.

1999 'Four Notes on the Size of Late Bronze Canaan', *BASOR* 313: 31–7 = *Canaan in the Second Millennium B.C.E.: Collected Essays*, Vol. II (Winona Lake, IN: Eisenbrauns, 2005): 134–44.

2000 'Three Notes on the Aramaic Inscription from Tel Dan', *IEJ* 50: 92–104.

2001 'An Assyrian Residence at Ramat Rahel?', *TA* 28: 260–80.

2002a 'The Abandonment of Cult Places in the Kingdoms of Israel and Judah as Acts of Cult Reform', *UF* 34: 585–602.

2002b 'In Search of Reality behind the Account of David's Wars with Israel's Neighbours', *IEJ* 52: 200–24.

2003 'Updating the Messages: Hezekiah's Second Prophetic Story (2 Kings 19.9b-35) and the Community of Babylonian Deportees', in Lester L. Grabbe (ed.), *'Like a Bird in a Cage': The Invasion of Sennacherib in 701 BCE* (JSOTSup, 363; ESHM, 4; Sheffield: Sheffield Academic Press): 201–20.

2005 'The Kingdom of Judah under Josiah', in Lester L. Grabbe (ed.), *Good Kings and Bad Kings: The Kingdom of Judah in the Seventh Century BCE* (JSOTSup, 393; ESHM, 5: London/New York: T&T Clark International): 189–247.

2007a 'Royal Inscription versus Prophetic Story: Mesha's Rebellion according to Biblical and Moabite Historiography', in Lester L. Grabbe (ed.), *Ahab Agonistes: The Rise and Fall of the Omri Dynasty* (LHBOTS, 421; ESHM, 6; London/New York: T&T Clark International) 145–83.

2007b 'The Northern Kingdom in the Late Tenth-Ninth Centuries BCE', in Hugh G. M. Williamson (ed.), *Understanding the History of Ancient Israel* (Proceedings of the British Academy, 143; Oxford: OUP for the British Academy): 399–418.

2008 'In Search of the Ancient Name of Khirbet Qeiyafa', *Journal of Hebrew Scriptures* 8.21: 1–8.
2009 'Saul, Benjamin and the Emergence of "Biblical Israel"', *ZAW* 121: 211–24, 335–49.
2010 'Khirbet Qeiyafa in Context', *UF* 42: 497–526.
2013 'The Kingdom of Judah in the 9th Century BCE: Text Analysis versus Archaeological Research', *TA* 40: 247–76.
2014 'Dismissing the Myth of a Flood of Israelite Refugees in the Late Eighth Century BCE', *ZAW* 126: 1–14.
2015 'Out of Egypt or Out of Canaan? The Exodus Story between Memory and Historical Reality', in Thomas E. Levy, Thomas Schneider, and William H. C. Propp (eds), *Israel's Exodus in Transdisciplinary Perspective: Text, Archaeology, Culture, and Geoscience* (Quantitative Methods in the Humanities and Social Sciences; Cham, Switzerland: Springer): 527–33.
2016 'The *lmlk* Seal Impressions Reconsidered', *TA* 43: 111–25.

Na'aman, Nadav, and Ran Zadok
1988 'Sargon II's Deportations to Israel and Philistia (716–708 B.C.)', *JCS* 40: 36–46.
2000 'Assyrian Deportations to the Province of Samerina in the Light of Two Cuneiform Tablets from Tell Hadid', *TA* 27: 159–88.

Nakhai, Beth Alpert
2001 *Archaeology and the Religions of Canaan and Israel* (ASOR Books, 7; Boston: American Schools of Oriental Research).

Naveh, Joseph
1982 'Some Recently Forged Inscriptions', *BASOR* 247: 53–8.

Nelson, Cynthia (ed.)
1973 *The Desert and the Sown: Nomads in the Wider Society* (Institute of International Studies; Berkeley: University of California Press).

Ngo, Robin
2014 *Canaanite Fortress Discovered in the City of David, Biblical Archaeology Sites, News*. 7 April 2014. Cited 27 June 2014. Online: http://www.biblicalarchaeology.org/daily/news/canaanite-fortress-discovered-in-the-city-of-david/.

Niccacci, Alviero
1997 'La stèle d'Israël: grammaire et stratégie de communication', in Marcel Sigrist (ed.), *Études égyptologiques et bibliques à la mémoire du Père B. Couroyer* (Cahiers de la Revue Biblique, 36; Paris: Gabalda): 43–107.

Nicholson, Ernest W.
1973 *Exodus and Sinai in History and Tradition* (Oxford: Blackwell).
1998 *The Pentateuch in the Twentieth Century: The Legacy of Julius Wellhausen* (Oxford: Clarendon).

Niditch, Susan
1996 *Oral World and Written Word: Ancient Israelite Literature* (Library of Ancient Israel; Louisville, KY: Westminster John Knox; London: SPCK).

Niehr, Herbert
1994 *'šāpaṭ', TWAT* VIII, 408–28.
1995 'Die Reform des Joschija: Methodische, historische und religionsgeschichtliche Aspekte', in Walter Gross (ed.), *Jeremia und die 'deuteronomistische Bewegung'* (BBB, 98; Beltz: Athenäum): 33–55.

Niemann, Hermann Michael

1993 *Herrschaft, Königtum und Staat: Skizzen zur soziokulturellen Entwicklung im monarchischen Israel* (FAT, 6; Tübingen: Mohr [Siebeck]).

1997 'The Socio-Political Shadow Cast by the Biblical Solomon' in L. K. Handy (ed.), *The Age of Solomon: Scholarship at the Turn of the Millennium* (SHCANE, 11; Leiden: Brill); reprinted in Niemann, *History of Ancient Israel, Archaeology, and Bible: Collected Essays/Geschichte Israels, Archäologie und Bibel: Gesammelte Aufsätze* (ed. Meik Gerhards; AOAT, 418; Münster: Ugarit-Verlag, 2015): 91–126.

2000 'Megiddo and Solomon: A Biblical Investigation in Relation to Archaeology', *TA* 27: 61–74.

2003 'Pentapolis', *RGG*[4] VI, 1087–88.

2007 'Royal Samaria – Capital or Residence? or: The Foundation of the City of Samaria by Sargon II', in Lester L. Grabbe (ed.), *Ahab Agonistes: The Rise and Fall of the Omri Dynasty* (LHBOTS, 421; ESHM, 6; London/New York: T&T Clark International): 184–207.

2013 'Neighbors and Foes, Rivals and Kin: Philistines, Shephleans, Judeans between Geography and Economy, History and Theology', in Ann E. Killebrew and Gunnar Lehmann (eds), *The Philistines and Other 'Sea Peoples' in Text and Archaeology* (SBLABS, 15; Atlanta, GA: Society of Biblical Literature): 243–64.

Noort, Ed

1994 *Die Seevölker in Palästina* (Palaestina Antiqua, 8; Kampen: Kok Pharos).

Norin, Stig

1998 'The Age of the Siloam Inscription and Hezekiah's Tunnel', *VT* 48: 37–48.

Noth, Martin

1930 *Das System der zwölf Stämme Israels* (BWANT, 4/1; Stuttgart: Kohlhammer).

1938 'Die Wege der Pharaonenheere in Palästina und Syrien IV', *ZDPV* 61: 277–304.

1960 *The History of Israel* (rev. trans.; London: A. & C. Black; New York: Harper & Row); ET of *Geschichte Israels* (Berlin: Evangelisch Verlagsanstalt, 3rd edn, 1956).

1962 *Exodus* (OTL; Philadelphia: Westminster Press).

1981 *The Deuteronomistic History* (JSOTSup, 15; Sheffield: JSOT Press); ET of Chapters 1–13 of *Überlieferungsgeschichtliche Studien* (Schriften der Königsberger Gelehrten Gesellschaft, Geisteswissenschaftliche Klass, 18. Jahr, Heft 2; Halle: Max Niemeyer Verlag, 1943): 43–266.

Oates, J.

1991 'Chapter 25. The Fall of Assyria (635–609 B.C.)', *CAH* III/2: 162–93.

O'Brien, Mark A.

1989 *The Deuteronomistic History Hypothesis: a Reassessment* (OBO, 92; Freiburg [Schweiz]: Universitätsverlag; Göttingen: Vandenhoeck & Ruprecht).

O'Callaghan, Roger T.

1948 *Aram Naharaim: A Contribution to the History of Upper Mesopotamia in the Second Millennium B.C.* (Rome: Pontifical Biblical Institute).

O'Connor, David

2000 'The Sea Peoples and the Egyptian Sources', in Eliezer D. Oren (ed.), *The Sea Peoples and their World: A Reassessment* (University Museum Monograph, 108; University Museum Symposium Series, 11; Philadelphia: University of Pennsylvania, The University Museum): 85–102.

Oded, Bustanay

1970 'Observations on Methods of Assyrian Rule in Transjordania after the Palestinian Campaign of Tiglath-pileser III', *JNES* 29: 177–86.

1972 'The Historical Background of the Syro-Ephraimite War Reconsidered', *CBQ* 34: 153–65.

1979 *Mass Deportations and Deportees in the Neo-Assyrian Empire* (Wiesbaden: Reichert).

1993 'Ahaz's Appeal to Tiglath-pileser III in the Context of the Assyrian Policy of Expansion', in Michael Heltzer, Arthur Segal, and Daniel Kaufman (eds), *Studies in the Archaeology and History of Ancient Israel, in Honour of Moshe Dothan* (Haifa: Haifa University): 63–71.

2000 'The Settlements of the Israelite and Judean Exiles in Mesopotamia in the 8th–6th Centuries BCE', in G. Galil and Moshe Weinfeld (eds), *Studies in Historical Geography and Biblical Historiography Presented to Zecharia Kallai* (VTSup, 81: Leiden: Brill): 91–103.

2003 'Where is the "Myth of the Empty Land" to Be Found? History versus Myth', in Oded Lipschits and Joseph Blenkinsopp (eds), *Judah and the Judeans in the Neo-Babylonian Period* (Winona Lake, IN: Eisenbrauns): 55–74.

Oden, Robert A.

1977 'Ba'al Šāmēm and 'ēl', *CBQ* 39: 457–73.

Ofer, Avi

1993 'Judean Hills Survey', *NEAEHL* III, 815–16.

1994 '"All the Hill Country of Judah": From a Settlement Fringe to a Prosperous Monarchy', in Israel Finkelstein and Nadav Na'aman (eds), *From Nomadism to Monarchy: Archaeological and Historical Aspects of Early Israel* (Jerusalem: Israel Exploration Society): 92–121.

2001 'The Monarchic Period in the Judaean Highland: A Spatial Overview', in Amihai Mazar (ed.), *Studies in the Archaeology of the Iron Age in Israel and Jordan* (JSOTSup, 331; Sheffield: Sheffield Academic Press): 14–37.

Oren, Eliezer D. (ed.)

1997 *The Hyksos: New Historical and Archaeological Perspectives* (University Museum Monograph, 96; University Museum Symposium Series, 8; Philadelphia: University of Pennsylvania, The University Museum).

2000 *The Sea Peoples and their World: A Reassessment* (University Museum Monograph, 108; University Museum Symposium Series, 11; Philadelphia: University of Pennsylvania, The University Museum).

Page, Stephanie

1968 'A Stela of Adad-Nirari III and Nergal-Ereš from Tell al Rimah', *Iraq* 30: 139–53.

Parker, Simon B.

1996 'Appeals for Military Intervention: Stories from Zinjirli and the Bible', *BA* 59: 213–24.

1997 *Ugaritic Narrative Poetry* (SBL Writings from the Ancient World, 9; Atlanta, GA: Scholars Press).

Parpola, Simo

1980 'The Murderer of Sennacherib', in B. Alster (ed.), *Death in Mesopotamia: Papers Read at the XXVI[e] Rencontre assyriologique international* (Mesopotamia: Copenhagen Studies in Assyriology, 8; Copenhagen: Akademisk Forlag): 161–70.

Pearce, Laurie E.

2006 'New Evidence for Judeans in Babylonia', in Oded Lipschits and Manfred Oeming (eds), *Judah and the Judeans in the Persian Period* (Winona Lake, IN: Eisenbrauns): 399–411.

2015 'Identifying Judeans and Judean Identity in the Babylonian Evidence', in Jonathan Stökl and Caroline Waerzeggers (eds), *Exile and Return: The Babylonian Context* (BZAW, 478; Berlin/Boston: de Gruyter): 7–32.

Person Jr, Raymond F.

1998 'The Ancient Israelite Scribe as Performer', *JBL* 117: 601–9.

Petschow, Herbert

1965 'Die neubabylonische Zwiegesprächsurkunde und Genesis 23', *JCS* 19: 103–20.

Piasetzky, Eli, and Israel Finkelstein

2005 '^{14}C Results from Megiddo, Tel Dor, Tel Rehov and Tel Hadar', in Thomas E. Levy and Thomas Higham (eds), *The Bible and Radiocarbon Dating: Archaeology, Text and Science* (London: Equinox): 294–309.

Pitard, Wayne T.

1987 *Ancient Damascus: A Historical Study of the Syrian City-State from Earliest Times until its Fall to the Assyrians in 732 B.C.E.* (Winona Lake, IN: Eisenbrauns).

1988 'The Identity of the Bir-Hadad of the Melqart Stela', *BASOR* 272: 3–21.

Popper, Karl

1959 *The Logic of Scientific Discovery* (London: Hutchinson); ET of *Logik der Forschung* (Vienna, 1935).

Porten, Bezalel

1968 *Archives from Elephantine: The Life of an Ancient Jewish Military Colony* (Berkeley and Los Angeles: University of California).

Propp, William H. C.

2015 'The Exodus and History', in Thomas E. Levy, Thomas Schneider, and William H. C. Propp (eds), *Israel's Exodus in Transdisciplinary Perspective: Text, Archaeology, Culture, and Geoscience* (Quantitative Methods in the Humanities and Social Sciences; Cham, Switzerland: Springer): 429–36.

Provan, Iain W.

1995 'Ideologies, Literary and Critical: Reflections on Recent Writing on the History of Israel', *JBL* 114: 585–606.

Provan, Iain, V. Philips Long, and Tremper Longman III

2003 *A Biblical History of Israel* (Louisville and London: Westminster John Knox).

Puech, Emile

1981 'L'ivoire inscrit d'Arslan-Tash et les rois de Damas', *RB* 88: 544–62.

1992 'La stèle de Bar-Hadad à Melqart et les rois d'Arpad', *RB* 99: 311–34.

Pury, Albert de, Thomas Römer, and Jean-Daniel Macchi (eds)
2000 *Israel Constructs its History: Deuteronomistic Historiography in Recent Research* (JSOTSup, 306; Sheffield: Sheffield Academic Press); French original, *Israël construit son histoire: l'historiographie deutéronomiste à la lumière des recherches récentes* (Le Monde de la Bible, 34; Geneva: Labor et Fides, 1996).

Pusch, Edgar B.
2001 'Piramesse', in Donald B. Redford (ed.), *Oxford Encyclopedia of Ancient Egypt* (Oxford: Oxford University Press): 48–50.

Raban, Avner
2001 'Standardized Collared-Rim Pithoi and Short-Lived Settlements', in Samuel R. Wolff (ed.), *Studies in the Archaeology of Israel and Neighboring Lands in Memory of Douglas L. Esse* (The Oriental Institute of the University of Chicago Studies in Ancient Oriental Civilization, 59; ASOR Books, 5; Chicago: Oriental Institute): 493–518.

Rad, Gerhard
1965 'The Form-Critical Problem of the Hexateuch', in *The Problem of the Hexateuch and other Essays* (trans. E. W. Trueman Dicken; Edinburgh: Oliver & Boyd): 1–78.

Rainey, Anson F.
1972 'The World of Sinuhe', *IOS* 2: 369–408.
1976 'Taharqa and Syntax', *TA* 3: 38–41.
1978 *El Amarna Tablets 359–379* (AOAT, 8; Neukirchen-Vluyn: Neukirchener Verlag, 2nd edn).
1984 'Early Historical Geography of the Negeb', in Ze'ev Herzog (ed.), *Beer-Sheba II: The Early Iron Age Settlements* (Publications of the Institute of Archaeology, 7; Tel Aviv: Tel Aviv University Institute of Archaeology): 88–104.
1994 '"The House of David" and the House of the Deconstructionists', *BAR* 20.6 (Nov./Dec.): 47.
1996 'Who Is a Canaanite? A Review of the Textual Evidence', *BASOR* 304: 1–16.
2001 'Israel in Merenptah's Inscription and Reliefs', *IEJ* 51: 57–75.
2015a *The El-Amarna Correspondence: A New Edition of the Cuneiform Letters from the Site of El-Amarna based on Collations of all Extant Tablets*, Vol. I (ed. William Schniedewind and Zipora Cochavi-Rainey; HdO, I/110; Leiden: Brill).
2015b *The El-Amarna Correspondence: A New Edition of the Cuneiform Letters from the Site of El-Amarna based on Collations of all Extant Tablets*, Vol. II (edited and completed by Zipora Cochavi-Rainey; HdO, I/110; Leiden: Brill).

Rainey, Anson F. (ed.)
1987 *Egypt, Israel, Sinai: Archaeological and Historical Relationships in the Biblical Period* (Tel Aviv University Kaplan Project on the History of Israel and Egypt; Tel Aviv: Tel Aviv University).

Ramsey, George W.
1981 *The Quest for the Historical Israel* (Atlanta, GA: John Knox).

Rawlinson, George
1864 *The Five Great Monarchies of the Ancient Eastern World* (4 vols; London: John Murray).

Redford, Donald B.

1963 'Exodus I 11', *VT* 13: 401–18.

1970a *A Study of the Biblical Story of Joseph (Genesis 37–50)* (VTSup, 20; Leiden: Brill).

1970b 'The Hyksos in History and Tradition', *Or* 39: 1–51.

1984 *Akhenaten: The Heretic King* (Princeton, NJ: Princeton University Press).

1986a *Pharaonic King-Lists, Annals and Day-Books: A Contribution to the Study of the Egyptian Sense of History* (Society for the Study of Egyptian Antiquities Publications, 4; Mississauga, ONT: Benben Publications).

1986b 'The Ashkelon Relief at Karnak and the Israel Stela', *IEJ* 36: 188–200.

1987 'An Egyptological Perspective on the Exodus Narrative', in Anson F. Rainey (ed.), *Egypt, Israel, Sinai: Archaeological and Historical Relationships in the Biblical Period* (Tel Aviv University Kaplan Project on the History of Israel and Egypt; Tel Aviv: Tel Aviv University): 137–61.

1990 *Egypt and Canaan in the New Kingdom* (Beer-Sheva, 4; Beer-Sheva: Ben-Gurion University of the Negev Press).

1992a *Egypt, Canaan, and Israel in Ancient Times* (Princeton, NJ: Princeton University Press).

1992b 'Execration and Execration Texts', *ABD* II, 681–2.

1993 'Taharqa in Western Asia and Libya', *EI* 24: 188*–91*.

1997a 'Textual Sources for the Hyksos Period', in Eliezer D. Oren (ed.), *The Hyksos: New Historical and Archaeological Perspectives* (University Museum Monograph, 96; University Museum Symposium Series, 8; Philadelphia: University of Pennsylvania, The University Museum): 1–44.

1997b 'Observations on the Sojourn of the Bene-Israel', in Ernest S. Frerichs and Leonard H. Lesko (eds), *Exodus: The Egyptian Evidence* (Winona Lake, IN: Eisenbrauns): 57–66.

1999 'A Note on the Chronology Dynasty 25 and the Inscription of Sargon II at Tang-i Var', *Or* 68: 58–60.

2000 'Egypt and Western Asia in the Late New Kingdom: An Overview', in Eliezer D. Oren (ed.), *The Sea Peoples and their World: A Reassessment* (University Museum Monograph, 108; University Museum Symposium Series, 11; Philadelphia: University of Pennsylvania, The University Museum): 1–20.

2003 *The Wars in Syria and Palestine of Thutmose III* (CHANE 16; Leiden: Brill).

2015 'The Great Going Forth: The Expulsion of West Semitic Speakers from Egypt', in Thomas E. Levy, Thomas Schneider, and William H. C. Propp (eds), *Israel's Exodus in Transdisciplinary Perspective: Text, Archaeology, Culture, and Geoscience* (Quantitative Methods in the Humanities and Social Sciences; Cham, Switzerland: Springer): 437–45.

Redford, Donald B. (ed.)

2001 *Oxford Encyclopedia of Ancient Egypt* (Oxford: Oxford University Press).

Redford, Donald B., and James M. Weinstein

1992 'Hyksos', *ABD* III, 341–8.

Redman, Charles L.
1999 'The Development of Archaeological Theory: Explaining the Past', in Graeme Barker (ed.), *Companion Encyclopedia of Archaeology* (London/New York: Routledge): 48–80.
Redmount, Carol A.
1995 'Ethnicity, Pottery, and the Hyksos at Tell El-Maskhuta in the Egyptian Delta', *BA* 58: 181–90.
Reich, Ronny
1992 'Palaces and Residences in the Iron Age', in Aharon Kempinski and Ronny Reich (eds), *The Architecture of Ancient Israel from the Prehistoric to the Persian Periods* (Jerusalem: Israel Exploration Society): 202–22.
2011 *Excavating the City of David: Where Jerusalem's History Began* (Jerusalem: Israel Exploration Society).
Reich, Ronny, and Eli Shukron
1999 'Light at the End of the Tunnel', *BAR* 25.1: 22–33, 72.
2003 'The Urban Development of Jerusalem in the Late Eighth Century B.C.E.', in Andrew G. Vaughn and Ann E. Killebrew (eds), *Jerusalem in Bible and Archaeology: The First Temple Period* (SBLSymS, 18; Atlanta, GA: Society of Biblical Literature): 209–18.
Reich, Ronny, Eli Shukron, and Omri Lernau
2008 'The Iron Age II Finds from the Rock-Cut "Pool" Near the Spring in Jerusalem: A Preliminary Report', in Lester L. Grabbe (ed.), *Israel in Transition: From Late Bronze II to Iron IIA (c. 1250–850 BCE): The Archaeology* (LHBOTS, 491; ESHM, 7; London/New York: T&T Clark International): 138–43.
Rendsburg, Gary
1981 'A Reconstruction of Moabite-Israelite History', *JANES* 13: 67–73.
Rendtorff, Rolf
1997 'Directions in Pentateuchal Studies', *CRBS* 5: 43–65.
Renfrew, Colin, and Paul Bahn
2004 *Archaeology: Theories, Methods and Practice* (London: Thames & Hudson, 4th edn).
Renz, Johannes
1995 *Handbuch der althebräischen Epigraphik: Band I Die althebräischen Inschriften: Teil 1 Text und Kommentar* (Darmstadt: Wissenschaftliche Buchgesellschaft).
Robertson, David A.
1972 *Linguistic Evidence in Dating Early Hebrew Poetry* (SBLDS, 3; Missoula, MT: Society of Biblical Literature).
Rogerson, John W.
1978 *Anthropology and the Old Testament* (Oxford: Blackwell).
1986 'Was Early Israel a Segmentary Society?', *JSOT* 36: 17–26.
Rogerson, John, and Philip R. Davies
1996 'Was the Siloam Tunnel Built by Hezekiah?', *BA* 59: 138–49.
Rollston, Christopher A.
2003 'Non-Provenanced Epigraphs I: Pillaged Antiquities, Northwest Semitic Forgeries, and Protocols for Laboratory Tests', *Maarav* 10: 135–93.

2004 'Non-Provenanced Epigraphs II: The Status of Non-Provenanced Epigraphs within the Broader Corpus of Northwest Semitic', *Maarav* 11: 57–79.

2005 'The Crisis of Modern Epigraphic Forgeries and the Antiquities Market: A Palaeographer Reflects on the Problem and Proposes Protocols for the Field', *SBL Forum*. Online: http://www.sbl-site.org/Article.aspx?ArticleId=370: 1–8.

2011 'The Khirbet Qeiyafa Ostracon: Methodological Musings and Caveats', *TA* 38: 67–82.

Rollston, Christopher A., and Andrew G. Vaughn

2005 'The Antiquities Market, Sensationalized Textual Data, and Modern Forgeries: Introduction to the Problem and Synopsis of the 2004 Israeli Indictment', *SBL Forum*. Online: http://www.sbl-site.org/Article.aspx?ArticleId=379: 1–8.

Römer, Thomas C.

2005 *The So-Called Deuteronomistic History: A Sociological, Historical and Literary Introduction* (London/New York: T&T Clark International).

2015 'The Revelation of the Divine Name to Moses and the Construction of a Memory about the Origins of the Encounter Between Yhwh and Israel', in Thomas E. Levy, Thomas Schneider, and William H. C. Propp (eds), *Israel's Exodus in Transdisciplinary Perspective: Text, Archaeology, Culture, and Geoscience* (Quantitative Methods in the Humanities and Social Sciences; Cham, Switzerland: Springer): 305–15.

Rosenberg, Stephen

1998 'The Siloam Tunnel Revisited', *TA* 25: 116–30.

Rosenfeld, A., S. Ilani, H. R. Feldman, W. E. Krumbein, and J. Kronfeld

2009 'Archaeometric Evidence for the Authenticity of the Jehoash Inscription Tablet', *Antiguo Oriente* 7: 57–73.

Rothenbusch, Ralf

2000 *Die kasuistische Rechtssammlung im 'Bundesbuch' (Ex 21,2-11.18-22,16) und ihr literarischer Kontext im Licht altorientalischer Parallelen* (AOAT, 259; Münster: Ugarit-Verlag).

Routledge, Bruce

2004 *Moab in the Iron Age: Hegemony, Polity, Archaeology* (Archaeology, Culture, and Society; Philadelphia: University of Pennsylvania Press).

2008 'Thinking "Globally" and Analysing "Locally": South-Central Jordan in Transition', in Lester L. Grabbe (ed.), *Israel in Transition: From Late Bronze II to Iron IIA (c. 1250–850 BCE): The Archaeology* (LHBOTS, 491; ESHM, 7; London/New York: T&T Clark International): 144–76.

Rowton, Michael B.

1965 'The Topological Factor in the *ḫapiru* Problem', in H. G. Gütersbock and Th. Jacobsen (eds), *Studies in Honor of Benno Landsberger on his Seventy-Fifth Birthday, April 25, 1965* (Oriental Institute, Assyriological Studies, 16; Chicago: University of Chicago Press): 375–87.

1976 'Dimorphic Structure and the Problem of the *'Apirû-'Ibrîm*', *JNES* 35: 13–20.

Rudman, Dominic

2000 'Is the Rabshakeh also among the Prophets? A Rhetorical Study of 2 Kings xviii 17-35', *VT* 50: 100–110.

Russell, Stephen C.

2015 'The Structure of Legal Administration in the Moses Story', in Thomas E. Levy, Thomas Schneider, and William H. C. Propp (eds), *Israel's Exodus in Transdisciplinary Perspective: Text, Archaeology, Culture, and Geoscience* (Quantitative Methods in the Humanities and Social Sciences; Cham, Switzerland: Springer): 317–29.

Ryholt, K. S. B.

1997 *The Political Situation in Egypt during the Second Intermediate Period c. 1800–1550 B. C.* (Carsten Nieburh Institute Publications, 20; Copenhagen: Museum Tusculanum Press).

Saggs, H. W. F.

1955a 'The Nimrud Letters, 1952 – Part I', *Iraq* 17: 21–56.

1955b 'The Nimrud Letters, 1952 – Part II', *Iraq* 17: 126–60.

1956 'The Nimrud Letters, 1952 – Part III', *Iraq* 18: 40–56 + plates 9–12.

Salzman, Philip Carl

1980a 'Introduction: Processes of Sedentarization as Adaptation and Response', in Philip Carl Salzman (ed.), *When Nomads Settle: Processes of Sedentarization as Adaptation and Response* (New York: Praeger): 1–19.

1980b 'Processes of Sedentarization among the Nomads of Baluchistan', in Philip Carl Salzman (ed.), *When Nomads Settle: Processes of Sedentarization as Adaptation and Response* (New York: Praeger): 95–110.

2002 'Pastoral Nomads: Some General Observations Based on Research in Iran', *Journal of Anthropological Research* 58: 245–64.

2004 *Pastoralists: Equality, Hierarchy, and the State* (Boulder, CO/Oxford: Westview Press).

Salzman, Philip Carl (ed.)

1980 *When Nomads Settle: Processes of Sedentarization as Adaptation and Response* (New York: Praeger).

Sandmel, Samuel

1979 'Palestinian and Hellenistic Judaism and Christianity: The Question of the Comfortable Theory', *HUCA* 50: 137–48.

Sass, Benjamin

1993 'The Pre-Exilic Hebrew Seals: Iconism vs. Aniconism', in Benjamin Sass and Christoph Uehlinger (eds), *Studies in the Iconography of Northwest Semitic Inscribed Seals: Proceedings of a Symposium Held in Freibourg on April 17–20, 1991* (OBO, 125; Freiburg [Schweiz]: Universitätsverlag; Göttingen: Vandenhoeck & Ruprecht): 194–256.

2005 *The Alphabet at the Turn of the Millennium: The West Semitic Alphabet ca. 1150–850 BCE: The Antiquity of the Arabian, Greek and Phrygian Alphabets* (Tel Aviv Occasional Publications, 4; Tel Aviv: Emery and Claire Yass Publications in Archaeology).

Sauer, James A.

1986 'Transjordan in the Bronze and Iron Ages: A Critique of Glueck's Synthesis', *BASOR* 263: 1–26.

Sawyer, John F. A., and David J. A. Clines (eds)

1983 *Midian, Moab and Edom: The History and Archaeology of Late Bronze and Iron Age Jordan and North-West Arabia* (JSOTSup, 24; Sheffield: Sheffield Academic Press).

Schaper, Joachim

2000 *Priester und Leviten im achämenidischen Juda: Studien zur Kult- und Sozialgeschichte Israels in persischer Zeit* (FAT, 31; Tübingen: Mohr Siebeck).

Schipper, Bernd Ulrich

1998 'Wer war "*Sō'*, König von Ägypten" (2 Kön 17,4)?', *BN* 92: 71–84.

1999 *Israel und Ägypten in der Königszeit: Die kulturellen Kontakte von Salomo bis zum Fall Jerusalems* (OBO, 170: Freiburg [Schweiz]: Universitätsverlag; Göttingen: Vandenhoeck & Ruprecht).

2000 'Salomo und die Pharaonentochter – zum historischen Kern von 1 Kön 7,8', *BN* 102: 84–94.

Schloen, David

2001 *The House of the Father as Fact and Symbol: Patrimonialism in Ugarit and the Ancient Near East* (SAHL 2; Winona Lake, IN: Eisenbrauns).

Schmid, Konrad

2015 'Distinguishing the World of the Exodus Narrative from the World of its Narrative: The Question of the Priestly Exodus Account in its Historical Setting', in Thomas E. Levy, Thomas Schneider, and William H. C. Propp (eds), *Israel's Exodus in Transdisciplinary Perspective: Text, Archaeology, Culture, and Geoscience* (Quantitative Methods in the Humanities and Social Sciences; Cham, Switzerland: Springer): 331–44.

Schmidt, Brian B. (ed.)

2015 *Contextualizing Israel's Sacred Writings. Ancient Literacy, Orality, and Literary Production* (Ancient Israel and Its Literature, 22; Atlanta, GA: Society of Biblical Literature).

Schmidt, Werner H.

1983 *The Faith of the Old Testament: A History* (trans. J. Sturdy; Oxford: Blackwell); ET of *Alttestamentlicher Glaube in seiner Geschichte* (Neukirchener Studienbücher, Band 6; Neukirchen-Vluyn: Neukirchener Verlag, 1968).

Schneider, H. D.

2001 'Horemheb', in D. B. Redford (ed.), *Oxford Encyclopedia of Ancient Egypt* (Oxford: Oxford University Press): II, 114–16.

Schneider, Nik

1952 'Patriarchennamen in zeitgenössischen Keilschrifturkunden', *Biblica* 33: 516–22.

Scott, James M. (ed.)

1997 *Exile: Old Testament, Jewish, and Christian Conceptions* (JSJSup, 56; Leiden: Brill).

Seidlmayer, Stephan J.

2001 'Execration Texts', in Donald B. Redford (ed.), *Oxford Encyclopedia of Ancient Egypt* (Oxford: Oxford University Press): I, 487–9.

Seitz, Christopher R.

1993 'Account A and the Annals of Sennacherib: A Reassessment', *JSOT* 58: 47–57.

Sergi, Omer

2013 'Judah's Expansion in Historical Context', *Tel Aviv* 40: 226–46.

Sergi, Omer, Avshalom Karasik, Yuval Gadot, and Oded Lipschits
2012 'The Royal Judahite Storage Jar: A Computer-Generated Typology and its Archaeological and Historical Implications', *TA* 39: 64–92.

Service, Elman
1962 *Primitive Social Organization* (New York: Random House).

Shalom Brooks, Simcha
2005 *Saul and the Monarchy: A New Look* (Society for Old Testament Study Monographs; Aldershot, Hampshire: Ashgate).

Shanks, Hershel
1996 'Fingerprint of Jeremiah's Scribe', *BAR* 22: 36–8.
2012 'When Did Ancient Israel Begin?', *BAR* 38.1: 59–62, 67.

Shanks, Michael, and Ian Hodder
1995 'Processual, Postprocessual and Interpretive Archaeologies', in Ian Hodder, Michael Shanks, Alexandra Alexandri, Victor Buchli, John Carman, Jonathan Last and Gavin Lucas (eds), *Interpreting Archaeology: Finding Meaning in the Past* (London/New York: Routledge): 3–29.

Sharon, Ilan, and Ayelet Gilboa
2013 'The *SKL* Town: Dor in the Early Iron Age', in Ann E. Killebrew and Gunnar Lehmann (eds), *The Philistines and Other 'Sea Peoples' in Text and Archaeology* (SBLABS, 15; Atlanta, GA: Society of Biblical Literature): 393–468.

Sharon, Ilan, Ayelet Gilboa, and Elisabetta Boaretto
2008 'The Iron Age Chronology of the Levant: The State-of-Research at the ^{14}C Dating Project, Spring 2006', in Lester L. Grabbe (ed.), *Israel in Transition: From Late Bronze II to Iron IIA (c. 1250–850 BCE): The Archaeology* (LHBOTS, 491; ESHM, 7; London/New York: T&T Clark International): 177–92.

Sharon, Ilan, Ayelet Gilboa, Elisabeth Boaretto, and A. J. Timothy Jull
2005 'The Early Iron Age Dating Project: Introduction, Methodology, Progress Report and an Update on the Tel Dor Radiometric Dates', in Thomas E. Levy and Thomas Higham (eds), *The Bible and Radiocarbon Dating: Archaeology, Text and Science* (London: Equinox): 65–92.

Shea, William H.
1985 'Sennacherib's Second Palestinian Campaign', *JBL* 104: 410–18.
1997 'The New Tirhakah Text and Sennacherib's Second Palestinian Campaign', *AUSS* 35: 181–7.
1999 'Jerusalem under Siege', *BAR* 26.6 (Nov./Dec.): 36–44, 64.

Shennan, Stephen J. (ed.)
1989 *Archaeological Approaches to Cultural Identity* (One World Archaeology, 10; London/New York: Routledge).

Sherratt, Susan
2003 'The Mediterranean Economy: "Globalization" at the End of the Second Millennium B.C.E.', in William G. Dever and Seymour Gitin (eds), *Symbiosis, Symbolism, and the Power of the Past: Canaan, Ancient Israel, and their Neighbors from the Late Bronze Age through Roman Palaestina: Proceedings of the Centennial Symposium W. F. Albright Institute of Archaeological Research and the American Schools of Oriental Research Jerusalem, May 29–31, 2000* (Winona Lake, IN: Eisenbrauns): 37–62.

Shiloh, Yigal

1980 'The Population of Iron Age Palestine in the Light of a Sample Analysis of Urban Plans, Areas, and Population Density', *BASOR* 239: 25–35.

1986 'A Group of Hebrew Bullae from the City of David', *IEJ* 36: 16–38.

Shiloh, Yigal, and David Tarler

1986 'Bullae from the City of David: A Hoard of Seal Impressions from the Israelite Period', *BA* 49: 196–209.

Shoham, Yair

1994 'A Group of Hebrew Bullae from Yigal Shiloh's Excavations in the City of David', in Hillel Geva (ed.), *Ancient Jerusalem Revealed* (Jerusalem: Israel Exploration Society; Washington, DC: Biblical Archaeology Society): 55–61.

2000 'Hebrew Bullae', in D. T. Ariel (ed.), *Excavations in the City of David*, Vol. VI (Qedem, 41: Jerusalem: Institute of Archaeology, Hebrew University): 29–57.

Shortland, A. J.

2005 'Shishak, King of Egypt: the Challenges of Egyptian Calendrical Chronology', in Thomas E. Levy and Thomas Higham (eds), *The Bible and Radiocarbon Dating: Archaeology, Text and Science* (London: Equinox): 43–54.

Silberman, Neil Asher, and David Small (eds)

1997 *The Archaeology of Israel: Constructing the Past, Interpreting the Present* (JSOTSup, 237; Sheffield: Sheffield Academic Press).

Simpson, William K.

1984 'Sinuhe', *LdÄ* V, 950–55.

Singer, Itamar

1988 'Merneptah's Campaign to Canaan and the Egyptian Occupation of the Southern Coastal Plain of Palestine in the Ramesside Period', *BASOR* 269: 1–10.

1991 'Appendix III: A Concise History of Amurru', in Shlomo Izre'el, *Amurru Akkadian: A Linguistic Study* (HSS, 40–41; Atlanta, GA: Scholars Press): II, 134–95.

2000 'New Evidence on the End of the Hittite Empire', in Eliezer D. Oren (ed.), *The Sea Peoples and their World: A Reassessment* (University Museum Monograph, 108; University Museum Symposium Series, 11; Philadelphia: University of Pennsylvania, The University Museum): 21–33.

2006 'The Hittites and the Bible Revisited', in Aren M. Maeir and Pierre de Miroschedji (eds), *'I Will Speak the Riddles of Ancient Times': Archaeological and Historical Studies in Honor of Amihai Mazar on the Occasion of his Sixtieth Birthday* (Winona Lake, IN: Eisenbrauns): 723–56.

2013 'The Philistines in the Bible: A Short Rejoinder to New Perspective', in Ann E. Killebrew and Gunnar Lehmann (eds), *The Philistines and Other 'Sea Peoples' in Text and Archaeology* (Society of Biblical Literature Archaeology and Biblical Studies, 15; Atlanta, GA: Society of Biblical Literature): 19–27.

Singer-Avitz, Lily
1999 'Beersheba – A Gateway Community in Southern Arabian Long-Distance Trade in the Eighth Century B.C.E.', *TA* 26: 3–75.
2002 'Arad: The Iron Age Pottery Assemblages', *TA* 29: 110–214.
Skjeggestad, Marit
1992 'Ethnic Groups in Early Iron Age Palestine: Some Remarks on the Use of the Term "Israelite" in Recent Research', *SJOT* 6: 159–86.
Smelik, Klaas A. D.
1992 'King Hezekiah Advocates True Prophecy: Remarks on Isaiah xxxvi and xxxvii//II Kings xviii and xix', in K. A. D. Smelik (ed.), *Converting the Past: Studies in Ancient Israelite and Moabite Historiography* (OTS, 28; Leiden: Brill): 93–128.
1995 'Moloch, Molekh, or Molk-Sacrifice? A Reassessment of the Evidence Concerning the Hebrew Term Molekh', *SJOT* 9: 133–42.
Smith, Mark S.
2001 *The Origins of Biblical Monotheism: Israel's Polytheistic Background and the Ugaritic Texts* (Oxford: Oxford University Press).
2002 *The Early History of God: Yahweh and the Other Deities in Ancient Israel* (San Francisco: Harper, 2nd edn).
Smith, Morton
1971 *Palestinian Parties and Politics That Shaped the Old Testament* (New York: Columbia).
Soden, Wolfram von
1935 'Eine babylonische Volksüberlieferung von Nabonidinden Danielerzählungen', *ZAW* 53: 81–9.
1970 'Zur Stellung des "Geweihten" (*qdš*) in Ugarit', *UF* 2: 329–30.
Soggin, J. Alberto
1984 *Storia d'Israele: dalle origini a Bar Kochba* (Biblioteca di cultura religiosa, 44; Brescia: Paideia Editrice); ET of *A History of Israel: From the Beginnings to the Bar Kochba Revolt, AD 135* (London: SCM Press, 1984).
1993 *An Introduction to the History of Israel and Judah* (London: SCM Press; Valley Forge: Trinity Press International, 2nd edn).
2001 *Storia d'Israele: Introduzione alla storia d'Israele e Giuda dalle origini alla rivotta di Bar-Kochbà* (Bibliotteca di cultura religiosa, 44; Brescia: Paideia Editrice, 2nd edn revised and expanded).
Sokolovskii, Servey, and Valery Tishkov
1996 'Ethnicity', in Alan Barnard and Jonathan Spencer (eds), *Encylopedia of Social and Cultural Anthropology* (London/New York: Routledge): 190–3.
Southall, Aiden W.
1956 *Alur Society: A Study in Processes and Types of Domination* (Cambridge: Heffers).
Sparks, Kenton L.
1998 *Ethnicity and Identity in Ancient Israel: Prolegomena to the Study of Ethnic Sentiments and their Expression in the Hebrew Bible* (Winona Lake, IN: Eisenbrauns).

Speiser, Ephraim A.
1964 *Genesis: A New Translation and Commentary* (AB, 1; Garden City, NY: Doubleday).
Spieckermann, Hermann
1982 *Juda unter Assur in der Sargonidenzeit* (FRLANT, 129; Göttingen: Vandenhoeck & Ruprecht).
Stade, Bernhard
1886 'Anmerkungen zu 2 Kö. 15–21', *ZAW* 6: 156–89.
Stager, Lawrence E.
1985a 'The Archaeology of the Family in Ancient Israel', *BASOR* 260: 1–36.
1985b 'Merenptah, Israel and Sea Peoples: New Light on an Old Relief', *EI* 18: 56*–64*.
1988 'Archaeology, Ecology, and Social History: Background Themes to the Song of Deborah', in J. A. Emerton (ed.), *Congress Volume: Jerusalem 1986* (VTSup, 40; Leiden: Brill): 221–34.
1998a 'The Impact of the Sea Peoples in Canaan (1185–1050 BCE)', in Thomas E. Levy (ed.), *The Archaeology of Society in the Holy Land* (London and Washington: Leicester University Press): 332–48.
1998b 'Forging an Identity: The Emergence of Ancient Israel', in Michael D. Coogan (ed.), *The Oxford History of the Biblical World* (Oxford: Oxford University Press): 123–75.
Staubli, Thomas
1991 *Das Image der Nomaden im Alten Israel und in der Ikonographie seiner sesshaften Nachbarn* (OBO, 107; Freiburg [Schweiz]: Universitätsverlag; Göttingen: Vandenhoeck & Ruprecht).
Stech-Wheeler, T., J. D. Muhly, K. R. Maxwell-Hyslop, and R. Maddin
1981 'Iron at Taanach and Early Iron Metallurgy in the Eastern Mediterranean', *AJA* 85: 245–68.
Steen, Eveline J. van der
2004 *Tribes and Territories in Transition: The Central East Jordan Valley in the Late Bronze Age and Early Iron Ages: a Study of the Sources* (OLA, 130; Leuven: Peeters).
2017 'The Archaeology of the Late Bronze Age in Palestine', in Lester L. Grabbe (ed.), *The Land of Canaan in the Late Bronze Age* (LHBOTS, 636; ESHM, 10; London/New York: Bloomsbury T&T Clark).
Steen, Eveline J. van der, and Piotr Bienkowski
2005 'Radiocarbon Dates from Khirbat en-Nahas: a Methodological Critique'. Online: http://antiquity.ac.uk/ProjGall/levy/index.html.
2005–2006 'How Old Is the Kingdom of Edom?'. Online: http://www. wadiarabah-project.man.ac.uk.
2006 'Radiocarbon Dates from Khirbat en-Nahas: A Methodological Critique', *Antiquity* 80 (no. 307): [no pagination].
Steiner, Margreet
1994 'Re-dating the Terraces of Jerusalem', *IEJ* 44: 13–20.
1998 'The Archaeology of Ancient Jerusalem', *CRBS* 6: 143–68.
2001 'Jerusalem in the Tenth and Seventh Centuries BCE: From Administrative Town to Commercial City', in Amihai Mazar (ed.), *Studies in the Archaeology of the Iron Age in Israel and Jordan* (JSOTSup, 331; Sheffield: Sheffield Academic Press): 280–8.

2003a 'Expanding Borders: The Development of Jerusalem in the Iron Age', in Thomas L. Thompson, with the collaboration of Salma Khadra Jayyusi (eds), *Jerusalem in Ancient History and Tradition* (JSOTSup, 381; CIS, 13; London/New York: T&T Clark International): 68–79.

2003b 'The Evidence from Kenyon's Excavations in Jerusalem: A Response Essay', in Andrew G. Vaughn and Ann E. Killebrew (eds), *Jerusalem in Bible and Archaeology: The First Temple Period* (SBLSymS, 18; Atlanta, GA: Society of Biblical Literature): 347–63.

Steiner, Margreet L., and Ann E. Killebrew (eds)

2014 *The Oxford Handbook of the Archaeology of the Levant, c. 8000–332 BCE* (Oxford: Oxford University Press).

Stern, Ephraim

1982 *Material Culture of the Land of the Bible in the Persian Period 538–332 B.C.* (Jerusalem: Israel Exploration Society; Warminster: Aris & Phillips).

1992 'The Phoenician Architectural Elements in Palestine during the Late Iron Age and the Persian Period', in Aharon Kempinski and Ronny Reich (eds), *The Architecture of Ancient Israel from the Prehistoric to the Persian Periods* (Jerusalem: Israel Exploration Society): 302–9.

1994 'The Eastern Border of the Kingdom of Judah in its Last Days', in Michael D. Coogan, Cheryl J. Exum and Lawrence E. Stager (eds), *Scripture and Other Artifacts: Essays on the Bible and Archaeology in Honor of Philip J. King* (Louisville, KY: Westminster John Knox): 399–409.

2001 *Archaeology of the Land of the Bible:* Vol. II. *The Assyrian, Babylonian, and Persian Periods (732–332 B.C.E.)* (The Anchor Bible Reference Library; New York: Doubleday).

Stern, Ephraim (ed.)

1993 *The New Encyclopedia of Archaeological Excavations in the Holy Land* (4 vols; New York: Simon & Schuster; Jerusalem: Israel Exploration Society).

Street, Brian V.

1984 *Literacy in Theory and Practice* (Cambridge Studies in Oral and Literate Culture; Cambridge: Cambridge University Press).

Swanson, Kristin A.

2002 'A Reassessment of Hezekiah's Reform in Light of Jar Handles and Iconographic Evidence', *CBQ* 64: 460–9.

Sweeny, Deborah, and Asaf Yasur-Landau

1999 'Following the Path of the Sea Persons: the Women in the Medinet Habu Reliefs', *TA* 26: 116–45.

Szuchman, Jeffrey (ed.)

2009 *Nomads, Tribes, and the State in the Ancient Near East: Cross-Disciplinary Perspectives* (University of Chicago Oriental Institute Seminars, 5; Chicago: Oriental Institute).

Tadmor, Hayim

1958a 'Historical Implications of the Correct Rendering of Akkadian *dâku*', *JNES* 17: 129–41.

1958b 'The Campaigns of Sargon II of Assur: A Chronological-Historical Study', *JCS* 12: 22–40, 77–100.

1961 'Azriyau of Yaudi', in Chaim Rabin (ed.), *Studies in the Bible* (Scripta Hierosolymitana, 8; Jerusalem: Magnes Press): 232–71.

1973 'The Historical Inscriptions of Adad-Nirari III', *Iraq* 35: 141–50.

1985 'Sennacherib's Campaign to Judah: Historical and Historiographical Considerations', *Zion* 50 (Jubilee volume): 65–80 (Heb.).

1994 *The Inscriptions of Tiglath-Pileser III King of Assyria: Critical Edition, with Introductions, Translations and Commentary* (Jerusalem: Israel Academy of Sciences and Humanities).

Tadmor, Hayim and Michael Cogan

1982 מאירועי שנת ארבע־עשׂרה לחזקיהו: מחלת המלך וביקור המשלחת הבבלית ('Hezekiah's Fourteenth Year: The King's Illness and the Babylonian Embassy'), *EI* 16: 198–201 (Eng. abstract 258*–59*).

Tapper, Richard

1990 'Anthropologists, Historians, and Tribespeople on Tribe and State Formation in the Middle East', in Philip S. Khoury and Joseph Kostiner (eds), *Tribes and State Formation in the Middle East* (Berkeley: University of California Press): 48–73.

Tappy, Ron E.

1992 *The Archaeology of Israelite Samaria*: Vol. I. *Early Iron Age through the Ninth Century BCE* (HSS, 44; Atlanta, GA: Scholars Press).

2001 *The Archaeology of Israelite Samaria*: Vol. II. *The Eighth Century BCE.* (HSS, 50; Atlanta, GA: Scholars Press).

Tarragon, Jean-Michel de

1980 *Le culte à Ugarit d'après les textes de la pratique en cunéiformes alphabétiques* (Cahiers de la Revue Biblique, 19; Paris: Gabalda).

Tatum, Lynn

1991 'King Manasseh and the Royal Fortress at Horvat 'Usa', *BA* 54: 136–45.

2003 'Jerusalem in Conflict: The Evidence for the Seventh-Century B.C.E. Religious Struggle over Jerusalem', in Andrew G. Vaughn and Ann E. Killebrew (eds), *Jerusalem in Bible and Archaeology: The First Temple Period* (SBLSymS, 18; Atlanta, GA: Society of Biblical Literature): 291–306.

Tetley, M. Christine

2002 'The Date of Samaria's Fall as a Reason for Rejecting the Hypothesis of Two Conquests', *CBQ* 64: 59–77.

Thomas, D. Winton (ed.)

1958 *Documents from Old Testament Times* (New York: Nelson).

Thompson, Thomas L.

1974 *The Historicity of the Patriarchal Narratives: The Quest for the Historical Abraham* (BZAW, 133; Berlin: de Gruyter).

1992 *Early History of the Israelite People: From the Written and Archaeological Sources* (SHANE, 4; Leiden: Brill).

1995a 'The Intellectual Matrix of Early Biblical Narrative: Inclusive Monotheism in Persian Period Palestine', in Diana V. Edelman (ed.), *The Triumph of Elohim: From Yahwisms to Judaisms* (CBET, 13; Kampen: Kok Pharos; Grand Rapids, MI: Eerdmans): 107–24.

1995b '"House of David": An Eponymic Referent to Yahweh as Godfather', *SJOT* 9: 59–74.

1995c 'Dissonance and Disconnections: Notes on the BYTDWD and HMLK. HDD Fragments from Tel Dan', *SJOT* 9: 236–40.

1995d 'A Neo-Albrightean School in History and Biblical Scholarship', *JBL* 114: 683–98.

2000 'Problems of Genre and Historicity with Palestine's Inscriptions', in André Lemaire and Magne Saebø (ed.), *Congress Volume: Oslo 1998* (VTSup, 80; Leiden: Brill): 321–6.

Timm, Stefan

1982 *Die Dynastie Omri* (Göttingen: Vandenhoek & Ruprecht).Tomes, Roger

1993 'The Reason for the Syro-Ephraimite War', *JSOT* 59: 55–71.

Toorn, Karel van der

1990 'The Nature of the Biblical Teraphim in the Light of the Cuneiform Evidence', *CBQ* 52: 203–22.

Toorn, Karel van der (ed.)

1997 *The Image and the Book: Iconic Cults, Aniconism, and the Rise of Book Religion in Israel and the Ancient Near East* (CBET, 21; Leuven: Peeters).

Trigger, Bruce G.

2003 *Understanding Early Civilizations: A Comparative Study* (Cambridge: Cambridge University Press).

Tucker, Gene

1966 'The Legal Background of Genesis 23', *JBL* 85: 77–84.

Tushingham, A. D.

1992 'New Evidence Bearing on the Two-Winged *LMLK* Stamp', *BASOR* 287: 61–5.

Tyldesley, Joyce

1996 *Hatchepsut: The Female Pharaoh* (London: Viking).

Tyson, Craig W.

2014 *The Ammonites: Elites, Empires, and Sociopolitical Change (1000–500 BCE)* (LHBOTS, 585; London/New York: Bloomsbury T&T Clark).

Uehlinger, Christoph

1993 'Northwest Semitic Inscribed Seals, Iconography and Syro-Palestinian Religions of Iron Age II: some Afterthoughts and Conclusions', in Benjamin Sass and Christoph Uehlinger (eds), *Studies in the Iconography of Northwest Semitic Inscribed Seals: Proceedings of a Symposium Held in Freibourg on April 17–20, 1991* (OBO, 125; Freiburg [Schweiz]: Universitätsverlag; Göttingen: Vandenhoeck & Ruprecht): 257–88.

1995 'Gab es eine joschijanische Kultreform? Plädoyer für ein begründetes Minimum', in Walter Gross (ed.), *Jeremia und die 'deuteronomistische Bewegung'* (BBB, 98; Beltz: Athenäum): 57–89 (for a revision and update in English, see 2005).

2003 'Clio in a World of Pictures – Another Look at the Lachish Reliefs from Sennacherib's Southwest Palace at Nineveh', in Lester L. Grabbe (ed.), *'Like a Bird in a Cage': The Invasion of Sennacherib in 701 BCE* (JSOTSup, 363; ESHM, 4; Sheffield: Sheffield Academic Press): 221–305.

2005 'Was There a Cult Reform under King Josiah? The Case for a Well-Grounded Minimum', in Lester L. Grabbe (ed.), *Good Kings and Bad Kings: The Kingdom of Judah in the Seventh Century BCE* (LHBOTS, 393; ESHM, 5: London/New York: T&T Clark International): 279–316.

Uphill, E. P.

1968 'Pithom and Raamses: Their Location and Significance', *JNES* 27: 291–316.

1969 'Pithom and Raamses: Their Location and Significance', *JNES* 28: 15–39.

Ussishkin, David

1976 'Royal Judean Storage Jars and Private Seal Impressions', *BASOR* 223: 6–11.

1977 'The Destruction of Lachish by Sennacherib and the Dating of the Royal Judean Storage Jars', *TA* 4: 28–60.

1980a 'The "Lachish Reliefs" and the City of Lachish', *IEJ* 30: 174–95.

1980b 'Was the "Solomonic" City Gate at Megiddo Built by King Solomon?', *BASOR* 239: 1–18.

1982 *The Conquest of Lachish by Sennacherib* (Tel Aviv, Publications of the Institute of Archaeology; Tel Aviv: Tel Aviv University).

1988 'The Date of the Judaean Shrine at Arad', *IEJ* 38: 142–57.

1994 'Gate 1567 at Megiddo and the Seal of Shema, Servant of Jeroboam', in Michael D. Coogan, Cheryl J. Exum, and Lawrence E. Stager (eds), *Scripture and Other Artifacts: Essays on the Bible and Archaeology in Honor of Philip J. King* (Louisville, KY: Westminster John Knox): 410–27.

1995a 'The Rectangular Fortress at Kadesh-Barnea', *IEJ* 45: 118–27.

1995b 'The Destruction of Megiddo at the End of the Late Bronze Age and its Historical Significance', *TA* 22: 240–67.

1997 'Lachish', in Eric M. Meyers (ed.), *The Oxford Encyclopedia of Archaeology in the Near East* (5 vols; Oxford: Oxford University Press): III, 317–23.

2000 'The Credibility of the Tel Jezreel Excavations: A Rejoinder to Amnon Ben-Tor', *TA* 27: 248–56.

2003a 'Jerusalem as a Royal and Cultic Center in the 10th–8th Centuries B.C.E.', in William G. Dever and Seymour Gitin (eds), *Symbiosis, Symbolism, and the Power of the Past: Canaan, Ancient Israel, and their Neighbors from the Late Bronze Age through Roman Palaestina: Proceedings of the Centennial Symposium W. F. Albright Institute of Archaeological Research and the American Schools of Oriental Research Jerusalem, May 29–31, 2000* (Winona Lake, IN: Eisenbrauns): 529–38.

2003b 'Solomon's Jerusalem: The Text and the Facts on the Ground', in Andrew G. Vaughn and Ann E. Killebrew (eds), *Jerusalem in Bible and Archaeology: The First Temple Period* (SBLSymS, 18; Atlanta, GA: Society of Biblical Literature): 103–15.

2007a 'Samaria, Jezreel and Megiddo: Royal Centres of Omri and Ahab', in Lester L. Grabbe (ed.), *Ahab Agonistes: The Rise and Fall of the Omri Dynasty* (LHBOTS, 421; ESHM, 6; London/New York: T&T Clark International): 293–309.

2007b 'Archaeology of the Biblical Period: On Some Questions of Methodology and Chronology of the Iron Age', in Hugh G. M. Williamson (ed.), *Understanding the History of Ancient Israel* (Proceedings of the British Academy, 143; Oxford: OUP for the British Academy): 131–41.

2008 'The Date of the Philistine Settlement in the Coastal Plain: The View from Megiddo and Lachish', in Lester L. Grabbe (ed.), *Israel in Transition: From Late Bronze II to Iron IIA (c. 1250–850 BCE): The Archaeology* (LHBOTS, 491; ESHM, 7; London/New York: T&T Clark International): 203–16.

2011 'The Dating of the *lmlk* Storage Jars and its Implications: Rejoinder to Lipschits, Sergi and Koch', *TA* 38: 220–40.

2012 '*Lmlk* Seal Impressions Once Again: A Second Rejoinder to Oded Lipschits', *Antiguo Oriente* 10: 13–23.

Ussishkin, David (ed.)

2004 *The Renewed Archaeological Excavations at Lachish (1973–1994)* (vols 1–5; Tel Aviv University Ronia and Marco Nadler Institute of Archaeology, Monograph Series, 22; Tel Aviv: Emery and Claire Yass Publications in Archaeology).

Ussishkin, David, and John Woodhead

1997 'Excavations at Tel Jezreel 1994–1996: Third Preliminary Report', *TA* 24: 6–72.

Van Beek, Gus W.

1982 'A Population Estimate for Marib: A Contemporary Tell Village in North Yemen', *BASOR* 248: 61–7.

Van De Mieroop, Marc

2004 *A History of the Ancient Near East ca. 3000–323 BC* (Blackwell History of the Ancient World; Oxford: Blackwell Publishing).

Van Seters, John

1966 *The Hyksos: A New Interpretation* (New Haven, CT: Yale University).

1975 *Abraham in History and Tradition* (New Haven, CT: Yale University).

1990 'Joshua's Campaign of Canaan and Near Eastern Historiography', *SJOT* 2/1990: 1–12.

2001 'The Geography of the Exodus', in J. Andrew Dearman and M. Patrick Graham (eds), *The Land that I Will Show You: Essays on the History and Archaeology of the Ancient Near East in Honour of J. Maxwell Miller* (JSOTSup, 343; Sheffield: Sheffield Academic Press): 255–76.

2010 'David the Mercenary', in Lester L. Grabbe (ed.), *Israel in Transition: From Late Bronze II to Iron IIA (c. 1250–850 BCE)*. Vol. II: *The Text* (LHBOTS, 521; ESHM, 8; London/New York: T&T Clark International): 199–219.

Vaughn, Andrew G.

1999a *Theology, History, and Archaeology in the Chronicler's Account of Hezekiah* (Archaeology and Biblical Studies, 4; Atlanta, GA: Scholars Press).

1999b 'Palaeographic Dating of Judaean Seals and its Significance for Biblical Research', *BASOR* 313: 43–64.

Vaughn, Andrew G., and Carolyn Pillers Dobler

2005 'The Probability of Forgeries: Reflections on a Statistical Analysis', *SBL Forum*. Online: http://www.sbl-site.org/Article.aspx?ArticleId=372: 1–6.

Vaughn, Andrew G., and Ann E. Killebrew (eds)

2003 *Jerusalem in Bible and Archaeology: The First Temple Period* (SBLSymS, 18; Atlanta, GA: Society of Biblical Literature).

Vaughn, Andrew G., and Christopher A. Rollston
2005 'Epilogue: Methodological Musings from the Field', *SBL Forum*. Online: http://www.sbl-site.org/Article.aspx?ArticleId=376: 1–4.

Veen, Peter van der, Christoffer Theis, and Manfred Görg
2010 'Israel in Canaan (Long) Before Pharaoh Merneptah? A Fresh Look at Berlin Statue Pedestal Relief 21687', *Journal of Ancient Egyptian Interconnections* 2: 15–25.

Veen, Peter G. van der, and Wolfgang Zwickel
2014 'Die neue Israel-Inschrift und ihre historische Implikationen', in Stefan Jakob Wimmer and George Gafus (eds), *'Vom Leben umfangen': Ägypten, das Alte Testament und das Gespräch der Religionen: Gedenkschrift für Manfred Görg* (Ägypten und Altes Testament, 80; Münster: Ugarit-Verlag): 425–33.

Veldhuijzen, Harald Alexander, and Thilo Rehren
2007 'Slags and the City: Early Iron Production at Tell Hammeh, Jordan, and Tel Beth-Shemesh, Israel', in S. La Niece, D. R., Hook, and P. T. Craddock (eds), *Metals and Mines – Studies in Archaeometallurgy Archetype* (London: British Museum): 189–201.

Vriezen, Karel J. H.
2001 'Archaeological Traces of Cult in Ancient Israel', in Bob Becking et al., *Only One God? Monotheism in Ancient Israel and the Veneration of the Goddess Asherah* (Biblical Seminar, 77; Sheffield: Sheffield Academic Press): 45–80.

Wachsmann, Shelley
2000 'To the Sea of the Philistines', in Eliezer D. Oren (ed.), *The Sea Peoples and their World: A Reassessment* (University Museum Monograph, 108; University Museum Symposium Series, 11; Philadelphia: University of Pennsylvania, The University Museum): 103–43.

Waddell, W. G. (ed.)
1940 *Manetho* (LCL; London: Heinemann; Cambridge, MA: Harvard University Press).

Wapnish, Paula
1997 'Camels', *OEANE* I, 407–8.

Ward, William A.
1972 'The Shasu "Bedouin": Notes on a Recent Publication', *JESHO* 15: 35–60.
1992 'Shasu', *ABD* V, 1165–7.

Ward, William A., and Martha Sharp Joukowsky (eds)
1992 *The Crisis Years: The 12th Century B.C.: From Beyond the Danube to the Tigris* (Dubuque, Iowa: Kendall/Hunt Publishing).

Watson, W. G. E., and Nicholas Wyatt (eds)
1999 *Handbook of Ugaritic Studies* (Handbuch der Orientalistik: Erste Abteilung, Der Nahe und Mittlere Osten, 39. Band; Leiden: Brill).

Wei, Tom F.
1992 'Pithom', *ABD* V, 376–7.

Weidner, Ernst F.
1939 'Jojachin, König von Juda, in babylonischen Keilschrifttexten', in *Mélanges Syriens offerts a Monsieur René Dussaud par ses amis et ses élèves* (Paris: Geuthner): II, 923–35.

Weinstein, James M.
1991 'Egypt and the Middle Bronze IIC/Late Bronze IA Transition in Palestine', *Levant* 23: 105–15.
1992 'The Chronology of Palestine in the Early Second Millennium B.C.E.', *BASOR* 288: 27–46.
1997a 'Hyksos', *OEANE* III, 133–6.
1997b 'Exodus and Archaeological Reality', in Ernest S. Frerichs and Leonard H. Lesko (eds), *Exodus: The Egyptian Evidence* (Winona Lake, IN: Eisenbrauns): 87–103.

Weippert, Helga
1973 'Das geographische System der Stämme Israels', *VT* 23: 76–89.
1988 *Palästina in vorhellenistischer Zeit* (Handbuch der Archäologie, Vorderasien, 2, Band 1; Munich: Beck).

Weippert, Manfred
1971 *The Settlement of the Israelite Tribes in Palestine: A Critical Survey of Recent Scholarly Debate* (Studies in Biblical Theology, 2nd Series, 21; London: SCM Press).
1974 'Semitische Nomaden des zweiten Jahrtausends: Über die Š3św der ägyptischen Quellen', *Bib* 55: 265–80, 427–33.
1978 'Jau(a) mār ḫumrî – Joram oder Jehu von Israel?', *VT* 28: 113–18.
1979 'The Israelite "Conquest" and the Evidence from Transjordan', in Frank M. Cross (ed.), *Symposia: Celebrating the Seventy-Fifth Anniversary of the Founding of the American Schools of Oriental Research (1900–1975)* (Cambridge, MA: American Schools of Oriental Research): 15–34.

White, Hayden
1978 *Tropes of Discourse* (Baltimore: Johns Hopkins University Press).

Whitelam, Keith W.
1996 *The Invention of Ancient Israel: The Silencing of Palestinian History* (London/New York: Routledge).

Whybray, R. Norman
1987 *The Making of the Pentateuch: A Methodological Study* (JSOTSup, 53; Sheffield: JSOT Press).

Williamson, Hugh G. M. (ed.)
2007 *Understanding the History of Ancient Israel* (Proceedings of the British Academy, 143; Oxford: OUP for the British Academy).

Wilson, Kevin A.
2005 *The Campaign of Pharaoh Shoshenq I into Palestine* (FAT, 2/9; Tübingen: Mohr Siebeck).

Wilson, Robert R.
1977 *Genealogy and History in the Biblical World* (Yale Near Eastern Researches, 7; New Haven, CT: Yale University Press).

Windschuttle, Keith
1996 *The Killing of History: How Literary Critics and Social Theorists Are Murdering our Past* (New York: The Free Press, rev. and exp. edn).

Wiseman, Donald
1958 'Historical Records of Assyria and Babylon', in D. Winton Thomas (ed.), *Documents from Old Testament Times* (New York: Nelson): 47–83.

Wood, Bryant G.

1990 'Did the Israelites Conquer Jericho? A New Look at the Archaeological Evidence', *BAR* 16.2 (March–April): 44–58.

2005 'The Rise and Fall of the 13th-Century Exodus-Conquest Theory', *JETS* 48: 475–89.

2007 'The Biblical Date for the Exodus Is 1446 BC: A Response to James Hoffmeier', *JETS* 50: 249–58.

Worschech, Udo

1997 'Egypt and Moab', *BA* 60: 229–36.

Wyatt, Nicolas

1996 *Myths of Power: A Study of Royal Myth and Ideology in Ugaritic and Biblical Traditions* (Ugaritisch-Biblische Literatur, 13; Münster: Ugarit-Verlag).

Yadin, Yigael

1979 'The Transition from a Semi-Nomadic to a Sedentary Society in the Twelfth Century B.C.E.', in Frank M. Cross (ed.), *Symposia: Celebrating the Seventy-Fifth Anniversary of the Founding of the American Schools of Oriental Research (1900–1975)* (Cambridge, MA: American Schools of Oriental Research): 57–68.

1982 'Is the Biblical Account of the Israelite Conquest of Canaan Historically Reliable?', *BAR* 8.2 (March–April): 16–23.

Yamada, Shigeo

2000 *The Construction of the Assyrian Empire: A Historical Study of the Inscriptions of Shalmaneser III (859–824 BC) Relating to his Campaigns to the West* (CHANE, 3; Leiden: Brill).

Yamauchi, Edwin M.

1973 'Cultic Prostitution: A Case Study in Cultural Diffusion', in Harry A. Hoffner (ed.), *Orient and Occident: Essays Presented to Cyrus H. Gordon on the Occasion of his Sixty-fifth Birthday* (AOAT, 22; Neukirchen-Vluyn: Neukirchener Verlag): 213–22.

Yasur-Landau, Assaf

2010 *The Philistines and Aegean Migration at the End of the Late Bronze Age* (Cambridge: Cambridge University Press).

Yoffee, Norman

2005 *Myths of the Archaic State: Evolution of the Earliest Cities, States, and Civilizations* (Cambridge: Cambridge University Press).

Young, Ian M.

1998 'Israelite Literacy: Interpreting the Evidence, Part I'; 'Israelite Literacy: Interpreting the Evidence, Part II', *VT* 48: 239–53, 408–22.

Yurco, Frank J.

1980 'Sennacherib's Third Campaign and the Coregency of Shabaka and Shebitku', *Serapis* 6: 221–40.

1986 'Merneptah's Canaanite Campaign', *JARCE* 23: 189–215.

1991 'The Shabaka-Shebitku Coregency and the Supposed Second Campaign of Sennacherib against Judah: A Critical Assessment', *JBL* 110: 35–45.

1997 'Merneptah's Canaanite Campaign and Israel's Origins', in Ernest S. Frerichs and Leonard H. Lesko (eds), *Exodus: The Egyptian Evidence* (Winona Lake, IN: Eisenbrauns): 27–55.

Zadok, Ran
1998 'On the Reliability of the Genealogical and Prosopographical Lists of the Israelites in the Old Testament', *TA* 25: 228–54.

Zagorin, Perez
1999 'History, the Referent, and Narrative: Reflections on Postmodernism Now', *History and Theory* 38: 1–24.

Zarins, Juris
1978 'The Camel in Ancient Arabia: A Further Note', *Antiquity* 52: 44–6.

Zarzeki-Peleg, Anabel
1997 'Hazor, Jokneam and Megiddo in the 10th Century B.C.E.', *TA* 24: 258–88.

Zertal, Adam
1989 'The Wedge-Shaped Decorated Bowl and the Origin of the Samaritans', *BASOR* 276: 77–84.
1990 'The Pahwah of Samaria (Northern Israel) during the Persian Period: Types of Settlement, Economy, History and New Discoveries', *Trans* 3: 9–30.
1994 '"To the Land of the Perizzites and the Giants": On the Israelite Settlement in the Hill Country of Manasseh', in Israel Finkelstein and Nadav Na'aman (eds), *From Nomadism to Monarchy: Archaeological and Historical Aspects of Early Israel* (Jerusalem: Israel Exploration Society): 47–69.

Zevit, Ziony
2001 *The Religions of Ancient Israel: A Synthesis of Parallactic Approaches* (New York and London: Continuum).

Zimhoni, Orna
1985 'The Iron Age Pottery of Tel 'Eton and its Relation to the Lachish, Tell Beit Mirsim and Arad Assemblages', *TA* 12: 63–90.
1997 'Clues from the Enclosure-fills: Pre-Omride Settlement at Tel Jezreel', *TA* 24: 83–109.
2004 'Chapter 25: The Pottery of Levels V and IV and its Archaeological and Chronological Implications', in David Ussishkin (ed.), *The Renewed Archaeological Excavations at Lachish (1973–1994)* (vols 1–5; Tel Aviv University Ronia and Marco Nadler Institute of Archaeology, Monograph Series, 22; Tel Aviv: Emery and Claire Yass Publications in Archaeology): IV, 1643–788.

Zorn, Jeffrey R.
1994 'Estimating the Population Size of Ancient Settlements: Methods, Problems, Solutions, and a Case Study', *BASOR* 295: 31–48.

Index of References

Index of Authors

Index of Subjects